MORE PRAISE FOR *HIGH COMMITMENT, HIGH PERFORMANCE*

"Michael Beer sheds a much-needed spotlight on building resilient, high-performance organizations—and the transformation process to get there. The research is compelling, the insights spot-on. A well crafted must-read for any executive faced with the challenge of driving effective change that recaptures leadership and enables a company to win in today's markets."

—Douglas W. Stotlar, president and chief executive officer, Con-way Inc.

"By unearthing the profound relationships between organizational, human, and competitive challenges, Mike Beer shows managers at all levels how they can navigate through these most trying economic times to build a strong and sustainable high performance organization. This book is essential reading."

—Danny Miller, professor, HEC Montreal and University of Alberta, author of *Managing for the Long Run*

"Mike Beer has done it, studied it, and now gives us a great guide that can help us create high performance organizations."

—Edward E. Lawler III, professor and director, Center for Effective Organizations, USC and author of *Talent: Making People Your Competitive Advantage*

HIGH COMMITMENT,
HIGH PERFORMANCE

HIGH COMMITMENT, HIGH PERFORMANCE

How to Build a Resilient Organization for Sustained Advantage

Michael Beer

In collaboration with Russell Eisenstat and Nathaniel Foote

JOSSEY-BASS
A Wiley Imprint
www.josseybass.com

Published by Jossey-Bass
A Wiley Imprint
989 Market Street, San Francisco, CA 94103-1741—www.josseybass.com

Readers should be aware that Internet Web sites offered as citations and/or sources for further information may have changed or disappeared between the time this was written and when it is read.

Limit of Liability/Disclaimer of Warranty: While the publisher and author have used their best efforts in preparing this book, they make no representations or warranties with respect to the accuracy or completeness of the contents of this book and specifically disclaim any implied warranties of merchantability or fitness for a particular purpose. No warranty may be created or extended by sales representatives or written sales materials. The advice and strategies contained herein may not be suitable for your situation. You should consult with a professional where appropriate. Neither the publisher nor author shall be liable for any loss of profit or any other commercial damages, including but not limited to special, incidental, consequential, or other damages.

Jossey-Bass books and products are available through most bookstores. To contact Jossey-Bass directly call our Customer Care Department within the U.S. at 800-956-7739, outside the U.S. at 317-572-3986, or fax 317-572-4002.

Jossey-Bass also publishes its books in a variety of electronic formats. Some content that appears in print may not be available in electronic books.

Library of Congress Cataloging-in-Publication Data

Beer, Michael.
  High commitment, high performance : how to build a resilient organization for sustained advantage / Michael Beer ; in collaboration with Russell Eisenstat and Nathaniel Foote.
       p. cm.
  Includes bibliographical references and index.
  ISBN 978-0-7879-7228-8 (cloth)
  1.   Organizational change. 2.   Industrial management.
I. Eisenstat, Russell A., 1955- II. Foote, Nathaniel. III. Title.
  HD58.8.B44 2009
  658.4′06−dc22

                                                                        2009013924

Printed in the United States of America

FIRST EDITION

HB Printing   10 9 8 7 6 5 4 3 2 1

CONTENTS

This book is dedicated to those from whom I have learned:
My clients
and
The giants in the field of organizational studies
on whose shoulders I stand

PREFACE

In my forty years as scholar and consultant I have made it my mission to help senior executives transform their businesses into high commitment, high performance organizations and to study their journey of change. As a nascent scholar-practitioner working at Corning Glass Works (now Corning Inc.) in the then emerging field of Organization Development, I was strongly attracted to the proposition that organizations can become less bureaucratic and more effective by appealing to people's desire for meaning, and their potential to learn and contribute. What I found to be effective and true to one company eventually became part of a larger sea change in management practice and studies.

In the past several decades, during which I have had the privilege of observing or partnering with many managers on a journey to high commitment and high performance, I have sought the answers to these fundamental questions. Why do some firms in every industry survive and outperform their peers over a long time frame, in some cases, over decades? Why do so many start-up firms fail in their infancy? Why do others become efficient and effective operations, only to lose their identity when there are major inflections and shocks in the industry? The core arguments that I make to answer these questions and others like them come from my hands-on experience in organizations as observer, case writer, consultant, and action researcher. They are also richly informed by the growing body of research and scholarship of my colleagues in the field of organizational studies as well as by my own research findings.

This book is about the challenges, rewards, dangers, and hopes inherent in the journey toward a high commitment, high performance (HCHP) organization. *By this I mean an organization that achieves sustained high levels of performance through organizing and managing to: (1) implement its strategy, (2) elicit commitment, and (3) enable ongoing learning and change.* Building an HCHP organization requires leaders to make a conscious choice. That choice involves promises; for example, leaders must maintain the firm's mission and cultural identity, maintain the "psychological contract" on which commitment has been built, and allow employees to have a voice in the affairs of the enterprise. It involves promises to customers inherent in the firm's brand and to those investors who seek sustained and predictable returns. Leaders of HCHP firms must be prepared to accept constraints with regard to firm purpose and values, strategy, financial and cultural risks taken, and the means they will employ to select, motivate, and organize people. Perhaps most essential, choosing to build an HCHP firm is to reject creative destruction of the marketplace as the only adaptive mechanism, and to substitute for it a resilient organization in which managers and front-line employees have a psychological and often an economic stake, as well as a voice.

Not all leaders can or should build HCHP organizations. If, for example, they choose to grow a business very rapidly through massive debt, acquisitions, and mergers, and then cash out, they will not build an HCHP firm. If their primary goal is to acquire money and power, building an HCHP organization will be beyond their reach. To choose HCHP is to trade off potentially very attractive expedient options for building an institution that will last. Some years ago I was teaching a case about an HCHP manufacturing plant to senior management of a company, when the CEO broke in during the discussion to say that he would not make the promises to employees embedded in the HCHP organization we were discussing. He could not, he said, promise the level of involvement, decision rights, development, and the implicit promise of long-term employment inherent in the way people were organized and managed in this organization, given market uncertainties and pressure from investors. Leaders like this CEO may choose not to impose constraints on their freedom of action because it prevents them from achieving their personal goals or because the challenge of building an HCHP firm is simply too great and would impose a leadership burden that does not fit with their values and skills.

The reader will learn that part of what makes building and sustaining an HCHP organization difficult is coping with undiscussable fault lines that develop in all organizations—for example, poor coordination, unclear priorities, and ineffective leadership behavior—when markets quake and historic patterns of management are no longer aligned with new competitive realities. These fault lines, which I call the "silent killers," arise from natural stress points inherent in all organizations which make them susceptible to low commitment and performance. They are not necessarily a manifestation of bad leaders. They do call for exceptional leadership—and most important, values and skills essential for confronting the truth, learning, and changing.

Research and experiences to which I refer throughout the book suggest that leaders *can* adapt their organizations to new circumstances by enabling honest, collective, and public conversations and, as I will show, realigning the organization as a total system. This not only enables an effective response to immediate market threats but builds commitment and resilience for the long run. The organization's redesign must focus on five organizational levers or subsystems, each intended to strengthen natural organizational stress points that otherwise would erupt and damage commitment and performance. Of these levers, the weakest found in most organizations is the learning and governance system which, if institutionalized, can ensure leaders' capacity to identifying emergent fault lines or barriers, including their own roles and behavior. And such a system enables leaders to solve problems in a way that maintains commitment and performance.

For fundamental change to occur, it's not enough to change only one aspect of the organization's design. All design levers available to management must be co-designed in a way that solves for both commitment and performance. It is leaders' commitment to this "simultaneous solve" that is at the heart of HCHP organizations. Such a simultaneous solve cannot be accomplished, I will argue, unless the means for change—the change process itself—enables the development of both high commitment and high performance. Exceptional leaders with whom I have worked and studied demonstrate that an organization can be transformed into an HCHP system if a leader consciously chooses to do so by employing the means discussed in this book.

Building an organization to last is a difficult and never-ending process. Each threat and opportunity will give rise to organizational fault lines that demand redesign of the organization and changes in leaders' roles and behavior. The leader's biggest challenge is to recognize demands for change in his or her role, values, and skills. The rewards for meeting these challenges are profound: serving customers with care; giving employees work that offers dignity, personal growth, and meaning; allotting shareholders good *and* steady returns, if not always the industry's highest; and developing a reputation as an extraordinary company, recognized for contributions to all stakeholders, including community and society.

A Short History of Management Thought

The history of management thought and practice has drifted between two different answers to the question of what constituted good management. Until the 1930s, management thought and practice was dominated by Max Weber's

conception of organizations as machine bureaucracies in which roles and relationships were tightly defined and hierarchically organized. Frederick Taylor's
scientific management reified this concept of organization and management.
Taylor provided a method by which managers could pursue efficiency, profits,
and, incidentally, increase their control over people.

Every revolution spurs a counterrevolution, and in this case, change was led
by the human relations movement. Research and theory turned to the causes
of alienation and its consequences for productivity and employee well-being.
The labor union movement in the United States, validated by legislation in
the 1930s, was the most powerful signal that bureaucracy and control had
human and performance costs. The landmark Hawthorne Studies, conducted
by Harvard Business School researchers, showed unequivocally how the social
context associated with bureaucracy and tight control undermines motivation
and productivity. It sent management scholars and managers in search of new
means for organizing and managing employees, means that would yield higher
commitment and performance. The Hawthorne Studies were the foundation
on which the human relations movement and participative management were
founded. And this research clearly identified the power of the *social system* to
govern attitudes, skills, and behavior.

In *The Human Side of Enterprise*, published in 1960 and arguably one of
the most influential management books, Douglas McGregor argued that the
social system is governed by leaders' assumptions about the nature of "man."[1]
Theory X managers—autocratic leaders focused on controlling people to achieve
efficiency, productivity, and profits—have pessimistic assumptions about the
motivation and potential of people to learn and perform. Their organizations
become bureaucracies. Theory Y managers—participative leaders who engage
and involve people in how to achieve productivity and profits—have positive
assumptions about people's capacity to commit and to learn. Their leadership
results in participative patterns of management and internal commitment. If
leaders' assumptions are false, not in touch with the consequences of their
organization's design or leadership, nor consistent with emerging knowledge
about how high commitment and performance can be achieved, then perhaps
enabling leaders to learn about their organization's behavior, and its causes
and consequences, could lead to significant improvements in leadership and
effectiveness. This idea gave rise to the field of organization development, a
theory and practice for planned organizational change aimed at overcoming the
problems of bureaucracy.

It only took a few decades for the management pendulum to swing back
to a preference for control and a dismissal of the positive view of people and
motivation, this time in the guise of a revolution in capital markets. With this revolution in the 1980s came the influence of economists on management thought.

Despite many positive outcomes of this revolution—management responsiveness to investors and, by extrapolation, sometimes to customers—there were also many unintended negative by-products. The market perspective that economists brought to the field of management favors Theory X assumptions about human nature. Incentives, instead of bureaucracy and autocracy, increasingly became the preferred means of control. Financial incentives, economists argued, are necessary to discipline irresponsible managers to become agents of investors. Though there is some truth in this observation, the consequence, with the exception of relatively few HCHP organizations and their leaders, was a short-term focus on profits to the exclusion of a longer-term concern for building identity and commitment. Managers' relationships to the firm became more transactional and short term, performed for money rather than love of the firm's mission, customers, or culture. Consequently, corporate leaders have been less motivated or found it more difficult to build a high-commitment system. This pattern of management unfortunately has become conventional wisdom and, in a different way than bureaucracy, has undermined the potential for high commitment and high performance.

In reality both financial performance and human commitment are fundamental to developing a great institution. So it is not surprising that the relatively few firms that have demonstrated sustained performance are also firms that achieve high commitment. They do not subscribe to the either-or assumptions inherent in the swing from profits and control to people and back again. As management scholars such as Jim Barron and Michael Hannan, Jeff Pfeffer and Charles O'Reilly, Jerry Porras, and Jim Collins have documented, truly great firms and their leaders embrace the tension of people and profits and have found ways to integrate these objectives. These scholars have described at a high level some of the principles and practices of high commitment, high performance firms and supplied empirical evidence for the claim that these firms are better for people and performance. The question of how to design and transform a company into an HCHP system has not, however, been tackled in a way that integrates theory and practice. I present a normative *systemic operating theory or model of HCHP organizations and situate it within the important question of change and transformation.* My "bottom-up" work with managers to change low or average performance and commitment organizations into HCHP organizations enables me to bring a grounded and action-oriented point of view that "top-down" normal science findings do not.

The Purpose of This Book

Unlike other volumes about high commitment and performance firms, I synthesize the perspectives and knowledge of a number of key disciplines; notably, strategic management, organization design, human resource management, culture and organization development, learning and change. Employing these diverse perspectives, I propose three paradoxical organizational outcomes needed to achieve sustained high commitment and performance, articulate five managerial levers for designing an organization to achieve these outcomes, and present a framework for change and transformation.

My hope is that this book will spur conversations about building HCHP organizations between CEOs, between CEOs and their next-generation leaders, between CEOs and their internal and external advisers, and between students of management. These necessary, stimulating communications will hopefully begin to form a new conventional wisdom about what constitutes excellence in organizing, managing, and leading organizations.

This book is about possibility. In a world in which capital markets have come to define success in financial terms only, a normative framework for "good" organization and management can hopefully contribute to the development of standards by which the work of CEOs might be judged, something that my colleagues Rakesh Khurana and Nitin Nohria have argued is essential if management is to be a profession.[2] What if we evaluated CEOs and key business heads inside the corporation on their progress and effectiveness in building an HCHP organization? What if we taught next-generation leaders how to build HCHP organizations? Without specifications this is not possible.

Although competitiveness and customers by necessity have to be the primary focus for high-performance organizations, it must be done in a way that simultaneously builds rather than destroys manager and worker commitment. This book discusses HCHP organizations through the lens of employees. Substantial and rigorous evidence exists that unless employees are highly committed, a business will not be able to obtain high customer commitment or high performance.[3] This lesson was brought home to me when I interviewed senior executives at Hewlett-Packard (HP) in 1995. Interviewees stressed the quality of HP's relationship with distributors, suppliers, and customers. "They prefer us to other companies because of the relationship of trust we have developed with them. We don't take advantage of them," one senior executive said. As the conversation progressed, it became clear that the high-commitment philosophy of management that guided HP as an organization was also the foundation for their relationship of trust with other stakeholders—yes, even investors.

Who Should Read This Book

Senior executives who aspire to build an HCHP firm can develop insights about the architecture of such firms and the process of transformation they must lead.

Senior human resource, organization development, and strategy professionals who are interested in new ways of thinking about how to build, transform, or maintain a values-driven firm should read this book. For teachers and students, I hope this volume, together with its accompanying full-length teaching cases, will provide the foundation for courses in HCHP organizations. Prospective managers ought to learn about what it takes to build a great institution, rather than simply how to manage for financial results, which is the perspective that dominates business education today. My fellow academics, with whom I have openly discussed, debated, and formulated many of the ideas in this book, will no doubt recognize places where I have benefited from their work. I hope they will find my insights useful and benefit from them, particularly about how their diverse research and theoretical lenses connect in the practical endeavor of organizing, managing, and leading HCHP organizations.

Executives who have the will to begin the journey to an HCHP organization face many uncertainties. What does this system look like? How do I diagnose my organization to determine what stands in the way of achieving high performance and commitment? What organizational levers can I exercise to improve performance and commitment? Where should the process of change begin? How do I assess progress and how do I know when I have strayed off the path? And perhaps the most important two questions: what leadership values and behavior are required? How do I develop my own leadership and that of leaders at lower levels to enable a successful transformation?

Unless senior leadership teams come up with solid, thoughtful answers to questions such as these, it is unlikely that they will succeed in building an HCHP organization. It is highly likely that they will be seduced by the latest fad or program. Leadership can all too easily be swayed by short-term business opportunities that may well waste scarce financial and human resources. Of these, leadership can least afford to waste employee trust, a resource hard-won and slowly gathered. In this book, I lay out a framework for both diagnosing organizational weakness and building a strong and resilient organization capable of sustained commitment and performance. I discuss three key outcomes that must be managed and five managerial levers that senior leaders can influence. Throughout, I advocate an honest, collective, and public conversation that is essential for the development of an HCHP organization, and I emphasize strategies for change that embrace the tension between the goals of high performance and high commitment.

Internal staff or consultants in human resource management, strategic management, and organization development will find in this book a comprehensive treatment of the knowledge domains they must master to help senior leaders transform their organization. I hope this framework can help these professionals in their conversations with senior leadership teams. Though I do not present the everyday details, I do specify the key principles for designing and changing the system.

Companies on the journey to HCHP can employ this book and its accompanying cases to educate next-generation leaders—those who will occupy top management positions in the next five to ten years. They are more likely to make wise choices if they understand the nature of these firms and what it takes to build and lead them.

December 1, 2008   Michael Beer
Concord, Massachusetts

HIGH COMMITMENT, HIGH PERFORMANCE

CHAPTER ONE

INTRODUCTION

My professional quest to study and build high commitment, high performance (HCHP) organizations began over forty years ago. Shortly after I joined Corning Glass Works (now Corning Inc.) in its corporate human resource department as a newly minted PhD in organizational psychology, I received a call from the plant manager of Corning's newest plant in Medfield, Massachusetts. He had read Douglas McGregor's *The Human Side of Enterprise* and wanted help in applying McGregor's ideas about participative management.[1] He aspired to develop a climate that would inspire commitment to the plant's unique mission—developing high-quality instruments for medical use. These demands required a different approach to managing people, he believed. Could I help?

I didn't have to think twice. My recently completed dissertation had been inspired by Douglas McGregor's arguments for participative Theory Y management and Abraham Maslow's view that people had high-order needs for achievement and self-actualization. Both thinkers believed that people could be motivated by organizations that engaged and stimulated people to realize their higher-order needs.[2] Working at the Medfield plant would be an opportunity to find out if an organization could truly be transformed to incorporate these ideas. I knew of one model for the kind of organization I had in mind—Non-Linear Systems, a small privately owned manufacturer of voltmeters in California that had been founded as a high-commitment organization by its owner.[3] But there existed no real road map for how this transformation could occur. My imagination sparked, I took my first of many trips to the plant.[4]

What emerged from this work was an eclectic approach to organization development, one that integrated multiple theories and perspectives in a practical way. After three years, the Medfield plant's approach to management had changed significantly, and so had the commitment of its employees.[5] Inspired by Frederick Hertzberg's ideas about the importance of work itself in motivating employees, we tore down assembly lines and gave employees the task of assembling an instrument in full, including the responsibility for ensuring that it met quality standards (except for auditing on a statistical basis).[6] The plant manager and his team participated in numerous workshops on how participative management could be applied in the plant.

Through day-to-day discussions with individuals on how to cope with numerous challenges that the plant faced, managers and engineers began to rethink their approach to management. For example, a manufacturing engineer, concerned about the lack of response from employees to his plan for changing the department's layout to incorporate new equipment, was advised to try again, this time explaining what prompted the need to change the layout and then asking for employee concerns and ideas. When employees responded with real and useful contributions, suggestions that this engineer had never imagined they were capable of making, he became a convert to the new philosophy of management. As other managers experienced similarly startling experiences, they began to transform their management philosophy and practices. Shop floor workers were encouraged to give tours to people working in other departments of the plant. Management soon discovered that these department tours, originally motivated by the desire to educate and build relationships, surfaced a number of significant manufacturing process problems previously hidden by the "walls" between departments. The result was an employee-led quality improvement process. Physicians were invited to make presentations about how test results were used in patient care to impress upon employees the importance of quality. Monthly sales and operating profits were posted on bulletin boards to develop an identity with the goals of the plant—a practice that the corporate control function quickly ordered to be stopped, rigidly believing that profit information needed to be kept proprietary lest employees share it with others to the company's disadvantage.

At the end of three years, employees at the Medfield plant had become an HCHP organization. Medfield workers developed high commitment to the mission of the plant and, combined with their growing skills, performance exceeded the division management's highest expectations. It was the most rapid start-up management had seen, not only in terms of operating margins, but also in customer and employee satisfaction.

Employee commitment manifested itself in several ways—positive attitudes reflected in employee surveys, low turnover, and, perhaps most graphically, by employee response to management's decision to loosen previously met quality standards. When employees spoke up and demanded to know why, management quickly realized that they could not make changes in standards without losing employee commitment. Consequently, management communicated extensively about the rationale behind the decision, thus alleviating employee concerns. High commitment, management learned, could not be retained unless they gave employees a voice in key decisions. Before long, Corning's top management began to talk about the "Medfield experiment" as a potential model and made sure to further Corning's reputation by talking to the business press, who were only too happy to write up Corning's success.

High-Commitment Manufacturing Plants

Some three years after the experiment at Medfield began, I received a call from managers at General Foods' Topeka, Kansas, dog food plant. Would I come out and share with them our experience at Medfield? Under the guidance of Richard Walton, later to become my colleague at Harvard and a key figure in the development of high-commitment manufacturing plants in several companies, the Topeka plant launched a much larger and more ambitious effort to create an HCHP system.

Spurred by Japanese competition in the late 1970s and 1980s, these early experiments, and others like them in numerous other companies, began to catch fire and spread. For example, General Motors collaborated with the United Automobile Workers (UAW) to launch a bold and visionary effort to incorporate high commitment, high performance ideas at its Saturn subsidiary, where the union president became an ex-officio member of the senior team. Goodyear Tire developed a systematic and long-term effort to transform all of its one hundred worldwide manufacturing plants into HCHP organizations. (This latter effort was led by senior management and was part of the company's organizational strategy to revitalize the company and compete in an increasingly difficult industry.) Similar efforts were launched at Cummins Engine, Procter & Gamble, and TRW, among others.[7]

In Europe, principally Scandinavia, a tradition of industrial democracy was leading practically minded academics to experiment with application of employee participation and job design in manufacturing settings. These innovations were motivated by efforts to counter the alienation so apparent in many traditional manufacturing plants where turnover and absenteeism were high, employees checked their brains at the door, and quality and productivity were low. The principles of scientific management, developed by Frederick Taylor, had spawned a work environment designed and controlled by engineers and supervisors that prevented workers' knowledge and needs from being incorporated. The purpose of innovations in these experimental plants was to shift from control to commitment as the dominant principle of management.[8]

Although most of the plant-level innovations were quite successful, they were not easily sustained or spread to other facilities of the corporation. In some cases, innovation disappeared as organizations confronted unanticipated technological or business changes that caused some in top management to move to a control mode; some corporate labor relations functionaries felt threatened by the new approaches; and some control-oriented leaders transferred into innovative plants were uncomfortable and unskilled in managing high-commitment organizations.[9] In other companies, the innovations remained isolated and did not spread to the rest of the organization. For example, General Motors had a number of successful high-commitment manufacturing plants, but these never impacted the practices of the company as a whole.

Failures to spread and sustain innovations in HCHP raise many questions about how a large-scale, multi-unit corporate transformation might be accomplished successfully, questions that I will address in the book.

Innovations at the Business Unit Level

Are high commitment and high performance principles that are successful in a manufacturing environment applicable to the strategic problems facing senior managers at the business unit and corporate levels? In the mid-1960s there were few if any planned change experiments that would answer this question. My own answer began to take shape when a new general manager of Corning's Electronic Products Division approached me for help after he had heard about the Medfield experiment. His division was underperforming and had significant morale and commitment problems.[10]

As my diagnosis of the division proceeded, it became clear that many of the ideas applied at Medfield also applied to management work, but that a whole set of new ideas about strategy, organization design, and management processes had to be incorporated. Although managers and professionals in the Electronic Product Division (EPD) had engaging and challenging jobs (unlike at Medfield), the division's performance suffered from a set of problems I also observed at Medfield: poor teamwork between key functions. In this case, revenues and profits suffered because EPD's functional departments, particularly marketing, manufacturing, and product development, were not coordinating their efforts to develop new cost-effective products. There was no shortage of commitment in EPD. The problem was that each manager was committed to his own functional department's goals rather than to the overall strategy and mission of the business unit. The consequence was an inability to respond to an increasingly competitive environment.

I learned that these problems had multiple root causes. A shift in the business environment and the division's strategy demanded far higher levels of coordination. The previous general manager, who led autocratically, had created an uncollaborative, highly politicized organization. Because all decisions went through him, the organization had not developed good cross-functional teamwork at lower levels. Nor did it possess the cross-functional team structure that would enable lower-level product development teams to work collaboratively. That this sorry state of affairs could not be discussed openly with the autocratic general manager increasingly threatened the division's survival.

Using a systemic diagnosis of the organization, the new, enlightened general manager made changes in the structure and management process of EPD. Within three years of his call for help he had succeeded in transforming the organization. Dramatic improvements were made in commitment to division goals, teams were trained to work together across functions, and overall leadership behavior, values, and culture changed. Unsurprisingly, the rate of new product development increased sharply, as did revenues and profits. From this experience I learned that, much like manufacturing plants, an underperforming strategic business unit with low commitment to mission could be transformed into an HCHP organization.

Similar efforts to implement change at the management level were under way at TRW's systems division. To serve the aerospace market, TRW's business model was heavily dependent on managing complex, cross-functional defense programs. Recognizing this challenge, Ruben Mettler, then president of TRW Systems, and Sheldon Davis, his vice president of human resources, pioneered in applying behavioral science ideas to program management. TRW found that planned changes in organization design, attitudes, and skills could enhance coordination and commitment to the mission of the company and improve results.

Academics Discover HCHP Corporations

In the early 1980s, the Harvard Business School, stimulated by innovations in industry, launched the first required course in human resource management. I was fortunate to lead that effort. The course aimed to educate prospective general managers about their responsibilities in creating an organizational system that produced commitment, coordination, and competence. Students were taught that these organizational capabilities were essential to the commitment of customers, employees, shareholders, and society.[11] The early manufacturing plant experiments provided rich cases, but were there examples of large high commitment and performance companies? Our search led to Hewlett-Packard (HP). Discovering HP was inspiring. Here was a remarkable and very different company built on values, objectives, and practices that deviated dramatically from conventional practice. It was a sophisticated corporate version of the small plant-level experiment I had helped shape at Corning. It reinvigorated my belief that large companies could be built on McGregor's Theory Y management assumptions and succeed financially. Over a forty-year time period, HP had achieved an annual growth rate in revenues and profits of 25 and 27 percent, respectively. By the late 1980s, Stanford researchers had identified and documented several other high-performance companies, such as Southwest Airlines, all led by CEOs who had systematically infused their companies with HCHP values, policies, and practices.[12]

In the 1990s, a number of systematic and rigorous research studies were published that supported the early experiments and case examples. These studies clearly showed that high-commitment practices and cultures are associated with sustained high financial performance. Some of the studies explored the relationship between high-commitment work practices and human as well as performance outcomes such as turnover, employee attitudes, productivity, and quality. Other studies showed that firm-level performance differences could be accounted for by differences in management philosophy, business policies, and culture. Virtually all the HCHP companies in these studies, however, were creations of their founders.

These studies showed *what* HCHP companies look like, how they are organized and managed, but they did not provide insights into *how* transformation happens, the distinctive focus of this book. I plan to integrate a comprehensive and systemic view of what HCHP firms look like, with a discussion of *how* average companies can be transformed. To understand how to change an organization requires one to be close to the action. It calls for studies that *focus on the process of change* through retrospective investigation or longitudinal research. Though less numerous, these studies have given us a real understanding of what leaders can do to transform their corporations into HCHP enterprises. A study of six corporate transformations, each with varying success, which my colleagues Russell Eisenstat and Bert Spector and I conducted in the mid- to late 1980s (when companies were responding to the Japanese challenge), as well as other such studies, inform many of the recommendations about how to bring about corporate change.[13]

Another way to learn about organizational change is for scholars to collaborate with managers, much as I did at Corning, in planning change and then researching the outcomes over time. This is called action research or action science.[14] Action research provides deep insights into the managerial assumptions, attitudes, and behaviors that enable or block a transformation in corporate culture. My own and others' action research informs this book. One action research program, which Russell Eisenstat and I conducted over a fifteen-year period, asked senior teams to utilize a task force of their own employees to inquire why their strategic intentions were not being implemented effectively. This study led to important insights about barriers to change and the means for transforming them into strengths through honest conversations.[15]

A number of excellent books have already been written about HCHP systems. Jeff Pfeffer's *Human Equation* is unequaled in making the case for high-commitment organizations through powerful evidence and arguments. Jim Collins's and Jerry Porras's seminal book, *Built to Last*, provides insights into the character of HCHP firms. Collins's *Good to Great* provides insights into the actions needed to develop an HCHP firm. This book builds on these works. It presents an operating theory of HCHP firms, demonstrates the architecture of HCHP firms, and integrates this perspective with a grounded discussion of the change process itself. I draw on multiple fields of management study that are not typically integrated into a whole systems perspective—for example, strategic management, organization design, culture, human resources management, leadership, and change. This book rests on the assumptions that soft cultural and leadership dimensions of high-commitment organizations must be integrated with hard dimensions such as strategic performance management and organization design. And it will focus on both *what* key HCHP organizational design levers look like, and *how* leaders can transform these levers and integrate them into a strategy for change.

Assumptions Underlying HCHP Organizations

A number of often unstated assumptions about organizations and management underlie high commitment, high performance organizations. CEOs or general managers wishing to transform their enterprise to HCHP organizations might do well to first reflect on the extent to which they share the perspectives detailed below. The discussion in this book is informed by these basic assumptions.

The Multiple Stakeholder Perspective

Shareholders are not the only constituent that HCHP firms serve. Employees, customers, community, and society are considered in all decisions. Top management attends to *multiple outcomes*, not just financial performance, in evaluating the performance of the enterprise and its managers. In effect, the firm must assess how well it is *providing value* for all its stakeholders. To what extent are employees committed and satisfied with their quality of life? To what extent are customers committed to the firm's offerings? To what extent are shareholders committed (invested for the long term)? To what extent is the firm making a contribution to the welfare of its community and society? Managers of HCHP organizations search for policies and management practices that *simultaneously* serve the interests of all stakeholders. A "simultaneous solve" produces surplus value for all. The organization is explicitly designed to produce economic, psychic, and social value for each party; leaders avoid decisions that privilege one party over another. This mentality requires the egalitarian philosophy that characterizes all HCHP firms, one that is decidedly absent in most average companies.

The Employee Influence and Learning Perspective

Developing employee commitment is seen as the primary means for meeting customer needs and achieving their commitment. To satisfy this objective, managers give employees at all levels a voice in the affairs of the enterprise, and influence on their immediate work, as well as on leadership, culture, policies, and management practices. This not only ensures fairness—what academics have called procedural justice—but enables senior management to learn whether their organization and leadership are effective. Senior managers at every level of the enterprise see themselves in partnership with employees in the quest to develop high commitment and high performance.

Unless mutual influence exists between management and employees or, for that matter, between management and each of the other stakeholders, cynicism develops about management's real intention. That cynicism will destroy trust and reduce the willingness of each side to risk revealing honestly their own thoughts and feelings about organization and leadership effectiveness. Problem solving, commitment, and organizational learning are impeded. For this reason, HCHP organizations create the means for honest interpersonal as well as organization-wide conversations about issues that matter. Figure 1.1 shows the virtuous cycle of communication, trust, risk taking, problem solving, and commitment—the development of a community of purpose—that honest conversations can foster. This requires more than skills. It demands that managers

FIGURE 1.1. THE VIRTUOUS COMMUNICATION AND LEARNING CYCLE.

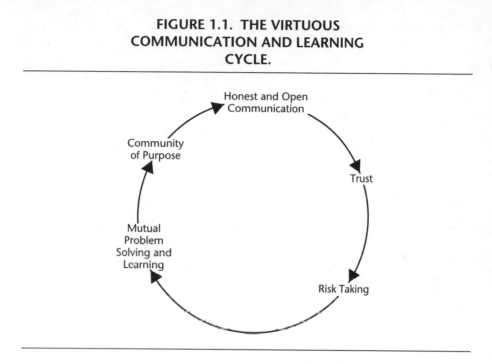

create the learning and governance mechanisms I discuss in chapter 7. Arguably, this is the most crucial design element, as it ensures continuous improvement in the quality of leadership and management practices.

The Systems Perspective

Organizations are complex, "high fit," multidimensional systems. Unless all facets of an organization fit together—that is, are internally consistent and externally relevant—the firm will not be able to create sustained high performance. These multiple facets—strategy, organization, people, and culture, for example—interact with each other in circular rather than linear ways. Cause and effect are often not connected in time and space, making analysis and solutions less obvious. In particular, I argue for a sociotechnical systems perspective which holds that harder "technical" changes in strategy, structure, and systems cannot succeed without changes in the social system of shared values, people, and culture. Yet in the majority of organizations it is the hard factors that get the most attention, in part because they are tangible and measurable.

Because change in the social system involves changes in people's minds, hearts, and skills, a transformation to an HCHP organization is a multiyear journey. Changing culture takes time, whether it occurs by developing existing employees and culture or through replacing people who do not fit. Equally important, managers who aim to transform their company to an HCHP organization will have to orchestrate change in many subunits of the enterprise—business units, country organizations, manufacturing plants, offices, stores, or branches—each with its own social system and leaders or, in the case of business units, a different business model.[16] And each subunit's efficacy is dependent on the larger organizational context of which it is a part.

The And/Also Perspective

Effective HCHP organizations are inherently paradoxical. Successful transformation leaders embrace opposites and find ways to make them work in harmony—people and profits, top-down and participative change, individual and team, hard and soft, technical and social. I learned this in 1981 when a senior manager at Hewlett-Packard pointed to the many contradictions inherent in the company. HP encouraged teamwork but at the same time differentiated individuals through a performance ranking system. It valued innovation and change but created many mechanisms for stability, including its employment security policy and emphasis on tradition. HP's objectives gave equal prominence to profits and to people-oriented goals such as individual dignity and teamwork. In this regard, leaders are uncompromising in their dedication to finding solutions that satisfy people and profits. A commitment to embracing paradox enables HCHP firms to weather all seasons.[17]

High commitment, high performance organizations are philosophically aligned with Taoist sage Lao Tzu, who pointed out that opposites coexist, and the presence of each demands the other.[18] For example, "convex cannot exist without concave, or as in the Chinese symbol, yin without yang."[19] At the heart of the and/also philosophy of HCHP firms is an intuitive recognition that people and life are full of contradictions and that great firms must be built on this premise. Seeking to understand what modern science (the theory of evolution, evolutionary psychology, social psychology, and biology) had to say about ancient philosophies regarding people, life, and society—about what makes for happiness—Jonathan Haidt found scientific evidence for the and/also. He concludes: "The East stresses acceptance and collectivism; the West encourages striving and individualism. But as we have seen [from scientific evidence] both perspectives are valuable. Happiness requires changing yourself and changing your world. It requires pursuing your own goals and fitting in with others."[20]

If people harbor contradicting needs and motives, HCHP organizations must be designed to appeal to striving and collectivism. Practicing the and/also enables HCHP firms to encourage the individual striving needed for innovation and the teamwork that enhances firm responsiveness and efficiency. It enables shareholder and employee commitment and thereby sustained advantage. HCHP managers must, therefore, embrace the *and/also as opposed to the either-or* perspective common in low-performance and low-commitment companies.

The paradox perspective has important implications for how managers ought to think about corporate transformation. As I elaborate in chapter 11, they need to avoid the temptation to view organizational change *only* through the prism of economic and shareholder value creation or *only* through the prism of human and organization development. Over his long tenure as CEO of General Electric, Jack Welch laid off 125,000 workers and earned the name Neutron Jack, yet in later years he embraced people, participation, and culture as keys to success. Archie Norman, CEO of Asda, a U.K. grocery chain now owned by Wal-Mart, led the company through a highly successful seven-year transformation that simultaneously restructured the company and involved people in building the new Asda.[21]

The Strategic General Management Perspective

The development of an organization's human system into an HCHP organization constitutes an important internal strategy worthy of the CEO's or general manager's continuous attention. It cannot be delegated to the human resource department. For the first fifteen years of Hewlett-Packard's life, its founders purposely avoided forming a personnel department because they regarded personnel, as it was called at the time, as a line management responsibility. When the corporate personnel department was formed, it played an important but supporting role. Archie Norman, who transformed Asda into an HCHP company, spent 75 percent of his time during the first three years of the journey as Asda's human resource director, according to his own estimate.[22] Jack Welch is widely quoted as having spent over 50 percent of his time on people issues.

A Social *and* Human Capital Perspective

The cost of hiring and developing people and the costs of developing organizational capabilities such as coordination, commitment, and competence should not be thought of as budgeted expenses. Rather, they are front-end investments that will yield a stream of benefits over time. They can create a flexible, creative, and productive workforce, as well as the underlying trust needed for adaptation to a rapidly changing competitive landscape. Human and social capital can, however, be easily degraded by neglect and poor maintenance, just as investment in financial and physical assets can.

HCHP companies establish business policies that will protect them from inadvertent liquidation of human and social capital. Very rapid growth, layoffs, frequent large acquisitions, and irregular investments in organization and employee development can undermine the virtuous cycle that underlies the sustained performance of HCHP companies. Of course this is not easy to do, and there are risks in estimating a future stream of benefits from an investment in social and human capital. Nevertheless, top management interested in developing an HCHP system should attempt to do so in both quantitative and qualitative terms.

The Normative and Situational Perspective

A debate in the field of organization studies has existed for a long time over whether there is one best way to manage *or* whether effective management practices depend on the situation—the industry, strategy, market, or country and national culture, for example. *The development of an HCHP organization demands both perspectives.* On the one hand, different strategic tasks demand different forms of organization, technologies, operating systems, leadership roles, and pay systems. On the other hand, building a high-commitment organization requires a normative perspective when it comes to people and culture. HCHP leaders believe that people are driven by *more* than their own self-interests to acquire money, status, privilege, and power, and that the politics and unethical behavior that can potentially arise from these drives are neither inevitable nor good for high commitment and high performance. They have an optimistic view of people—that under the right organizational circumstances, people want to commit to an organization's mission, want to work collaboratively with others who share similar values, and will work unselfishly toward organizational goals.

Is this assumption naive? My colleagues Paul Lawrence and Nitin Nohria plumbed the depth of multiple scientific traditions (evolutionary biology, psychology, anthropology, economics, neuroscience, and others) and found support for the "optimistic" view of people. They found that human development has genetically hardwired people to bond and learn, drives that enable them to behave beyond their self-interest.[23] Leaders of HCHP organizations believe this intuitively, and thus organize and manage their enterprises to appeal to and encourage the responsible and collaborative behavior of which all human beings are apparently capable.

The Head and Heart Perspective

HCHP organizations require leaders who lead from the heart *and* manage with their heads. Employee commitment, as I suggest above, is an emotional quality. It arises when organizations enable fulfillment of fundamental and universal human needs for meaning and making a difference.[24] Commitment cannot be developed through logical argument. To stimulate these needs, managers must lead with the heart. But they must create policies and practices with their heads. One way to do this is to be honest with themselves and their employees about what is in their hearts—their feelings and thoughts—so that the policies they have designed can be stress tested through honest conversations. Good analytical thinking about a host of business problems is also essential. High performance demands that managers view the firm through the lens of hard facts and that these facts govern managerial decisions as much as the ideals do. The head *and* heart perspective is rarely found in one single manager. Leaders may have to combine their good head with the heart of others or their good heart with the good heads of others.

The Change Perspective

Most HCHP companies are "born right," shaped by the vision and values of their founders. But what about the majority of firms not born right? Can they be transformed into HCHP organizations in adolescence or adulthood? My view is yes; this is not only possible, but very much worth the prize. The transformation of such companies as Asda, Becton Dickinson, General Electric, and New United Motor Manufacturing, among others (see next chapter), demonstrates that the DNA of older companies with bureaucratic patterns of management can be transformed with remarkably positive human and economic outcomes. As I will show, not just any change process will do. The means for change must be consistent with the aspiration to build an internally consistent system that enables commitment and continuous learning.

Summary

Our knowledge about how to build high commitment and high performance organizations has evolved in the last fifty years from early experiments in small companies and manufacturing plants to an understanding of how to build large multi-unit HCHP corporations. Doing this involves knowledge about how the system should be designed—its management policies and practices—as well as knowledge about how to lead fundamental cultural change and enable continuous learning and improvement.

Plan for the Book

The book is divided into five parts, each composed of one or more chapters—each building on the former to tell the story of what it takes to build an HCHP firm.

Part One: The High Commitment, High Performance Organization

Chapters 2, 3, and 4 make the case that HCHP organizations are complex systems that must be consciously chosen and involve the acceptance of a disciplined approach to building the HCHP system.

Chapter 2 presents three HCHP outcomes—the pillars of *performance alignment*, *psychological alignment*, and the *capacity for learning and change*—that must be developed by leaders who aspire to build an HCHP organization. It provides the reader with the look and feel of an HCHP company—Southwest Airlines—and the critical role that leaders' management philosophy plays in building these companies. And it discusses how applicable the HCHP concept is to different national cultures.

Chapter 3 goes deeper. If CEOs or general managers are to invest in transforming their organizations, it is important that this be a conscious choice, one that involves acceptance of certain values, principles, and assumptions about how to organize and manage. Not only do these choices diverge from the conventional and easy, they create constraints that CEOs must be willing to accept.

Chapter 4 makes the case for why the systems perspective is essential in building HCHP organizations, outlines key levers for change, and introduces the multilevel and multi-unit systems perspective needed to transform a large corporation.

Part Two: What Stands in the Way

Chapter 5 presents organizational and managerial barriers that I call the silent killers, barriers that stand in the way of developing HCHP organizations and leadership practices. The fact that these barriers are difficult to discuss publicly makes it challenging for organizations to examine and change them into strengths. Without confronting and changing the silent killers, leaders succeed in changing only the technical system and not the social and human system so central to HCHP organizations.

Part Three: Leadership and Learning Change Levers

Chapter 6 is about the leadership needed to build an HCHP organization. It discusses what leaders must do, who they must be, and what they must know in order to stimulate and facilitate a collective action learning process that enables redesign and realignment of the HCHP system.

Chapter 7 discusses the system of learning and governance needed to continuously improve the quality of leadership and management. Such a system enables truth to speak to power and helps managers to see the total system and barriers to change. It enables them to transform their organization with commitment—to build a community of purpose.

Part Four: Organization Design Change Levers

Chapters 8, 9, and 10 discuss three facets of the organization that must be redesigned in order to build an HCHP organization, illustrating how a learning and governance process can facilitate change in each of these organizational domains.

Chapter 8 discusses the role of strategic performance management in HCHP organizations. It outlines why organizations fail to execute and achieve sustained high performance, the essential qualities of high-performing cultures, and illustrates the role of learning and governance in strategic performance management.

Chapter 9 discusses the role of organization design and periodic redesign in developing and sustaining performance alignment and psychological alignment. Design logic and alternative organizing models are discussed, as well as the role of learning and governance processes in enabling rapid realignment of the organization without loss of commitment.

Chapter 10 is about developing human and social capital through the design of an HCHP human resource system—a set of HR policies and practices for attracting, selecting, socializing, developing, and rewarding people—found in the most advanced HCHP companies. It argues that social capital—a collaborative team culture—is underemphasized and underdeveloped in most firms when compared to human capital, yet differentiates HCHP firms from other companies.

Part Five: Transforming the Organization

Chapter 11 describes stark differences between two archetypal strategies for change—Theory E, which focuses on the firm's economic health, and Theory O, which focuses on the firm's organizational health. It argues that both are necessary and must be integrated into a strategy for each of eight dimensions of change. The chapter also illustrates how leaders can integrate E and O in managing eight facets of strategic change through the lens of an exceptional example of corporate transformation.

How to Read This Book

Senior executives and their advisers—strategic management or human resource executives as well as organization development consultants—should read chapters 1–7 closely. Although chapters 8, 9, and 10 may also be of interest to senior executives, they provide in-depth information that may be of most interest for advisers to senior management. Chapter 11 should be read by top management as well as their advisers.

PART ONE

THE HIGH COMMITMENT, HIGH PERFORMANCE ORGANIZATION

CHAPTER TWO

PILLARS OF HIGH COMMITMENT, HIGH PERFORMANCE ORGANIZATIONS

Working here is truly an unbelievable experience. They treat you with respect, pay you well, and empower you. They use your ideas to solve problems. They encourage you to be yourself. I love working here.

—EMPLOYEE AT SOUTHWEST AIRLINES[1]

High commitment and high performance companies are able to deliver sustained performance because they have developed the following organizational pillars:

1. Performance alignment
2. Psychological alignment
3. Capacity for learning and change

Performance alignment occurs when the total organization system —structure, systems, people, and culture—fits performance goals and strategy. *Psychological alignment* is the emotional attachment of people at all levers, particularly key unit leaders, to the purpose, mission, and values of the company. And if the firm is to sustain both performance and psychological alignment, it must also have the *capacity for learning and change*. Taken together, these three pillars create the resilience essential for a company to weather inevitable inflections in the business and social environment as the firm grows (see Figure 2.1). Strength in all areas markedly increases the chances that a firm will be able to sustain high commitment and high performance over an extended period of time, sometimes over decades.

It's not enough for a company to have one or two of these pillars in place at a given time. The CEO of an HCHP firm must be able to *simultaneously solve* for all three of these organizational outcomes. That is one reason why competitors of Southwest Airlines, an exemplary HCHP organization for almost four decades,

FIGURE 2.1. PILLARS OF HIGH COMMITMENT, HIGH PERFORMANCE ORGANIZATIONS.

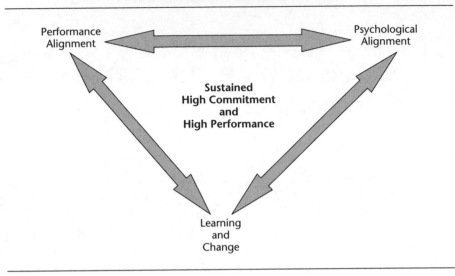

have not been able to emulate its success.[2] Competitors were able to copy certain operational practices and gain some semblance of performance alignment in a short period of time (however, in all cases this was incomplete), but they could not develop psychological alignment or the capacity to learn and change in a short time frame. To simultaneously solve for all three outcomes, leaders must have the will and skill to consider all three pillars when making decisions about strategy, business policy, and human resource practices.

How has Southwest been able to develop psychological alignment, capacity for learning, and such a remarkable performance? Does Southwest have secret "high tech" tools to select the smartest and brightest? The answer to this is a decided no! Southwest and other HCHP organizations achieve extraordinary results through finding ordinary, competent people with great attitudes who fit their culture. Organizing, managing, and the company's underlying philosophy come first. Profits and commitment will follow.

The thesis of this book is that sustained commitment and performance emerge when the *organizational system*—hard formal structures and systems as well as the soft leadership, people, and cultural characteristics—is explicitly designed by leaders to solve for all three organizational outcomes. The system and its three strong pillars enable a virtuous cycle as depicted in Figure 2.2.

FIGURE 2.2. THE VIRTUOUS HCHP CYCLE.

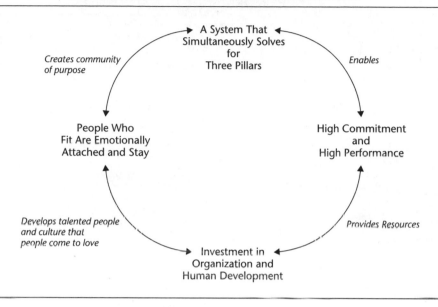

Are HCHP Organizations a Realistic Objective?

You may ask whether it is realistic to think that organizations can be created where people are so committed that they subjugate individual career and department interests to the purpose and objectives of the larger organization. Aren't politics inevitable when large numbers of people are brought together to achieve a common purpose? Won't managers' commitment to their own interests and that of the departments they manage always trump their commitment to the mission of the company? Is it really possible for companies to enable people to speak truthfully about the challenges the organization faces, including the behavior and policies of top management?

Though difficult to create and sustain, the success of Southwest Airlines is not an aberration brought about by the particular circumstances of the airline industry. Nor is the company's success *only* due to founder Herb Kelleher's unique skills in relating to people, though, as we shall see, his values and vision have been critical to Southwest's success. Table 2.1 provides an illustrative list of HCHP companies in industries as diverse as retailing, steel, education, sports, and high technology. All have outperformed their peers for many years and,

TABLE 2.1. HIGH COMMITMENT, HIGH PERFORMANCE COMPANIES.

Airlines	Southwest Airlines
Software	SAS Institute
Technology	Hewlett-Packard (until late 90s)
Telecommunication	Cisco
Consulting	McKinsey
Investment Banking	Goldman Sachs
Sports	New England Patriots
Steel	Nucor
Pharmaceuticals	Johnson & Johnson
Hotels	Marriott
Computers	IBM (until 80s)
Electrical Equipment	Lincoln Electric
Grocery	Costco
Education	Harvard Business School
Automobiles	Toyota

in some instances, for decades. None fits perfectly the ideal HCHP model for organizing, leading, and managing discussed in this book, but all bear substantial similarity to it.[3]

Founded as HCHP companies, these firms have demonstrated that the HCHP model of management delivers superior value to employees, customers, and shareholders. The companies are not identical in their organizational arrangements or HR policies and practices, but they have all developed performance and psychological alignment, as well as the capacity to learn and change.

Competitors have a very challenging time gaining an advantage over these companies, because their organizational system and the high-commitment culture are difficult to imitate in the short run, if at all. To gain a detailed understanding of what an HCHP company looks and feels like, I will provide an overview of Southwest. It makes for an excellent illustrative case because it has been so well researched and its policies and practices so well documented.

Southwest Airlines: An Illustrative Case[4]

By now it's no secret that Southwest Airlines, founded in 1971, has been the most successful airline company in the United States for over thirty years. From its inauspicious beginnings, flying out of Love Field in Dallas with only three airplanes, the company has grown into a major player in the industry. By 2004 it served fifty-nine cities and employed thirty-four thousand people. Its annualized returns to stockholders from 1972 to 2002 were 25.99 percent, the best among all U.S. stocks and above high-performing companies like Wal-Mart (by a very small amount), as well as Walgreens, Intel, and Comcast.[5] As of 2004 it outperformed all other airlines on a number of critical operating dimensions. It is the only airline to have made a profit every year for the past thirty years. Southwest's operating costs are 20 percent below the rest of the industry, despite the fact that it is 80 percent unionized.[6] In 2005, Southwest's market capitalization exceeded that of all the other airline companies combined, many founded well before Southwest. Even more impressive is that Southwest's returns exceed those of many companies in industries advantaged by technology and a favorable competitive environment. In other words, Southwest has achieved sustained high performance in what most regard as a terrible industry, one that since its deregulation in the late 1970s has presented a very tough challenge.

Southwest's success was accomplished with a strategy and a set of management policies and practices that were, and in many instances still are, very counterconventional. Southwest's original strategy, to serve nonbusiness customers with low fares that would compete with bus fares on the same route, was at first thought to be impossible and probably a prescription for disaster. They have been able to maintain competitively low fares by creating a community of people who relentlessly focus on controlling costs. Here's Colleen Barrett, executive vice president of customers:

> We're one big family, and the family members expect a lot of each other. Part of that means watching our costs carefully. We can't compete unless our costs are as low as, or lower than our competitors, which mean everyone has to take part. For example when the price of jet fuel skyrocketed during the Persian Gulf crisis, Herb [the company's CEO] sent a letter to every pilot asking if she or he would contribute ideas on how to save fuel. The pilots developed a new procedure for takeoffs and landings that was just as safe and saved a significant percentage of the fuel used in those maneuvers.[7]

But unique practices and management do not end with an emphasis on low cost. Southwest developed an operating system that supported the low-price, low-cost, on-time departure strategy. When the company was founded, the system violated every prescription in the airline industry. That model includes flying only one type of aircraft (the Boeing 737), fast turnaround of airplanes, timely departure, high utilization of airplanes, flexible work roles, and a friendly and fun environment for customers. The company flies out of secondary, noncongested airports and offers point-to-point service only; passengers cannot connect to other cities through the traditional hub-and-spoke system thought to be essential for success. And contrary to the practice of other airlines at the time, from the outset, Southwest did not provide assigned seats, served only peanuts and drinks, and did not check luggage through to another airline when a passenger wanted to make a connection.

Southwest has reversed the conventional wisdom that low cost means less attention to customers. The company earned the Triple Crown award—best on-time performance, fewest complaints, and fewest bags lost—for five years in a row, something that no other airline has achieved. The company was ranked first in the industry, with the fewest customer complaints, for thirteen consecutive years. They have not done this by offering meals and other high-end services, but rather by offering passengers fun and friendliness. As one flight attendant stated, "We are all dedicated to the delivery of positively outrageous service to customers—with a sense of pride, warmth and friendliness."[8] As Herb Kelleher, CEO during the first three decades, likes to point out, "It's easy to offer great service at high cost. It's easy to offer lousy service at low cost. What's tough is offering great service at low cost, and that's what our goal is."[9]

The secret to the low-cost, low-price, and friendly service model lies in Southwest's equally unconventional approach to managing people; one that outsiders often find hard to believe really works. One employee, who had worked at several other large companies, said, "I was pretty dubious at first, having been at places where everyone but the top two or three people were considered commodities, but I have come to appreciate a place where kindness and the human spirit are nurtured."[10] A keen observer and expert on the airline industry observed, "At other places managers say that people are the most important resource, but no one acts on it. At Southwest they have never lost sight of that fact."[11] This observation is supported by Southwest's consistent place in Fortune Magazine's list of the "Fortune 100 Best Companies to Work For." In 1998 it ranked number one in that list. Southwest's approach to managing people stems from a unique culture, one created and sustained by the company's founders. The company enjoys a culture of teamwork and selfless contribution that is not the norm in U.S. society. It took imagination, leadership, and courage to create the culture described by a manager as follows: "At Southwest, the community is most important. People have to let go of their personal egos. Without the success of the community, you can't have personal success. The U.S. needs a heavy dose of Southwest's culture. It needs people who are more community-minded and less self centered."[12]

Southwest's high performance capabilities and culture are robust enough to repeatedly beat off challenges by competitors. Fearing revenue loss in the California market, United Airlines (45 percent of its revenues came from its California hubs at the time) tried to compete on the San Francisco–Los Angeles route, only to fail miserably. Continental tried to compete with its "Continental Light" flights, which served only peanuts and drinks, but failed to make any money, and ultimately abandoned this concept. Experiencing continued performance problems in the face of Southwest's increasing success and growth, competitors are again trying to emulate their model. Only time will tell how many will be successful in the long run. Below I illustrate the HCHP three pillars through the lens of SWA.

Three Pillars of HCHP Organizations

Performance Alignment

High performance cannot be achieved unless all aspects of the organization's design are aligned or fit together and in turn are aligned with or fit the strategic task of the organization.[13] Crucial to this multi-alignment is that management maintains internal consistency across design levers and throughout all corporate subunits and levels. Why is this quality of organizations so important?

Strategy Must Be Distinctive, Focused, and Values-Based. A focused and distinctive strategy for delivering value to a targeted customer segment is essential for sustained competitive advantage. Southwest realized before anyone else that if they could make airfare as cheap as ground transportation and provide friendly service as well, they would be able to create a new market that no one else was serving. They have focused on this strategy relentlessly. In choosing this strategy, management made a conscious *choice* not to cater to business travelers. Gary Kelly, now CEO of Southwest, captured the strategic choice that underpins the company's success as follows:

> First of all the company just had a great idea. And it really was—through the lens of 20–20 hindsight—it was brilliant. In the late '60s, early '70s, it was a very humble idea to the founders. But nonetheless, it was visionary. The second aspect is that they were remarkably disciplined in their focus on the strategy over decades, and they resisted the temptation to chase other distractions. They knew what they were good at, and they just worked harder and harder to perfect that.[14]

A focused strategy freed management to hire only people who were aligned with low-cost and friendly service. Its organizational design, operating system, and human resource policies were intended to compete with the car, bus, and train travel typically used by leisure travelers. Perhaps unsurprisingly, in recent years, SWA has also become attractive to business travelers who value low-cost, on-time flights. Making a clear choice enabled Southwest to avoid the mistakes that often plague underperforming companies like Continental (up to the late 1990s) and United when they attempt to serve low-end *as well as* high-end customers, what Michael Porter has called straddling.[15]

Perhaps less well known is the fact that HCHP firms' strategic choices emerge from their hearts as well as their heads. Strategy typically reflects senior management's desire to create a better world, to make a contribution. The value-based component of the strategy is what enables the company to avoid distractions, as Kelly put it. Hewlett-Packard's concern with gaining customer respect and loyalty by providing quality products had a deeply human quality. Engine manufacturer Cummins Engine's long-standing commitment to the environment was central to their recent turnaround.[16] Gary Kelly sees human values as the underpinnings of Southwest's strategy: "A huge component of the strategy wasn't necessarily a thought. It was more visceral. It was just an appreciation for people. It was a very deep understanding that we're here to serve customers and that to serve customers well, you have to have great people, and you have to take great care of those people."

The Organization Must Fit the Strategy.
A clear strategic choice makes it possible to fit the organization and its people to the strategy. By organization I mean the roles, responsibilities, and relationships that enable specialization and coordination. Structure and systems define these formally, but in HCHP companies the culture and norms play an especially important role in shaping organizational behavior. Without alignment the strategy will not be implemented effectively and performance will be severely compromised. Implementation is about more than setting goals and following up. It is about creating a design that enables execution.

Southwest's strategy requires fifteen-minute airplane turnarounds and continuous emphasis on keeping costs low. The operating system (using only one type of plane to ensure low maintenance, no assigned seating, and so on) and organization were purposely designed to achieve low cost. Unlike its competitors, Southwest Airlines created the position of airport station manager, whose job is to develop a tight-knit team that coordinates maintenance, pilots, and ramp and customer-service employees for the fifteen-minute turnaround. Cross-functional teams are empowered to be responsive to local station conditions rather than driven by rules and processes created by distant corporate staff. Cross-functional processes imposed by corporate staff are likely to suppress initiative and prevent teamwork at the local unit level. By balancing the need for top-down control with local autonomy, Southwest has managed to increase the organization's capacity, as well as increase the number of decisions and the amount of work that can be accomplished in a cost-effective manner. The decentralized structure enables coordination, communication, and creativity, and it develops leadership competence, all capabilities that characterize HCHP organizations.

On the people side, Southwest's low-cost friendly and fun service strategy demands managers who are not elitist or particularly concerned about status, and employees who are relationship oriented and relatively uninhibited. Even pilots must have these qualities, regardless of their proficiency. Without a relationship orientation, pilots would not collaborate with flight attendants in cleaning an airplane or meet the fifteen-minute turnaround objective, nor would they be able to relate to passengers in the friendly manner expected of all Southwest employees. A customer's experience with a company must be consistent for loyalty to truly develop.

High-performance organizations like Southwest are clear about the attitudes, capabilities, and behaviors needed to implement the strategy. They recruit and select people who fit these criteria. They are also clear about qualities they don't want and consciously avoid making hiring mistakes. A highly proficient pilot who was rude to a secretary was not hired. That pilot probably would have been hired by an underperforming company, on the assumption that success comes from hiring the candidate with the best functional skills. Mistakes in hiring are costly and reduce the value proposition for customers and shareholders. Indeed, a study of Southwest Airlines shows that coordination based on relationships, rather than structure or incentives, is at the heart of the company's high performance.[17] Continental's and United's failure to woo away Southwest's customers can be traced to an inability to fit their organization (particularly the company culture) and operating system to the low-cost and friendly service strategy they tried to emulate.

Organizational Design Levers Must Be Internally Consistent. Employees must become convinced that management means what they say. For this, internal consistency between the various organization design levers is important. The firm will most likely not be able to implement its strategy without it. Consistency is essential for developing employee trust and commitment to the goals, values, and strategy of the enterprise. Southwest's low-cost and rapid airplane turnaround would not be possible, as noted above, without relationships of trust and good communication. Consider the following description of how cross-functional communication at SWA enables both an aligned and internally consistent organization: "There is a constant communication between customer service and the ramp. When planes have to be switched and bags must be moved, customer service will advise the ramp directly or through operations. If there is an aircraft swap operations keeps everyone informed. It happens smoothly."[18]

Inconsistent policy and practice erode the effectiveness of other policies too. Consider the training in interpersonal relationships and teamwork that employees receive at Southwest's People University. Without a structure that demands accountability for broad performance measures at the station level where functions come together, leaders that embody core principles, good union management relationships, and broad job descriptions, the training investment would be largely wasted. Similarly, a structure that enables station managers to be accountable for broad measures of performance would be ineffective without station managers who know how to lead a team.

Internal Consistency and Competitive Advantage. Internal consistency makes it very difficult for a competitor to copy a firm's formula for success. Copying one practice may be relatively easy; copying a large set of policies and practices that are internally consistent is far less likely. This is in part a function of statistical probabilities, as Michael Porter has argued.[19] If the probability of copying any one policy is .9, the probability of copying many consistent policies is far lower. But copying a firm's internally consistent policies is also made difficult by the fact that this consistency emerges from the CEO's values. If competitors do not have a CEO who possesses the "right" values, they cannot create consistent policies and practices. Surprisingly, few firms actually use the value lens in hiring CEOs.[20] Leaders at every level of the company must possess the same management philosophy and values as the CEO. Such leadership consistency takes a long time to develop. Southwest achieved it through many years of careful selection and development of their managers. Conversely, the leadership gap prevented United and Continental Airlines from competing successfully with Southwest.

Inconsistency led to Continental's failure to compete with Southwest. In 1993, Robert Ferguson announced his plan to split the company into two operations; one would concentrate on short-haul, low-fare flights (named Continental Light or CA Light), and the other would feature first-class service at business-class prices. Ferguson believed a cost structure lower even than Southwest's would enable Continental to compete successfully. CA Light cut its fares and cut its meal service, but much of the rest of its operating system—multiple airplane types, a reservation system, and hub-and-spoke system—remained the same. More important, the company was unable to replicate Southwest's HCHP culture. Continental flight attendants, when asked to emulate Southwest practice by helping to clean cabins between flight segments, complained about increased workloads and short break times. Though ground crews tried hard they still took thirty minutes to turn around an airplane rather then the twenty minutes they hoped for (a goal that was still five minutes more than Southwest's typical performance). And pilots were upset until the company provided meals during their busy schedules.

It takes years to create the Southwest culture and employee attitudes. Perhaps more important, Robert Ferguson at Continental did not possess the values and style required of a CEO who wants to create an HCHP system. He was described as a taskmaster who was "harsh and uncommunicative" and who drove employees away. He admitted to not suffering fools gladly and said "he would tell you in front of 20 people or 100 people if you were not doing a good job."[21] This is not the inspiring and caring leadership style of high-commitment leaders like Herb Kelleher.

Psychological Alignment

The Southwest employee who says she "loves working here" captures exactly the type of emotional attachment to the firm that defines psychological alignment. Love of company mission and values is a central characteristic of an HCHP system, research has found.[22] Organization structure, the performance management system, and incentives—the hard aspects of an organization—can *move* people to work together, if only temporarily. But employees who are psychologically aligned with the mission and values of the organization are *internally motivated*. With psychological alignment, firms become *communities of purpose*. Relationships and teamwork become central drivers of behavior. People become willing to sacrifice their immediate self-interest for the demanding goals required for high performance. The sense of family that pervades HCHP organizations and the attention to people required to achieve that feeling are reflected in what Southwest's Kelly reported to me in a 2008 interview: "There's a real celebration of success and individual achievements. The family-like feel is accomplished through not only what we do here at Southwest Airlines, but also by appreciating people for who they are, their personal accomplishments. And simple things, like recognizing birthdays, weddings, and anniversaries. Many companies do those things, but it comes across disingenuous. Here it really is a celebration."[23]

Firms seeking psychological alignment consciously develop a *distinctive "psychological contract"—a high-investment, high-return exchange* between the firm and its employees (managers and workers). This is not a written contract. It is what employees and top management, representing the shareholder, believe they are giving and getting in the relationship. In a high-commitment culture, the psychological contract is the set of high mutual expectations and obligations that create high value for both parties. The unwritten contract is based on positive assumptions about people, what they aspire to, and what they are capable of.[24]

At a minimum, all organizations expect managers and workers to reliably perform assigned tasks and to achieve performance standards. But in HCHP organizations with high psychological alignment, management expects that employees will take initiative, work collaboratively, supervise and regulate themselves, work unselfishly, and continually change and adapt. HCHP companies consciously draft a psychological contract that will elicit emotional commitment from their employees to the community.

At a minimum, all employees, the highest-level managers as well as the lowest-level workers, expect the organization to provide fair treatment, fair pay, and benefits, and some involvement in decisions affecting their work and work life. But employees in HCHP organizations expect much more than money and fair treatment. They expect management to live by the values that bind them to the community. They expect open and trusting relationships, achievement, involvement, challenge, responsibility, personal growth, and meaning. Although not all employees have these needs, HCHP organizations select employees who do have these needs. When they are managed as responsible citizens of the organization, employees' latent needs can be unleashed. Because making an emotional commitment means they are willing to give their all, employees in HCHP firms expect a voice in the policies and practices that govern their lives and a substantial voice and influence over the firm's affairs.

In effect, the enterprise cedes substantial influence over goals and process to employees in return for dedication and commitment to the community and its purpose. This is what *aligns employees' hearts and minds* with the enterprise's mission and values. With a positively aligned psychological contract, employees have the interests of the company and its customers at heart, are flexible in the work they do (they do not insist on adhering to the letter of their job descriptions), and engage the work with their hearts and heads, as opposed to just their hands. They approach the problems of the firm with the customers' and firm's interests in mind. "We're one big family," Colleen Barrett at SWA explained, "and the family members expect a lot of each other. Part of that means watching our costs carefully. We can't compete unless our costs are as low as, or lower than our competitors, which mean everyone has to take part." A ticket agent at Southwest illustrated this commitment to keeping costs low when she pursued a three-dollar stapler she had lent to a colleague at another airline. In most companies, employees would not think it worth the time and trouble. They might even take the stapler home. The sense of community and commitment to the firm's mission enables employees, managers, and workers to sacrifice their egos for the greater good.

TABLE 2.2. THE HCHP PSYCHOLOGICAL CONTRACT.

Management Expects	Employees Expect
Dedication to mission and strategy	Non-political culture—management does the "right" thing
High performance	Be on winning team working with best of best
Behavior consistent with values	Leader behavior consistent with values
Initiative	Delegation of authority
Collaboration and teamwork	Coworkers who share common values
Self-management	Participation in goal setting
Flexibility	Autonomy
Unselfish contribution	Unselfish and egalitarian behavior at top
Openness to feedback and learning	Opportunity to speak truth to power
Commitment to the firm	Employee development; above average pay and benefits; good faith effort to avoid layoffs

Partnership, created by a process of mutual influence, is at the heart of an HCHP system. It is not about money, though HCHP firms typically pay their employees above-average wages. *Involvement* enables employees to develop commitment and willingness to learn, accept, and even drive change. Table 2.2 summarizes the high-stakes psychological contract that HCHP organizations forge—what management and employees expect from each other.

At its most basic level, Southwest's success can be attributed to the partnership between senior managers and lower-level managers, and between managers and their thousands of employees. Everyone—the community—is involved in making the business and work life better. In sharp contrast, a United Airlines mechanic reported: "You've got to hope that the way we do things will change. [United] is the kind of place where management usually thinks they are way up there and the rest of us are way down here. They want to make sure the shareholders get what they want, but they don't care much about the employees. All that's got to change [if we are going to compete with Southwest]."[25]

Employees want to work for a successful organization, not only for the sake of pride and a sense of efficacy, but also because a winning company is able to offer personal development, career opportunities, job security, and financial rewards such as stock options. HCHP companies are able to provide these tangible benefits because the level of worker commitment produces extraordinary financial results. This is what creates the virtuous cycle found in HCHP firms (see Figure 2.2).

The shareholders at Southwest have achieved remarkable returns on their investment—in 2002 its market value of $9 billion was larger than all other airline companies combined. But high profits were also used to invest in employee training and to carefully select and develop leaders to manage the high-commitment way. Because all employees own stock, the consistent rise in price made employees richer and offset the slightly lower-than-average industry wages they receive.

Stock ownership is a double-edged sword, however. As the airline business became more challenging and new competitors emulated Southwest more effectively than United and Continental had, Southwest returns suffered (though still better than the industry standard), and the yearly stock growth its employees have come to expect is no longer a given. What was a positive symbol of community now threatens to be a source of dissatisfaction. Though Southwest's many other positive features still give it a huge advantage in retaining employees, this problem illustrates the challenge of maintaining the virtuous cycle in the face of uncertainties in the business environment.

The work of developing psychological alignment begins during the recruitment and selection process. Applicants are carefully screened for their fit with the company's values and culture. New hires are clearly told what they can expect and what will be expected of them. In 2003 Southwest hired only .04 percent of their 202,357 job applicants. Such a low selection ratio enables a company to reject employees that don't fit. Of course, the company would not have so many people who want to work there unless they had first created a reputation as a great place to work. A socialization process also shapes the psychological alignment. New employees participate in an educational process about the company's values, culture, and operating and service principles, an education that is reinforced throughout their employment.

Psychological alignment is particularly vulnerable to inconsistencies between how higher- and lower-level employees are treated. HCHP organizations typically practice symbolic egalitarianism, which means that they make a concerted effort to create common policies and practices for upper and lower levels. Southwest, like other HCHP companies, is relentless about vertical consistency. The profit-sharing plan, for example, pays all levels the same percentage of profit even though senior managers receive more profit dollars than lower-level employees. HCHP firms typically also make no distinctions between levels with regard to office (most have an open office landscape with similar cubicles for all levels) and other status symbols such as company cars.

United Airlines, conversely, never developed psychological alignment, even after its employees became owners. That is because its leaders, as a flight attendant testifies, did not care about its employees, develop an egalitarian climate, or create a sense of consistent and fair practices across levels.

We've always been treated like angry children who don't deserve what they get. Upper management has been adversarial and confrontational with us for over 10 years now; I don't think Mr. Wolf liked the flight attendants at all. We are managed differently from other groups. We're disciplined if we're sick more than 3 days per month or if we arrive late for a flight. We're the only group that has to hop on a scale every month. Pilots certainly aren't held to those standards. When it comes to the boys in the cockpit, things are different. The pilots stay in downtown hotels, and we are stuck out at the airport. When we have to deadhead, they fly in first class and we're in the back of the plane. That says it all . . . The irony, of course, is that the bosses ought to think a lot harder about how we feel if they want to keep their customers happy. We're the people who spend all the time with passengers. To the public we are United.[26]

Capacity for Learning and Change

We live in a time of unprecedented change. Global competition as well as rapid changes in technology and markets require organizations to be adaptive and capable of transformation. Robert Bauman, former CEO of SmithKline Beecham and an experienced change leader, captured the importance of the capacity for learning and change as a key to competitive advantage. "Most important in implementing change in the near term is about instilling the capacity for change within the organization in the long term. In my view the capacity for ongoing change is the ultimate source of competitive advantage."[27]

Unfortunately, the evidence points to the exact opposite. Most firms do not adapt and therefore lose their performance edge and eventually die. Of the original Forbes 100 companies named in 1917, sixty-one ceased to exist by 1987. Of the remaining thirty-nine, only eighteen stayed in the top hundred, and their return was 20 percent less than the overall market for that period. Of the companies named in the original S&P 500 in 1957, only seventy-four remained in 1997 and of these, only twelve outperformed the S&P 500 during that period.[28] Jim Collins's study of 1,435 companies on the Fortune 500 list between 1965 and 1995 found that *only* eleven were able to move from simply good performance to great performance, defined as cumulative stock returns 6.9 times the general market for a period of fifteen years or more, and this after a concerted effort to transform them.[29] Since the completion of the study the performance of approximately half of these companies has declined below the level that qualified them as great companies.[30] The difficulty firms have in adapting to environmental challenges can also be seen in the steady decline in CEO tenure—from 10.5 years in 1990 to less than four years in 2000.

In a groundbreaking study of why successful firms decline, Danny Miller concludes that the very alignment of leadership behavior, policies, and management practices that make companies successful are also the source of their demise.[31] Alignment, paradoxically, is also the reason for failure. Firms, he finds, tend to accentuate the strategy and management practices that gave them success and suppress divergent views and practices. According to Miller: "[Firms] choose one set of goals, values, and champions, and focus on these more and more tightly as they are enveloped by crisis. The powerful get more powerful and defend against contrarian views about what the firm's strategy should be or how the organization should be changed to implement this strategy. Those who disagree with those in power become disenfranchised. Consequently, firms move first toward consistency, then toward obsession and excess."[32] Why?

Over time firms tend to attract, select, promote, and terminate people based on their fit with the distinctive qualities and attitudes of the firm.[33] This phenomenon reduces diversity, an essential quality of the workforce if firms are to adapt to new circumstances. Yet we know that diversity promotes different perspectives; if those different perspectives are joined in a dialogue, new and creative solutions can be created. Firms die because there is too little honest dialogue about external and internal realities.

If organizations are purposely "built for high fit," can they also be built to adapt? My answer to this question is a qualified yes, so long as the firm practices honest and fact-based self-inquiry and has created a safe environment where truth can speak to power. Indeed, designing into the organization the paradoxical qualities of a strong, high-fit culture that creates common habits and the capacity for learning and also change that will challenge those habits before they become entrenched is a real challenge for HCHP leaders. Herb Kelleher solidly met this challenge. Southwest's capacity for change and learning enabled it to adapt from a small Texas company that attracted customers with flight attendants in "hot pants" to a firm that today has a diverse workforce. It survived the oil shocks of the 70s by engaging employees to solve problems. This capacity to adapt is what allowed the airline to grow from a small regional carrier to a large national carrier. Most recently, Southwest scored highest in a study that compared turnover and return on investment of ten airline companies in the post-9/11 environment, further proof of its capacity to adapt to catastrophic events.[34]

What enables HCHP systems to adapt despite the tight configuration of people, organization, culture, and strategy? The key is diversity in functional expertise and personal background such as race and ethnicity. The latter is particularly important given the diversity of customers and firms that global companies serve. When people with various backgrounds, from different levels and parts of the organization, interact with different elements of the firm's environment—customers, suppliers, investors, community, or competitors—and engage with their disparate perspectives, then real organizational learning and change are possible. The problem is that in most firms people with diverse views are often not encouraged to engage in honest dialogue. Hierarchical structures make it difficult for employees to risk voicing new ideas and engaging in debate with those in entrenched positions of power. As we shall discuss further in chapter 5, most companies have a culture of silence.

HCHP firms have a number of interrelated characteristics and practices that make it more likely that senior management and lower levels will engage in honest, collective, and public conversations that matter, fact-based conversations about business and organizational realities. Below I list some of these core characteristics.

Caring About Customers and Performance. In most companies, senior management carries the burden of identifying problems and launching initiatives to improve performance, usually with the help of corporate staff groups. Not in HCHP companies. Employees at all levels from top to bottom care about the customer, performance, and company success. This enables flexibility, learning, and change. As a customer service supervisor at Southwest put it: "The main thing is that everybody cares. We work so many different areas but it doesn't matter. It's true from the top to the last hired.... Sometimes my friends ask me, why do you like to work at Southwest? I feel like a dork, but it's because everyone cares."[35] Employees who care about the customer are motivated by the company having first cared about them.

Mutual Respect. People are selected for their human and interpersonal qualities such as respect for others and the capacity to voice their views openly and honestly. A variety of mechanisms encourage and exercise these qualities. At Hewlett-Packard, management expected, even demanded, that individuals speak their minds. Management by walking around (MBWA) was a practice that all managers were expected to follow. This developed relationships of trust and enabled open dialogue. Southwest Airlines has a similar culture. It values the dignity of the individual and encourages mutual respect.[36] This respect permeates vertical and horizontal relationships. With mutual respect comes the capacity to have a multilevel and multifunctional dialogue about problems, and this dialogue fosters learning and change.

The importance of mutual respect became clear to me when I consulted with a business unit at Hewlett-Packard in the mid-1990s. Senior management not only embraced my suggestion that they hear the unvarnished truth from lower levels about why the business was underperforming, but they took this type of honest and collective process of organizational learning to a new level and institutionalized it. They wanted to hear from their people because they respected them. And the process gave them an even greater respect for their people.

Egalitarian Culture. HCHP firms tend to be less hierarchical and bureaucratic.[37] All of them have an egalitarian culture created through the elimination of status symbols such as offices, private parking spots, and titles.[38] Less differentiation makes senior managers much more approachable. It creates a firm where the hierarchy of ideas matters more than the hierarchy of position. Unsurprisingly, in such a firm, diverse ideas are more likely to be heard and become part of the organizational conversation. This is one of the reasons Southwest has been able to win in a very tough industry. An operations manager at Southwest characterized the company's egalitarian culture by contrasting it with that of American Airlines. "I would never work at American Airlines. The animosity there is tremendous. Here it's cool. Whether you have a college degree or a GED it doesn't matter. There is no status here, just a good work ethic."[39]

Honest Conversations and Constructive Conflict. Relationships of trust, so carefully fostered in HCHP companies, enable managers and workers to have *open and honest conversations* across levels and functional department divides. Such conversations make it possible for the organization to solve problems based on facts. Problems are approached by thinking about what is best for the firm and its customers, as opposed to what is best for my department or me. This must begin at the top. At Southwest Herb Kelleher exemplifies listening and openness. A pilot observed, "I can call Herb today. You just call and say there's a problem. He'll say, 'Think about it and tell me the solution that you think will work.' He has an open door policy. I can call almost 24 hours a day. If it's an emergency he will be back to me in 15 minutes."[40]

Research shows that in uncertain and turbulent environments, where learning and change are essential for survival, high-performing companies are differentiated from low-performing companies by a culture that encourages employees to confront the inevitable conflict between different perspectives.[41] In HCHP companies these conflicts do not erupt into win-lose arguments, nor are they smoothed over. Conflicts are resolved through problem solving. Confronting differences constructively is seen as the best way to maintain relationships. Consider the following perception of an employee at Southwest Airlines:

> What is unique about Southwest is that we are real proactive about conflict. We work very hard at destroying any turf battles once they crop up—and they do. Normally they are not malicious or ill intentioned. Sometimes it's a personality conflict. Sometimes it's bureaucracy.[42]
>
> —Manager

Because we are moving at a fast pace, miscommunication and misunderstanding happen sometimes. We take great pride in squaring it away as quickly as possible. Pilots and flight attendants—sometimes an interaction didn't go right between them. They are upset, then we get them together and work it out, it's a teamwork approach. If you have a problem, the best thing is to deal with it yourself. If you can't, then we take the next step—we call a meeting of all the parties.[43]

—Pilot

The capacity of an organization to maintain a culture that is both performance-oriented and fosters trust and constructive conflict is key to sustained high performance. But HCHP companies are not automatically immune to the decline that afflicts most firms. Trust and open dialogue can easily erode, particularly when the conflict is about fundamental strategic issues that promise to alter the company's historic business model. The evidence we cited earlier about how few companies survive or sustain high performance suggests that high fit, as desirable as it is, can also rigidify the organization and prevent it from reinventing itself. To prevent this, HCHP organizations must create a learning culture, one that *institutionalizes* the learning and governance systems I discuss in chapter 7.

Southwest has a culture committee, composed of employees from all levels and parts of the company, that is charged with assessing all Southwest initiatives (business and human resource) for fit with the culture. And, as described earlier, the company fosters an open-door policy that enables employees to skip levels if they want to deliver an unwelcome message or air a grievance. Asda, a U.K. grocery chain now owned by Wal-Mart, institutionalized a number of mechanisms by which senior teams at the corporate and store levels obtained feedback from customers and from employees about organization and leadership effectiveness. At Lincoln Electric, for many years an HCHP company, an advisory committee to the CEO provided employees with influence on work practices and the incentive structure so central to its high productivity.

Why then do I qualify my support for the thesis that HCHP companies can, realistically, be both aligned and adaptive? Though the firms discussed here are clearly more adaptive than the average firm, there is also evidence that the capacity for learning and adaptability is the least developed of the three outcomes. Consider the decline of IBM in the 1980s and Hewlett-Packard's decline between 1995 and 2004. Learning requires multiple levels of the organization—the board, the CEO, the top team, and lower-level leaders—to engage in fact-based inquiry, reflection, diagnosis, and action planning that are responsive to the diagnosis. This process inevitably threatens self-esteem and careers and therefore requires the type of culture that Southwest Airlines clearly has. Just as it took several decades for strategic planning to become institutionalized, so will it take at least that much time to integrate honest, collective, and public conversations into the strategic management process of HCHP firms and to create real accountability for learning.[44]

Southwest, according to Gary Kelly, improved its system in 2005 in response to the tectonic forces buffeting the industry. In a 2008 interview, Kelly described the changes in strategic management that he initiated within the senior team and with the larger extended group of senior managers:

> We changed the way we worked together dramatically. We have much more frequent interaction. We have much more formalized planning sessions where we all participate . . . . You know, it's not just sitting down with a whiteboard. It's making sure that we give all of our officers a seat at the table to understand what the challenges are, where we want to be, and what it is we're going to have to do to close the gap. I wanted to hear what they had to say. So it's been a very empowering effort for all of us.[45]

Kelly also noted:

> It required some patience and some nurturing. It required being vulnerable. You've got to be honest and say, you know what? You're right, I don't understand. Or, you're right, the way we did this wasn't as good as it could be. Because many people are going to be defensive and reject suggestions to do things a little different, you have to have honest conversations and trust. Without these traits, a company can not challenge tradition, which is necessary to improve performance.[46]

Southwest's capacity for learning and change has enabled the company to adapt to numerous changes in the industry. In very difficult times, with oil at $140 a barrel, it is still profitable, albeit at lower levels than before. Its employees remain committed despite a profit-sharing plan and stock option plans that are not paying off as much, if at all.

Solving for All Three HCHP Pillars Simultaneously

Could a company be successful in the long run if it had high-performance alignment but low psychological alignment and commitment? Under these circumstances alignment would be obtained through hierarchy and incentives rather than emotional attachment and commitment. People would do things

FIGURE 2.3. ALIGNMENT AND ORGANIZATION TYPE.

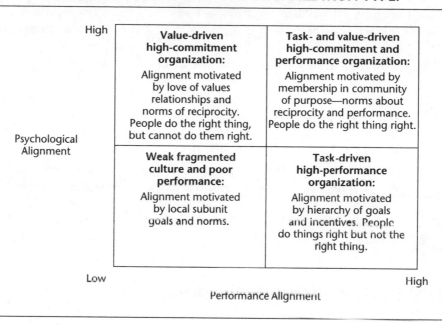

High

Value-driven high-commitment organization:	**Task- and value-driven high-commitment and performance organization:**
Alignment motivated by love of values relationships and norms of reciprocity. People do the right thing, but cannot do them right.	Alignment motivated by membership in community of purpose—norms about reciprocity and performance. People do the right thing right.
Weak fragmented culture and poor performance:	**Task-driven high-performance organization:**
Alignment motivated by local subunit goals and norms.	Alignment motivated by hierarchy of goals and incentives. People do things right but not the right thing.

Psychological Alignment

Low   High

Performance Alignment

right—follow rules and procedures—but would not extend themselves to do the right thing when unique problems arose (see Figure 2.3).[47] For example, at Southwest, low psychological alignment would undermine its strategy. Pilots would resist cleaning the airplanes ("It's not in my job description"). Maintenance and other support groups would not cooperate without top-down control. More airplane cleaners and maintenance supervisors would have to be hired and coordination would be reduced. Southwest's low-cost rapid turnaround and on-time departure and arrival policy would all be undermined.

The performance of a firm with high psychological alignment but lacking a performance alignment would also be unsuccessful. In such an organization people would focus on mission and relationships. They would do the right thing, but without strategically aligned structure, systems, and processes, they would not be able to do things right to implement strategy (see Figure 2.3). The organization would be inefficient and less than fully effective despite high commitment. Moreover, psychological alignment would itself suffer a sharp decline as frustration with ineffectiveness and poor performance rose. I saw this result in an HCHP business unit at Hewlett-Packard in the mid-1990s. An unclear strategy and organizational design that made needed coordination difficult undermined morale and commitment. Functional conflict and frustration with poor results increased. Consider what would have happened to psychological alignment at Southwest if the company had not created the role of station manager to align structure. Coordination would be lower than required despite high commitment. Frustration would mount and undermine commitment as well as performance.

Psychological alignment opens up the solution space. People find many more ways to solve problems, and the organization executes effectively and efficiently. Performance alignment creates the formal conditions for efficiency and effectiveness, but without commitment to structure, systems rules and procedures become brittle and are not adapted to ever-changing problems.

Performance alignment and psychological alignment would create high performance for some period of time. But without the capacity for honest dialogue about changing realities, companies would not be able to adapt to inevitable market and technological upheavals, as illustrated by Southwest Airlines' success. Without honest conversations and people's willingness to be vulnerable, as Gary Kelly put it, a company could not challenge tradition and deeply held assumptions needed to improve performance.

The simultaneous solve I am advocating poses a leadership challenge. Performance alignment requires that managers engage their *heads*. Aligning the organization with strategy is a rational design process. Psychological alignment requires that managers engage their *hearts*. It requires them to be in touch with their humanity and their values. Without this they cannot define the type of management philosophy that will inspire and elicit commitment, something that Herb Kelleher's philosophy clearly accomplished. Learning and change require secure *senior managers able to hold their egos in check*. Such individuals are not threatened by truth that contradicts their view of reality. Few leaders possess these qualities in equal measure, but effective leadership teams can when different perspectives are embedded in the kind of honest conversations Gary Kelly saw as an essential part of the Southwest Airline's adaptation to new competitive realities.

Leader Values and Philosophy

When HCHP systems emerge from the philosophies and values held by founders or CEOs, they are not easily copied. If it were that simple, Southwest Airlines' success would have been easy to imitate, and their success would not have been sustainable over nearly four decades. There is a remarkable similarity between the philosophies that HCHP leaders follow. Consider the philosophy of Herb Kelleher, Southwest's CEO:

> We've never had layoffs . . . we could have made more money if we furloughed people. But we don't do that. And we honor them constantly. Our people know that when they are sick, we will take care of them. If there are occasions for grief or joy, we will be there for them. They know we value them as people, not just as cogs in a machine.[48]

And consider the philosophy of Patrick Kelly, CEO of PSS World Medical:

> Business people don't like to talk about values. But without these, all business is about is making money. . . . To me, achieving business goals is great. But no business goal is worth sacrificing your values. If you have to treat people poorly or cut corners in your dealing with customers, forget it. . . . You can build an organization based on mutual loyalty, even in today's economy. But you can't do it if you treat people as disposable.[49]

CEOs of HCHP companies espouse management philosophies that reflect inner beliefs and values about life, the role of business organizations in society, and the nature of people at work. Without a clear set of the "right" values, CEOs aspiring to build an HCHP company will be unable to enact their management philosophy authentically or be able to endure the difficult task of making internally consistent business and human resource decisions. Nor would they be able to persevere in confronting the many external forces that can cause the firm to abandon the path to high commitment and performance; for example, short-term pressures from capital markets or the lure of deceptively quick-and-easy wins such as acquisitions or mergers.

A large-scale Stanford study of high-technology start-ups clearly shows how a founder's underlying values and premises about how to build a successful firm influenced the organizational system that the firm ultimately adopted.[50] Consider how the values and assumptions of the founder or CEO of one such start-up high-technology company made HCHP impossible. He opted for a less participative Theory X philosophy of management because he thought it would allow him to pay lower wages.[51] Here is what he said to researchers: "This 'settling for less [participation]' is also driven in part by greed. I simply don't want to give up the [stock] options it would take to get a high caliber person."[52]

Leaders make many choices that in subtle ways shape the organizational system. These choices are connected to their personal assumptions, often untested and erroneous, about human nature and human systems. The CEO in the Stanford study chose a more hierarchical system than Southwest's because of his own greed and his assumption that generous stock options are the primary attraction for highly capable people. But he also made an assumption, one that the Southwest Airlines story and that of many other HCHP firms belie; namely, that monetary incentives must be a precondition for participation and involvement. That is why an open learning environment is so essential to the development of an HCHP system. The CEO, not just employees, must be in a continuous learning process that examines and tests assumptions that govern how the business organizes and manages people.

Even leaders who start with an HCHP philosophy must be open to feedback about the consistency of their decisions and actions. Consistency prevented employee cynicism at Southwest. Kelleher mandated an open-door policy and truly listened. He also happened to be the lowest-paid CEO among high-performing companies, and on a day-to-day basis showed no interest in differentiating himself from the *community of employees*. He eschewed the typical trappings of hierarchical power typically accumulated by CEOs and general managers and interacted unpretentiously with customers and employees at all levels. For example, he showed up in "drag" at a maintenance hangar at 2:00 AM, and consistently stopped to talk to employees, listened to problems they served up, and engaged fellow employees to come up with solutions. These were an expression of his personality and values—caring for people and the desire to enjoy a fun environment. Perhaps most important, he believed that employees must be treated in the same way as customers if customers are to be treated well by employees.

Can Companies Not Born Right Be Transformed?

Unfortunately, companies like Southwest are in a decided minority, despite the assertions of many annual reports that people are the most important asset. Less than half of today's managers believe that people really matter when it comes to meeting financial objectives.[53] Half or less of this subgroup act upon their belief with the conviction and persistence needed to develop their organization's system and move it toward the HCHP model.

For companies that are not HCHP organizations, the challenge is to transform. Though difficult, the prize is well worth it to all stakeholders. The five companies (an illustrative list) described below demonstrated that, with effective leadership and a well-thought-out transformational strategy, change is possible (see Table 2.3).

TABLE 2.3. SUCCESSFUL HCHP TRANSFORMATIONS.

Asda	Grocery
Becton Dickinson	Medical technology
General Electric	Conglomerate
IBM	Information technology
New United Motor Manufacturing Inc. (NUMMI)	Automobile

Asda

Asda's CEO, Archie Norman, and his deputy, Allen Leighton, took the company from the brink of bankruptcy in 1991 to high commitment and performance by 1999. In eight years Norman and Leighton changed an authoritarian and bureaucratic organization into a store-centered, customer-focused, participative, listening organization. They created an HCHP company in which employees and management at every level were partners committed to their low-price value strategy. During seven of the eight years it took to transform the company, Asda consistently beat competitors in like-for-like sales, and profits improved steadily. When the company was sold to Wal-Mart in 1999, Wal-Mart executives said they bought it because they recognized that Norman and Leighton had done much more than cut costs. They had created an HCHP culture that Wal-Mart executives saw as "more like Wal-Mart than Wal-Mart's culture was like Wal-Mart." Recognizing the economic value of the high-commitment culture Asda had developed, Wal-Mart paid eight times what Asda's market capitalization had been when Norman took over the company in 1991.[54]

Becton Dickinson

In the late 1980s Becton Dickinson (BD) was an average company. It had established a strong product position in the medical field with its blood syringe and blood collection products and had entered the diagnostics business. But despite the fact that its ten business units were number one or two in their markets, the firm was far from an HCHP company. Analysts rated it a hold, not a buy, and its CEO in 1990 described the company as having "good strategy but unable to implement it." The company was failing to implement its global strategy because of poor coordination and collaboration between U.S. product divisions and country organizations. Business unit managers complained that corporate R&D was disconnected from their businesses. Divisions were not collaborating to implement a new supply chain and corporate marketing strategy. Employees felt the company lacked caring and human values. Managers saw little management development or internal promotion. In short, performance was average and commitment to the larger mission was low. Beginning in the early 1990s, three successive CEOs worked to transform the company into an HCHP company. In 1990 Ray Gilmartin, a former strategy consultant, clarified the corporate and business unit strategies and began the process of strategic and psychological alignment by introducing a learning and governance system in multiple parts of the company that enabled truth to speak to power. Under Clateo Castellini's leadership, the company went further in developing HCHP values and better communication, and continued its march toward greater openness, alignment, and commitment. BD's current CEO, Ed Ludwig, continued these initiatives, further strengthened BD's value-driven management as well its leadership development, and introduced Six Sigma. By 2005 the company was a long way down the road to becoming an HCHP company.

General Electric

Jack Welch took over a bureaucratic General Electric company in the early 1980s. Frustrated by the bureaucracy he had experienced rising in the company, Welch began the company's journey to HCHP in the early 1980s when he made massive cost-cutting reductions by laying off 125,000 employees. Had Welch stopped there, I would not be listing GE as an example of a largely successful transformation. In the late 1980s Welch introduced values that added a necessary human dimension. By demanding not only performance but also adherence to new values, by stimulating honest conversations about bureaucratic barriers, and placing emphasis on identifying and developing managers, Welch was able to make large strides in moving the company from a bureaucracy toward an HCHP organization. The outstanding performance of GE during Welch's tenure has been frequently and widely chronicled in the business press. GE's market capitalization increased 2,637 percent during this period, and its senior executives have ended up running many companies.[55]

IBM

IBM was an HCHP company from its founding (see earlier list of companies "born right"). Thomas Watson Jr., the founder's son, strengthened and expanded high-commitment values and practices introduced by his father: full employment, an egalitarian culture, open communication, and gains sharing.[56] The company was for many years the fastest-growing and most profitable company in the United States. It adapted to several technological revolutions, including the emergence of the personal computer, before it ran into serious difficulties in the 1980s and early

1990s. When Louis Gerstner became CEO in 1992, financial losses threatened its survival and its top management considered breaking up the company. The company's reemergence as an HCHP company is attributable to Gerstner and his CEO successor, Sam Palmisano. Gerstner broke the psychological contract when he laid off thousands of employees, a necessary step in restoring IBM's financial fortunes. He then restored performance alignment by introducing a worldwide "matrix" structure that moved power from hardware divisions and country organizations to industry segment leaders, and he introduced a culture that encouraged people to confront facts and improve performance. In an effort, still under way, to restore psychological alignment, Palmissano reintroduced values that supported the collaborative structure Gerstner introduced earlier. By 2005 IBM had transformed itself from a hardware company with multiple computer and computer-related products into a highly profitable information systems solutions provider and an undisputed leader in the field.

NUMMI

A joint venture of General Motors and Toyota set up in 1984, NUMMI made astounding productivity and employee satisfaction gains with largely the same unionized and "hostile" workforce that had led General Motors to shut down its Fremont, California, plant in 1982. Managers who worked at the plant before the transformation characterized the old relationship with the union as a "war." Under new leadership the company transformed its union-management relationship and made significant changes in human and performance outcomes. For example, under the old Fremont plant system of management, absenteeism averaged almost 20 percent, and over five thousand grievances were recorded during the three-year labor contract. With the same union and employees, working in the same plant with largely the same equipment, absenteeism dropped to 3 percent after the transformation. What accounts for these changes at NUMMI? New leaders with new values changed the organizational system, its management practices, and ultimately, the culture.[57]

Does National Culture Pose a Constraint?

National cultures differ on important dimensions that affect the likelihood and difficulty of building an HCHP organization. Research has shown, for example, that countries differ in the extent to which their cultures accept or reinforce unequal power, value the reduction of uncertainty and ambiguity, and value individualism or group identity.[58]

National differences reflect an average, however. Individuals in any one country are likely to differ widely, enabling companies to select for fit with HCHP practices. Nevertheless, national differences on these dimensions affect the extent to which leaders are likely to employ HCHP practices and the difficulty of doing so should they or expatriate leaders make an attempt. Imagine how much more difficult it would be to create *psychological and strategic alignment* in organizations operating in highly individualistic national cultures than in cultures where group membership is emphasized. How much more difficult it would be to develop the *capacity for learning* and change in national cultures high in deference to authority and low in individualism, cultures where managers and workers are unlikely to speak up to those in authority, or to be inclined to break with group norms, or take the initiative to innovate.

In sum, each national culture poses different challenges. Individualism in the United States may help leaders create a meritocracy, a practice that may spur individual performance, but it is also a barrier to U.S. executives who want to build a culture of participation and partnership. On the other hand, Japan's collectivism has clearly been an aid to Toyota's leaders in shaping its team-based culture, a culture that has enabled process improvements that vaulted the company to its now dominant position in the automobile industry. But the desire not to stand out could discourage honest conversations in the workplace. (In Japan, honest conversations are encouraged but occur in bars at night.) A recent study found that a productivity program that required employee participation was more successful in northern European countries high in collectivism and low in power distance, and less successful in the United States, a country high in individualism.[59]

Nevertheless, HCHP organizations have been and can be built in a variety of national cultures, despite differences in assumptions about appropriate behavior. In each country some compromises may have to be made to accommodate accepted local practice and laws. Consider Hewlett-Packard, whose leaders succeeded in establishing the "HP Way" in some sixty different countries across the globe. HP systematically selected and developed country managers and workers inclined to adopt the HP Way. When Samsung, their business partner in Korea, objected to some of the values and practices in the late 1980s, HP withdrew from the Samsung partnership so that it could go it alone and build a country organization with an HP Way culture. Just how true HP was to its philosophy in countries with different cultures is illustrated by a Mexican executive in my class who exclaimed in a case discussion about HP, "Now I understand what those crazy managers [in HP's Mexican subsidiary] on the fifth floor of my building are doing." He was referring to the countercultural egalitarian practices that were visible to him—no private offices for anyone including the managing director, and picnics at which managers cooked for employees, egalitarian practices uncommon in Mexican corporations.

If culture does not have to pose a constraint, then the will of the senior executive could. The collaboration that my TruePoint colleagues and I had with managers in India, Japan, and several Latin American countries demonstrates that leaders with the will to lead an HCHP transformation can employ countercultural practices. Despite the emphasis on deference to authority in Latin America, for example, committed leaders were able to employ a high-involvement learning and governance process that enabled truth to speak to power and brought about change. Moreover, there are examples of organizations founded on HCHP principles in a variety of countries with different national cultures; Toyota is one such example.

Research by Robert House and his colleagues may explain why determined leaders succeed despite potential cultural barriers. In a large cross-cultural study they found that people valued quite similar things—fairness, trusting relationships, community, and making a difference, all values that underlie HCHP organizations. And this despite national cultures that may have institutionalized laws, regulations, and practices not supportive of these values.[60] This suggests that the introduction of HCHP practices will stimulate commitment, teamwork, and community, just as HP found. A recent study found positive performance effects after HCHP human resource practices were introduced in several different cultures.[61] The key in all cultures, including the United States, is finding leaders who have the values and will to lead an HCHP transformation.

The Challenge

Although the transformation to HCHP presents leaders with a challenge, as the stories in this chapter illustrate, it's well worth taking on such a challenge given the value that can be created for all stakeholders. This book advocates that CEOs consider adopting an organizational change strategy that will put their companies on the path to HCHP. Such a journey, as has been pointed out, will take years and requires that the CEO be dedicated to this purpose, often in the face of resistance from managers who do not believe in this vision or its potential to achieve high performance. Demands from the environment—capital market, competition, boards of directors who may not understand or be committed to HCHP, and social and political forces—could easily push the company off the path to HCHP.

The antidote to straying from the path is commitment to the HCHP destination. This will only occur if building an HCHP organization is an informed choice. The CEO and his or her top team must explore their values and the legacy they want to leave. In my experience, when leaders explore who they are and what they want to leave behind, an HCHP vision comes into focus. When they understand the evidence that HCHP firms are more resilient and have sustained advantage when compared with other firms, they are more likely to choose that direction. Just as high-commitment organizations enable employees to make informed choices to gain their commitment, so top management must understand the conditions and constraints they must accept should they embark on the journey to HCHP, the subject of the next chapter.

Summary

High commitment and high performance organizations are characterized by three pillars:

*   *Performance Alignment*—structure, systems, and people's capabilities fit the strategy.
*   *Psychological Alignment*—people are attached to the mission, values, and culture of the company emotionally. They love the company.
*   *Capacity for Learning and Change*—the organization and its leaders promote fact-based inquiry about external market and internal organizational realities by enabling truth to speak to power.

Developing and maintaining all three outcomes is only possible if leaders solve problems with all three in mind and find solutions that deliver all three. An organization that is aligned with strategy and performance goals will not reach its performance potential unless its employees are psychologically aligned. Committed people will be able to execute strategic intent in smart and flexible ways. Alignment is known to cause rigidity, however. Habits and ideologies make it difficult to learn, particularly at the top. Only by enabling truth to speak to power can those at the top learn about barriers that threaten to undermine alignment. Substantial evidence exists that business failures occur when top managers do not learn and adapt.

An HCHP system is hard to emulate. Establishing the system requires leaders with an HCHP management philosophy. It is their commitment to these values that enables development of the system and enables them to resist pressures and enticements that could easily take the firm off the path to HCHP.

HCHP organizations can and have been built in many different regions of the world despite differences in culture. Though cultural practices may differ, people's values are similar and aligned with HCHP practices, which appeal to fundamental human needs. Moreover, there is considerable variability among people, making selection of people who fit HCHP practices an important strategy. What is essential is a leadership team committed to HCHP values that can lead the building process. And these leadership teams must go through a process of informed choice. They must grapple with the question of who they are, what legacy they want to leave, and what constraints and responsibilities they are willing to incur in order to succeed.

Senior teams who wish to assess their purpose and organization will want to discuss the following questions:

1. Do we have the desire to build an HCHP system?
2. Do our beliefs and motives match those of lead HCHP organizations?
   a. The purpose of a firm is to serve multiple stakeholders.
   b. People have potential that is underutilized.
   c. Teamwork and collaboration are critical to success.
   d. Building an institution is a worthwhile goal that will leave a legacy.
   e. Stretch goals and meritocratic culture can stimulate high performance.
   f. Are we willing to lead change with all the conflict and potential resistance associated with it?
   g. Are we willing to learn about how effectively we are leading the organization?
3. Is our organization now characterized by the three pillars of HCHP organizations?
4. What aspects of our national culture are potential barriers to developing an HCHP organization? What are the implications?

CHAPTER THREE

PRINCIPLED CHOICE AND DISCIPLINE ARE ESSENTIAL

Although most corporate leaders would acknowledge the demands of the increasingly competitive environment in which their firms operate, and many may espouse a desire to build an HCHP enterprise in response, few understand the discipline and the courage that are required. To build enduring HCHP institutions, leaders *must consciously choose and stick to* the firm's

1. Purpose and guiding values
2. Strategy
3. Risk profile
4. Basis for motivating, organizing, and managing people

Without conscious choice, the system's design emerges through multiple decisions made in many parts of the organization and without benefit of a common vision. Without conscious choice, leadership teams cannot develop understanding and commitment to HCHP principles. Without commitment and discipline it is all too easy for CEOs and their top teams to liquidate investments made in firm identity and brand, capabilities, and culture. In times of crisis, when capital markets may demand expedient decisions that could take the firm off the HCHP path, commitment to principles enables CEOs to go against conventional wisdom in decisions about strategy, debt, growth rate, acquisitions, and layoffs. Research tells us that corporate leaders tend to imitate other firms' practices when faced with ambiguity about what constitutes effective high-performance management.[1] Without fully understanding and committing to HCHP principles, the pressure to imitate other firms cannot be resisted. Nor can the pressure to keep up with others in the industry—even when, in their heart of hearts, leaders know they are compromising their own integrity and that of their firm. And adhering to HCHP principles does not introduce rigidity; instead, it enables flexibility without erosion of purpose and sustained high performance.

The Case of NICO[2]

The remarkable case of National Indemnity Company (NICO), an insurance company that has outperformed the insurance industry by a wide margin, illustrates the kind of steadfast commitment and courage needed to make decisions required of HCHP leaders.

NICO is owned by Berkshire Hathaway, an investment company with a portfolio of businesses managed for investors by Warren Buffett, who is acknowledged as an investor without equal. Today, NICO is a star performer. Yet when NICO was purchased in 1967 it did not have unique advantages. It was not known, had no special actuarial capabilities, and was not the lowest-cost operator. Like everyone else in the industry, it sold through agents, a method that many thought was outdated.

From the very beginning, NICO's CEOs made conscious choices about the purpose of the firm, its strategy, the basis on which they wanted to motivate their managers and employees, and the constraints they would impose on themselves to build sustainable commitment and performance. Having made clear and informed choices gave them the courage to withstand short-term pressure that threatened long-term success.

Between 1986 and 1999, when the rest of the industry cut prices to grow more rapidly and boost stockholder returns, NICO's four CEOs refused to do so. Consequently, they lost market share. But NICO's CEOs saw that in cutting prices to gain market share their competitors were taking unwise actuarial risks. NICO watched as the rest of the industry gained revenue while their revenues dropped 85 percent and market share and profits declined. Most companies cut their staff. Not so at NICO. Its top management promised employees that no one would be fired. This preempted the "fear factor" and its undesirable consequences, especially the temptation by lower managers to accept riskier policies that would improve their individual performance. And a refusal to cut staff meant the firm did not liquidate its investment in people—their commitment, experience, and knowledge.

By making these "against the grain" decisions, NICO's CEOs avoided a breakdown in underwriting discipline and habits of mind required to maintain a focused and distinctive strategy. To complement the no-layoff policy, NICO was also very careful not to overstaff. Buffett describes the type of courage CEOs must have to manage for the long term: "It takes real fortitude—embedded deeply within the company culture . . . . Living day to day with dwindling volume—while competitors are boasting of growth and reaping Wall Street applause—is an experience few managers can tolerate. NICO had four CEOs . . . . and *none* of them have bent. It should be noted that only one of the four graduated from college. Our experience tells us that extraordinary business ability is largely innate."[3]

Sure enough, when other insurance companies were inevitably hit by natural calamities and had to pay policyholders beyond their ability to do so, they were forced to fire still more people, thereby unwinding the company's infrastructure. They liquidated the very assets that they needed to succeed in the future. Meanwhile, NICO's steady-as-you-go approach enabled them to compete for future customers more effectively, which in the long term has yielded committed people, quality customer service, and a reputation for paying willingly and quickly. Its performance has been outstanding and has provided its parent with such excellent returns that Warren Buffett featured NICO in Berkshire Hathaway's annual report.

Undoubtedly, NICO's CEOs could manage for the long term more easily than their publicly traded competitors because they were owned by Berkshire Hathaway and worked for Warren Buffett. But it is also true that Buffett bought NICO because of the quality of their CEOs and the guiding values of the company. Consider how different NICO's philosophy of management is from that followed by CEOs of many of Wall Street's financial institutions in 2008. In an effort to increase revenues, market share, and profits in the booming mortgage-backed securities market, these CEOs strayed from their strategies and took unwise and unsustainable risks, thus ignoring potential long-term consequences. The result was liquidation of the very kinds of assets that NICO's management sought to protect, the long-term performance, commitment of their people, and survival of their business.[4]

Firm Purpose and Values: The Multiple Stakeholder Model

In contrast to the many firms that, as we discovered, contributed to the economic meltdown of 2008 because they operated without regard to their multiple constituents and to society as a whole, HCHP firms like NICO operate with a multistakeholder model. Moving in that direction requires that CEOs and their senior teams spend time clarifying their purpose and values and developing firm objectives that reflect the multistakeholder perspective. In effect, these objectives serve as the constitution for the firm. They are broad, even vague, because they are intended as guidelines. The development of these objectives requires confronting a fundamental question. Is the firm's purpose to increase shareholder value, or to enrich senior management, or is it to serve other stakeholders as well—customers, employees, community, and society? In a 1957 retreat, almost twenty years after the firm's founding, Bill Hewlett and David Packard and their key managers met to discuss a set of objectives David Packard had drafted earlier. Consider the multistakeholder objectives that emerged from these discussions:[5]

1. *Profit:* To recognize that profit is the best single measure of our contribution to society and the ultimate source of our corporate strength. We should attempt to achieve the maximum possible profit *consistent with our other objectives* [emphasis mine].
2. *Customers:* To strive for continued improvements in the quality, usefulness, and value of the products and services we offer to our customers.
3. *Fields of Interest:* To concentrate our efforts, continually seeking new opportunities for growth but limiting our involvement to the field in which we have capability and can make a contribution.
4. *Growth:* To let our growth be limited only by our profits and our ability to develop and produce innovative products that satisfy real customer needs.
5. *Our People:* To help HP people share the company's success, which they make possible; to provide employment security based on performance; to ensure them a safe and pleasant work environment; to recognize their individual achievements; to value their diversity; and to help them gain a sense of satisfaction and accomplishment from their work.
6. *Organization:* To maintain an organizational environment that fosters individual motivation, initiative, and creativity, and wide latitude of freedom in working toward established goals.
7. *Citizenship:* To meet the obligations of good citizenship by making contributions to the community and the institutions in our society that generate the environment in which we operate. [Later changed to include other nations and societies.]

Unless leaders see value creation for all stakeholders as a fundamental objective of the firm, they will be unable to build a great company that will endure. Note that profit is the first of HP's objectives, a reflection of the founders' unsentimental and pragmatic view that profit is essential if the other objectives are to be achieved. Managing a multistakeholder firm requires that leaders make synergistic decisions that allow for simultaneously delivery of a "value surplus" to all stakeholders (that is, each party receives far more than they invest) while simultaneously enabling sustained competitive advantage.[6]

Employment security at Hewlett-Packard, for example, had economic value—retained essential skills and capabilities and developed teamwork, but it simultaneously contributed to employee well-being. Employee stock ownership made it harder for other firms to acquire HP (employees who love their company would not give their proxy to a prospective buyer) while at the same time creating economic and psychological value for employees.

This is yet another example of how HCHP firms manage paradox; in this case, the paradox between achievement of altruistic goals and economic gain. John Young, CEO of Hewlett-Packard in the 1980s, captured the essence of the multistakeholder perspective of HCHP companies when he said: "Maximizing shareholder wealth has always been way down the list. Yes, profit is a cornerstone of what we do—it is a measure of our contribution and means for self-financed growth—but it has never been the point in and of itself. The *point* in fact, is to *win*, and winning is judged in the eyes of the customer and by doing something you can be proud of. There is symmetry of logic in this. If we provide real satisfaction to real customers—we will be profitable."[7]

Bill George, former CEO of Medtronic, who transformed his company into an HCHP company, argues that it is not altruism that drove him to follow the multiple stakeholder perspective, but pragmatism. "It works."[8] Competitive advantage comes from investing for the long term, not from maximizing short-term profits, he argues. Focusing on how to improve customer and employee commitment, rather than only on shareholder gains, fosters an investment mentality.

Isn't the multistakeholder perspective inconsistent with the need for strategic focus that is also the hallmark of high performance? Not when the organizational solution—a constellation of policies and practices—enables implementation of a focused strategy and simultaneously solves for the interests of all key stakeholders. Management develops and communicates a story about the connection between stakeholders—how employees must be served in order to serve customers, and how serving customers will result in shareholder value. That logic makes clear to managers the virtuous cycle on which success is founded and sends an unmistakable message that focusing on one stakeholder will undermine the system that produces profits.

Managers in HCHP organizations utilize the principle of *informed choice*. Stakeholders are *told the truth* about the challenges facing the firm and how they will be affected. They are invited to give their thoughts and reactions to inform management's decisions. Although management is not obliged to follow advice from lower levels, they are obliged to explain their actions in light of the feedback they receive. In this way the firm builds relationships of trust with stakeholders that develop into problem-solving relationships. In 1996, the president of HP's computer business said that HP's collaborative approach with distributors gave the company a distinctive advantage. "Competitors keep distributors in the dark," he said, and argued persuasively that this enabled HP to develop loyalty from distributors that other firms could not. And he argued that HP's collaborative internal culture is what had enabled the positive relationship with distributors.

To be credible, the multiple stakeholder perspective must permeate all levels of management. All decisions must be made with this perspective, not only the easy ones. By consistently applying the values inherent in the multistakeholder perspective, HCHP firms reduce their risk of making short-term, expedient decisions that are inconsistent with the vision of an enduring enterprise. They protect the investments in culture and brand made over the years. Senior Hewlett-Packard executives in Harvard's Advanced Management program, in which I taught in the 1990s, made it clear that the multistakeholder perspective was part of every HP manager's DNA. In contrast to other executives in the program, who typically framed decisions in financial terms only, HP executives consistently framed decisions in terms of their effects on all the stakeholders and went on to talk about how they might involve them in decisions.

HCHP firms can institutionalize the multistakeholder perspective through various mechanisms. Holding managers accountable for living to articulated principles is one way. The "balanced scorecard" approach to setting objectives and measuring results can help in this regard so long as profit is not framed as the reason for meeting customer, employee, and community goals, something that could lead to cynical decisions. Selecting, socializing, and promoting people whose values fit the multistakeholder perspective is another key way in which this perspective can be developed and sustained.

The choice of purpose and values is a declaration about how the company will be organized and managed for years to come. It must therefore involve all key leaders of the organization—the board of directors, the CEO, and the top team. Consider the introduction to a memorandum issued by the chairman of a health care company, at the beginning of their journey to HCHP. Later parts of the document elaborate on this vision.

> The purpose of this document is to articulate a shared understanding
> between the Board of Directors and the President and CEO about our
> mutual desire for a more democratic way of governing our organization. We

recognize that we are seeking to achieve a form of governance that will require significant transformation from our current state. It is likely to take years of persistence to make the changes that will be needed, spanning multiple management teams. Therefore, it is our intent that this document outlives the tenure of the current board members and president and CEO in order that this more democratic way of governing can be attained and maintained.[9]

The power of values and multistakeholder objective to shape a great company, if consistently applied, was eloquently stated by David Packard when he wrote:

> Any organization, any group of people who have worked together for some time, develop a philosophy, a set of values, series of traditions and customs. These are, in total, unique to the organization. So it is with Hewlett-Packard. We have a set of values—deeply held beliefs that guide us in meeting our objectives, in working with one another, and dealing with customers, shareholders, and others. Our corporate objectives are built upon these values. The objectives serve as a day-to-day guide for decision making. To help us meet our objectives, we employ various plans and practices. It is the combination of these elements—our values, corporate objectives, plans and practices—that form the HP Way.[10]

Strategy

There is no one strategy type that differentiates HCHP firms from others. Numerous strategies can lead to high performance. However, high-performance firms do make a conscious choice about strategy. *Strategy is distinctive*—it offers a product or service to a well-defined and understood customer segment in a way that is different in some important aspect from rival firms. As my colleague Michael Porter has shown, distinctiveness is achieved by performing activities in the value creation chain that are different from those of competitors, or by executing the same activities as competitors in different ways.

Strategies of HCHP firms are also distinctive in that they reflect leaders' animating beliefs about the firms' purposes and values. Consider how Cummins Engine's long-standing commitment to socially responsible behavior, as well as its expertise in pollution control devices, led it to build a distinctive source of competitive advantage by becoming the leading manufacturer of environmentally friendly engines.[11] When beliefs motivate strategy, it becomes loftier, gives meaning, and creates more commitment than a more calculative strategy.

Senior teams of high-performing companies are very clear about who the firm is and are extraordinarily disciplined in maintaining the firm's strategic focus. They know what they want to do and which customers they want to serve. They know what they do *not* want to do and which customers they do *not* want to serve. This prevents what Michael Porter has called *straddling* fundamentally different strategies, which is ineffective because it requires fundamentally different organizations, capabilities, and cultures, and because it blurs the company's identity and brand. The economic meltdown of 2008 can in part be blamed on companies that strayed from their core strategy in order to take advantage of large profits to be found in risky, mortgage-backed securities.

No strategy, however successful, will succeed forever. Leaders of HCHP firms are constantly scanning the environment for new trends and their rivals' moves. When their business is threatened by shifts in the environment, HCHP firms recommit—as did NICO—to who they are. They redouble their efforts to do what they do, but find ways to do it better—and differently, if necessary. This does not preclude making bold strategic moves when they see strategic inflections coming. Collins and Porras found that HCHP companies set "audacious goals."[12] Indeed, in an aggressive market for corporate control, being proactive about sustaining profitable growth is essential. It reduces "governance risk"—the risk that the firm will become an attractive takeover target and will be run in the interests of shareholders only.

Bold strategic initiatives are always connected to the firm's core capabilities, beliefs, and values. Evolution of the business is continuous and devoid of delusion. Hard facts are assessed and strategic changes made, but always keeping in mind the principles of distinctiveness and alignment with existing capabilities. What this means is that HCHP firms tend to grow their businesses by using existing capabilities in new markets, the approach that Hewlett-Packard employed when it used its core technical capabilities and collaborative culture to enter new product or market domains and new geographies.

HCHP firms reduce the risk of new strategic initiatives through informed, fact-based deliberation and through flawless execution. Strategic decisions are made without delusion. They are informed by facts, not politics, something that an HCHP culture enables and others cannot emulate. Strategic decisions or initiatives occur only after honest, fact-based discussions by multiple key people, and not according to the CEO's whim. Consider how Southwest Airlines' fact-based discussion led the company to settle a controversy over its historic open seating policy. All along, some vocal customers and industry observers had criticized Southwest for not moving to the assigned seating systems employed by its competitors. After years of criticism there were strong, emotionally laden opinions among key managers on both sides of the question. Here's how Southwest Airlines' CEO, Gary Kelly, describes the deliberations.

> It was remarkable. All the officers lived through this. They all witnessed the effort that we went through; they all went through the emotion surrounding the question of assigned seating. The facts were laid out and compared to our objectives. Operationally, we proved that it was definitely slower to assign seats. Customers told us by a margin of 2 to 1 that they preferred open seating. So they had those facts. And, it was just so simple to go to all of our employees and say, "This is what we're doing, this is why we're doing it, and we're going to be proud of it."[13]

For these reasons, egocentric and narcissistic CEOs are not found running HCHP firms. Of course, HCHP CEOs have a strong point of view that they articulate but they enable the kind of fact-based conversation and decision-making process described by Gary Kelly. These characteristics allowed HP to enter and succeed in businesses as diverse as test and measurement instruments, computers, and printers. By staying focused on who they are and by careful evolution of their business model through experimentation, HCHP companies mitigate the risk inherent in strategic choice.[14]

In many ways HCHP firms are like "the little engine that could." They put a premium on boring, steady, and continuous progress. Southwest Airlines' response to the continuing turmoil of the airline industry following September 11, 2001, as well as to the increasing number of competitive low-cost carriers, has been to work harder at doing what they do better and, if necessary, differently.

In effect, HCHP firms take strategic risk by innovating in domains in which they have distinctive capabilities and they limit their strategic risk through experiments that must prove their worth before further steps are taken. They avoid "betting the farm." For this reason, a robust strategic performance management process, discussed in chapter 7, is so important.

Risk

Building an HCHP culture takes years and is easily liquidated with a few bad decisions. Consider the subprime mortgage crisis of 2007–2008. Lacking institutionalized business policies and norms to limit risk, leaders' greed and desire to keep pace with competitors' growth regardless of risk went unchecked.

HCHP firms are conservative. To build an institution that will outperform over a long time, it is essential to manage financial and cultural risk. It requires a perspective about risk that differs significantly from what we now learn was the practice at Wall Street banks, mortgage companies, buy-out firms, or hedge funds. NICO's management avoided long-term financial and cultural risk by refusing to accept risky business in order to match competitors' growth rates. HCHP firms institute and institutionalize *business policies and guidelines designed to prevent current and future leaders from putting sustained commitment and performance at risk.* Among these business guidelines are policies about debt, growth, mergers and acquisitions, employment stability, forward pricing, and percentage of revenues for a given customer or customer segment. Like Ulysses on the open sea, these policies, which must be enforced by the board of directors, prevent leaders from being pulled off course by the "sirens" of greed and rapid unsustainable growth. They tie a succession of CEOs to the mast of their corporate ship.

Limits on Debt

Long-term debt incurs interest costs and the strictures of bank covenants. During periods of economic decline or unexpected "business shocks," management may be forced to liquidate investments in employees, customers, and new business development to meet creditors' demands. Large-scale layoffs jeopardize employee and customer commitment, trust, and loyalty.

During its first five decades of high commitment and high performance, Hewlett-Packard followed a self-financing policy that avoided long-term debt. Southwest Airlines' debt limiting policy and its fuel hedging policies in recent years are both intended to prevent business shocks, such as high fuel costs or spiraling interest cost, from eroding the integrity of their strategy and organization. Their wisdom was borne out by how well the company fared, compared to its competitors, after volume declined dramatically following 9/11. It is the only company in the industry that avoided layoffs and continued to be profitable in the years that followed. Its stock price recovered quickly after 9/11 while the stocks of other airline companies continued to languish.[15] The company's capacity to sustain environmental shocks is again being born out during the industry turmoil of 2008. Southwest Airlines remains profitable while most others are reeling from huge losses that threaten their survival.

The economic meltdown in 2008 is the most recent illustration of how excessive debt threatens survival and undermines the long-term interests of investors, employees, and customers. Interestingly, Goldman Sachs, the only HCHP investment bank that I know of (see chapter 2), has fared far better than others. And it garnered a financial infusion from Warren Buffett, an investor who takes an interest in firms that operate according to HCHP principles, such as NICO. Though risk and debt are part of any investment bank's business model,

Bear Stearns and Lehman Brothers, founded in roughly the same time period as Goldman, no longer exist because they did not manage risk as well. According to Charles Ellis, Goldman's sustained success has a lot to do with how the firm has been managed over the years—the humility of its leaders, their sense of stewardship, and the firm's culture of teamwork.[16] It is not hard to extrapolate that values like these translate into more conservative risk management.

Smart Growth

HCHP companies must of course grow to provide opportunities for their employees and to stay competitive. They strive for controlled growth, however. Rapid growth demands new people, particularly leaders—a lot of them—who share the company's values and have capabilities aligned with the business model, making it likely that managers will be forced to hire people who do not fit the firm. Very rapid growth also outstrips the firm's capacity to socialize new employees and develop HCHP leaders, thus causing erosion of the HCHP culture.

Despite the obvious attraction of rapid growth, Southwest Airlines limited itself by entering only two new cities a year, resisting pressures from many cities for their service, in order to keep to their commitment to manageable growth. Hewlett-Packard's self-financing policy served to limit its growth to between 20 to 25 percent in its first four decades. Bob Wayman, HP's longtime chief financial officer, told me more than once that HP's self-financing policy was designed to prevent erosion of the HP Way, the company's unique culture.

Acquisitions

Many companies use acquisitions as a means to get out of trouble and grow. HCHP companies recognize, however, that acquisitions are risky. Acquisitions have the potential to swamp their carefully developed HCHP culture. When acquisitions make strategic sense, HCHP companies acquire small companies or limit the number of acquisitions at any given time. They also develop capabilities to integrate companies rapidly. Cisco acquires only small companies that they can absorb easily. Chris Richmond, head of GE's commercial leasing business, whom we will meet in chapter 8, employed carefully selected and timed acquisitions. More important, he succeeded because he developed a standard process for integrating acquisitions, one that was recognized as a best-in-class practice within GE and in the larger business community. Hewlett-Packard (until the late 1990s), Southwest Airlines, and Nucor have grown organically and purposely limited their acquisitions. Arguably, HP's demise as an HCHP company came about in part as a result of its acquisition of Compaq.

Pricing Policies

Aggressive pricing policies to gain market share in new product or market domains can be risky. Managers come to believe that the new product or service is a winner and invest more. The new product or service is not tested on the basis of its inherent value. When competitors with equal or better values move in, the business begins to fail. For years, Hewlett-Packard had a policy of no forward pricing to ensure that growth was slow and steady and that the fundamental value of new products was tested from the start.

Employment Stability

Many of the policies above are intended to maintain employment stability. HCHP companies avoid layoffs at all costs, in effect granting some employment stability to their people, though not promising lifetime employment. Research has shown, as I will elaborate in chapter 10, that companies with employment stability policies outperform their competitors.[17]

◆ ◆ ◆

In summary, strategic management in HCHP companies includes policies and values intended to impose boundaries on managerial decisions and behavior. Their purpose is to reduce the all-too-human tendency to be attracted by the "sirens" of easy but unprofitable and unsustainable growth.

Motivating, Organizing, and Managing People

CEOs who wish to build an HCHP company will have to

- Examine their assumptions about human nature and motivation
- Consciously choose an approach to organizing and managing the enterprise that will foster their view of what drives people at work

In the last two decades, a large body of convincing research, some reviewed at the end of the chapter, supports the proposition that it matters how people are organized and managed—how much they are involved, how much voice they are given, and how much and how well teams are used to integrate value-creating activities—and in the long run, this may be the only thing that matters.[18] Firms that engage their employees in a way that produces commitment outperform on a number of outcomes such as return on sales, return on assets, employee satisfaction, employee turnover, customer satisfaction and loyalty. They also outperform on management and leadership development. In addition, there is a considerable body of case research, some presented in the book, which shows that interventions aimed at changing the way people are organized improve human and financial outcomes.

Do employee attitudes and motivation created by the organizational system lead to positive financial outcomes? Or do positive outcomes lead to high employee satisfaction and commitment? That question has not and will probably never be fully resolved given the circular nature of the relationship between employee commitment and performance. For example, employee involvement has been shown to lead to high productivity in many studies, but other research finds that the firm's financial performance leads to employee satisfaction and attachment, which in turn fosters employee willingness to put larger goals ahead of their own self-interest.[19] The fact that interventions aimed at improving efficiency and effectiveness have been shown to improve both performance and employee commitment *only* when employees are involved in those efforts, and that change strategies aimed at improving financial returns without involving employees typically do not, suggests that motivation and how people are engaged does matter.[20]

Additionally, decades of psychological research have shown that an "internal commitment" model of motivation, one that focuses on goals, is far superior to a compliance model.[21] Internal commitment occurs when (1) the goals are seen as important and meaningful—employees are engaged and feel they are making a difference and identify with the firm's mission; (2) goals, tasks, and decisions about employee welfare are agreed to mutually by managers and their people; (3) the individual defines the behavior required to perform the task; and (4) the organization and its cultural values are designed to enable the accomplishment of the task.

CEOs who aspire to build an HCHP organization must examine their assumptions about people and motivation in the context of what we know from scientific research. They must then make a conscious choice about the primary way in which people will be motivated in their company and consequently the policies and practices that will have to be designed to that end. Research facts help, but managers will have to use feedback to explore their personal assumptions in the context of that research.

Misconceptions About Motivation and Management

One of the most common misconceptions is that people are motivated by a single need or drive. When leaders spend time and energy designing compensation systems to solve morale problems, for example, and do not consider how well people are involved or how much top-down control is being exercised, they betray the false assumption that people are motivated only by money. In fact, people have multiple needs and drives and there are many effective ways to manage, although the position of this book is that HCHP firms are founded by appealing to some needs more than others. Below I discuss five motives and their corollary implications about how to organize and manage people. Some of my discussion draws on Ed Schein's foundational writing on this subject.[22] Each motive is framed as a core assumption about who we are as human beings:

Rational-Economic. People are motivated by economic incentives and will decide what to do to maximize their gains. They behave in a self-centered manner, seeking rewards and avoiding responsibilities that do not pay off. Top managers who operate according to these assumptions view the relationship between the firm and its employees as calculative. People are attracted and motivated, some would say moved, by incentives of money, security, status, and position. If incentives are properly aligned with firm goals, *performance alignment* is enhanced. However, hierarchy, managerial authority, and rules will be needed to ensure that people do not take advantage of the system to maximize their personal gains. Consequently, psychological alignment or commitment to firm goals and capacity for learning and change are not necessarily enhanced.

Social. People are motivated to develop trusting relationships and to bond with others. This provides a sense of identity with the group or organization of which they are a part. Managers who operate on this assumption organize people into task teams and develop shared values and strong cultures. These strategies are intended to meet employees' needs for affiliation, and obtain in return high levels of commitment to achieve group and organizational goals. Strong group and cultural norms cause behavioral and performance standards to be internalized by group members and they develop pressures to meet group expectations. Organizations that appeal to "social man" foster performance and psychological *alignment*.

Achieving.[23] People—individually and in groups—are motivated by goals; by the desire to achieve them as well as by feedback about whether they have been achieved. Organizations that want to appeal to this need and gain the benefits of goal-directed behavior ensure that people at all levels have clear, ambitious goals and can see the results of their own actions. When goals are properly tied to strategic tasks, the firm ensures *performance alignment*.

Self-Actualizing. People are motivated by meaningful work that allows them to become all they are potentially capable of becoming. They want to grow and learn on the job. Organizations that want to meet these needs and exploit them provide challenging work and opportunities for learning and development; they enable career mobility across different types of jobs and functions, and provide education and training. Organizations that enable self-actualization increase strategic and psychological alignment as well as *capacity for learning and change*.

Participating. People desire to be involved in an enterprise that is bigger then themselves, something that gives meaning and purpose beyond simply having a job and earning an income. Such a "community of purpose," as Charles Heckscher has called it, cannot be built unless people are given a voice in the community.[24] Voice increases identification with the community's purpose—the company's goals, strategies, and values—and increases the sense of control that people have over their lives, as well as protects their dignity. Organizations that want to meet needs for participation and exploit its potential to develop commitment place goals in the context of mission and values, employ organizational mechanisms for participation and voice, and seek to develop a long-term employment relationship. *Performance alignment, psychological alignment, and capacity for learning are enhanced.*

I will refer to needs for participation in a higher purpose, self-actualization, and achievement as "higher-order" needs. Organizational psychologists have argued that these higher-order needs become salient only after basic needs for security, money, and relationships have been satisfied.[25] Although there is no consistent empirical support for this formulation—on the contrary, highly paid executives seem to want even more money and bigger stock options—higher-order needs do offer the greatest potential for developing all three pillars of HCHP organizations: psychological alignment, performance alignment, and the capacity for learning and change.

Recent research by Paul Lawrence and Nitin Nohria, cited briefly in the introduction, supports the limitations of the rational-economic model if it is the only model employed in managing people. Their work supports the position that commitment can be gained by appealing to people's many sides and needs.[26] Based on a review of research in fields as diverse as evolution, psychobiology, biology, evolutionary psychology, and psychology, they suggest rather convincingly that evolution has developed in humans four hardwired and equally important needs. These needs, Lawrence and Nohria argue, have become part of our DNA. Humans need not only to *acquire* (extrinsic rewards such as money, power, promotion, status, and so on) but also to *bond* (to have trusting relationships with others, often expressed as being part of a family or larger community), to *comprehend* (to grapple with challenging work, to understand, and learn), and to *defend* (resist and fight when threatened).

The need to acquire is one that economists have used to argue for incentives that are instrumentally tied to results, and has led organizations to emphasize promotions, titles, and money as the primary incentives. The finding that humans are also hardwired to bond with others and to learn suggests that organizations can indeed motivate on the basis of needs for participation, self-actualization, achievement, and affiliation. People will and do operate beyond their narrow self-interest. It is beyond the scope of this book to review the diverse literature that led Lawrence and Nohria to these conclusions. It is important to note, however, that they cite a number of studies that show people will sacrifice money to preserve relationships.

Historically, decisions about how to organize and manage have been driven primarily by the rational-economic assumptions about people. This is despite substantial evidence that people are complex and can be motivated by all five perspectives and assumptions described above. There are *two primary errors* that managers make when they form their assumptions about motivation and make decisions about the best way to organize and manage people.[27]

First, managers form erroneous assumptions about people from their observation of behavior within the organization. They then attribute the behaviors they see to individual character and motives. If people do not strive to achieve or do not collaborate, it is assumed that they are unmotivated and need to be pushed and controlled. There is considerable evidence, however, that employee behavior is less about individual motivation and at least as much a function of the social system in which they are working—leadership behavior, the nature of the work itself, the extent to which a productive team culture has been developed, and how much employee involvement is allowed or encouraged. In other words, it is a mistake to assume that some people are motivated and others are not, when how they are managed is an important cause of their behavior.[28] This error leads to a self-fulfilling prophecy. As management applies control to what they see as unmotivated employees, employees reduce their commitment, which makes management apply even more control, thus further reducing employee commitment.

Second, managers erroneously assume that the need patterns with which people first come into the organization are not changeable. If this were true, the only way managers could develop an HCHP organization would be to rely solely on selection when hiring. The reality is that human needs change in response to the situation into which they are placed. My own and others' studies of the effects of organization change show fairly dramatic changes in attitudes and behavior as a result of planned change. For example, studies of the effects of the Scanlon Plan, a gains sharing plan that gives people a voice in productivity improvements, showed that commitment and performance improve after the plan is introduced.[29]

Recently, behavioral economists have demonstrated the power of suggestion to change attitudes. What is interesting about these studies is that they come from economists who have historically embraced the rational-economic view of man and recommended that managers employ incentives to motivate.[30]

Implications for Managerial Choice

Following are means that senior management can employ to make an informed choice about how to motivate, organize, and manage their people.

Reflect and Clarify Assumptions. If managers believe in the power of the rational-economic model of motivation, they are likely to erroneously design an organization that will appeal to this side of people but will not develop high commitment and performance. Making a valid choice requires senior executives to examine their assumptions. Introspection alone will not suffice. This requires honest feedback from others about behavior they see followed by an exploration of underlying assumptions. CEOs who aspire to lead an HCHP system would be well advised to foster such a conversation in their leadership team in advance of developing their management philosophy and designing management practices. And leadership teams would be well advised to enable lower levels in their organization to tell them the truth about how they experience organizational life. The conversation about assumptions is not a one-time proposition. It has to be revisited periodically when the firm is challenged by internal and external threats and opportunities.

Consciously Choose How the Firm Will Be Organized and Managed. Once assumptions about motivation at work have been clarified, senior teams must turn to the questions of how to organize and manage the firm. They must translate their assumptions into policies and practices. The following questions can help them define the essential practices that determine the character and culture of the company:[31]

1. *On what basis will we primarily attract and attach employees to the firm?* Will employees be attracted and motivated through *emotional appeal* to the mission of the company and values such as participation, self-actualization, challenging work, and teamwork, *or* will our appeal be more instrumental, based on opportunities for personal advancement or money?
2. *On what basis will we primarily select employees?* Will we select based on intelligence, collaborative attitudes and, most important, a capacity to learn and grow, *or* will selection be based on functional skills, past job experiences, and professional reputation?

3. *On what basis will we primarily control and coordinate the work of our employees?* Will people be brought together into a *community of purpose* through challenging goals and a culture of teamwork, *or* will we rely on top-down control—structure, systems, processes, financial incentives, and managerial oversight?

4. *On what basis will we primarily evaluate and promote employees?* Will promotion be based on adherence to the company's values of teamwork and continuous striving to contribute to the larger purpose of the firm and win, *or* will it be based on individual results—financial, operating, and technical?

Answering these questions can lead to rich discussions by senior teams about the management practices and human resource policies required to develop a "community of purpose." It is important to remember that HCHP firms eschew the either-or and embrace the and/also. Thus, the answers to the questions above are not about choosing one or the other but rather about primary versus secondary emphasis.

Sustaining a journey to HCHP requires that senior teams continuously assess how well their organization is aligned with their HCHP vision. To do this, managers will have to collect honest views from employees about their experience in working in the organization, analyze and discuss the data, and take actions to modify policies and practices as needed. A collective and public conversation within the senior team and between the senior team and lower-level employees is essential if senior management is to understand life in the organization. Employee surveys are not enough. Direct conversations that produce rich qualitative and emotionally charged information will give senior management a real understanding of the firm's psychological contract.

What HCHP Firms Are Not

Senior teams can enhance understanding of what an HCHP organization is by having knowledge of alternative models for organizing and managing people, in effect what HCHP firms are not. Each of the models below fails to create policies and practices that will unleash the full potential of which most people are capable. A seminal Stanford study of start-up firms found these organizing models for young start-ups achieved lower levels of commitment and operating performance when compared with about a third of firms they defined as high-commitment firms.[32] These are pure types, and about half of the companies they studied were not, nevertheless the description of the pure type can help senior teams aspiring to build an HCHP organization clarify to which type they are closest and what they want to avoid.

Professional Model

The motivation in this organizational model is challenging professional work. People are attracted to becoming part of an organization that will be at the frontier of professional achievement. Challenging work is the attraction and the source of tremendous motivation to achieve, but it can also be too narrow a source of motivation to encourage responsiveness to customers—performance alignment—or to enable flexible response to market realities—capacity for learning and change.

Selection is based on professional skills. As in the commitment model, control and coordination are based on norms and peer pressure more than on incentives and formal controls. The norms, however, are focused on making breakthrough professional achievements, as opposed to customer satisfaction. If management were to emphasize commercial goals in response to competitive pressures, they could expect considerable resistance. Employees would perceive this change as being in conflict with the firm's identity as a leading-edge professional organization.

Performance is evaluated on professional skills and accomplishments, and therefore promotions are likely to be filled by outsiders if their skills are thought to exceed the best available inside the firm. Employees are motivated primarily by challenging work and its leading-edge nature. Not surprisingly, approximately 40 percent of the high-technology start-ups in the Stanford study fell into this category. They underperformed the commitment model. Most, but not all, professional service firms, health care systems, universities, and research laboratories typically fit the professional model.

Though it can breed initial success based on innovations in technology or services, the professional model will ultimately run into trouble. Apple Computer in the 1990s was such a company. Its distinctive technology was the reason for its great success between 1977 and the late 1980s. Commitment to the mission of developing the best computer technology was very high and drove employees who "worked 90 hours a week and love it."[33] However, Apple's inability to compete in the emerging personal computer market of the 1990s, despite its superior technology and products, illustrates the inability of the professional model to adapt to new circumstances and realign around new strategic realities. Customer focus and teamwork were difficult to achieve in a firm of engineers who came to Apple because they wanted to do leading-edge technical work and were not interested in helping the company enter the competitive business computing market. The passion for the work, though highly motivating, made it hard for management to reorient the firm to practical realities of a marketplace that preferred cost-effective rather than best-in-class technology.

Our work with hospitals illustrates the same difficulties. Here the professional model is built around doctors. Improvements in health care systems require the transformation of the traditional professional model into a high-commitment community model where collaboration and coordination are needed to improve patient care and safety.

The Star Model

The motivation in this organizational form is to advance in one's professional field; unlike the professional model, the referent for advancement is standing in the industry or professional field rather than standing inside the firm. As in the professional model, employees join the firm because of the nature of the challenging work offered. But unlike the professional model, people are selected based exclusively on their talent and reputation in the field rather than on their potential to become committed to the enterprise. Control is achieved through professional norms rather than organizational norms. People aspire to develop their reputation in the field. Consequently, employees are likely to be more motivated by personal *career ambition* than by their commitment to organizational mission or goals. The star firm seeks the best talent and might buy it as readily as it might develop that talent internally. This leads to selection of an elitist workforce. Consequently, the behavior of employees is far less subject to demands of the business or its leaders, particularly if these demands are framed in terms of organizational mission and goals.

Universities, particularly elite universities, and some consulting firms, law firms, and investment banks operate on the star model. Because employees are likely to be motivated by self-interest, it is more difficult to develop teamwork aimed at customer satisfaction and economic value creation. It is possible to build a professional service firm that avoids these pitfalls. McKinsey, the large, well-known management consulting firm, has from its founding emphasized adherence to company norms and standards as well as teamwork, although that may have weakened some in the late 1990s. In the financial services industry, Goldman Sachs is another example of a team-based HCHP firm.

Star systems can have extraordinary success at the outset. Ultimately, however, the lack of commitment to mission, firm goals, and teamwork can result in trouble when competition becomes more intense. Many law firms faced that problem in the 1990s. Emphasis on individual professional accomplishment, unconstrained by strong organizational norms, made it difficult to cross-sell and coordinate the activities of diverse practice groups so necessary to deliver a customer solution. Consider a Wall Street law firm to which I was a consultant. By all accounts the reputations of its professionals were among the best in their fields, but the firm was having difficulty growing its revenue and profits because it was unable to foster cross-selling. Instead, each elite professional group was focused on its own practice.

The star system does not create a source of sustainable advantage, because its leaders assume that organizational performance is a function of the cumulative talents of individuals. In fact, the only true sustainable source of advantage, one that is hard to replicate, comes from developing a collaborative culture and social capital (see chapter 10).

The Bureaucratic Model

Bureaucratic organizations motivate largely on the rational-economic model of man. Employees are hired based on the skills and experience they possess and to fill a current opening, as opposed to their potential for growth. Control and coordination are based on formal structure, defined work processes, and measurement and incentive systems. Behavior is driven principally by compliance and less by internal motivation and commitment. As Charles Heckscher and Nathaniel Foote argue, bureaucracies, and for that matter, the autocracies discussed below, are governed by norms of *deference* and *autonomy*.[34] Deference ensures compliance and discourages challenging authority. Autonomy emanates from the central thesis of bureaucracy; namely, that each department has a defined sphere and resources to do its job and is accountable for delivering on its goals. This discourages the interdepartmental coordination and collaboration required to meet customer needs.[35]

Relatively few founders, the Stanford research discovered, seek to create this model at the outset. Many firms, however, drift into bureaucracy over time, perhaps because founders *do not have the will and skill* to sustain their initial aspiration to build an HCHP organization. Managing a bureaucracy demands less from leaders; it is easy to see how under conditions of stress, when creativity is required to sustain a high-commitment system, CEOs give in to the relative simplicity of using rules and systems to control behavior. In other cases, the drift to bureaucracy occurs because successors do not share the founders' conviction.

General Motors, which under Alfred Sloan was an innovative model of management, is an example of a company that has slowly drifted over several decades from HCHP to bureaucracy. Its market share and performance have steadily declined and, in 2008, GM required a bailout by the U.S. government to avoid bankruptcy.

The Autocratic Model

Autocracies, firms run single-handedly by the founders or successor CEOs, motivate by the rational-economic model of man. Employees are attracted to these firms largely because of their financial rewards. Selection is based on experience and skills to do a specific job. Control and coordination in these firms are achieved through the CEO's personal oversight, and less by formal systems. Managers and workers are motivated by a combination of fear and greed. Relatively few firms in the Stanford study started this way and few survived in the long run. Why? As the firm grows in size, oversight by the CEO is no longer an effective means of control. Low performance and commitment lead to the replacement of the CEO.[36]

Harold Geneen, who grew ITT by acquisition in the late 1960s and 1970s, was an autocrat who managed to avoid this outcome longer than most others. A photographic memory enabled him to personally control a sizable firm.[37] He was well known for the quarterly reviews he held around the world with some 200–300 key managers. Managers from diverse businesses presented their financial results. Geneen's exceptional grasp of detail, combined with his photographic memory, enabled him to question each executive about his or her results. Although these meetings fostered dread and fear, they moved people to produce results at any cost given the financial incentives the firm offered for achieving results. In the late 1970s unethical behavior and declining performance led to Geneen's ouster and the ultimate demise of the firm.

No firm is, of course, a pure organizational type; even those I employ as examples were not. Nevertheless, senior teams may find that these alternative models help them diagnose their organization's current state and steer a course toward an HCHP organization.

Evidence for HCHP Success

Many CEOs might not agree with my view that making a conscious choice about their organizing and management model is a crucial priority. A well-known entrepreneur and founder-CEO of a highly successful Silicon Valley company opined that "[Choosing an] organizing model [is] a source of failure for start-ups.... In order to have a successful company organization, one must first have a successful company. Companies that strive to put in place organizational norms and models, cultures from the outset are working on the wrong things."[38]

I strongly disagree with this perspective. Capital markets have caused leaders to increase their focus on financial objectives to the exclusion of building a great company for the long run. For those who still believe that shareholder value is created by a focus on operating and financial performance, I provide a sample of rigorous evidence—from multiple research traditions, often ignored—that show the opposite.

In the seminal study of high-tech start-ups cited earlier, Stanford researchers were able to document the performance of these companies over time. They conclude:

> Our first main finding is that organization-building and high commitment [human resource management] seems to pay, even in the turbulent "built to flip" environment of Silicon Valley. High commitment firms [compared to other organizing models discussed earlier], had lower administrative overhead—fewer managers and staff specialists—making them more cost effective and more innovative and adaptive. And this benefit of the commitment model extended over time even after the founders who chose the model had left the company and a new CEO was in charge. This effect can be directly attributed to the self-management ethos of the commitment model. Moreover, high commitment start-up firms went public faster than firms with any of the other models of management or companies with no clear model. High commitment firms were also *less* likely to fail subsequent to going to public. Firms founded on the autocracy model, on the other hand, had the highest failure rate. The next highest failure rates were among companies that followed the bureaucratic and professional models.[39]

By correlating employee survey results with financial performance one to five years after a standardized employee survey was conducted in a sample of companies he studied, Dan Dennison found that businesses with high employee participation—those firms whose organizational design enabled employees to work effectively, and where information was openly shared, where human resources was emphasized, and where coordination was high—outperformed companies low on these organizational characteristics in their return on sales and return on investment. The differences in financial performance were substantial and increased over time, demonstrating that how people organized and managed does matter in the long run.[40]

Jim Collins and Jerry Porras's seminal study of paired high- and low-performing companies in the same industry found that they differed in a number of characteristics that I ascribe to HCHP companies. Among other characteristics, their founders were motivated to build an enduring firm, not to enrich themselves; measured success not just by profits, but by the firm's contribution to customers, employees, and society; embraced paradoxical management practices; had distinctive and strong cultures; grew leaders from within; and continually renewed their products and practices while maintaining their core management philosophy. Between 1926 and 1990, the high-performing companies returned $6,356 for every dollar invested while comparison companies returned $955 and the general market $415.[41]

In a study of a large set of paired high- and low-performing companies, John Kotter and Jim Heskett found that over an eleven-year period, high-performing companies with strong cultures that were aligned with strategy and that developed leaders at multiple levels increased revenues by an average of 682 percent versus 166 percent. As compared to low-performing companies, HCHP companies expanded their workforces by 282 percent versus 36 percent, grew their stock prices 901 percent versus 74%, and improved their net incomes by 756 percent versus 1 percent."[42]

A study by Jim Collins found that companies that achieved extraordinary results—an average cumulative stock return of 6.9 times the general market over a fifteen-year period following a corporate transformation—held leadership and cultural characteristics that are remarkably similar to those in HCHP organization as I define and describe them in this book. For example, Collins's extraordinary companies, like HCHP companies, had focused strategies rooted in core capabilities and they confronted "brutal facts."[43] Collins's study found that the extraordinary results were not due to high-profile celebrity leaders, executive compensation, strategy, technology, mergers and acquisitions, change programs, or the industry in which they operated. Leaders had the paradoxical qualities of personal humility and the will to lead change. Though Collins does not say so explicitly, we can infer that these leaders practiced and encouraged participation, teamwork, and involvement as a means of developing commitment.

Many studies conducted in the last two decades show that high-commitment work practices are associated with better productivity, financial performance, and employee well-being. These work practices include high involvement, self-directed teams, flexible work design, extensive investment in training, reduced differentiation in status symbols and in pay between top management and lowest-level employees, and organization-wide reward systems, rather than those directed toward individual or business units.[44]

In an award-winning study, Mark Huselid found that there is a substantial economic reward for firms that employ high-commitment work policies and practices. Companies in the upper 16 percent of firms with such practices experienced 7.05 percent less turnover, substantially more sales per employee ($27,004), higher capitalization per employee ($18,641), and high profits ($3,814).[45]

From a recent study commissioned by the Corporate Leadership Council, we can conclude "that every 10% improvement in commitment can increase employee's discretionary effort by 6% and performance by 2%; highly committed employees perform at a 20% higher level than uncommitted employees."[46] Other studies have shown that high-commitment practices are linked to a high quality of work life, for example, greater empowerment, greater satisfaction, fewer occupational injuries, and lower levels of work-family conflict.[47]

Fortune magazine's annual "100 Best Companies to Work For"— companies whose employees are engaged and committed—have higher average stock returns, higher operating performance [ratio of operating income to assets], higher return on assets, and higher returns on capital employed compared to companies not so classified. In addition, they receive almost twice the number of applicants (1.9 times) compared to companies in their industries that are not on the list, and they also have much lower turnover (12.6 percent versus 26 percent)."[48]

Working Mother's annual "100 Best Companies" list, largely made up of public companies that follow the HCHP model, consistently outperformed the S&P 500 Index (an index of 500 U.S. companies typically employed for comparative purposes) between 1996 and 1998.

Research conducted at MIT into differences in the manufacturing performance of automobile plants around the world found that plants that incorporated high-commitment work practices had higher productivity and quality than plants that did not employ these practices. When these plants also incorporated so-called "lean manufacturing" process (just-in-time inventory and kanban methods), their performance was especially high, indicating that high performance requires not only commitment but also efficient and effective business practices that align with competitive realities, what I defined as performance alignment.[49] Many of the human resource and manufacturing processes had their origin in the Japanese manufacturing industry, particularly Toyota, which outperforms American companies such as General Motors and Ford in both productivity and quality.

Research by Ben Schneider and his associates has demonstrated a relationship between positive employee attitudes in bank branches and positive customer attitudes. They conclude: "The simultaneous delivery and receipt of service in the face-to-face, for profit services sector brings employees and customers physically, organizationally and psychologically close.... [Customers] often equate services with the employees who render them.... [Employees] and customer perceptions, attitudes, and intentions share a common basis and are related to each other."[50]

Researchers at the Harvard Business School have extended these findings by linking service to profits in what they called the "service profit chain." Positive employee attitudes lead to positive customer attitudes, which in turn lead to higher profits that can be used by the company to invest in its employee and organization development.[51]

Danny and Isabelle Le Breton-Miller find that family-run or family-dominated companies have higher margins, more stable earnings, better cash flows and sales per employee then the average company listed in the *Business Week* 1000.[52] They also grow faster and have higher returns on assets and equity. And they survive twice as long as companies that are not family owned or run. Concerned about their legacy, family executives develop HCHP policies and practices, for example, long-term relationships with their employees, customers and community—a multi-stakeholder philosophy. They invest in R&D, quality improvement, and develop customer loyalty even during the worst of times, thus serving as an example of how not to allow short-term pressures to deter from managing for the long term. With regard to employees, they adopt a "collective orientation," carefully avoiding the professional, star, bureaucratic, or autocratic models. Family companies develop a community of purpose by attaching employees to mission and values and by motivating through intrinsic rather than extrinsic rewards (money, power, and promotion). To seal this psychological contract, senior executives are paid 20 percent less than they would be in privatized companies, and non-executive staff is paid 10 percent more. Not surprisingly, these companies recruit and select people to fit the community of purpose they are building.

◆ ◆ ◆

High-commitment companies produce sustained high performance over long periods of time because they are simply more resilient. According to the Stanford researchers, even financially driven venture capitalists believe in the resilience of the HCHP model. Venture capitalists have told them that "the technological and economic uncertainties inherent in high-tech entrepreneurship, combined with the interpersonal stress involved, puts a premium on employees and organizational designs that can cope and adapt. In their judgment, [organizational] blueprints that manage to capture the hearts and minds of employees up front can better achieve adaptation."[53]

Resilience comes from the *capacity to learn and change*. Managers and workers who are committed to the mission and values of the firm are more likely to make sacrifices to maintain the firm's competitive position.[54] Change involves inevitable losses in influence, sense of competence, esteem, relationships, position, identity, and security.[55] If the attachment of managers and workers is to the company's mission and values, as opposed to an attachment to furthering their careers (*star model*) or only the challenge of the work itself (*professional model*), they are more likely to accept these losses. The *bureaucratic model* and the *autocratic model* are even less resilient. Those at the top are insulated from challenges to their assumptions and mental models. Political correctness, denial, arrogance, and entrenched ideas simply prevent new competitive realities from intruding on past habits of mind and heart.[56]

Summary

The development of an HCHP organization, which this book advocates as the best of several alternative organizational systems, represents a choice. Too often leaders make this choice implicitly. Making a conscious, informed choice creates the conviction that leaders will need to resist moving off the path to HCHP posed by continual threats and opportunities in the life of a firm. Making a conscious choice will give CEOs the courage to resist conventional wisdom that is often wrong. Choice of the HCHP model of management will require the discipline to maintain the path discussed in this chapter.

Embedded in the choice of a high-commitment model are assumptions about four crucial strategic choices leaders of HCHP firms make.

The purpose of the firm. HCHP organizations are based on a multistakeholder perspective. These firms create policies and make decisions in a way that adds value for investors, customers, employees, community, and society.

The strategy of the firm. HCHP firms develop focused and distinctive strategies. These are built on a clear idea of whom the firm will serve, the capabilities and culture the firm possesses or intends to build, and equally clear ideas of whom the firm will *not* serve and who they are *not*. When presented with threats and opportunities, HCHP firms make incremental strategic advances that extend capabilities, rather than make opportunistic moves that distract the firm away from its core capabilities.

The risk profile of the firm. Building a resilient firm that survives and prospers in the long run requires management to weigh carefully the financial and cultural risks associated with decisions about growth rates, debt, pricing, mergers and acquisitions, and layoffs. They develop a number of business policies that constrain managers from liquidating investments in people and culture.

The basis of motivation and how people will be organized and managed. HCHP firms extend their view of motivation well beyond the calculative, rational-economic view of man. Though they ensure satisfaction of multiple needs, from money to self-actualization and participation, they are built to stimulate and "exploit" higher-order human needs, in particular the human desire to participate in a firm that has a higher purpose, enables achievement, and bonds people into a community of purpose.

Senior teams that want to build an HCHP organization will find it valuable to discuss the following questions and design the organization's management policies and practices accordingly.

1. On what basis do we now attract and attach employees to the firm, and what basis do we want to use in the future?
2. On what basis do we now select and promote employees, and what basis do we want to use in the future?
3. On what basis do we now control and coordinate the work of our employees, and what basis do we want to use in the future?
4. On what basis do we now evaluate and promote employees, and what basis do we want to use in the future?

Discussions of these questions cannot be just intellectual. They must delve into the assumptions that senior team members make about human motivation and the purpose of business organizations in society. In effect, senior team members must answer the questions of who they are and what is their deepest purpose as managers. Without these clarifying discussions, organization design decisions are not likely to be sustained. That is because the conviction needed to stay the course as the organization is confronted with challenges will not have been developed.

CHAPTER FOUR

BUILDING THE HIGH COMMITMENT, HIGH PERFORMANCE SYSTEM

For every problem there is a solution that is simple, direct . . . and wrong.

—H. L. MENCKEN[1]

An HCHP firm's sustained advantage does not come from its portfolio of assets, products, technology, acquisitions, mergers, or best practices. It comes from the organizational system and culture developed over a number of years, a system that is impossible to replicate in the short run and difficult to imitate in the long run.[2] Clateo Castellini, a CEO who led an HCHP transformation at Becton Dickinson, which we will discuss further in chapter 10, captured this perspective when he said: "I always thought that the way a corporation was organized, the way it was functioning, was a very important indicator of its earning potential. In fact I always told ... [Wall Street] analysts that in their job of studying a corporation and publishing a report, they should look at its culture and organization, besides looking to the products, the strategy and the skills of the CEO! They should be very careful [not] to invest in the long run in a company with a poor organizational approach."[3]

If a business is failing, the senior team must analyze why the current system is failing, experiment with change in multiple parts of the system, engage in continuous learning as to whether changes have been successful or unsuccessful, and then adapt the system over time. The task of building an HCHP firm is therefore one of aligning the total system with strategy and HCHP values. This cannot be done through the shortcuts I see many companies taking; for example, paying big money to recruit the smartest people with the most relevant functional knowledge, or by engaging smart and expensive consultants, or putting thousands of employees through management training and education to teach values and best practices. As important as it is to have smart people, engage good consultants, or train and educate managers and front-line workers, these methods alone will not revive a failing business or build an HCHP system.

Shortcuts bypass the pattern and quality of relationships and decision making—within the leadership team, between top and lower levels, and between different parts of the organization—that are needed for the organization to work efficiently and effectively. Relationship quality and decision-making processes underlie virtually all core challenges, and those challenges invariably stem from the organizational context—leadership team values and behavior, organization structure, management practices, and human resource policies.

Doesn't a company's success and failure depend largely on its leaders? The answer is yes and no. *Yes*, because uncommon values, wisdom, and the collective intent of leaders—the CEO, the top team, and the board of directors—are essential preconditions for the development of an HCHP system of management. *No*, because that is not enough. Successful transformation leaders cannot rely on themselves as the only lever for change.[4] Nor can they rely only on selecting and developing lower-level leaders, as important as that is. They recognize that the most important product they produce is the organizational system itself. Winning products and services, they understand, will be made possible by the well-designed and well-led HCHP system they are working to build. And HCHP leaders recognize that their journey is never over. Changes in markets, technology, and competition continually challenge HCHP leaders to adapt the organization's system of management without losing its soul.

Herb Kelleher's unique and people-oriented style, an important part of the Southwest Airlines story, is not what underlies the company's success. A sound organizational system does. That is why the company will probably continue to be successful under Gary Kelly, who in a recent interview acknowledged that he is a very different person from Herb Kelleher and could not and would not emulate him. Kelly made it quite clear that the key to success has been the system of organizing and managing people and the business, as well as its governing philosophy introduced by Kelleher and the executives with whom he built the company. His job, Kelly said, is to maintain that philosophy and the organization's essential features while adapting the system to new market realities.[5]

In their seminal 1994 book, *Built to Last*, Collins and Porras conclude that companies that were "built to last," companies that sustained high performance over a period of decades, were founded by leaders who focused on what they called "clock building" as opposed to "time telling."[6] In other words, the system of organization and management built to support the company's strategy and values, and not charismatic leadership, was what distinguished companies built to last from companies that did not sustain high performance. In a second study, Jim Collins found that the leaders who led a transformation from "good to great" were humble and focused on the team rather than on themselves.[7] And a recent rigorous study confirms the view that CEO centrality—the relative importance of the CEO within the executive team in terms of ability, contribution, and power—is *inversely* related to several important performance outcomes.[8] The more the CEO played a strong and central role in running the company, the poorer the firm's performance. Although the leader's high-commitment management philosophy was the foundation, as the Stanford study of start-up companies cited in chapter 3 found, it was the high-commitment "employment system" that shaped the company's culture and accounted for its results.[9]

When I studied Hewlett-Packard in 1980, and wrote a case about this remarkable company, well before *Built to Last* was published, interviewees spoke about the firm's values and the system of management that HP's founders had put together to support those values. Nobody mentioned HP's products or technology. The oscilloscope, HP's hugely successful first product, was not what drove the founders to start HP. The oscilloscope actually emerged after several other earlier product introductions. It should come as no surprise that David Packard saw his and Bill Hewlett's primary task as building a system that would be profitable and aligned with their values.

Collins and Porras report on how David Packard saw the task of building HP as articulated in a 1964 speech and a 1973 interview: "The problem is, how do you develop an environment in which individuals can be creative? I believe that you have to put out a good deal of thought to your organizational structure [system] in order to provide this environment." In 1973, an interviewer asked Packard what specific *product* decisions he considered the most important in the company's growth. Packard's response did not include a single product decision. He answered entirely in terms of organizational decisions: developing an engineering team, a pay-as-you-go policy to impose fiscal discipline, a profit-sharing program, personnel and management policies, the "HP Way" philosophy of management, and so on. In a fitting twist, the interviewer titled the article, "Hewlett Packard Chairman Built Company by Design, Calculator [a product] by Chance."[10]

The challenge of building an HCHP system from its inception is of course very different from building an organization from the ashes of poor performance and low commitment. Founders have the advantages of shaping the culture by selecting key people consistent with their intentions from the very beginning. They can invent the company incrementally. Founders do not have to overcome deeply embedded *patterns of relationships and behavior,* nor do they have to cope with "culture drag." Giving birth is simply easier than resurrecting an organization from the depth of low commitment and underperformance; this is the focus of this chapter and book.

Barry Oshry, who has devoted his professional career to understanding organizations as systems and helping leaders change them, observes that overcoming deeply embedded patterns of behavior is especially difficult because managers have a tendency to attribute organizational failures, and I would add successes, to individuals rather than to the system of policies and practices and the recurring patterns of behavior to which they give rise. He observes: "Our tendency is to explain [this pattern of behavior] in terms of character, motivation and abilities of the individuals involved—*that's just the way they are*—or in terms of the specific nature of one's organization—*that's just the way we are*. If our explanation is personal, then our solutions are also personal: fix the players, fire them, rotate them, divorce them. If our explanations are specific to our organization, then we fix the organization: reorganize, reengineer, restructure."[11]

A recent study of CEOs who are successfully transforming their companies into HCHP systems, conducted by my colleagues and me at the TruePoint Center for High Commitment and High Performance, found that these CEOs understand quite well that attitudes, skills, and behavior are shaped by the total system and that they have to redesign it to transform it. One CEO observed: "So the question is then why doesn't it happen? If everyone is for it, then why doesn't it happen? And the truth is that figuring out the mechanics of the system of activities that need to go in place . . . is actually a bit tricky. I mean, it actually takes some creativity to invent those processes."[12]

My experience in working with and studying many underperforming businesses has shown me that taking the total systems perspective is essential. Two key things must be considered by leaders who aspire to build an HCHP organization:

1. A systems framework to guide diagnosis and redesign of the organization
2. A multilevel and multi-unit view of the corporation

Over the years I have been struck by how easily fundamental truths about how to build HCHP systems are forgotten as managers embrace new fads and folderols. Their failures confirm again and again that there are no simple formulas—that the hard and continuous task of building a system over time is the difference between success and failure.

Diagnosing and Rebuilding the System

There is no simple way to draw a map of an organizational system. One reason is that at any given point in time, there are many moving parts interacting with each other. That is why there are so many different models proposed by academics and consultants, each representing some aspect of a complex system. Moreover, organizations are open systems, as opposed to closed mechanical systems, meaning that they are subject to influence from their changing environments, and consequently their design must be constantly adapted to fit new circumstances. Complexity makes diagnosing and then redesigning an organization a continuous problem-solving process.

Diagnosing the organization is not a simple task, however. The truth about the organization's strengths and weaknesses must be surfaced. Unfortunately, organizational silence, the reluctance of lower levels to tell senior management the truth about dysfunctional patterns of behavior that block commitment and performance, prevents senior teams from learning about barriers to effectiveness. For this reason real change requires what I call *honest, collective, and public conversations* (to be discussed in chapters 6 and 7) about how the organizational system is functioning. Only then can senior teams see the "whole system," perform a valid diagnosis of root causes, and develop solutions that fit the real causes of poor performance and low commitment. Open and searching conversations are the key to transforming the system. No rigid framework can simplify the task.

Nevertheless, I have found that leadership teams seeking to diagnose and develop their organizations find it useful to refer to a map of the territory like the one in Figure 4.1, if only as a starting point.[13] The model emerged from my

FIGURE 4.1. THE HIGH COMMITMENT, HIGH PERFORMANCE SYSTEM.

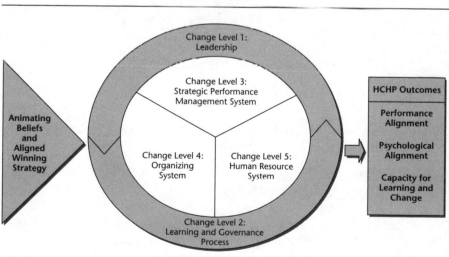

work with senior teams engaged in a diagnosis of why their organizations have been (1) unable to implement their strategic intent and achieve desired levels of performance, and (2) unable to develop commitment to goals and strategy.

The five change levers shown in Figure 4.1 have an empirical base. Senior teams that I worked with and studied typically identified deficiencies in five organizational and managerial capabilities. Each of these domains had become misaligned with new strategic realities. Each ultimately had to be changed to turn around the fortunes of the organization. That is why I call them change levers. Each one is a subsystem that must be redesigned to align the organization and its people with the organization's goals and strategy. And of course they must be internally consistent. Figure 4.2 shows the capabilities senior teams had to develop and the subsystem they redesigned and changed over time. Redesigning these subsystems created a new management discipline that "forced" new behavior and ultimately "hardwired" that behavior, thereby putting the organization on a path to sustained high commitment and performance. The five change levers are shown in Figure 4.2.

1. *Leadership:* The role and responsibilities of the leader and senior team—the direction they provide, their effectiveness in confronting the truth about barriers to implementing their direction, and their will and skill in leading change.

2. *Learning and Governance System:* A structure and process that enables senior teams to lead an honest, collective (organization-wide), and public conversation

FIGURE 4.2. FIVE CRITICAL CAPABILITIES AND CHANGE LEVERS THAT SHAPE THEM.

Critical Organizational Capabilities	Change Levers
1. Clear top-down direction and the willingness to confront and resolve internal tensions blocking performance and commitment	1. Leadership—leader and top team
2. Honest and open communication within and between the senior team and lower levels about barriers	2. Learning and Governance System
3. Translation of strategic direction and values into effective execution	3. Strategic Performance Management System
4. Coordination between value-creating activities	4. Organizing System
5. Capable people, particularly leaders, who fit strategy and animating beliefs and values	5. Human Resource System

that reveals how the organizational system is functioning and mobilizes commitment to change.

3. *Strategic Performance Management System:* The process by which strategy and goals are set, results are measured and reviewed, and financial and human resources requirements are defined, targeted for development, or reallocated to enable effective and timely execution.

4. *Organizing System:* The formal organizational arrangements. Its design defines roles, responsibilities, and relationships of value-creating activities, and specifies mechanisms for integration, such as cross-cutting teams.

5. *Human Resource System:* Policies and practices that define how people will be recruited, selected, evaluated, developed, rewarded, and terminated.

Change levers 1 and 2—Leadership and the Learning and Governance System in the outer circle in Figure 4.1—mobilize energy for change and guide the process of direction setting, diagnosis, and redesign. The leadership team (lever 1) must have the vision and motivation to engage relevant managers and front-line employees to learn about and change the total system as well as their own role and behavior. The Learning and Governance System (lever 2) is their platform for engaging the organization in a safe, effective, honest, collective, and public conversation, something that is otherwise difficult if not impossible. Change Levers 3, 4, and 5 are design levers. They are critical subsystems of the organization that, as I have observed in successful change efforts, are redesigned by the senior team. They transform the hidden barriers to performance and commitment that I discuss in the next chapter into strengths.

For the redesign and change process to result in an HCHP system, its leaders must be animated by deep beliefs about life and people and a strategy that is consistent with those beliefs and which also positions the company to win in the marketplace (see Figure 4.1).[14] The result is a "powerful internal and external brand." By brand I mean a genuine emotional connection between people (employees, customers, even investors) and the organization and its products or services. Southwest Airline's distinctive strategy, organization, and operating system, and the tight alignment between all design elements, are each a function of passionate beliefs about how they want to treat and manage people, about which customers they want to serve, and how they want to serve them.

There is a remarkable similarity in beliefs held by leaders of HCHP firms operating in very different industries, as discussed in the previous chapter. They believe that the purpose of the firm is to serve all stakeholders. They have ambitious aspirations to build a great business and organization. They believe that people want to make a difference, contribute, and grow. And they are open to learning, one of the reasons they are comfortable with the honest, collective, and public conversations needed to build an HCHP system. It is these beliefs that enable them to create an HCHP company. Should senior leadership teams not hold these beliefs, they will have to learn their way into them or be replaced before a fundamental transformation can occur.

A systems model like that in Figure 4.1 can guide senior teams through the following series of questions:

1. What are our distinctive energizing beliefs about life and people? What distinctive strategy is consistent with those beliefs?
2. What is the gap in performance and commitment that concerns us, given our strategic intent?
3. How do we evaluate the organization with respect to the three essential HCHP outcomes or pillars—performance alignment, psychological alignment, and capacity for learning?
4. Which of the levers or subsystems as currently designed and implemented cause deficiencies in organizational outcomes?
5. How should we redesign the system—all five levers—to overcome our shortfall in organizational and performance outcomes?

Systemic change cannot be achieved without a collective learning process rooted in the truth. Without knowledge from *all* parts of the organization, senior management cannot obtain a rich multilayered view of the organization or come to understand the circular and complex connections between multiple facets of the system. They need to see the whole system as well as their role in it. Once the truth is on the table, the systems framework enables a rigorous analysis and redesign that is consistent with the diagnosis. That's because the systems framework and the truth will not allow senior teams to overlook aspects of the system they may otherwise ignore or avoid because it happens to be personally, politically, or culturally difficult to deal with. The systems framework helps senior leaders to avoid, in H. L. Mencken's language, identifying "one solution that is simple, direct, and wrong." Metaphorically, managers will avoid doing "surgery without a diagnosis," something that medical doctors would be called to account for, because of their rigorous professional standards.

A systemic approach to change encourages the formation of a holistic vision regarding how the business will be organized and managed to align with new realities. It allows multiple levers for change to be addressed simultaneously. This last point is important because the changes in one design lever often demand a complementary redesign of one or more of the others. Only by working with a systemic approach to change will problems be connected to the multiple design levers that are causing them.

As a practical matter, all levers cannot be changed at once. Certainly they cannot progress at the same rate of change. Resources and time do not permit that. Such was the case in Corning's Electronic Products Division, to be discussed in the next chapter. A learning and governance process enabled senior management to implement simultaneous changes in the structure of the organization, their leadership role, and their strategic performance management system. What took much longer was a full transformation in their beliefs and skills, and in those of the many key people whose alignment was necessary to enact the new organizational design. These beliefs and skills evolved over time, and as the leadership team learned from implementation. Recruitment and development of key people who are needed to enact new organizational arrangements proceed more slowly. In effect, the new system is designed and launched before all requisite skills and knowledge are developed. Education and training follow the design and launch. To sustain change, those who cannot or will not learn new ways, particularly leaders, must be replaced.

Leadership teams can take many actions to remedy low commitment and failing performance; for example, a new enterprise system, a new incentive system, firing and hiring people, initiating programs like Six Sigma, or developing down-the-line leaders. Yet too often, I have seen how prematurely launched change initiatives—before a diagnosis is performed reduce a leader's motivation to change fundamental underlying problems. This is particularly true if those changes have occurred independent of a learning and governance process that provided honest feedback. Leaders embrace quick fixes and ignore fundamentals, probably because the fundamentals are painful and difficult to change. If fundamental problems have not been confronted, or the organization has not been redesigned to overcome them, premature change initiatives will outstrip the capacity of the organization and its leaders to absorb their potential value.

Organizations Are Multilevel and Multi-Unit Systems

A corporation has many cultures, not one. Each subunit is likely to vary in its level of performance alignment, psychological alignment (emotional attachment to the company and its values), and its capacity to learn and change. HCHP transformations therefore demand systemic change at multiple levels and in each of many subunits of the corporation, each with its own distinctive alignment and culture, as Figure 4.3 shows, a subject to which I will return in chapter 11. By subunits I mean the corporate top management unit (CEO, key line and staff executives), major business units, regional organizations, corporate functional staff units, and major operating units such as manufacturing plants, stores, or

FIGURE 4.3. CORPORATE TRANSFORMATION INVOLVES MULTILEVEL AND MULTI-UNIT CHANGE.

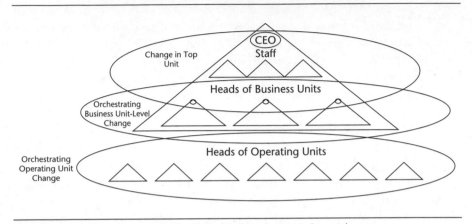

Source: Adapted from Beer et al., *The Critical Path to Corporate Renewal.*

large offices. The amount of variability in cultures will depend on whether the company has grown organically or has grown by acquisition.

A corporate transformation requires changes in each of the corporation's subunits—the top unit and the many subunits below. In effect, each subunit is a system in its own right. An HCHP transformation will require each leadership team to shape their subunit into an HCHP organization. That means they will have to replicate the corporate change process discussed above—engage managers and employees in a collective learning and change process that results in redesign of the system. Of course, lower-level units have fewer degrees of freedom. They cannot change corporate policies and practices, unless the company is a holding company, but they can adapt their strategy, structure, leadership, and local culture, and they can identify corporate barriers. For these reasons the process of building an HCHP company *ideally* starts at the corporate level. It can also start in business units at lower levels, though this is a much slower and riskier path that depends on spontaneous diffusion of HCHP practices or the rise of an innovative manager to the top job. Wherever the transformation starts it must eventually spread to all units. The role of corporate leaders is to urge, orchestrate, and support such a process in all of the corporation's major business units, just as business units have to motivate a process in operating units.

A multi-unit learning process is a potential source of learning for both the unit leaders and top management. If top management encourages lower-level leaders to begin organizational learning in their subunit, and holds them accountable for reporting what they learned and plan to change, management will discover many important things. Are their leaders willing to engage in honest conversations? Are they able to lead systemic change with commitment? Are they able to learn about themselves? Of course such transparency will not be possible unless top management adopts a development stance along with its findings. If they replace general managers upon hearing an honest, self-critical report about what they have learned regarding their organization and leadership weaknesses, it will discourage transparency, though replacement may be necessary and will be seen as fair if problems persist over time.

To change a larger corporation may seem overwhelming to top management. Changing all facets of the organization at once is impossible. Encouraging and overseeing innovations in all subunits is overload. For this reason many transformations start with top management commissioning planned experiments in one or two subunits of the company; smaller size and lower risk allows radical departure from traditional patterns. The model organizational subunits become leading-edge units from which top management can learn. If the model organizations are successful, top management's task is to spread well-tested ideas to other subunits.

Summary

Building an HCHP organization requires a systems perspective and framework. It gives leadership teams a systems template for diagnosing and changing their organization—its hard, structural elements as well as its softer human, behavioral, and cultural characteristics. And to actually "see" the whole system, the senior team must enable lower levels to talk honestly about barriers to commitment and performance. This enables a deeper diagnosis, one that will focus on a total system redesign. Renovating all aspects of the system increases the likelihood that previously unsuccessful patterns of leadership, management, and organizational behavior will actually change and that change will be sustained. Figure 4.1 provides a practical framework that has been used successfully by senior teams to engage the multiple causal factors underlying low performance and commitment. Redesigning leadership roles and behavior and the four other levers for change enables senior management to hardwire an effective pattern of management, one that strengthens five core capabilities essential for sustained performance (see Figure 4.2).

Large organizations are composed of multiple subunits—a top management unit, business units, key functional units, and operating units—and each is a system with its own subculture. Successful HCHP transformations require change in each subunit. Leadership teams in each subunit will have to engage employees in a collective learning process, conduct a diagnosis, and employ all five change levers. Successful change in multi-unit organizations often starts with planned experiments in a few subunits. These models are then spread to all other units.

Leadership teams that want to transform their organization into an HCHP system will want to discuss the following questions:

1. What are our beliefs about life and people, and do we have a strategy consistent with those beliefs that also positions the company to win?
2. Are we engaging the organization and ourselves in an honest, collective, and public conversation about our organization's strengths and weaknesses?
3. Have we diagnosed the root causes of our underperformance and commitment?
4. Has a systemic vision for change been developed?
5. Has that vision been stress tested with lower levels in a way that allows modification and builds commitment?
6. Have we avoided starting with educational programs aimed at changing attitudes and skills and instead employed education and facilitation to support changes in roles and responsibilities?
7. Have we changed formal structure and policies to reinforce and hardwire new patterns of management if they prove effective?
8. Do we have a plan for change that encompasses all subunits and their senior teams?
9. Are we continuing to employ organization-wide honest conversations to assess progress in our efforts to build an HCHP system?

PART TWO

WHAT STANDS IN THE WAY

CHAPTER FIVE

HIDDEN BARRIERS TO SUSTAINED HIGH COMMITMENT AND HIGH PERFORMANCE

What would one hundred key people in a company say if they felt safe enough to speak candidly about organizational strengths and about barriers to commitment and performance? For the past fifteen years, my colleague Russ Eisenstat and I have had the privilege to work with CEOs and business unit general managers who had the courage to actively solicit such candid views of key people in their business, employing a process we call the Strategic Fitness Process (SFP).[1]

The SFP requires leaders and their senior teams to commission a task force of eight of their highest-potential people to interview approximately one hundred key people in the organization. The interviewees are first asked to describe what they see as the organization's strengths. Next, they are encouraged to talk openly about existing barriers that prevent implementation of the organization's strategy and values. In turn, we consultants interview senior teams about *their* perceptions of organizational strengths and barriers. Interestingly, senior teams see the same barriers in place as do the task forces, although typically not with the same emotion or sense of urgency. Knowing is apparently not the same as doing. As we discovered, doing requires the will to confront difficult, emotionally charged problems and find ways to engage people at lower levels in what we have come to call *honest, collective, and public conversations.*

People are motivated to speak openly for two reasons. First, senior teams make it clear that the feedback they receive will be made public (shared with the wider organization) and acted upon, thus assuring interviewees that their opinions will be heard. Second, the SFP process is designed to create anonymity for interviewees and "psychological safety" for task force members (see chapter 7 for how this is done). In other words, no repercussions will occur if employees speak negatively about the organization. In our experience, one cannot overestimate how essential these two conditions are if truth is to speak to power. Perhaps even more essential, if truth cannot speak to power the organization will fail to achieve sustained commitment and performance.[2]

Over the course of fifteen years, we have *not* been surprised to find that task forces consistently identified a single organizational strength: competent and motivated employees. (In every organization there were, of course, some people underperforming.) This finding is completely consistent with the systems perspective of this book; namely, that the system of organizing and managing bears the primary burden for dysfunctional and unmotivated behavior. Change the pattern of management, and the potential for commitment and performance can be unleashed, though some people, particularly key managers, may have to be replaced.

What did surprise us from task force reports was the consistent and emotionally charged nature with which people talked about six core barriers that undermine commitment and performance. In most cases, the interviewees had been part of organizational life for some time and were frustrated with failed top-management initiatives that ran afoul of these hidden barriers. They were angry that leadership teams had been unwilling to confront what to them were obvious deficiencies in how the enterprise was organized, managed, and led.

The six barriers almost always appeared as a group, suggesting that they are a manifestation of a management system that is unaligned with the strategic task for the organization. The six core barriers are:[3]

1. Conflicting priorities, unclear strategy, or unclear values
2. An ineffective senior team
3. Top-down or laissez-faire leadership
4. Poor horizontal coordination and communication
5. Inadequate leadership development and paucity of down-the-line leaders
6. Poor vertical communication

We call these barriers "silent killers." Silent because, though known to most key employees and discussed in private with trusted friends, senior teams had never openly acknowledged the barriers. The lack of public discussion about the barriers is a manifestation of a pervasive phenomenon in organizations (to which I will return in chapter 7), one that academics call "organizational silence."

Open discussion will not occur if people—even key managers—perceive that they cannot *speak* openly and, in particular, if they perceive they cannot *speak up*.[4]

Industry surveys and studies consistently confirm the pervasiveness of organizational silence. In one survey, for example, only 29 percent of front-line supervisors and 38 percent of middle managers agreed that their organization encouraged employees to express their opinions openly.[5] Another survey found that 70 percent of employees were hesitant to speak up about problems at work, either out of fear of repercussions or out of cynicism that speaking up would simply not make a difference.[6] When asked which types of work problems were most likely to be avoided in discussion, nearly half the respondents mentioned "management practice." Without a psychologically safe opportunity to speak about concerns, people will avoid talking publicly about problems with supervision, organizational processes, and performance; neither will people offer suggestions for improvement, disagree with company policies and decisions, or voice opinions on career and fairness issues.[7]

Furthermore, studies show that fear and cynicism do not simply apply to lower hierarchical levels. "There was no basic difference in un-discussables," Jim Detert and Amy Edmondson concluded, "from one level of the organization to the next."[8] It might also be said that managers often don't speak truthfully to employees about the real challenges the organization is facing for fear of reducing employee commitment and thus causing increasing turnover. Ultimately, these tendencies are destructive to an HCHP culture.

We use the term "killers" for these six barriers because, like cholesterol and hypertension, which cause unexpected heart attacks in humans, the silent barriers are *symptoms of low performance alignment, low psychological alignment, and low capacity for learning and change*. Like high cholesterol and hypertension, which are problems that can mount over time, these silent killers erode an organization's capacity to adapt to changing business realities long before they are actually discovered. Although numerous separate studies have identified each individual barrier, to my knowledge, their interconnection as a *syndrome* that blocks high commitment and performance has not been previously shown.[9]

At some point, every organization will face the challenge to achieve integration and unified commitment to an ever-changing direction set by top leaders. The silent killers are *organizational stress points* that exist in all organizations. They are a product of challenges incurred when human beings are brought together into a hierarchical, task-driven organization. My message is that, if not confronted, the silent killers will erupt into major fault lines, especially when markets quake, that is, strategic inflections challenge the business's ability to compete. Once confronted with the silent killers, senior leaders must be willing and able to lead their organizations through a learning process to better align with the new strategic task. Much as earthquakes make manifest hidden fault lines, new competitive realities shock the organizational system and make manifest the six previously hidden barriers.

The difficulty of preventing these barriers from becoming major fault lines in the organization, and overcoming barriers when they arise, is one of the major reasons for the relative paucity of HCHP firms. However, we have found that determined, courageous, and exceptional leaders, such as the ones profiled in this book, *can* successfully develop barriers into strengths.

Again and again, we have found that when leaders enable honest, collective, and public conversations about organizational barriers, they not only develop performance and psychological alignment, but also begin to develop the capacity for learning and change. When these conversations become an accepted norm, the organization becomes a resilient HCHP organization. Determined, courageous, exceptional leaders with whom I have worked have been able to confront and overcome the silent killers and go on to build an HCHP organization. CEOs who fail to make discussable the six hidden barriers are ultimately replaced.

Although HCHP organizations make it less likely that the six stress points will become major barriers to adaptation and performance, even they are not immune to the silent killers. Especially when organizations are shocked by unprecedented competitive upheaval or when their historic business models are challenged, HCHP organizations will begin to see organizational fault lines. They reflect the difficulties that organizations have in adapting. High levels of commitment and a capacity for learning, however, enable HCHP companies to overcome hidden barriers quickly, and before they become major, threatening fault lines. This capacity is what makes these companies resilient. In a recent interview with Gary Kelly, CEO of Southwest Airlines, he described how he had to change the role of his highly committed senior team once he realized that new competitive realities of the airline industry in the post-9/11 environment required much closer coordination between key activities.[10]

In the remainder of this chapter I will illustrate the six silent killers by describing how they undermined commitment and performance in Corning's Electronic Products Division (EPD). This is a case I lived through as a consultant several decades ago. It suggests that the syndrome of hidden barriers was as fundamental to understanding underperformance then as now; and, as I will show, transforming the silent killers was fundamental to EPD's transformation into an HCHP organization. Silent barriers can be turned into organizational capabilities through redesigning five change levers, as defined and discussed in chapter 4 (see Figures 4.1 and 4.2), and elaborated in the next two sections.

Corning's Electronic Products Division (EPD)

In the late 1960s, I was approached by Don Rogers (a pseudonym), the vice president and general manager of the Electronic Products Division, a business unit of Corning Glass Works (now Corning Inc.) where I was working as an internal organization development consultant. Rogers had taken charge of the division two years before we met, following the untimely death of its previous general manager, Joe Bennett. Over lunch, Rogers described a business facing fierce competition and major organizational problems.[11] He reported:

> We have had some difficult times in my division over the past two years. Sales have been down due to the general economy and the effects on the electronics industry. But our problems are greater than that. Our business is becoming fiercely competitive. To deal with the downturn in business we have had to reduce the number of people and expenses sharply. This has been painful, but I think these actions have stemmed the tide. We are in control again. But the business continues to be very competitive, morale is low, there is a lot of conflict between groups that we can't seem to resolve. There is a lack of mutual confidence and trust. The organization is just not pulling together and the lack of coordination is affecting our ability to develop new products. Most of my people believe that we are having conflicts because business is bad. They say that if business would only get better we will stop crabbing at each other. Frankly, I am not so sure if they are right. The conflicts might be due to pressures we are under but more likely they indicate a more fundamental problem. Can you and your group help determine if the conflict between groups is serious and if so what might be done about it?[12]

I told Rogers I would be happy to help. Corning's EPD manufactured high-reliability electronic components for defense and commercial markets. Founded by Joe Bennett, the business had performed very well until just a year before Rogers took charge. Since then, sales in its core business—high-reliability components sold primarily into the defense industry—were in alarming decline, due to a slowdown in defense spending, while sales and profits in more competitive commercial markets were not increasing at a sufficient rate. The latter depended on new products, too few of which were coming out of the new-product development pipeline, and when they did, the process was painful and took too long.

Despite significant cost cutting and the replacement of most of the senior team by Rogers, the business was falling short of corporate expectation for a 10 percent annual rise in revenues and profits. Managers reporting to Rogers felt that corporate expectations were unrealistic given that EPD operated in a much more competitive landscape compared to Corning's other businesses, where Corning's technology and manufacturing capabilities were a distinctive advantage. Managers were certain that EPD would never meet the expectations for a 10 percent revenue and profit rise; some wondered if EPD would be better off with a corporate parent in the components business.

After what my team and I learned about EPD from three months of data collection and diagnosis, the division's underperformance was not surprising. The three pillars of HCHP, essential for sustained performance and commitment (see chapter 2), were dangerously low.

Performance Alignment

EPD's organization and management processes were not aligned with new strategic realities. Although the decline in the defense business and the emergent needs of TV and computer manufacturers for reliable but cheaper components called for a new strategy, the senior team, who were aware of this shift, had not articulated the new strategy or requisite new-product development priorities. EPD's functional structure and management processes needed to foster coordination and had not been realigned to fit the much faster pace of product development required in commercial markets. Performance measures that worked in a defense-oriented business, a system that held manufacturing plants responsible for gross margin, for example, undermined responsiveness to shifting customer needs in a fast-moving commercial market. All of this resulted in very poor coordination.

Psychological Alignment

Managers in various parts of the organization made decisions to maximize the performance of their own department or activity, particularly a powerful manu-facturing function, as opposed to supporting the EPD's overarching objectives for revenue and profit growth. Adversarial relationships between functional depart-ments undermined any sense of common purpose. For example, manufacturing plant managers resisted requests from marketing and product development for trial runs of new products on their manufacturing lines because such trials under-mined plant gross margins; poor margins could undermine their career progress. A history of top-down autocratic management by Bennett had caused managers to become protective of their departments and themselves. Though Rogers had replaced most of the senior team and was an open and participative manager, his laissez-faire style, more appropriate to the corporate research and development division from which he came, was not sufficient to bring together rival functional departments. Morale and commitment were extremely low, suggesting poor psychological alignment.

Capacity for Learning and Change

Though key people often met in small groups at the water cooler and behind closed doors to air their frustrations, these frustrations were not openly shared and discussed with the relevant parties or within the top team. Consequently, frustrations turned into deep distrust. Although individual senior team members, indeed many key people beyond the senior team, were aware of many of EPD's problems, distrust and a lack of mechanisms for an honest, collective, and public conversation prevented the senior team from confronting problems openly, diagnosing root causes, and reinventing the organizational and management system to fit new competitive realities.

The stakes were high. For Corning, failure would mean an eventual exit from a business that was to be the foundation for entry into the larger electronics market. As a new general manager just two years in his job, failure to turn around EPD's performance would probably derail Rogers' promising career, one widely seen as having great potential.

Silent Barriers to Commitment and Performance

What had so dangerously lowered the three pillars of high commitment and performance and threatened EPD's survival? Although my consulting team at Corning and I identified the barriers discussed below, it was not until dozens of task forces in the last fifteen years reported the same six barriers that the silent killer syndrome came into clear focus.[13] Below I describe the barriers that task forces reported to their senior team, and illustrate how they prevented EPD management from responding in a timely and effective way to a specific strategic inflection that their business was experiencing. As I will show, the inability to discuss them openly made it impossible to overcome them; conversely, exceptional leaders who enabled such a discussion were able to eradicate the barriers.

Conflicting Priorities, Unclear Strategy, and Unclear Values

Senior teams heard that many key employees saw conflicting priorities fostered by an unclear mission, goals, and values.

Conflicting Priorities. Sustained high performance can only come after the business's senior team has defined clear priorities. Common priorities enable coordinated effort. Each part of the organization allocates the same level of effort and resources to each initiative. Lower levels in underperforming businesses reported that different functional departments, businesses, or geographic regions were operating according to different priorities, thus frustrating execution.

In Corning's EPD, key people reported considerable confusion about the relative priority of nine new-product development projects. Marketing and product development were pouring resources into the development of one new product which manufacturing and sales had stopped working on because they felt it would not succeed. Given the strategic importance of new-product development, this barrier loomed large in the business's underperformance.

Unclear Strategy and Goals. We heard task force after task force tell senior teams that the people they interviewed felt confused about business strategy; some had not heard what the strategy was until presented with it in the interview. Others said the strategy made no sense given what they knew about the market and customers. In one underperforming business the lack of clarity and agreement about strategy was described as follows: "We have two competing strategies that are battling each other for the same resources. The resultant factions around these two strategies are tearing this organization apart."[14] Although most key managers in EPD sensed that they were experiencing a strategic inflection—a shift from defense to commercial markets with different requirements and characteristics—this sense had not yet been fully acknowledged or communicated to the larger organization.

Lack of common direction in many companies was not restricted to strategy. In many cases, the organizations we studied also lacked clear operational objectives. In Corning's EPD a key executive said: "There are no operational objectives. I get the feeling that everyone is concerned, but no clear objectives are set."[15] That many organizations do not have a clear, comprehensive, and disciplined system for integrating the goals of many diverse functions and businesses with strategy has been confirmed in numerous studies, most recently by Robert Kaplan and David Norton.[16] That is why formalizing a coherent strategic performance management system (chapter 8) is so important.

Unclear Values. Without clear, understood, and accepted HCHP values to govern leadership and organizational behavior, individuals and departments will be guided by their own. In one corporation, clearly not an HCHP company, a task force reported to the CEO and his top team that the company lacked "human values."

EPD was governed by a set of implicit values. Under Bennett, it had been governed by noncollaborative norms. Leadership had not defined values that would invest its employees with a sense of meaning and mission. Rogers had also not articulated a set of HCHP values, although his behavior as a leader demonstrated them. He was more participative than Bennett and urged better teamwork, though he required help in developing it throughout the organization. Such values are an essential complement to formal structures and incentives, and distinguish HCHP firms from their peers. They enable the spontaneous teamwork needed in the dynamic and rapidly changing competitive environments of the twenty-first century. EPD's problems in coordination could be explained in part by leadership's failure to articulate their expectations for collaboration, and the consequences for those who did not comply.

◆ ◆ ◆

Without a common direction in strategy and values, it is of course impossible to begin the process of fitting or aligning the organization, which is an essential condition for HCHP.

Ineffective Senior Teams

"You as a senior team are ineffective as a group." This was the message conveyed to senior teams by SFP task forces in every one of the underperforming organizations and low-commitment organizations we worked with and studied. The correlation between the top teams' effectiveness and company performance is corroborated by numerous studies.[17] For example, Kathy Eisenhardt and Claudia Schoonover studied ninety-eight of the 102 firms in the semiconductor industry between 1978 and 1988, and found that top team effectiveness was associated with the financial success of the firm at the end of two years. This performance advantage became even stronger by the end of six years.[18] Our finding that top team ineffectiveness was perceived to be a major problem by all task forces in our study is confirmed Don Hambrick, a leading expert on top teams. He writes that "the widely used expression 'top management team' is a misnomer for the groups that exist at the apex of many firms."[19] When senior teams, confronted by feedback about their ineffectiveness, dug into why they were ineffective, they discovered the following sources of ineffectiveness:

Low Team Cohesion and Collaboration. Teams were often not cohesive enough and lacked the trust to be able to engage difficult issues. Lower levels sensed this from their bosses and saw it as affecting decisions and undermining teamwork. An executive in Corning's EPD described the senior team under Rogers' predecessor, Joe Bennett, as follows: "There is little group activity and decision making except when there is a specific problem. It is not a natural group. We are never together. I don't think we have been together, except for formal manager's meetings [where financial results are reviewed and administrative issues are discussed], once in the last three months or so. There is not cohesiveness in the group."[20]

Teams Infrequently Review Strategy or Discuss and Agree on Values. Despite the assertion of senior executives that strategy matters, many senior teams met too infrequently to review strategy implementation, make midcourse corrections by reallocating resources, or redesign the organization to enable better execution. Very often senior teams found safety and comfort in agendas that included administrative but not strategic issues. "We discuss vacation policies and review financial results instead of tackling really important strategic issues," reported one senior team member.

Recent research by Kaplan and Norton finds that 85 percent of senior teams spend less than one hour per month discussing their strategy, with 50 percent not spending any time on this. The same study finds that top teams in companies that manage strategy well usually meet once a month for four to eight hours. Meeting regularly for at least a half day naturally leads to a continuous review of strategic initiatives and, as required, the reallocation of human or financial resources. Though EPD had regular reviews of new-product development projects, these were operational as opposed to higher-level strategic reviews.

At the Hewlett-Packard Santa Rosa Systems Division, a senior team that did not meet regularly to review the cross-functional business teams charged with implementing their new strategy undermined its execution. Lacking oversight, functional departments fought for scarce engineering resources and inexperienced team leaders did not receive coaching.

Teams Are Poorly Constituted. Many senior teams were simply too big to enable a meaningful and candid dialogue about strategic issues. In Corning's EPD new-product development, reviews typically involved some fifteen to twenty people. In other cases, senior teams did not include key managers outside the organization whose resources were essential to strategy implementation. Corning's EPD is a good example. It depended mightily on support from a corporate R&D function that was widely perceived to be unresponsive to the division. Yet the director of the relevant R&D activity was not invited to new-product development reviews. In another company, neither front-facing marketing units charged with business development nor sales and back-end operations units were represented on the business unit's senior team.

Conflict Not Confronted and Managed. Senior teams discovered that one of the central problems underlying their ineffectiveness was their inability to manage conflict. Fearing that differences in views might erupt in angry and unconstructive confrontations that would undermine relationships, senior teams avoided engaging the strategic issues facing the business. Corning's EPD serves as an illustration of what we have seen in many other top teams. As a consultant to EPD, I recorded the following observations of product development reviews: "While problems encountered were always described, the issue of slippage in goals and the underlying reasons for it were rarely discussed. Differences in opinions usually proved hard to resolve. People would end them by agreeing to disagree and moving on to the next item on the agenda. While tempers flared occasionally, open hostility or aggression was rarely expressed at meetings. Afterwards, however, people split off to continue the debate, often in pairs or small groups in the hallways, over coffee, or in other offices."

The senior team's inability to confront conflict was in part due to general manager Don Rogers, who was described by one of his senior team members as follows: "He does not listen too well. His interruptions of others prevent him from hearing others' opinions and make it seem as if he really does not want criticism."[21]

An inability to confront tough issues caused EPD's new-product development effort to suffer. The senior team was unable to kill projects and reallocate resources. EPD's market development manager, who chaired the top team's product development reviews, said: "Projects are slipping badly and we just can't seem to get them moving. In my opinion, we also have some projects that should be killed but we can't seem to be able to do that either."[22]

Research shows that constructive, issue-oriented conflict is essential. It leads to the consideration of more alternatives; better understanding of the possible choices; and overall, significantly more effective decision making. Constructive conflict has been found to be associated with both high performance in business and effective public policy decisions.[23]

Top-Down or Laissez-Faire Leader

Corporate CEOs and general managers of underperforming businesses facing strategic challenges were always implicated in the silent killers. They were either too top down, and in some cases, autocratic, or they were seen as laissez-faire. Top-down managers viewed it as their prerogative to make all major decisions. This led them to undervalue and underinvolve their senior team in key decisions. Strategic decisions were often made in one-to-one meetings. On the rare occasions when one senior team met to discuss strategic issues, senior team members had the distinct feeling that a decision had already been made. The consequence was a political environment with low trust, not only within the senior team, but also among key managers at lower levels who, as task forces found, knew very well that the CEO or general manager was directive and the senior team ineffective.

In Corning's Electronic Products Division, founding general manager Joe Bennett was too top down. This made it impossible for the senior team to engage in constructive dialogue needed to confront strategic and organizational problems. "Joe is very autocratic with me and others. As a result, those working for [him] who are most successful are political and manipulative. People around here do not extend themselves very much to disagree with [him]," reported one member of Bennett's senior team.[24] This management pattern had created a closed, low-trust, and political environment that was still present some two years after Rogers, Bennett's successor, had taken charge, illustrating the remarkable resilience of established patterns of behavior.

Asda, a U.K. grocery chain once known for top management's autocratic and regal style of management, suffered a ten-year decline in performance and commitment. Store managers, who knew their policies and practices were failing, feared confronting senior management and a powerful trading department at the corporate center.[25]

Laissez-faire CEOs or general managers who did not engage their senior teams and other key managers in confronting business and management problems were also seen as ineffective. The causes were multiple. Some were spending too much time away from their business on outside activities or assignments. Others were uncomfortable with the potential conflicts that might arise when strategic issues were engaged, did not listen when they were discussed, or were not demanding enough. In describing Don Rogers' laissez-faire approach to management, one interviewee said, "[H]e has been soft on me. He should be holding me to my goals. I have not met some of these goals and he should be climbing all over me." [26]

At the low-performing Santa Rosa Systems Division of Hewlett-Packard, its general manager's laissez-faire style led to a one-on-one approach to managing the senior team.[27]

Both top-down and laissez-faire approaches to management prevent CEOs and general managers from gaining the benefits of diverse views. Neither approach confronts poor business and human outcomes, or is capable of revitalizing the business. Usually it's impossible to know whether the leader's style produced ineffective senior teams, or whether the leader's style was a response to a lack of success in developing an effective senior team, but both were probably true. What is clear is that the leader's style and the top team's effectiveness are deeply connected and together create a vicious downward spiral.

Poor Coordination and Collaboration

Task forces in underperforming and low-commitment organizations unanimously reported: "We have poor teamwork and collaboration in our organization." Depending on the size and scope of the business, inadequate teamwork occurred across functions, business units, and geographic regions. As an array of research shows, coordination and collaboration between value-creating activities is essential for the efficient and effective implementation of strategic intent.[28] Without coordination it is impossible to create an integrated firm in which multiple knowledge resources are mobilized to formulate and implement the firm's strategic tasks. Good relationships between people and departments, often based on a norm of reciprocity ("I will help you because you helped me"), are what enables companies like Southwest Airlines to achieve extraordinary coordination and high performance.[29]

In Corning's EPD, poor relationships between marketing, product development, R&D, and manufacturing slowed the development of essential new products. At Asda, the U.K. grocery chain that was close to bankruptcy, customer defection became the end result of poor coordination between the operating function responsible for all two hundred stores and the trading department that purchased what stores sold. The trading department simply did not listen to store managers who knew what their customers wanted.[30] At Becton Dickinson in the 1990s, low collaboration between U.S. product divisions and country organizations blocked execution of the company's ability to penetrate overseas markets with successful domestic medical and diagnostic products.[31]

Collaboration in HCHP firms extends to relationships with critical partners outside the organization's immediate boundaries—interdependent departments not reporting to the general manager, such as other divisions, geographic regions, suppliers, and key customers.[32] Collaboration in HCHP companies like Southwest Airlines also extends to unions and is one of the factors in their extraordinary success.[33] The cost of poor or no partnership with those outside the organization's immediate boundaries is evident in the following views, expressed by EPD's new-product development manager, about corporate R&D—views that had not been shared with the relevant executive in R&D: "It is difficult to get a time schedule from them. Their direction is independent of ours since they report elsewhere. They will not wring their hands if they are behind schedule. They will more quickly try to relax requirements for the development if it is behind schedule. I need more influence on specifications when it comes to things they are working on. I often have to go upstairs to solve the problems that occur with this group."[34]

Horizontal collaborative relationships are essential if bureaucratic solutions such as "going upstairs" are to be avoided. These slow down coordination and create hostility. That success in a knowledge economy depends on collaboration has been argued persuasively by a number of management scholars.[35] As we shall see, by putting in place structures and processes for horizontal coordination, EPD was able to increase coordination and induce collaboration.

Inadequate Development of Down-the-Line Leaders

"We do not have adequate leadership development and sufficient down-the-line leaders" was another unanimous complaint task forces reported to senior teams. Virtually all the underperforming companies lacked managers at the middle level who had a general management perspective, multifunctional experience, and interpersonal skills to lead interdependent functions and activities.[36] In EPD, inadequate leadership skills and the inexperience of "product development specialists" in marketing (their responsibility was to integrate the activities of marketing, manufacturing, product development, R&D, and sales) was one of the reasons for the crisis in coordination and new-product development.

The inadequately prepared product development specialists ran into great difficulties persuading more senior plant managers to run trials of new products, or persuading R&D to align their research priorities with the needs of EPD. Similarly, in Hewlett-Packard's Santa Rosa Systems Division, cross-functional business teams were ineffective in part because section managers in R&D lacked the business and general management perspective to enable the proper conversations and decisions. Becton Dickinson's failure to implement effectively a new global strategy was in part caused by the parochial U.S.-centric perspective of U.S. division heads charged with leading worldwide business teams.

The leadership gap in these organizations occurred because most managers had come up through their home function, business unit, or region, and never acquired the broader general management perspective needed to understand and manage cross-boundary activities. Managers also lacked leadership skills—managing meetings, confronting conflict, and enabling group consensus, for example. In many of the companies, ineffective senior teams did not spend time developing common values and perspective about what constituted good leadership. Many of the companies lacked a coherent internal process for early identification and development of managers consistent with common company values. EPD was no exception.

Poor Vertical Communication

Dozens of task forces identified poor vertical communication—upward and downward—as a key barrier. Most damaging was the paucity of open *honest upward communication* in any of the organizations studied. Most task forces communicated anxiety prior to presenting their findings about barriers to senior teams by evoking the well-known phrase: "Don't shoot the messenger." One task force even brought lapel buttons that communicated this anxiety to the senior team. Though, as I will show in chapter 7, a well-orchestrated conversation can enable task forces to speak truth to power.

Interviews, task force members reported, took much longer than we or they expected. People were eager to talk at length to their peers on the task force. They were emotional; some were moved to tears about problems that had frustrated them for some time. Consistent with much other research, the emotional nature of the interviews suggests that key people were most frustrated by the inability to report to senior teams about barriers to effectiveness, honestly and directly, and to see subsequent changes.[37] They always regarded the opportunity to do so as positive, particularly because they understood the senior team would inform the larger organization about what they had learned from the collective voice of the organization and what they planned to change.

The anxious response of employees to being selected as a task force member was a telltale sign of deep fears in reporting the truth to senior teams. At Becton Dickinson in 1990, a task force had to be disavowed of their belief that they had been given a "career-limiting opportunity." Once they returned from their interviews and collectively identified the six barriers, along with other problems, they became even more anxious.

A task force in a Canadian corporation was so fearful about negative repercussions that they spent several hours the night before their feedback session expressing their grave concerns. Consider what a task force member in another company recounted about his experience giving feedback to the top management team: "Just before we went into the conference room, I looked outside at Bodega Bay. It was an overcast and dreary day, and I imagined the sharks out in the water, circling their prey. As the task force entered into the room, I couldn't help but wonder if we too, would soon be swimming with the sharks."[38]

The problems and barriers in Corning's EPD had been around for four years. Bennett's autocratic style—"People around here do not extend themselves very much to disagree with Bennett"—created fear. His unwillingness to hear the truth became evident when, as part of an organization development program called the Managerial Grid, he became quite angry when told of interfunctional disputes between departments. His anger effectively squelched open, honest discussion about a difficult and ultimately damaging company dynamic inherited by his successor, Rogers.

A variety of fears prevent truth from speaking to power: fear of losing favor with those in power, fear of damaging long-standing relationships, hurting other people, and even job loss. Past experience leads many people to believe that speaking up will not lead to change. Previous efforts to do so may not have been acted on or, if acted on, senior management had not bothered to inform employees about the resulting changes.[39] This leaves employees believing that the risk of speaking up is not worth the benefit.

Problems in upward communication were complemented by inadequate and ineffective *downward communication*. When presented with a two-page statement of strategic and organizational direction developed by senior teams, key employees often said they had not been made aware of management's strategic intent or that they disagreed with some or all of it. These knowledge gaps stemmed from inadequate communication by the CEO and each top team member to their respective functions, regions, or business units.

Senior teams were generally surprised to find that their strategic intent was not well understood. They had made speeches and used other media to communicate strategy and values, but failed to understand that communication is a two-way dialogue that must allow lower levels to express their doubts. Nor did senior management grasp that to obtain the unvarnished truth they must go out of their way to ask for feedback and create safe conditions for the conversation. These deficiencies were compounded by the immense challenge of creating such a dialogue with large numbers of people.

Poor vertical communication is what makes these six barriers silent; it is the barrier most responsible for senior teams' inability to learn about inadequate alignment and low commitment. CEOs are human; they are just as prone as all of us to want to avoid confronting "brutal facts" that are painful and have the potential to break relationships and careers, including the CEO's.[40] Our work with underperforming organizations suggests that the truth has a powerful effect and creates a mandate for change. Consider how a senior team member described the power of the truth: "I was taking a lot of notes, but all I could think of the whole time, was 'how did it get this bad?' The discussion between the top team and how we worked together was even more painful. The whole thing was easily the worst day in my [company] career. In my room at night I was considering writing a resignation letter, until I realized that Scott (the general manager) wouldn't accept it. It hit me that we were in it up to our necks now and there was no turning back."

All organizations, as noted earlier, will be confronted with the silent killers when old patterns of management are no longer aligned with strategy. We have established that leaders who are willing to learn the truth, as did the senior manager above, can eradicate the silent killers. Open and honest vertical communication, if built into the lifeblood of the organization, can help organizations adapt to strategic challenges.

The Silent Killers: A Mutually Reinforcing Syndrome

The six silent killers presented themselves as a cluster in virtually all of the companies we studied. Their causal relationship is circular and mutually reinforcing, and the pattern is self-sealing. That is why we call them a syndrome: once the barriers are in place their very nature and their relationship to each other prevent leadership and organizational learning. Only exceptional leaders open to learning are able to confront them and transform them into organizational strengths. Figure 5.1 illustrates that the silent killers undermine three essential functions that an organization needs to "adapt and cope" with its ever-changing

FIGURE 5.1. HOW THE SILENT KILLERS AFFECT EFFECTIVENESS, COMMITMENT, AND PERFORMANCE.

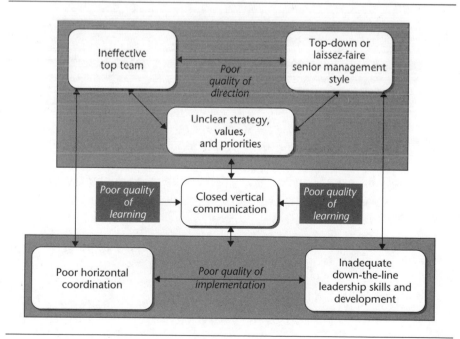

environment—setting a high-quality direction, implementing that direction, and learning from experience about problems in execution or problems in the direction itself.[41]

The first three barriers—conflicting priorities and unclear strategy and values, an ineffective senior team, and top-down or laissez-faire leadership—*make it difficult for the organization to develop a high-quality direction.* Both top-down and laissez-faire leaders are unable to create an effective senior team. Both styles prevent the engagement and constructive conflict essential for the development of an effective senior team. Without the whole team working together to shape a direction, it is not surprising that the direction is unclear and that there are conflicting priorities. Lack of debate in such teams is likely to undermine the substantive quality of the direction. And lack of agreement about strategy, priorities, and values in turn undermines cohesion in the top team. Moreover, ineffective senior teams can cause leaders who are conflict averse to become directive or to adopt a laissez-faire style out of frustration. I worked with a business unit manager who managed his team in a one-to-one manner, rarely bringing them together, because he feared that to do so would cause tensions between senior team members to erupt into uncomfortable conflict.

The barriers of poor coordination, inadequate leadership development, and insufficient effective down-the-line leaders sharply reduce the top team's capability to implement their direction. These barriers arise when ineffective senior teams are unable to speak with one voice and march to the same priorities. Such teams are also unlikely to have confronted how the organization's design—roles, responsibilities, and required relationships—may account for poor coordination. Discussions about the organization's design are threatening because they could result in changes and loss of power.

An ineffective senior team is also unable to identify and develop managers who can lead cross-enterprise teams needed to execute the strategy (as described in Corning's EPD) or align people around their values. They are unable to come to agreement about what constitutes effective leadership. And they are also unlikely to have the motivation or discipline to manage the succession and leadership development process. All of this undermines both performance and psychological alignment.

Poor or closed vertical communication, the sixth barrier, *undermines the quality of organizational learning,* a function that is essential for sustained alignment and performance. Without an honest two-way conversation between the senior team and key people at lower levels, senior teams are unable to learn. Consequently, they are precluded from changing their assumptions, role, or behavior, or how the business is organized and managed. Only open vertical communications will

FIGURE 5.2. THE EFFECTIVE AND RESILIENT HCHP ORGANIZATION.

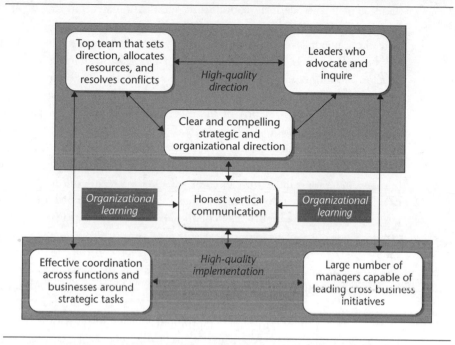

transform the silent killers into strengths and create an effective and resilient HCHP system as shown in Figure 5.2.

One might assume that simply replacing leaders would enable a turnaround. Though new leaders may have the will to lead change, as did Rogers at EPD, new leaders must also have access to the truth about the organization they are taking over to make a valid assessment of the organization's problems and develop legitimacy for the radical changes they may have to implement. The EPD story illustrates this quite well. Rogers was new, but had he not led an honest, collective, and public conversation he would not have been successful in transforming EPD into an HCHP organization.

Root Causes of the Silent Killers

The hierarchical nature of organizations is the core reason for their susceptibility to the silent killers. Organizations have to develop *horizontal differentiation* to implement their strategic tasks. Differentiated functions or departments, each with different goals, people, and time horizons, are needed to implement the many activities needed to produce and sell a product or service. It is only when this "value chain" of activities, as Michael Porter has called them, is integrated that the firm can operate efficiently and effectively and create economic value.[42]

Coordination is difficult in a hierarchical organization because departments develop a distinctive culture and identity in order to be effective at their differentiated task. Each differentiated department vies for resources, making coordination difficult. Heads of these activities compete with one another for recognition and promotion. As organizations grow they also become *differentiated hierarchically*. They develop more levels and more power differentials. These give rise to organizational silence and the inability of truth to speak to power. And because those who ultimately become CEOs have worked a lifetime to achieve that lofty and powerful position, it is likely that they will be oriented to using that power, adding to the hierarchical quality of their organizations.

It is not hard to see how these inherent properties of organizations create silent killers such as an ineffective top team, poor coordination, and silence. It takes courageous, determined, and exceptional HCHP leaders to confront them and develop a culture that mitigates the effects of hierarchy. Exceptional HCHP leaders function in an anti-hierarchical manner by reducing power differentials within the senior team and between the senior team and lower levels. Engaging a sufficiently large swath of key people in honest and public conversations about the silent killers is one way that leaders send a powerful message that deference to authority is no longer expected or valued. Such conversations signal that the CEO or general manager is not only open to learning but is also interested in creating a collaborative and less hierarchical organization. Many HCHP firms also typically reduce the effects of hierarchy by injecting a dose of symbolic egalitarianism. They eliminate formal power distinctions in offices, titles, and vastly unequal compensation.

The Transformation of Corning's Electronic Product Division

Don Rogers succeeded in transforming an underperforming business into a very successful one by enabling an honest and public conversation about the silent killers. He commissioned my team of consultants and me to interview some forty key people in all parts of the organization. A survey was then sent to all key employees to verify that our initial findings represented the pattern of management in the larger organization.

The unvarnished truth about the silent killers was fed back to Rogers' team—not an entirely comfortable experience. Also presented were initial ideas for steps needed to change EPD as a total system. The honest conversation that began within the senior team was then extended into a collective organization-wide conversation in twelve different division locations. At each location the entire senior team was present—to tell people the whole truth about what they had learned from the feedback employees had provided, and about their plan for change. At each location Rogers and his staff were challenged by lower levels, sometimes quite emotionally, about the plans. In every location it became clear that the senior team had been given unvarnished feedback, had accepted it, and was now acting on it. The fact that Rogers had the courage to make public the feedback about his laissez-faire leadership reinforced the belief that the truth had been put on the table and that he was open to learning and change.

It was this open organizational conversation that enabled the leadership team to see the system and implement simultaneous changes in all five change levers discussed in the last chapter. The following changes were announced and executed:

- *Clarify Strategy and Priorities:* A meeting to develop and articulate a new strategy consistent with EPD's changing environment and to prioritize new-product development initiatives had already been held and the strategy and priorities that emerged were presented.
- *Develop an Effective Senior Team:* The senior team changed its role into a strategic one. They did this by making changes in format and frequency of meetings (described below) as well as by undertaking team development activities with me as coach.
- *Rogers' Leadership Behavior:* Honest feedback for Rogers from consultants about perceptions of his leadership and how he might engage the organization more effectively primed the pump. Ongoing coaching and consultation became the means for learning.
- *Organizing System:* A frame-breaking reorganization was undertaken. EPD's functional organization was transformed into a matrix-like project team organization. Cross-functional teams, one for each new product, were led by marketing specialists. This constituted a radical shift in power for function heads, particularly for manufacturing which had the most power, and was met with many questions and some initial resistance. This change was aimed at improving coordination and the speed and efficacy of the new-product development process. Giving leadership of new-product development teams to marketing not only increased the influence of marketing, but also helped create an outward perspective needed in the fast-changing commercial markets EPD had entered.

- *Strategic Performance Management System:* The top team put in place a new process for reviewing new-product development initiatives. It eliminated the large and unwieldy new-product development meetings in favor of quarterly reviews of each new-product development team. Their role was to evaluate progress and, based on what they learned, to reprioritize these initiatives as needed and reallocate financial and human resources accordingly. These meetings were also intended for strategic discussions that would lead to commissioning teams to evaluate new product opportunities.

- *Learning and Governance:* Periodic assessment of progress in order to make midcourse corrections occurred, using the same high-involvement learning process that facilitated the original transformation. In effect, that process became the governance process for managing ongoing change. My consulting team was engaged to facilitate this process and coach the senior team and each new cross-functional new-product development team.

Modifications in all five change levers were made within a short period of time. EPD was reorganized and its leadership team adopted its new strategic role. Cross-functional teams experienced growing pains but kept meeting, reviewing their progress with the senior team. By leading a collective learning process Rogers was able to garner commitment and improve performance. Two years after my initial meeting with Rogers the following performance changes were evident:

- Within a year the silent killers became strengths and the organization much more effective. Interfunctional conflict was replaced by teamwork and commitment to common goals.
- The rate of new-product development for new commercial markets, a necessary strategic response, increased significantly.
- EPD's performance improved dramatically in the first year and steadily improved over the years. It beat the corporate standards for revenue and profit growth that many managers had been certain, at the beginning of the transformation journey, could not be attained.

Corning's top management saw EPD's management, particularly its planning and strategic management, as the best in the company. Don Rogers, a new general manager no one thought was a candidate for a corporate top management position, was promoted to head a much larger division. Five years after I first met with him he was promoted to president of Corning, bypassing a number of more senior and seasoned candidates for the job.

Given that *culture* has to be the ultimate target of any HCHP transformation, you may wonder whether EPD's culture changed. Consider the quotes below from key people who were deeply involved in new cross-functional teams two years after the transformation began:

A manager:

Problems are shared and understood. If things don't happen, I don't start placing blame. I have better understanding of why it didn't happen. Now I ask how I can help to make it happen. It is important to have empathy for the other guy, but not sympathy.[43]

A marketing specialist and project team leader regarding how to handle conflict:

Sam [the OD consultant who was working with his team], we have been having some problems and I decided it was time to get to the causes. We are just not working together effectively, and we all see a need for improvement. For example, I find myself going around the system to get something done. I am going over [one of my project team member's] head. I think we should all get together and put the technical tasks aside and take a closer look at our process.[44]

Two events are illustrative of the extent to which EPD's culture changed.

- EPD's top team's commitment to a new set of assumptions and beliefs about how to manage the business was strong enough for them to challenge Rogers' successor, whom they feared would bring assumptions and beliefs rooted in the Bennett era. The successor was told *not* to make any decision without first talking to key people about the changes that had occurred in EPD, and to me, the consultant who had collaborated with the senior team in planning and implementing the transformation.
- A few years after the transformation began, a manufacturing plant manager—a powerful and prestigious role in EPD—accepted the job of head of marketing, an indication of how perceptions of the value and influence of marketing had changed in this previously manufacturing-dominated business.

◆ ◆ ◆

A collective learning process led by Rogers had revealed the truth about EPD's silent barriers to effectiveness, commitment, and performance and transformed

EPD into an HCHP system. The next two chapters will explore in more depth the type of collective leadership process and learning and governance process that enabled fundamental change in EPD and many other organizations that we have worked with and studied.

Summary

The paucity of HCHP firms is a function of silent barriers to effectiveness, commitment, and performance that undermine the capacity of the organization to adapt and cope with its ever-changing environment. The silent killers, as I call them, are a syndrome of stress points that can quickly become fault lines when the corporation is challenged competitively. They are difficult to confront and discuss openly. That makes this syndrome self-sealing. Exceptional HCHP leaders are able, however, to overcome the silent killers by engaging key people in an honest, collective, and public conversation about the barriers and solutions to eliminate them. In this way they ensure sustained performance and psychological alignment as well as the organization's capacity to learn and change.

The six barriers are:

1. Unclear priorities as well as unclear strategy and values
2. An ineffective senior team
3. A leader who is either a top-down or laissez-faire manager
4. Poor coordination across functions, business units, or geographic regions
5. Inadequate development of down-the-line leaders
6. Closed vertical communication that prevents truth from speaking to power

The silent killers are barriers to (1) setting a high-quality strategic and values direction, (2) implementing that direction, and (3) learning from experience about problems in execution or problems in the direction itself. If the senior team cannot learn about the silent killers they cannot overcome them. Organizational decline and destruction will follow.

The root cause of organizational silence is the hierarchical nature of organizations. It leads to competition between managers and their departments for resources and rewards, breaking down integration at the top and lower levels.

Leadership teams who want to overcome the silent killers and build an HCHP organization will want to foster an honest, collective, and public conversation so that they can answer the following questions:

1. Is our strategic and organizational direction valid, understood, and are people committed to it?

2. Have we designed the organization and our role as a senior team for good coordination and successful implementation of our strategic intent?
3. Do we have a sufficiently large cadre of leaders needed to implement our direction and a good process for identifying, developing, and deploying them?
4. Have we institutionalized a process that will enable us to continue to learn about hidden barriers to HCHP?

PART THREE

LEADERSHIP AND LEARNING CHANGE LEVERS

CHAPTER SIX

LEAD A COLLECTIVE LEARNING PROCESS

Change Lever 1: Leadership

Lives of great men all remind us. We can live our lives sublime.
And departing, leave behind our footprints on the sands of time.

—LONGFELLOW[1]

A leader is best when people barely know he exists, not so good when people obey and acclaim him, worst when they despise him. "Fail to honor people—they fail to honor you." But of a good leader, who talks little, when his work is done, his aims fulfilled, they will all say, "We did this ourselves."

—LAO TZU[2]

So you start off with a company that's in disarray with low morale. They want direction and it's no good coming in and saying, well, hey guys, I'm here now. I'm going to listen. They all think, well, that's pretty disappointing. We want to know which way to march. So you tell the troops which way to march, in a broad direction, and then create some time for yourself to understand the steps you really need to make.

As far as the leadership is concerned, the point is not just listening, and it's not just acting. It's being able to combine the two.

—ARCHIE NORMAN,
FORMER CEO, ASDA[3]

Leadership by CEOs and their senior teams is without question *the* key factor in successful transformations to HCHP.[4] Our work with and study of leaders who successfully changed their organizations suggests that transformational *leadership is a collective action learning process.* These leaders engaged key people in defining and developing the conditions that enabled performance alignment, psychological alignment, and the capacity for learning and change, the three outcomes essential for sustained HCHP.[5]

HCHP leadership is not about exercising influence through the formal authority vested in one's position, nor is it about influence through superior knowledge and intelligence. Smart CEOs with a strong will to merely impose their ideas do not succeed in building an HCHP company. The distinctive HCHP outcomes of psychological alignment and capacity for learning not only require leaders with an emotional commitment to a well-thought-out vision, but also require deep involvement in an action learning process that surfaces the truth about how the organizational system is currently functioning and provides as many people as possible the opportunity to contribute. This HCHP approach to leadership is grounded, operational, and puts a premium on collective learning and, as I show below, is much less dangerous than the mythical heroic view of leadership.

Why Heroic Leadership Fails

"There are no great men. There are only great challenges that ordinary men like you and me are forced by circumstance to meet," observed Admiral William F. "Bull" Halsey, a man who saw leaders tested by challenges far greater than those faced by business leaders. Yet, the Great Man theory of leadership is still alive and well. Heroic, decisive, and charismatic leaders who impose their strategic vision and solutions are widely celebrated in the business press.[6] When companies outperform, success is attributed to the CEO's leadership. When companies fail, the CEO is blamed and usually fired. Quite often the same CEO is celebrated and later fired. Jeff Skilling, Enron's leader in the 1990s, was widely hailed for several years as the leader who had created a new business and organizational model, and was then later blamed for the company's demise and convicted for mismanagement and misdeeds.[7]

Attributing success to personal qualities—the CEO's brilliance, vision, and style of management—is not only dangerous but dead wrong. A firm's behavior and performance tend to be path dependent, research shows. As Warren Buffett has observed, when you bring good management into a bad business, it is the reputation of the business that quite often survives. Much academic research supports this view. In *Built to Last*, Collins and Porras conclude that the key to sustained success was not visionary *leadership* (which was their proposition at the beginning of the research), but visionary *organizations*. For these reasons quick fixes and inspirational speeches do not transform organizations. Transformation requires leaders committed to the long-term development of the organization. These leaders draw on knowledge about the business and the organization extant in the firm, and they commit people to change.

For several years now my Harvard Business School colleagues Michael Porter, Jay Lorsch, and Nitin Nohria have been running a workshop for CEOs who recently took charge of their companies.[8] Seven lessons about leadership emerge from discussions with these CEOs; all point to the fallacy of top-down, single-handed, and single-minded leadership and the importance of collaboration with all stakeholders.

1. You can't run the company.
2. Giving orders erodes other managers' confidence.
3. It's hard to know what is going on in your organization.
4. You are always sending a message, but not necessarily the one you intend.
5. You're not the boss—the board is.
6. Pleasing sharcholders is not your goal.
7. You're still human.

Why is the heroic CEO exactly the wrong leader? Ron Heifetz reminds us that "in a crisis . . . we call for someone with answers, decisions, strengths, and a map of the future, someone who knows where we ought to be going—in short someone who can make hard problems simple . . . . Instead of looking for saviors, we should be calling for leadership that will challenge us to face problems for which there are no simple, painless solutions."[9]

Hubris causes heroic leaders to impose their strategic and organizational solutions without testing either their validity or the company's capacity to execute them. Imposing ideas from previously led organizations or copying from other firms fails to honor the past, fails to mobilize people to tackle tough problems, and reduces the willingness of people throughout the firm to partner with the CEO. Heroic leadership fails to integrate listening and decisive action into a seamless, iterative, and continuous learning process. Most important, heroic leadership fails to perform the central function of leadership—engaging employees *authentically* in a process of organizational learning and development from which they as leaders also learn.[10]

Our findings are that CEOs can learn a great deal from those at lower levels who are in touch with the day-to-day realities of the marketplace and the efficacy of the organization in execution. Andy Grove, the cofounder and long-time leader of Intel, discovered that lower-level managers recognized long before he and his senior team did the strategic inflection point that Intel faced as the market shifted away from memory chips to microprocessors; with that discovery, Grove began to reorient the focus of the company.[11] The leaders featured in this book—Don Rogers, Henry Gullette, Grey Warner, Chris Richmond, Scott Wright, Ed Ludwig, and Archie Norman—are all strong leaders who motivated a collective process of learning because they knew that they did not have all the answers and that they needed others to help move the organization forward.

To share the responsibilities of leadership, transformational CEOs or business unit general managers develop and come to rely on their *leadership team*.[12] This requires a sustained effort to build that team and to develop together a vision of the firm—its purpose, its strategy, and its values, as well as the legacy they want to leave and the principles for organizing and managing that they will employ. Most important, HCHP leaders recognize that the leadership team that they must develop is composed of not only their direct reports and a larger circle of key managers, but also the board of directors, who must share the senior team's vision, values, and strategic intent. The process of transformational leadership I discuss in this chapter applies to the CEO's relationship with lower levels as well as his relationship with the board. In a recent study of HCHP CEOs, my colleagues at the TruePoint Center for High Commitment and Performance and I were struck by how much care these leaders take to partner with their boards, not only with their own team. Indeed, the leadership model proposed here is one that leaders in the corporation's multiple subunits will ultimately have to adopt if the transformation of the larger organization is to be complete.

Unfortunately, the charismatic and heroic model of leadership is the dominant perspective in selecting CEOs, according to the research by my colleague Rakesh Khurana. He finds that when a crisis of performance hits, a company board of directors inevitably does the wrong thing. They go "in search of a savior," a charismatic and dynamic leader who is associated with a celebrity company or CEO.[13] Khurana shows that in many cases this approach fails to deliver a sustained turnaround. That was exactly the story at Hewlett-Packard where an ineffective board selected Carly Fiorina, a charismatic leader who not only failed to turn the company around but managed to liquidate the HCHP culture built by its founders and successors (see chapter 9). The failure of heroic leaders to be open to the truth about the efficacy and ethics of their business model and organization is certainly a major reason for the failures of banks and mortgage companies in 2008.

In a systematic study of senior GE executives who became CEOs in other companies, my colleagues Boris Groysberg and Nitin Nohria found that the performance of these transplanted senior executives was far from uniformly positive. Success depended on a good fit between their leadership skills, values, and business knowledge with the firm's business and organization challenges.[14] Obviously, being a celebrity leader who comes from a celebrity company was not the key factor. And what if the fit of the CEO is not perfect, which is usually the case? Then the leader's ability to engage people and learn is even more crucial.

The leadership and learning perspective I am proposing requires leaders to embrace *paradox*. On the one hand, as Archie Norman suggests (see quotation at the beginning of the chapter), leaders must have strength of purpose. *They must have a point of view about the general direction of the firm* and must be willing to articulate that view clearly and firmly if they hope to bolster employee confidence and raise hope that successful transformation to HCHP is possible. On the other hand, *leaders must also be able to suppress their egos and enable others to lead*, as suggested by Lao Tzu's quote at beginning of the chapter. Jamie Houghton, the successful former CEO and chairman of Corning Inc., concludes from his experience that leaders are better able to listen and learn if they are *not too sure of themselves*. And, he notes, "History tells us that those in leadership positions who do not listen eventually fail."[15] Confidence is needed but so are the will and skill to lead a collective learning process.

Henry Gullette[16]

In September 2002, Henry Gullette was hired as chief operating officer at Clean Lodging (a pseudonym) with the understanding that he would succeed chairman and CEO, Joseph Stemson. Stemson's leadership of the firm had moved it from a relatively unknown but strong brand with seventy-five family-oriented motels in 1992 to a much larger player with 225 units in 2002. Under Stemson's leadership the company had received numerous honors and was cited in 2002 by a major business magazine on its list of *Best Small Companies*. Stemson hired Gullette as someone who could bring a fresh and more sophisticated marketing and management thinking to a company whose leaders were largely homegrown and lacking in advanced training in business and management.

When Gullette arrived, he found the company's sales per existing unit were in decline, something he had not expected. It seemed the company's previous growth, fueled by opening new units, had masked some underlying problems that would pose serious challenges to the company's future. Gullette recalled: "I came in assuming that I had plenty of time to learn the business, that I could lay low and then slowly and quietly begin to move some pieces around, but soon I learned differently. The situation was much more challenging than I realized." Despite these challenges, Gullette believed that Clean Lodging had a strong foundation on which to build.

Gullette, an experienced executive, was new to the hospitality industry. Though his first priority was to turn around the business, particularly to grow same-unit sales, he also knew Clean Lodging had to increase the number of motel units and to move into new geographic markets. To this strategic task Gullette brought an HCHP management philosophy that he had developed over the years and believed in strongly.

By the end of 2005 Gullette had achieved a remarkable improvement in firm performance. Revenues and profits had grown, stock price doubled, and dramatic improvements had been made in turnover of front-line employees (from 220 to 126 percent), as well as unit, district, and regional managers (49 to 26 percent), all of which were well above industry averages. That meant that each year twenty thousand associates and about five hundred managers did not have to look for a job somewhere else, because Clean Lodging was a better place to work. These turnover improvements enabled service improvements that came from a more stable workforce and allowed millions of dollars in reduced training and hiring costs, which were in turn invested into improvements in customer service. Indeed, these changes were accompanied by significant improvements in customer satisfaction. A cultural transformation was under way and Gullette had been promoted to CEO, with Stemson continuing as chairman.

In 2006, however, Gullette faced a new challenge, one born of higher gasoline prices and stronger competition from lower-cost motels that had recently invested in improved appearance, new products, and service. Clean Lodging's revenue flattened, profits declined somewhat, and stock price lost half its gains. Gullette was now faced with a more fundamental challenge—how to completely reinvent the company's business model.

This became a personal challenge as well as a business and organizational challenge for Gullette. His leadership of the first wave and now the second wave of change are clear illustrations of how HCHP leaders go about transforming their companies. Henry Gullette's role in leading a collective learning process is woven into the principles detailed below.

What HCHP Leaders Must Do, Be, and Know[17]

Leaders of HCHP companies are first and foremost action oriented. Vision without execution will not lead to success. That is why I begin the discussion of leadership with what general managers—CEOs or business unit heads—and their leadership teams must *DO* to develop HCHP outcomes. Research evidence and my own work with and study of HCHP leaders point to what they must *BE* and what they must *KNOW* if they are to take the key actions necessary to

TABLE 6.1. WHAT HIGH COMMITMENT, HIGH PERFORMANCE LEADERS MUST DO, BE, AND KNOW.

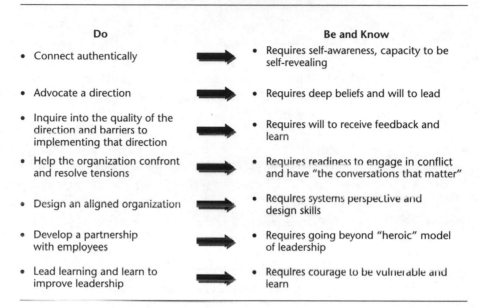

Do	Be and Know
• Connect authentically	• Requires self-awareness, capacity to be self-revealing
• Advocate a direction	• Requires deep beliefs and will to lead
• Inquire into the quality of the direction and barriers to implementing that direction	• Requires will to receive feedback and learn
• Help the organization confront and resolve tensions	• Requires readiness to engage in conflict and have "the conversations that matter"
• Design an aligned organization	• Requires systems perspective and design skills
• Develop a partnership with employees	• Requires going beyond "heroic" model of leadership
• Lead learning and learn to improve leadership	• Requires courage to be vulnerable and learn

lead an HCHP organization. Table 6.1 provides an overview of the leadership dimensions discussed below.

Leaders Connect Authentically

What Leaders Must Do. Leaders cannot mobilize followers on a journey to HCHP unless they can convince people that they approach their task with high moral purpose. Their aspirations must go far beyond the usual financial and strategic goals most CEOs enunciate. Leaders do this by revealing to others who they are, what they believe in, and what motivates them. Because first impressions are hard to change, this must happen very early in the CEO's tenure. Communicating who you are and what your higher purpose is engages people emotionally. It allows them to hope that their own aspirations to do something meaningful and important—to leave their legacy—will be fulfilled by committing to the leader's agenda for change.

Within three months of his arrival, Henry Gullette revealed who he was and what his purpose was in front of a large group of managers when he talked about his father—a successful businessman who became a minister, and never actually had a ministry, but applied his moral purpose in another pursuit. Gullette recalled:

> I was doing my first strategic plan direction presentation. And in a way, it was the first time I stepped from just executing and following other people's footsteps to laying out, here's the path we're going to go on, and it's going to be different, and it's going to be exciting, and it's going to be worthwhile. I thought that people should know what I thought about it . . . . [It became] clear in my own mind and I decided to tell people. And I talked about—I well up every time I do this, so forgive me. But I talked about being with my father when he died . . . . And he was an incredibly good guy . . . and had lived a really worthy life and he's sort of my [inspiration] . . . . Anyway, I decided to share that story. And I think it allowed people to connect with me in a way that they knew I was real.

There are of course many ways for leaders to reveal who they are. But to convey authenticity, the communication will inevitably have to reveal the wellspring of emotions from which deep purpose arises, emotions that accompanied Gullette's recollections and undoubtedly showed in front of the senior management group he addressed. Being in touch with one's inner feelings, beliefs, and values—rare in most business settings—is actually a powerful source of inspiration to others. It enables leaders to develop psychological alignment, to transform the psychological contract from transactional to one based on commitment. Gullette observed:

> The ability to lead and energize and inspire others stems directly—I mean . . . directly—from the ability to lead and energize and inspire myself. In those moments when I am crystal-clear about what I stand for, and what I'm doing, and why I'm doing it, and why it matters, I can talk to anybody and get them fired up . . . . Being authentic with people . . . [about] the way I am and the way I work is absolutely essential for getting it to come out right. And [what's] been true of the board, true for the investment community, that's true of my associates, is that I have to speak from the heart.

What Leaders Must Be and Know.[18] Several personal qualities enable HCHP leaders like Gullette to be authentic. They are *self-aware*—they are clear about their core values, in touch with their emotions, able to display them in communication with their followers, and clear about their own motives, values, and goals. Authentic leaders have a strong sense of who they are and can articulate this to others.

HCHP leaders are able to develop trust because they are *objective about themselves*. They know their own strengths and weaknesses and can talk about them with others. They do not deny their weaknesses in these conversations. This builds credibility. High levels of self-esteem and personal security enable authentic leaders to be honest with themselves and others about who they are.

Authentic leaders are *transparent*. They are able to express their true emotions to followers and do it in an appropriate manner, avoiding the expression of emotions that can be hurtful and destroy trust. As Gullette's example illustrates, authentic HCHP leaders are able to be transparent in front of large groups. It is this that enables them to mobilize people. Don Rogers, with whom I worked at Corning (see chapter 5), surprised his managers with his candor and was able to obtain their commitment to the transformation he led. He inspired others in the organization and gained their commitment to change when he made public the feedback he had received about his leadership style.

In summary, authentic leaders lead from the heart, not from the head. Authenticity is not developed through knowledge, but through reflection about one's self and one's experiences. Authentic leaders are believable because they allow their heart to shape the direction in which they take the organization—always, of course, using their heads to check that the direction they are setting is fact based and realistic.

Leaders Advocate a Direction

What Leaders Must Do. Leaders who succeed in transforming their corporation have a strong point of view about strategy, values, and how to organize the enterprise, and advocate this new direction to their people. In general, there are two waves of change when new leaders take charge, according to seminal research by my colleague Jack Gabarro.[19] In the first wave, successful leaders may begin to articulate values and principles they believe in, but they focus change resources on fixing operating problems in the business that must be solved in the short term, buying time for more fundamental change to come later. These are standard turnaround practices that are critical for survival, but they do not build an HCHP firm. Gullette took a number of steps in the first year in response to unexpected, declining like-for-like unit revenue—he expanded the use of credit cards, introduced family-friendly services, commissioned an initiative to make service faster, and closed underperforming motels.

The second wave of change—one that begins the process of building an HCHP organization—occurs over a longer period of time. Successful leaders advocate a new, long-term vision for the company, how it will compete, and the management philosophy and values by which it will be governed. This comes from their deep sense of purpose. In this second wave of change, leaders ensure that the business and value components are internally consistent and reinforce each other. They define the animating beliefs that will govern all business and management decisions. The vision that CEOs articulate defines how performance and psychological alignment, two of the three pillars of HCHP, will be developed.

Gullette's strategic and organizational vision was called the Virtuous Cycle, loosely defined as how the company's key constituents (guests, associates, shareholders, and leaders) could best fuel one another's success, commitment, and satisfaction. The Virtuous Cycle's distinctive power to gain commitment from all stakeholders came from putting the firm's leaders first. By a policy of supporting leaders and associates first, and putting guests ahead of shareholders, Clean Lodging would have a sustainable high-performance business model that would engender commitment from all. Gullette explained his underlying "servant leadership" philosophy as follows:[20]

> What we talk about is building Clean Lodging into a world-class institution that is a shining example of the power that is unleashed when we enable each other to achieve our full potential through service to others—appealing to "our better angels" as it were. And if making a difference is really about serving each other then the question is "how do we serve each other?" Well, leaders serve associates by helping them achieve their potential; associates care for guests on the front lines. Our guests reward our shareholders. Shareholders benefit from financial returns and some of our returns are reinvested into our leaders and associates. This is our Virtuous Cycle.

HCHP leaders aspire, as Gullette's quote above illustrates, to build an institution—an organization that will have sustainable advantage. They, like Gullette, are motivated to leave a legacy, and they are not bashful about advocating the general direction required to succeed in this. And HCHP leaders are visible throughout the organization, communicating strategy and, as I will discuss below, engaging people in a dialogue. A current study of HCHP CEOs that I am conducting with my colleagues at the TruePoint Center for High Commitment and High Performance finds that they spend enormous amounts of time advocating their vision and values—the same message over and over again to the point of boredom—to all levels of the company.

What Leaders Must Be and Know. HCHP leaders like Henry Gullette are very different from average CEOs and general managers. First, they all have strong conceptual capabilities that enable them to be strategic and form a vision of the future they are trying to create. Secondly, they have what Jim

Collins calls a strong professional will, or what Marvin Bowers, the founder of McKinsey, called the will to manage.[21] These leaders care deeply about creating a high-performance winning enterprise. They are laser focused on achieving strategic objectives.

But high-commitment leaders also have a moral purpose. In forming their goals and vision, they do not start by looking to others—Wall Street analysts, the board of directors, the business press, the attractive deal, or conventional wisdom. Instead they start from a deep set of beliefs about the purpose of the firm and their role as leaders. As the noted historian James MacGregor Burns has observed, "Transformational leadership must elevate followers to a moral level."[22] HCHP leaders apply their beliefs to a given situation by crafting a practical strategic and organizational direction. They are inner rather than outer directed.

Like most HCHP CEOs, Gullette had thought deeply throughout his career about his own beliefs; over time, he integrated his beliefs into a management philosophy. Like most high-commitment CEOs, he read numerous books on business, management, and philosophy. Like most highly principled leaders, Gullette encouraged his key executives to read the books he read. *Man's Search for Meaning*, a book by Viktor Frankl, a holocaust survivor and psychiatrist, played a particularly important role in shaping Gullette's philosophy.

Experiences throughout an executive's career also shape philosophy. Sometimes working for a bad manager informs high-performance leaders about what not to do just as great bosses act as role models to emulate. Or previous business challenges can have a profound influence. In Gullette's case, taking charge as president at his previous company, a struggling business with low morale, made him conclude, similar to Frankl, that there were three core values that provide meaning in people's lives:

- People want an opportunity to make a difference
- People want to be able to enjoy the journey
- People want to be part of doing the right thing

Gullette was aware that his explicit values orientation was unusual for a corporate CEO, but felt that it was core to his leadership philosophy:

> I used to wrestle a lot with whether I should work for a nonprofit organization, because that was the place where meaning was clearer. And what I figured out over time was that meaning should not be reserved for people who work for hospitals, that everybody deserves the right to find meaning for themselves in their work. And this work really does make a huge difference for all the people

who touch it. In fact 90 percent of the population doesn't work in a hospital or a food bank and each of those people deserve the right to have meaning for themselves and their life at work. Learning how to bring meaning to people at work is worth my life.

These beliefs guided Gullette's vision for Clean Lodging and he used them to evaluate the actions he took to shape the company.

Joseph Stemson, who selected Gullette to succeed him and to lead Clean Lodging to new heights, saw in Gullette many of the qualities that in my own observation characterize HCHP leaders. Stemson explained:

In interviewing Henry, it was clear he was bright. Henry is philosophical. By that I mean [that] Henry has the capability to conceptualize the big picture. You know there are lots of successful executives that are not conceptual. And if you are not conceptual, it's very difficult to be strategic. Because one has to be conceptual in order to put themselves in a different place, in a different experience—where they cannot be dependent on what they have learned, but they have to be dependent on what they're going to learn, and how to deal with what they're going to learn in a new environment with new challenges.

Being bright, philosophical, and, above all, conceptual enables leaders to advocate departures from the current and prevailing status quo. With these qualities, they create vision and goals that stretch the organization to achieve levels of commitment and performance previously thought to be impossible.[23] They are leaders with the capacity to learn in unfamiliar territory.

Leaders Inquire

What Leaders Must Do. The evidence is overwhelming; declines in organizational performance are almost always caused when leaders avoid realities that are known to everyone. Consider Roy Ash, who was CEO of Addressograph in 1976, a name that you may not recognize because the company went bankrupt. Ash is an example of the visionary heroic leader who thought he had a vision that would allow him to dominate such companies as IBM, Xerox, and Kodak in the emerging field of office automation. Ash became so wedded to his vision that he refused to confront mounting evidence that his plan was not working. To enable his vision to live on, he milked profitable businesses while throwing money at a plan that could not succeed.[24] Our experience with companies like Addressograph, as I will show in chapter 7, is that in virtually every one of these instances people at lower levels across multiple functions know the truth.

Similarly, it is becoming clear that the failure of financial institutions in 2008 was evident to people below the top well before the collapse.

Only actively soliciting unvarnished feedback and promoting an honest fact-based dialogue—what I mean by inquiry—can prevent this. Top leaders, according to a Center for Creative Leadership study, are faced with overwhelming barriers to learning and growing. Executives and professionals whom they interviewed said the following:[25]

- "There is a tendency for the environment at executive levels to be feedback poor."
- "When you're a manager, you develop a set of people you can get feedback from—a web, a grapevine. But as you rise in the hierarchy, it withers and by the time you get to the top, it's dead."
- "The higher you go the more constricted the feedback channels become."
- "In most corporations senior executives don't get much feedback on their weaknesses. There is not that candor in executive suites."

These conditions can easily induce leaders to enter an unconscious collusion with those around them to avoid discussions of what is not working. Gullette observed: "There's only one thing worse than being in a tight spot, and that's not knowing anything about it." HCHP leaders like Gullette go to great lengths to learn about their effectiveness. And because reflection is difficult in the action-oriented environment of an HCHP firm and silent collusion so easy, a disciplined process for feedback and reflection is important, as I discuss in chapter 7.[26]

Leaders who aspire to build HCHP organizations must inquire into the quality of their plans as well as the effectiveness of their organizations and their own leadership if they are to succeed. Without inquiry, leaders cannot learn that their plans and vision are doomed to failure and they will be unable to lead the continuous improvement necessary for sustained HCHP. *It is the capacity for continuous learning that distinguishes HCHP leaders.* A continuous learning process is particularly important in value-driven HCHP organizations because it is inevitable that the leader's behavior will at times deviate from his or her espoused values and principles; this is simply because each situation is subject to varied interpretations.[27]

Inquiry is essential to prevent values from backfiring when disenchantment rises and commitment declines. It allows leaders to evaluate the gap between their espoused strategies and principles and the reality experienced by others in the organization. Consider how in 2008 inquiry might have changed the course of history had CEOs of financial institutions valued inquiry. Inquiry legitimizes leaders' demands of others to adhere to espoused goals and values and to strive for continuous improvement. It buys them trust and makes their high-commitment vision believable and credible. A manager on a task force employed by Gullette to inquire into the firm's strategic plan explained his response to the inquiry: "They changed the whole plan. They listened to us and they reacted. I came away from the process with a reinforced belief that no one person is as smart as all of us and a realization that Henry is not afraid of someone's ideas."

Without inquiry, people in the organization are likely to be cynical about the grand vision and the invitation to participate and make a difference. Moreover, modeling inquiry enables top leaders to expect lower-level managers to lead honest conversations in search of continuous improvement. Gullette believed that only through continuous improvement would Clean Lodging achieve the vision and strategy he and his leadership team were developing. He explained:

> The way to lead is to have a fact-based assessment and then provide a clear direction. You get unvarnished input from associates, you change your plans, you communicate and align, perform to plan, track results and optimize, and finally you learn to improve. The point is that anytime you do anything of significance you go through these steps as a leader. You slow down long enough to get unvarnished input. This is a way of doing work that gives people a chance to make a difference. I adopted most of these steps from [Dr. W. Edward] Deming, with the exception that we have added the listen and change steps.

Shortly after Gullette arrived at Clean Lodging, he and his leadership team appointed a task force of eight of their best people to interview key people about their views of the plan. As a result of this inquiry, Gullette learned that people thought the plan was great and that it generated a lot of positive energy, but some were concerned that the plan was too ambitious to implement. As a result, he reduced the number of initiatives. Gullette recalled, "Going from 12 to 5 saved our bacon because had we worked on 12 we would have done all of them poorly. As it were we were stretched at 5." In subsequent iterations, the Strategic Dialogue Process (SDP was modeled after the Strategic Fitness Process described in chapter 7), as it became known in the company, was integrated into the strategic planning process every year to obtain feedback about the strategy *and* the barriers to implementing it.

Open dialogue is not an easy experience for leaders, even for someone like Gullette who believes in feedback. Learning that lower levels did not see the leadership's plan as entirely positive made that first year difficult. Nevertheless, continuous improvement through honest conversations became the centerpiece of Clean Lodging's leadership model—one that leaders at the regional, district, and motel unit level were expected to follow. Gullette explained the profound effect of SDP on his leadership credibility and legitimacy:

> So if I were to think about the key things that we focused on—well, first of all, from an annual planning process . . . just the dialogue (SDP) premise has absolutely been, I think, one of the reasons that the first few years were successful, and the fact that I personally have credibility with the organization. The ripple effects of, he really does care about what we think, and they really do change their plans based on the truth of what's going on, especially for some of those coming in from outside the industry, has been absolutely essential. I can't imagine—I would not have survived had I not done that, I'm absolutely clear about that, because it changed our plans several times significantly.

What Leaders Must Be and Know. In order to conduct an open inquiry, leaders must have the *will to receive feedback and learn.* It's difficult and disorienting for any human being to be disconfirmed, but because HCHP leaders define themselves rather than allowing outside forces and people to define them, they are able to learn from honest conversations without being personally devastated. Ed Ludwig, CEO of Becton Dickinson (chapter 10), recalled how difficult it was for him to hear that the enterprise IT system he had been stewarding was not achieving its goals and needed to be abandoned or relaunched. He acknowledged what he heard, took responsibility for the failure, and asked for help in fixing the system and a number of problems that surfaced.

The will to inquire is not enough. High-commitment leaders *know that their position of power creates a huge barrier to honest conversations* that they must overcome if they are to learn the unvarnished truth. When leaders aspire to develop an HCHP firm, what leadership behavior and qualities should they display in order to invite employees to speak up about their concerns and improvement ideas? A large-scale study by Jim Detert and Ethan Burris shows that when leaders appear open and engage in coaching-oriented behavior, subordinates can voice their ideas about required improvements.[28] But the leader's behavior is not sufficient, according to Detert and Burris. Readiness to speak up is significantly influenced by the employee's perception that it is *safe* to voice ideas for improvements; speaking up is normally perceived as risky. HCHP leaders must, therefore, know how to design honest, collective, and public conversations—a learning and governance process I discuss in chapter 7.

Help Organization Confront Conflict and Manage Tensions

What Leaders Must Do. Transformational leaders must help their senior team and the organization to resolve tensions productively.

Organizations, like all other social systems, including the family, have tensions. Leaders in underperforming companies tend to be conflict averse. Instead of dealing directly with tensions and conflict, they dictate solutions, smooth it over, or work one-on-one with other executives. They do not know how to work constructively in teams with diverse views (see chapter 5). They do not understand that tension and conflicting perspectives are natural by-products of differentiated roles and responsibilities. Marketing, operations, and research and development do not and should not have the same perspective. Higher levels see things differently than lower levels. Bringing different views and perspectives into the open, confronting differences, and finding the best solution—one that is integrative—is what enables creative problem solving, continuous improvement, and sustained performance. Kathleen Eisenhardt and her associates have found that the best top teams know how to have a "good fight." These teams argue, debate alternatives, and find a way to create an integrated solution to the problems they are facing.[29]

More importantly, transforming a business into an HCHP organization requires that leaders in the organization confront the root causes of the current organizational state, including their own roles. Organizations develop a pattern of behavior, beliefs, values, and skills that over time take on meaning and legitimacy. People become emotionally invested in this system because it has worked and enabled them to feel effective. This "moral order," as Larry Hirschhorn calls it, is heavily defended by employees, creating barriers to change.[30] People invest a moral order with legitimacy. If asked, they would say, "It is the right way to do things." Changing a system inevitably involves personal and emotionally charged losses in power, relationships, rewards, competence, esteem, and identity. These can be deeply distressing and will inevitably be resisted consciously and most often subconsciously.

Conflict, emotions, and the aggressive behavior that they spawn are an essential part of the transformation process.[31] Without it the underlying psychological contract—the deep understandings of mutual obligations that have come into existence over time—cannot be changed. In effect, leaders must enable conflict to purge the organization of the old order and establish a new moral order. This organization-level process may be thought of as similar to the emotional process that individuals undergo in deep change such as in psychotherapy. Emotions such as authenticity, sympathy, hope, fun, and attachment are all important for the development of an HCHP organization. A change process devoid of these emotions and leaders who cannot attend to and develop them, Quy Huy finds, cannot possibly create an HCHP organization.[32]

What Leaders Must Be and Know. Leaders who intend to build an HCHP system must be comfortable with and able to lead honest conversations that matter. We found that the best transformational leaders, like Henry Gullette, Ed Ludwig at Becton Dickinson (chapter 10), or Archie Norman and Allen Leighton at Asda (chapter 11), did this naturally or learned very quickly about its value. They all recognized the importance of exploring differences, and the potential emotional conflict that arises when these differences are rooted in different values, preferences, principles, and personalities.

Leaders who manage conflict well are likely to be centered, inner directed, and secure—they know who they are and what they stand for. This makes them less defensive and less likely to react to conflict in aggressive and potentially destructive ways—arguing back, blaming, or making attributions. They are more likely to employ both head and heart, and can feel empathy when approaching conflict. This is reflected in what research and experience tells us that leaders must be in order to manage conflict effectively:[33]

- *Perspective taking:* Effective leaders try to understand the other person's views, perhaps by focusing on the other person's words and asking why he or she may have that emotional view. According to Runde and Flanagan, perspective is "perhaps the most powerful of the constructive behaviors."
- *Creating solutions:* Leaders must work with others to explore options and alternatives for a solution that will improve performance as well as resolve the conflict.
- *Expressing emotions:* Because feelings are often at the root of conflict, effective leaders encourage people to express their emotions individually and collectively rather than signaling that emotions should be restrained. Feelings can be powerful sources of energy and commitment for change and renewal. In my experience, this is not practiced often enough, even by HCHP leaders, and is particularly important, as discussed earlier, in transforming the organization.[34]
- *Reaching out:* HCHP leaders are likely to take the first step to break an impasse or a deadlocked negotiation. This opens up communication and prevents conflict from escalating.
- *Reflective thinking:* Effective leaders weigh the pros and cons of a conflict situation and think about the best resolution to the problem.
- *Adaptive behavior:* Leaders who manage conflict well are flexible and try to make the best of the situation they face; they can let go of an ideal solution they may have had in mind.

In our work with leaders, we find that typical fears about conflict—that it will escalate into uncontrollable fights, will undermine relationships, and make things worse—are not well founded so long as a structured, regulated, and safe "container" for the conflict is employed. Gullette's Strategic Dialogue Process is one such container. Hirschhorn calls this a *counterstructure* and argues that leaders must trust that a structured container for potentially emotional feedback is a necessary part of a fundamental transformation; indeed, it is needed to "undermine the inherited structure while at the same time providing a new basis for cohesion [commitment]."[35] Hirschhorn argues that a counterstructure provides "a safe way in which aggression can be mobilized and . . . a new psychological contract between leaders and employees" can be built.[36] Asda's Allan Leighton created a forum where store managers and the corporate trading department (purchasing department), who had historically been in conflict, could each share with the other their concerns and complaints. Leighton regularly pushed both parties to confront each other, not shying away from the emotions that were aroused. He maintained control and enabled these exchanges to be constructive by introducing humor.

The idea that leaders must bring out feelings, emotions, and conflict as part of the transformation process is a counterconventional view for many CEOs who pride themselves on staying rational and unemotional. Transformational leaders become comfortable with and knowledgeable about how to design a counterstructure, such as the Strategic Dialogue Process used at Clean Lodging. They employ it actively to surface the emotion-laden truth, help create new relationships, and mobilize and direct feelings in new ways. That is why learning and governance systems discussed in the next chapter are an essential lever in transformations to HCHP.

Design an Aligned Organization

What Leaders Must Do. The energy released in an emotionally charged change process must lead to a strategically and psychologically aligned organization. To take advantage of such a process, *CEOs and the senior team must also be architects.* They must be personally involved in designing a structure, processes, and systems that fit the business. And they must be concerned with building an HCHP culture.

Henry Gullette discovered that the field organization's regional structure did not align with television markets. Because television promotions are one of the means for generating revenue and must be coordinated with other initiatives to increase volume, division managers in charge of a geographic area could not be held fully responsible and accountable for revenue and profits. Gullette and his senior team reorganized the field structure around television markets to make division managers accountable, and thereby improved the company's alignment with its strategy. Similarly, one of Louis Gerstner's first initiatives when he took charge of a failing IBM in the early 1990s was to realign the organization around customers. Such realignments were part of all transformations we studied. Recall that reorganization was central to the successful transformation of Corning's Electronic Products Division discussed in the last chapter. Reorganizations reshape roles, responsibilities, and patterns of interaction. If properly supported with coaching and training, they change attitudes and behavior.

Although one cannot directly affect culture, the design of a new human resource system—what types of people are selected and how they are evaluated, developed, and rewarded—is also part of the design challenge, as I will discuss in chapter 10. Under Gullette's leadership, changes in human resource management resulted in significant reductions in turnover of front-line employees and managers.

What Leaders Must Be and Know. To play the architect role effectively, leaders must have a systems perspective as discussed in chapter 4. They must instinctively understand that the behaviors they see and the attitudes they hear are in part a function of the organization's formal design. And they must be willing and able to spend significant time with their senior team, usually with the help of a thought partner from outside the organization, analyzing the organization's alignment and changing it as necessary. This means that the leader must see organizational design as an important part of management work, and must be knowledgeable about how to design an HCHP organization (the core knowledge and perspective needed by leaders will be discussed in chapters 8 through 10). Too many leaders delegate this task in its entirety to consultants and wait for the solution to be presented. Though consultant expertise is valuable, I argue that there is no substitute for senior team involvement.

Gullette again turned to analyzing and realigning his organization when the company experienced flat sales and lower profits in 2005 and 2006. This time the realignment had to be more fundamental. Starting from first principles—the promises that Clean Lodging wanted to make to guests, employees (particularly leaders), and investors to enable sustained performance—Gullette and his senior team, along with the help of consultants, commissioned a set of teams to examine the organization's core processes. These teams then developed and made recommendations for structure, roles, responsibilities, measures, and IT systems that would allow the company to fulfill its promises. Gullette and his senior team were deeply involved in this realignment and communicated its purpose to analysts on Wall Street. The importance of making this realignment work known to investors and analysts is borne out by the fact that Clean Lodging's stock price remained relatively high despite its flat earnings during this period.

Developing a Partnership with Employees

What Leaders Must Do. To build a collaborative community of purpose, HCHP leaders must act in a way that makes employees at all levels feel they are partners in the mission. This is particularly important with respect to members of their top team, and to relationships between the senior team and the larger body of managers and front-line workers. Power asymmetries within the senior team and between the senior team and lower levels lead to coercion and the resulting anger and distrust, and thus reduce collaboration and commitment. Without collaboration and commitment, the potential for value creation—improved decisions, innovation, and process efficiencies—is significantly reduced.[37]

Leaders must create a partnership culture, one in which participation in decisions is not based on hierarchical position but on knowledge and proximity to the problem. In a partnership culture, commitment to mission and reduced hierarchical barriers enable people throughout the corporation to engage spontaneously and fluidly to solve mission-critical problems. Charles Heckscher calls this a collaborative enterprise.[38] He argues that an economy in which customers want solutions rather than products demands much higher levels of integration across boundaries, what Jack Welch called the boundaryless organization.

Slogans are easy. Many leaders espouse partnership but employees observe that their actions and organizational behavior do not reflect it. The following steps are ways in which leaders can develop a partnership culture.

Personal Behavior. To foster an effective partnership culture, leaders must be role models. This means being visible in all parts and levels of the organization, as well as interacting with employees in planned and spontaneous forums. These interactions humanize leaders to employees. Leaders succeed by being open about challenges faced, admitting errors and mistakes, and enlisting help from people at all levels to meet the challenges. It is not done through PowerPoint slides.[39]

Henry Gullette met with a task force of front-line employees in one of the company's motel units that had recently applied the Strategic Dialogue Process. When Gullette learned that at least part of the problems they identified lay with a practice in a corporate staff department, he did not defend it or argue with the task force; instead, he thanked the task force for the feedback and engaged people in solving the problem. Herb Kelleher at Southwest Airlines regularly dressed in "drag" and visited hangars at midnight. IBM's CEO, Sam Palmisano, fostered worldwide "jam sessions" over the Internet that personally engaged thousands of employees around the world in conversations about the company's values.

One of the first steps that Archie Norman and Allan Leighton took in transforming Asda, a U.K. grocery chain, was to meet quarterly with all two hundred store managers (by region) and foster honest conversations about what was and was not working. It is important to note that they institutionalized this process and continued it over an eight-year period. Norman thought that "it made [store managers] feel they were managing [Asda] because they met the chief executive, or Allan or I, or both of us mostly, and said, look this is the problem and somebody screwed up here and can't we do this and can't we do that? And then they saw something happening, so they felt appreciated, recognized, valued, and they also felt the message was getting through." [40]

Shape Policies and Practices. HCHP leaders design policies and practices that foster an egalitarian, self-effacing culture. This is done through many of the human resource policies discussed in chapter 10—ensuring that senior management do not have special pay packages, removing status symbols such as offices and parking spots, even for themselves, sharing the pain of downturns in business by cutting their own pay, creating profit-sharing plans that are the same for all employees regarding percentage of profit to salary, and demanding that employees at all levels be paid in accordance with performance. If top management must be more egalitarian in its distribution of rewards, so must lower levels share more responsibility for performance. Nucor Steel's sustained high performance was based in part on the premise that employees are partners in responsibility for performance; they shared the rewards of good performance and the pain of poor performance.[41]

Build Supportive Empowering Relationships. Partnership requires supportive relationships based on caring, mutual respect, and empowerment. HCHP leaders must display these qualities themselves if they want to spread the spirit of partnership. Clearly, this means delegating and entrusting people with authority at the lowest possible levels. One of Gullette's early efforts to reduce top-down management and improve commitment and performance was to introduce a planning process to all 275 motel unit managers. He and his team traveled around the country to meet with unit managers and teach them the planning system. They asked each unit manager to develop a plan and coached them on how to implement it. Gullette saw the role that this process played in shaping a partnership culture as follows: "I believe this was a pivotal moment for me and Clean Lodging. It said we will share the challenge with you, we value your ideas and how to get it done and we want you to lead the way in your motel units. We believe in your power to make a difference and we believe in the power of the people in your motel to make a difference."

Ann Mulcahy, who is transforming Xerox into an HCHP company, says: "I get things done by identifying with people in the company and trusting them. I care most about building a good team to lead the company."[42] Doug Conant, CEO of Campbell Soup, writes personal notes to employees to celebrate distinctive accomplishments or performance, as well as to offer encouragement. So did Jack Welch at GE. Archie Norman at Asda spent each Sunday reading every suggestion that came to him through the "Tell Archie" suggestion system he designed, asked the individual employee's supervisor to respond, and personally checked to see that they did. If they did not respond he sent a jar of molasses to their desks to signal that they were too slow to respond.

What Leaders Must Be and Know. Leaders are best able to develop a partnership culture if they have the human qualities required to do so. They start with the premise that all people have ideas and want to contribute. Henry Gullette operated from a deeply held assumption that people want to make a difference and can. And this assumption guided every policy and practice he employed to transform Clean Lodging. According to Bill George, who has been studying authentic HCHP leaders, the premise that people are a resource causes leaders to emphasize the "we" rather than the "I."[43]

The idea that the leader does not have all the answers was evident at a 2007 conference of HCHP leaders I held at the Harvard Business School. Despite different personalities and styles, to a person these CEOs were similar human beings in that they had an optimistic view of people—they believed people are the key to developing a high-performance firm. This was reflected in practices such as listening, involving their senior team in decisions, empowering people, mentoring, and developing leaders. What drives this behavior are three seemingly paradoxical qualities: deep caring about people and their lives, strong caring about the performance of the firm, and the strong will to create an HCHP organization.

The "we not I" perspective is only possible if the leader is not arrogant, and indeed is humble, something I saw in participating CEOs. Jim Collins observed: "Those who worked with or wrote about the good-to-great leaders continually used words like quiet, humble, modest, reserved, shy, gracious, mild-mannered, self effacing, understated, did not believe in his own clippings."[44] The humble quality of HCHP leaders has been found over and over again by other researchers and is one in which we can be quite confident.[45] This is not to say that HCHP leaders do not have egos or yearn to be recognized for their accomplishments. Of course they do. They simply hold their egos in check.

In my interviews and many interactions with Henry Gullette I never once found a shred of arrogance. He always talked in terms of the team and credited others for their help. When we developed a written case about Clean Lodging, he had me remove all references to him as the responsible executive and asked that the attribution be to his top team. When confronted with the challenge of declining like-for-like sales early in his tenure, before he fully understood the lodging business, Gullette was humble enough to raise the question of whether he was the right person to lead the company. His team responded to this display of humility by assuring Gullette that he had the leadership skills the company needed and that they would help with their years of hospitality business experience.[46]

Lead Learning and Learn How to Lead

What Leaders Must Do. As I have made clear throughout this chapter, HCHP leaders see the process of change as a collective learning process, one in which iterative advocacy and inquiry leads to deeper and ever-changing understanding of the business, organization, people, and their own leadership. Leading a transformation journey is not about aligning the company with the leader's ideas. It is about enabling leaders and their people to learn together about the problems they face and the actions they must take.

Such a collective process of learning will inevitably provide top managers with feedback about their own effectiveness, feedback to which they must respond if the larger corporate transformation is to succeed. A recent McKinsey study of transformational leaders found that a corporate transformation journey is typically preceded or accompanied by the leader's personal transformation journey: "You have to sacrifice yourself for a big cause before you can ask others to do the same," observed one CEO.[47]

My own experience confirms these findings. If leaders do not respond and change their role and behavior, not only are they undermining commitment, but also organizational effectiveness and performance improvements. Henry Gullette learned that his strength—analyzing problems and coming up with systemic solutions—led him to underinvolve his senior team in shaping solutions and also resulted in too many ideas and an overload of change initiatives. By accepting this feedback and increasing his top team's involvement, he undercut potential cynicism that might have arisen given his strong espousal of participation and involvement. By reducing the number of change initiatives significantly he also, of course, ensured better execution of the remaining change initiatives.

In my experience with honest, collective, and public conversations, the leader's core strengths and weakness—her personality and intellectual capabilities—did not change as a result of feedback. What changed was leaders' understanding of the role the organization required them and their top teams to play. Changing their leadership role enabled enactment of a new approach to organizing and managing. By changing their role and behaviors, managers begin to learn about their assumptions regarding leading and managing. When organizational changes lead to improved effectiveness and performance, new assumptions are shaped and reinforced.

What Leaders Must Be and Know. For managers to lead learning efforts from which they also learn requires them to make themselves vulnerable. Their readiness to confront painful truths about their own deficiencies as leaders is motivated by their commitment to making a difference and to deeply held values of servant leadership. Because they put the welfare of the enterprise first, they are willing and able to sacrifice themselves for the larger good. They follow Mahatma Gandhi's philosophy, "For things to change, first I must change."[48] When Gullette faced new challenges in 2005, he said, "I am deeply frustrated that I/we are not further along on the journey [of change]. There is nothing I hate more than facing my own integrity gaps." Courage is only possible when one has high aspirations. Gullette's vision that Clean Lodging should be "a workplace that is worthy of the human spirit" enabled him to also say, "In retrospect, the fact that it is difficult is why doing this work is so important."[49]

Being humble and willing to learn is often not enough, we have learned. Having the means—knowledge and tools—for orchestrating personal and organizational learning is also important. What stops some managers from leading learning that will make themselves vulnerable is the lack of knowledge about how to do this effectively and safely. Gullette had the values but lacked the means. Having a well-tested process like the Strategic Dialogue Process was invaluable, according to his own assessment; organizations can increase their leaders' willingness and courage to learn by providing them such a process.

Surviving and Thriving in the Leadership Role

The pressure for performance that began to be exerted by capital markets in the late twentieth century and the increasingly short-term perspective of most boards of directors have created a challenging environment for CEOs who wish to build a great institution. (Although a strong market for corporate control has also had the salutary effect of focusing CEOs on results and shareholder interests.) CEOs who wish to transform their corporations find themselves pushed and pulled between pressures for financial results and their aspiration to build a great firm capable of sustained performance and commitment.

The stress generated by the multistakeholder perspective of HCHP CEOs makes their job much more difficult than that of CEOs who are directive or see the shareholder as their only constituency. Gullette wryly described his leadership role, particularly during the period of declining sales and flat profits, by invoking the advertisement that Ernest Shackleton, the commander of the historic and ultimately failed mission to the South Pole, might have answered: "Men wanted for hazardous journey. Small wages, bitter cold, long months of complete darkness, constant danger, safe return doubtful, honor and recognition in case of success."

CEOs of HCHP companies motivated by a higher and longer-term purpose must be able to survive and thrive in what Thomas Rice, my colleague at TruePoint, calls the *leadership crucible*. The crucible is the intensely "hot" space in which conflicting interests of multiple stakeholders are felt by CEOs. The strong value system that drives HCHP CEOs makes it certain that at some point what one or more stakeholders are pushing them to do will come into conflict with their own belief system and long-term purpose. HCHP leaders who hope to be in their jobs long enough to see their aspirations realized must be able to make decisions and take actions in a way that will retain the commitment of *all* stakeholders.

Multiple demands can cause the leader to burn up psychologically, Rice argues, and in some instances lose his job. Gullette, who found Rice's crucible metaphor very useful, observed: "So the underlying premise of the crucible is that most leaders don't actually survive . . . . Most leaders emerge as crispy critters because they couldn't keep everyone happy and ended up imploding. And [it] feels to me to be very real, based on people I know in [the] industry." Gullette then posed the question that I hope to answer in this section: "What do people who thrive in the leadership crucible do?"

To thrive in the "hot space," CEOs must find ways to gain *support from external resources*—that is, multiple stakeholders. In this section I focus on the top team, investors, and boards of directors. But this is not enough. Unless leaders strengthen their will and resolve to succeed, replenish their commitment to their moral purpose, and develop into better leaders, they will be unable to survive in their continuously changing and challenging circumstances.

Managing Stakeholders

Leaders cannot allow themselves to be pulled in different directions—responding today to intense pressures from investors, and tomorrow responding to equally intense dissatisfaction from employees, customers, or community and society. This process is likely to create unintended consequences and stir distrust in the leader's intentions.

In order to survive and thrive in this crucible of multiple demands and pressures, leaders must frame their task in a way that enables them to align the interests of multiple stakeholders prior to making decisions and taking actions. It requires leaders to develop relationships of mutual trust and respect. Research shows that partnership relationships, which HCHP firms are uniquely capable of developing, will improve relationships with suppliers, joint ventures and alliances, and performance. Jamie Houghton, former CEO of Corning, insisted on fifty-fifty ownership in all of Corning's partnerships because he believed that without equal power a relationship of mutual trust and collaboration would not develop. A study conducted by Miller and Miller of why and how family-owned or family-dominated enterprises perform better than public companies supports this conclusion. Managers of these HCHP firms spend a great deal of time cultivating long-term relationships and creating a sense of partnership with all of their stakeholders—employees, suppliers, investors, and communities.[50] Separate research in the automobile industry shows, for example, that a partnership relationship—one in which manufacturers with high power do not take advantage, but instead rely on trust and cooperation—actually has positive effects on the manufacturer's performance.[51] All this suggests that the principles of collective learning discussed in this chapter apply to the problem of integrating multiple stakeholder interests into a solution that works for everyone.

Relationships of mutual trust are built by being open with stakeholders about the circumstances facing the firm and the leader, and discussing plans for change needed and their likely effects on each stakeholder. Henry Gullette employed exactly this approach when he faced declining revenues and flat profits. He brought his leadership team into the process of analysis; together, they forged a plan for reinventing the business and company. He then communicated honestly and forthrightly with employees, the board, and Wall Street about the present situation, the plan for reinventing the business model and company, and the time it would take to show results. He recalled: "So in order for the board to be productive, they need to know what the real issues on the business are. In order for Wall Street to know what a reasonable expectation is, they just have to know the facts, so they see what associates and guest challenges are, and the fact you are actually dealing on the right issues."

This process leads to feedback responses from each constituency regarding their expectations, and enables the leader to search for an integrative solution, which in turn must be communicated back to each constituency.

Without honest conversation with employees about what Wall Street expects, it is hard to create a case for improvement or sacrifice. The more direct the communication from analysts to employees, the more believable the CEO's message will be. Without telling Wall Street what the company must do to invest in employees and how it relates to the business model, it is difficult to get acceptance for long-term investments. And without being clear about the time line of the long-term investment strategy, analysts on Wall Street will lose patience when quarterly earnings fall below expectations. HCHP leaders hold the center between these potentially conflicting forces.

When I asked Archie Norman about the pressures he must have felt from the City—the United Kingdom's equivalent of Wall Street—when he took charge of nearly bankrupt Asda (discussed in chapter 11), he said he was quite clear with them about the circumstances he faced, his plans, and that a turnaround should not be expected for three years. This gave him the running room to establish credibility should he be faced with any additional or unanticipated difficulties. And it gave him time to invest in transforming the business and organizational model. Had he promised the City to deliver short-term results and then failed, his credibility would have been reduced. Successful CEOs build social capital with all their stakeholders in this way.

Faced with declining revenue and the task of reinventing the firm, Gullette told Wall Street analysts it would be eighteen months before he could roll out the reinvented Clean Lodging. Interestingly, Wall Street bought the story and, instead of dropping significantly, the stock price continued to reflect the value that analysts saw in the reinvention of the company. Indeed, Gullette learned that the best analysts on Wall Street understand that short-term predictions of success—without a long-term investment story—are not to be believed.

To enable the long-term perspective that building an HCHP corporation requires, CEOs of HCHP companies, I found, pay particular attention to the selection and development of investor relationships. Some CEOs, Gullette included, are making efforts to choose investors who are specifically looking for long-term sustained performance. They do this by carefully preselecting the audiences to which they pitch the company and its stock. Mike Eskew, CEO of United Parcel Service (UPS), has found that by communicating UPS's long-term strategy effectively, "we can attract investors who will stick with us for the long haul."[52]

There are two constituencies to which leaders must pay particular attention: the leadership team and the board of directors.

The Leadership Team. The leadership team atop an HCHP organization must be a high-performing team capable of integrating the firm. Don Hambrick, who has studied top teams for decades, argues that "organizations that are loose amalgamations of business units, collections of regional subsidiaries, or portfolios of unrelated activities are at a crippling disadvantage in an era requiring the creation and leveraging of core competences, the exercise of global clout, and the ability to engage periodically in fast sweeping company-wide changes."[53] And higher levels of top team effectiveness and cohesion have been shown to be associated with firm performance in a number of studies.[54] Though the extent of top team cohesion required is contingent to some extent on the firm's strategy and structure—decentralized structures versus matrix organizations, for example (see chapter 9)—CEOs aspiring to HCHP must move their top teams significantly toward ever higher levels of integration to find opportunities for value creation through synergy and coordination.

The top team at Southwest Airlines meets frequently and often for extended periods of time and, according to Jody Gittell, who observed the top team in action, functioned well without Herb Kelleher, despite the potential for succession rivalries (at the time Kelleher was planning to retire). "Managers from different business areas," Gittell reports, "spoke knowledgeably about issues beyond the expertise suggested by their titles, and they repeatedly built on their thoughts. It was like stepping into a conversation in which these managers had been engaged for many years."[55] Colleen Barrett, Herb Kelleher's partner in leading the firm, observes: "Titles mean very little here. Most people overlap in functionality. You would not get an accurate impression of Southwest from interviewing us individually about our areas of expertise."[56] And as I discussed earlier, I learned from Gary Kelly in a 2008 interview that he has increased the level of top team interaction and cohesion even further in response to competitive pressures and a rapidly changing environment.

Hambrick's and Gittell's observations are supported by our findings that in underperforming businesses people below the top team see their leader and top team as causal to conflicting priorities, poor coordination, and poor performance (see chapter 5). That causal relationship is also borne out by many examples of turnarounds in coordination, commitment, and performance that we have observed *after* underperforming top teams have successfully improved their effectiveness.[57]

Aligning the top team with the leader's direction and philosophy is critical. All successful transformation leaders find that they must replace some if not all members of their top team relatively early in the company's journey. David Lawrence, who led Kaiser Permanente, found that he had to make changes in his senior team in order to progress along the transformation journey. Dissenters had to be removed; senior executives brought in committed to the change Lawrence was leading from the start. He recalled, in a 1996 conference, that he needed a top team on whom "I could be 100 percent dependent" and who "would be fighting in the same way I was trying to make the changes."[58]

The top team is not only important to the implementation of the transformational agenda, according to Asda's CEO, Archie Norman (see chapter 11), but it can help the CEO survive and thrive in the leadership role.

There is no substitute for leadership . . . and that doesn't just mean individual leadership. It means a team that is going to lead and work together. And I think the team is very, very important because when things are pretty tough, and it's not all fun, and it is pretty grim, and you all wonder whether you made the right decision [to undertake the CEO job] and whether you've sacrificed your career to a company that can never change, then being together is extremely powerful, and being able to refer ideas and think about ideas and play a different role is extremely powerful . . . . So that's the first thing you [have to undertake]—it's very, very important to create that team.[59]

Ultimately, the top team must be involved in leading the collective learning process outlined in this chapter. Creating a top team aligned with their goals not only makes it easier for CEOs to achieve their purpose but also makes it easier to survive and thrive in their pressure-filled role.

The Board of Directors. More than any other stakeholder, the board can limit the CEO's freedom to act. If the CEO has made the board partners in the journey it reduces heat in the crucible. More importantly, the board can do a lot to support and help. And they can make the CEO a better leader. Once again the experience of David Lawrence at Kaiser Permanente is relevant. He observed, "[T]he board has been absolutely essential . . . . They have been an important source of stability and support; at the same time, by being better educated [about the challenges] they are placing higher demands on me."[60]

CEOs can create a partnership with the board in two ways. First, they work with the board's nominations committee to ensure that members are selected to fit their leadership philosophy as well as to provide differing points of view or expertise. Though CEOs do not have the unilateral power in the United States that they had prior to scandals and reforms between 2000 and 2006, they can still have substantial influence. Even in the United Kingdom, where a non-executive is chairman by law, the CEO can influence changes in the board composition. One of Alan Parker's first successful initiatives in his efforts to transform Whitbread, a U.K. hospitality company, was to change the composition of his board.

Secondly, a partnership means that the CEO brings the board into the discussion of key issues—strategy, key executives' promotions, and organizational changes. So concludes Jay Lorsch, an expert on boards.[61] Transparency about the effectiveness and culture of the organization, even when it reflects on the CEO, is essential. Clateo Castellini, former CEO of Becton Dickinson, a company that has been on a twenty-year journey to HCHP, shared with the board of directors feedback about the company's health that he had received from a task force commissioned to conduct an honest, collective, and public inquiry. Ed Ludwig, his successor, also believes in this kind of transparency.

The leader's skill in facilitating a productive board discussion is important. Does the CEO come in with a PowerPoint presentation to tell the board what he or she is planning to do? Or does the CEO frame issues for discussion? Gullette learned, over time, that "from a board facilitation perspective ... it's important the way I frame the questions. Strategic questions for the board to consider [are important], and then I become the 'note-taker' for their dialogue." Gullette learned that he and the board learned more and came to a better mutual understanding when he created space for discussion by framing the issues, as opposed to simply presenting his plans.

Of course, to develop a partnership with the CEO—for open discussions of issues to take place—the board itself must be effective. It must possess the characteristics of the effective leadership teams discussed earlier. The CEO can take a leadership role and suggest, as some have, off-site sessions facilitated by a coach or consultant to help develop common goals, mutual understandings, and role definition of its members. Facilitating such a board discussion several years ago, I learned how critical discussions led by an outside consultant can be in bringing problems to the surface and building a more effective board. Many issues that surfaced in the board team-building meeting I facilitated had been known to all but never discussed.

There is no less important an issue than CEO succession if the company is to experience continuity in its transformation and stay on the path to HCHP. CEOs who have worked hard to build HCHP organizations therefore work closely with the board to develop the specifications for their successor and discuss candidates within that specified framework. Too many journeys to HCHP have been derailed because the board of directors did not understand the distinctive qualities of the HCHP strategy and culture that their CEO had built.

The importance of an effective board and a CEO's partnership with the board of directors is illustrated by the experience of Henry Gullette. His transformation of Clean Lodging was interrupted after five years by a board of directors that ultimately did not commit to his HCHP vision. Gullette described the situation as follows:

> I joined the company knowing that three-quarters of the board [had been around a long time and were wedded to a cost rather than service strategy]. I believed that there was a tremendous opportunity to transform the board as well as the company. Five years later and they are all still there.... I still

had the two former CEO's on the board, one of whom was the chairman. Perhaps even more importantly was that our belief systems were fundamentally different on a wide range of issues. As a result they supported me to some degree when things went well, but when the company's underlying strategic issues surfaced they insisted on reverting back to their old ways. Because the brand faced some important strategic challenges, and the board was unwilling to confront these issues head on, it was simply time to go.

The implications are clear. CEOs who wish to lead a transformation must have a board that is willing. Beyond the quality of the conversations between the CEO and the board, conversations that Gullette did try to fashion, the board's composition must be favorable—composed of people who are open to a partnership and to learning. It is unlikely that board members whose identity is strongly tied to the past will be able to adapt their vision of the future.

Failure to achieve board alignment around an HCHP vision can be fatal to its achievement. After Gullette's departure, the board of directors pushed the company back to its legacy: a cost-driven rather than service-driven business model, and an autocratic rather than commitment model of management. Clean Lodging's performance and stock price declined sharply and the company's survival is now in doubt.

Managing Self

The most important resource in the HCHP journey is the leader. This is not surprising given that leading a transformation to HCHP is much more difficult than leadership in a normal state. An HCHP journey requires frame-breaking cultural change. The normal state is business-as-usual dominated by activities and satisfying everyone, but achieving little that is extraordinary. Gullette described his experience when faced with making a fundamental transformation in both the business and cultural model of Clean Lodging in 2005: "About a year ago, I started a grieving process around the loss of the easy dream. Because when I first came, it looked . . . this was just not hard. You focus on a few measures, you get a little better each year, you sort of tweak the organization . . . and the results are terrific."

It is not surprising, therefore, that CEOs who lead transformations to HCHP companies must commit themselves to developing themselves and *finding and holding on to their personal center*—what they believe in and what they aspire to do as leaders.

Along the journey to HCHP, leaders encounter crises that require them to be extraordinary. During these periods they and the company can easily be pulled off the HCHP path. To be at their very best, leaders must enter what Robert Quinn has called the "fundamental state of leadership."[62] It requires leaders to move from comfort with activities to a focus on results, from self-absorption to commitment to mission and higher purpose, from focus on self to focus on others, from being internally closed to being externally open, and, in my view, from hiding the truth to embracing the truth. It requires leaders to answer questions my colleague Thomas Rice asks leaders: "Who are you?" or "What do you stand for?" Gullette found that the stamina and personal inspiration he needed required "reading, meditation, exercise and personal prayer . . . there has to be a regular grounding, in what are my intentions." Gullette went on:

> If you are *not* strong enough as a human being to withstand a fair amount
> of heat, and basically know *why* [emphasis mine] you're doing what you are
> doing, and to energize and inspire yourself in a very grounded way, the odds
> of your coming out of this alive are almost zero because it's too hard. When
> leaders do not know who they are, what they are trying to do and, importantly,
> why they respond to stress by being hard on others [it] . . . does not lead to
> high commitment or performance.

Despite all the books and training courses, leaders are at their best, according to Robert Quinn and Bill George, when they don't copy others.[63] One cannot be in the fundamental state of leadership all the time, but HCHP leaders have to enter it at critical junctures. It is then that they draw on their deepest instincts, values, and capabilities.

What is the best way for leaders to hold the center, to stay true to their HCHP aspirations in the face of short-term pressures to accede to the wishes of various stakeholders? Leaders might start by asking themselves a set of questions, according to Quinn. He argues that leaders have to learn how to use these questions in times when extraordinary leadership is required. This applies to HCHP leaders in particular because their aspirations are unconventional and lofty. Below are four questions that Quinn suggests and a fifth I have added:[64]

1. *"Am I results oriented?"* Has the leader articulated the outcome he wants to create? In our normal state we are in our comfort zone by being activity focused.
2. *"Am I internally directed?"* To do difficult things the leader must leave the normal state of complying with what others—employees, investors, or the board, for example—want done.

3. *"Am I other focused?"* To transform an organization, the leader must leave the normal state of self-absorption and self-interest. It requires focus on the welfare of the organization and all of its stakeholders.

4. *"Am I externally open?"* Sustained improvement and change require that leaders are open to signals that change is needed. In the normal state, leaders are too busy and defensive to hear those signals.

5. *"Am I hiding the truth?"* All of the questions above require the leaders to be truthful with themselves and with others. There is a natural human tendency to avoid the truth.

Leaders who enter the fundamental state—who confront the facts of the business and who stay true to who they are and what they believe in—will, like Henry Gullette, be able to look upon their efforts with honor regardless of the ultimate outcome. Consider Gullette's reflections on his experience after leaving Clean Lodging:

> A critical idea that I have learned over the years is the truth espoused by Socrates and Plato—that no one can hurt one's honor besides oneself. I leave Clean Lodging having met my five-year commitment that I gave to the board and having fought for what I believe to be right through the very last minute I was there (and beyond). I had opportunities to abandon ship which would have been much more profitable for the shape of my career and I did not take them. I was pressured to take actions that would have been on a path I could not support and I did not take them. As a result I can sleep well.

Summary

HCHP leaders are the antithesis of the heroic leader. Single-handed and single-minded leaders do not engage employees, key executives, and other stakeholders in the type of collaborative learning process required to develop strategic and psychological alignment, or the capacity to learn and change that I argue are imperative for sustained commitment and performance. HCHP leadership is a collective action learning process—one that engages people around ambitious, difficult, and lofty goals.

Instead of starting with the conventional list of characteristics that great leaders possess, this chapter focused first on what transformational leaders must *DO* to develop a collective process of organizational learning and adaptation.

Research evidence and my own experience in working with and studying transformational leaders point to what leaders must *BE* and what they must *KNOW* to succeed. Senior executives who want to lead a journey to HCHP should be able to answer in the affirmative to the following questions:

Do	Be and Know
1. Do I connect authentically with people in my organization?	Am I open with others about my beliefs, motives, values, and emotions?
2. Do I have a well-defined view of the direction—strategy, values, and organizational culture my company should take?	Do I have the will to lead the company in that direction?
3. Do I enable inquiry into the quality of our direction and into barriers to implementing it?	Do I have the will to receive feedback and learn?
4. Do I help the organization and its people to confront and resolve tensions?	Am I ready to have the conversation that matters and engage the tensions and conflicts it will produce?
5. Do I and my senior team play a leadership role in designing our organization to achieve its purpose?	Do I have the systems perspective and knowledge about organizational design?
6. Do I develop a partnership with employees at all levels and with other stakeholders?	Am I humble enough to do this? Do I have the interpersonal skills to do it?
7. Am I leading an organizational learning process from which I and my leadership team are also learning?	Do I have the courage to make myself vulnerable so my leadership team and I can learn?

Leading an organization on the never-ending journey to HCHP is difficult. Leaders are confronted with multiple demands from a variety of constituents—shareholders, employees, capital markets, and community. They find themselves continuously seeking solutions that will meet the interests of all. This is emotionally difficult and cannot be achieved without an aligned senior team and board of directors. For this reason HCHP leaders spend considerable time and effort developing an effective senior team and board of directors. Both groups must come to share the values and vision of the CEO. Unless they do, the journey to HCHP is likely to be difficult or unsuccessful.

Surviving and thriving in this crucible of conflicting demands is no easy task. It requires that leaders strengthen and develop their internal resources. They must learn to enter the fundamental state of leadership when faced with challenges—a state that demands that they dig deep into their values and purpose. That fundamental state of leadership requires leaders to move from comfort with activities to focus on results, from self-absorption to commitment to mission and higher purpose, from focus on self to focus on others, from being internally closed to being externally open, and from hiding the truth to embracing the truth.

CHAPTER SEVEN

ENABLE TRUTH TO SPEAK TO POWER

Change Lever 2: Learning and Governance Systems

[Leadership] is [about having] enough modesty to constantly doubt, be open, and listen.... It is the ability to hear and accept bad news—and then move on, using the experience as a tool for future improvement.[1]

—JAMES HOUGHTON, FORMER CHAIRMAN AND CEO OF CORNING INC.

If building an HCHP organization is the aspiration, and hidden, undiscussable managerial problems are consistently identified by lower levels as barriers (see chapter 5), it stands to reason that leaders and senior teams must find a way to *learn the truth* about their organization and leadership. Difficult and necessary as it may be to learn the truth, it ensures continuous improvement in the quality of leadership and management—the elusive but essential ingredient for a successful journey to HCHP. Though there is wide acceptance and adoption of quality improvement systems like Six Sigma at the operating level, few organizations have institutionalized such a system of learning and continuous improvement.

In this chapter I argue that, to meet this major challenge, HCHP leaders require a *learning and governance system* that enrolls the larger organization in a collective learning process. Such systems enable *iterative, honest, collective, and public conversation about the state of the business and organizational system*. By honest I mean that the unvarnished truth about the business and organization is made discussable. By *collective* I mean that key people in all of the firm's value-creating activities are involved in the conversation. By *public* I mean that everyone in the organization knows that an honest assessment led by the senior team and/or the board of directors is in progress and they are kept informed about what was learned and what actions will be taken. This collective learning process is a powerful means for leaders to "hear and accept [good] and bad news—and then move on," as James Houghton puts it in the quotation introducing this chapter.

The business landscape is littered with companies that failed to sustain their performance trajectory because senior leaders were unable to learn from lower-level managers or employees. Samsung Motors' disastrous foray into the automobile business is a case in point. Although many of Samsung's managers and the majority of the group's employees opposed the idea at the time, arguing that "going into an overcrowded auto market without any existing competencies in producing and selling cars was too risky," top management went ahead.[2] In today's business landscape, bold and innovative ideas are not enough. Exceptional leaders will ensure that those ideas become reality by engaging their employees in an organizational conversation about the firm's strategic direction and barriers to achieving it.

Consider also how the economic meltdown of 2008 might have been averted if failing banks and mortgage companies with bad lending practices had had an institutionalized system that enabled truth to speak to power—to top management or, if necessary, to boards of directors. Our research findings and that of many others clearly show (see chapter 5) that people below the top know well in advance of the crisis that there are problems of strategy, integrity, commitment, and organizational effectiveness. We are learning that this was of course also true with regard to risky loans that were being issued by mortgage companies and banks. Key people below the top who saw the problems were unable to come together, pool their observations, discuss their meaning, and communicate them *as a group* to top management or the board of directors. Those charged with the stewardship of the firm were unable to learn that the quality of management was bad and threatened the firm's effectiveness, performance, and integrity. Taking action after the crisis is in full-blown ascendance is hardly a prescription for continuous learning and sustainable high performance.

Promoting honest conversations that matter is easier said than done. Lou Gerstner, in recounting his early days at the helm of IBM in 1992 (IBM had lost its HCHP edge when it failed to respond to tectonic change in the industry), gives an idea of how difficult it was to do this even though he was a new leader not responsible for IBM's problems and wanted people to speak up. Gerstner held his first meeting, with his corporate management board, made up of the top fifty company executives, on the afternoon of the formal announcement of his appointment. He laid out his views, hopes, and values. The corporate management board listened attentively. At the conclusion, Gerstner asked for questions. "There were none," he recalled. Less than a month later, he held his first meeting at the lab, which he calls "the soul of IBM." There, Gerstner went through essentially the same talk he had made to the management board. At the end of the speech, the attendees applauded. But as he left the meeting, Gerstner realized that he "wasn't sure what they were thinking."[3] This, he recalled, was diametrically opposite to the open and fact-based conversations at McKinsey, the consulting firm listed in chapter 2 as an HCHP firm, where he started his career and rose to be a partner.

Simply asking for questions or expecting employees to be open about their ideas and feelings will not turn a failing organization into a thriving HCHP company. This is because managers and front-line employees have long been complicit in enabling organizational silence. Typically, they are reluctant to tell top management the truth because they fear negative consequences. They are unwilling to go through the emotional stress that delivering unwelcome news involves. And they have learned that speaking up does not lead to change.

Leaders, too, no matter how well intentioned and motivated, do not develop overnight into HCHP executives. They are prone to the human tendency to avoid confronting difficult issues, particularly if that means exposing problems that could be attributed to their performance or to ineffective managers whom they will have to confront. In addition, the CEO role tends to induce a certain degree of arrogance and distance, which means that only the most humble incumbents who actively seek honest conversations are likely to learn the truth or establish genuine partnership with lower levels.

Stanley Finkelstein argues that failures are caused by leaders' belief that they know the answer and have the solutions, whether it is a new strategy or organizational solution.[4] How can companies enable honest dialogue? Most corporations do employ some means for managers to learn from front-line workers what they think about how they are managed. Usually, employee surveys or informal interactions with leaders are initiated. But most of these methods are too superficial or sporadic to enable top management to obtain the rich, multifaceted, and valid assessment of the organization needed for a valid diagnosis.

Most HCHP firms go beyond surveys. They employ a variety of ways to involve their people directly in collecting information about the state of the enterprise. Sometimes these mechanisms are standing committees or task forces, such as Southwest Airlines' culture committee. Sometimes they are special forums, such as town meetings where employees voice their views directly to senior management. What's important is that management is in direct face-to-face communication with employees, hearing their views, engaging in a conversation that matters, closing the loop later by telling employees what they heard and the decisions they have since made, then opening up the conversation again for their reactions and suggestions. When employed iteratively, these forums become learning and governance systems. What they have in common is genuine dialogue.

Dialogue, according to Peter Senge, is a structured and collective thought process.[5] The purpose of dialogue is to move beyond the understanding of any one individual or group and create an enriched and shared understanding.

Senge adds: "In dialogue, a group explores complex difficult issues from many points of view. Individuals suspend their assumptions but ... communicate [them] ... freely. The result is a free exploration that brings to the surface the full depths of people's experience and thought and yet can move beyond their individual views."[6]

In a few HCHP companies, learning and governance processes have been applied at multiple levels and units, making senior teams accountable to top management and to employees. General Electric's Work-Out process, introduced by Jack Welch, required all managers to meet with key employees, converse about barriers to bureaucracy, and commit, on the spot, to action. The Strategic Fitness Process (SFP), which Russ Eisenstat and I developed in 1990 for Becton Dickinson, a global medical technology company, played an important role in that company's corporate transformation (see chapter 10). Since then nearly three hundred different organizations at the corporate, business, and operating unit level have employed SFP. Our research into the process and effects of SFP has revealed essential principles that inform how learning and governance systems should be designed and inform this chapter.[7] Merck's Latin American region serves as an illustrative case.

Merck Latin America[8]

Grey Warner, the newly appointed head of Merck's Latin American region, faced a major challenge in 1993. Although viewed within Merck as a successful "can-do" executive, Warner had never been a country manager, never held an international position, did not speak the languages of the region, and had visited Latin America only twice in his life. Merck corporate executives had already targeted Latin America for fast growth in sales and profitability after a decade of economic turbulence. A marked rise in democratic institutions, an expanding middle class, and a strengthening commitment to free market forces in the 1990s promised an increasingly fertile economic environment. What's more, Merck had just reacquired 100 percent ownership of all ten country organizations from local partners, all under ineffective and autocratic management. Underperforming, with little teamwork, poor communication, low trust and commitment, Warner's ten country organizations were bureaucracies easily cast as prototypes for the deadly "silent killers."

From his headquarters in Whitehouse Station, New Jersey, Warner recognized that his organization would have to become better and quicker in developing new products and identifying new markets if they were to take advantage of the growth opportunities offered by Latin America's increasingly robust economy. He needed to find ways of aligning ten foreign country organizations with his vision.

Warner brought with him several overarching principles that would make a difference. In his view, strategic planning should involve lower-level employees in his country organization. Transparency, which Warner described as something greater than honesty, as it entailed telling the "whole truth," should be the rule that guided all discussions and decisions. He believed that "how" leaders managed mattered as much if not more than "what" they brought with them as substantive solutions to problems. He knew that his country managers needed a process by which to establish a positive "how" with their people. Sorely needed was honest conversation within the senior team itself and between the senior team and lower levels, most crucially about the business strategy and the barriers to strategy implementation, performance, and commitment. As a solution, Warner asked each of his ten country managers to utilize the Strategic Fitness Process. He positioned this with his country managers as a means by which each country manager and his senior team could lead a process of organizational learning and change from which they, in turn, could improve the quality of their leadership and management.

Merck's Mexican subsidiary illustrates the challenge that each of the ten country organizations faced. It also illustrates what an organization with low commitment and performance feels and looks like.[9] When Warner took over, there existed in Merck Mexico a command and control management, hierarchical functional structure, lack of cross-functional cooperation, shortage of skilled or experienced employees, and business values still not aligned with those of the corporation. A sales representative reported the following: "When we were not owned by Merck there was chaos and people did what they wanted. The culture was very paternalistic, very authoritarian. People felt underestimated in their abilities and underappreciated."[10]

One of the roots of the problem was an ineffective senior team. The new country manager who had been transferred to Mexico from Merck Spain described it as follows: "It was each for his own and not a lot of cooperation. There were different visions of where the organization should go, not necessarily wrong visions, just different, and that caused a fair amount of friction. And because everyone was busy, doing their own thing, people were not naturally talking to each other."

Although an effective relationship between marketing and sales was critical to long-term success, an employee reported the opposite:

> The relationship between marketing and sales was dysfunctional, and at times, destructive. Their staffs seldom spoke cross-functionally. There were stories of sales managers telling their sales reps not to speak with anyone in marketing. If a rep had a question about marketing, the rep should speak with his or her sales manager. The sales managers would ask a marketing person the question and

then relay the response back to the rep. In the field, if a rep could not answer a doctor's question that required input from marketing, it could take a week or two for the response to work its way through the chain and back to the doctor.

In short, having no cross-functional communication between sales and marketing was blocking company responsiveness and performance.

Warner began by introducing strategic planning across the region. Knowing that strategy clarification would not lead to results unless the organization and its people were aligned, Warner introduced the Strategic Fitness Process. In each country organization, the learning process began with an announcement by the country manager to employees that the senior team was launching an inquiry into the organization's effectiveness. It explained that management would receive direct feedback about findings and would then communicate changes they planned to the whole organization. The SFP process puts senior teams at the center of the conversation. Facilitated by a third party—initially my colleague Russ Eisenstat, and later by Merck's internal human resource and organization development professionals—the first step in the process is an off-site meeting. The senior team collaborates to write a short strategic and organizational direction that describes goals, strategy, and values for managing the organization (see Figure 7.1 for the sequential steps in the Strategic Fitness Process).

FIGURE 7.1. THE STRATEGIC FITNESS PROCESS.

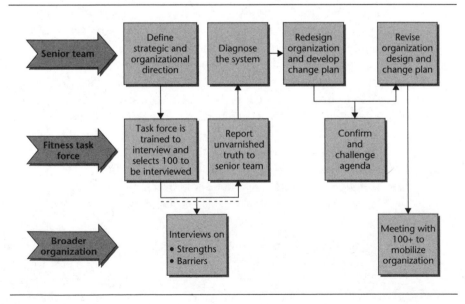

Next, an employee task force of eight high potential and performance employees, usually key managers or employees one or two levels below the senior team, are commissioned by the organization's senior team to interview approximately one hundred other employees about *strengths and barriers* to implementing the new direction. (Knowing strengths that must be reinforced and sustained is as important as knowing about barriers that require change.) Confidentiality is assured to all interviewees. The task force then analyzes the interview data and identifies key themes and prepares to present their findings at a three-day meeting specifically designed for feedback, diagnosis, and action planning.

On the first day, the task force reports their findings to the senior team. To ensure a rich and honest discussion, task force members are seated at a table to discuss what they'd learned, as opposed to making a presentation. The senior team, seated in an outer circle of tables, listens, takes notes, and is asked to restrict their questions to requests for clarification. The "fishbowl" arrangement, as it is commonly called, allows the task force to speak as a group of reporters and thus provides psychological and career safety. A ground rule set in advance of the feedback is that perceptions reported by the task force are to be treated by the senior team as facts. Challenging the validity of the findings is off limits because the task force's reports are based on a rigorous analysis of their interview findings and reflect what a majority of employees perceived. The task force in Merck Mexico reported and discussed the following themes for several hours and then left the room to allow the senior team to begin its own deliberations.

1. Leadership: the right leadership was not in place; there was no confidence in the current leadership.
2. Communication: both vertical and cross-functional communication were poor.
3. Teamwork: people did not know how to work together.
4. Management style: managers gave orders and employees were fired for questioning orders.
5. Marketing and sales were not aligned.
6. People in the field felt alone.
7. Accountability: few employees took responsibility for their work.
8. Salaries and benefits were not competitive.

After the task force left, the SFP facilitators presented the senior team members' views of Merck Mexico's strengths and barriers that they had collected from interviews with team members in advance of the meeting.

Merck Mexico's senior team spent the next two days in discussions about what they had learned and what they planned to do. The facilitators helped the senior team conduct a systemic diagnosis of the organization and develop an action plan. The following week the action plan was reported back to the task force by the senior team for their critique. If the task force believed the action plan was not responsive to the data they presented or would face implementation problems, the two groups met again until they found common ground. Once consensus was reached, the senior team, accompanied by the task force, held a one-day meeting with the hundred interviewees and other key people. In these meetings, senior teams summarized what they had learned and what changes they'd planned before opening up for further discussions on the proposed plans. Typically, major concerns do not arise at this state, but if they do they have to be resolved. Communication to everyone in the organization follows.

Two years after Warner's appointment, all ten Latin American country managing directors had implemented the governance and learning process described above. In each case, results were shared with Warner by the country managing director, accompanied by the consultant to the process, who served as an honest broker. Sometimes task forces accompanied the general manager to present their findings to Warner directly. This upward feedback about findings and plans for change from each country manager gave Warner in New Jersey access to the leadership and organizational problems that each organization faced. It allowed Warner to evaluate plans for change and coach managing directors. Though replacing managers immediately based on findings would have defeated the efficacy of the process, Warner did not shy away from replacing country managers if they were unable or unwilling to learn from the process and the coaching they received following the process. This *"learn, change, or go"* principle makes learning and governance systems a means for holding managers accountable for that most elusive and poorly measured business asset, leadership quality and organizational effectiveness.

In the hands of an exceptional value-driven leader like Grey Warner, the SFP played a role in positive outcomes achieved by Merck's Latin America region. The region achieved a compounded annual growth of 20 percent in the years that followed. Ten years later, the attitudes of employees at Merck Latin America were higher than corporate and national norms.

How and Why Learning and Governance Systems Work

Governance and learning systems that foster honest conversations are a powerful platform for *leaders to speak truthfully* to employees about challenges faced by the organization and for *employees to speak truthfully* to those in power about barriers to organizational effectiveness and health. In a much shorter time frame than otherwise possible, leaders can learn about the root causes for low commitment and performance that could escalate into a significant problem. In dozens of organizations, ranging in size from corporations and country organizations like Merck Mexico to operating units as small as sixty people, we have helped senior teams apply versions of the Strategic Fitness Process. This has given us the opportunity to see how a learning and governance system that enables truth to speak to power works and why it is essential.

Honest collective and public conversations reveal the full set of problems and outcomes that leaders need to know. Data about the organization's strategic and psychological alignment as well as its capacity to learn and change are brought to the surface, thereby enabling a holistic diagnosis of the system. This data enables deeper conversations about how the business should be organized, managed, and led. Unfortunately, too many corporations spend time and money on multiple, narrow data-gathering forays into specific problems and therefore miss the systemic underpinnings for symptomatic problems. Enabling truth to speak to power brings into stark relief the big "boulders" that must be dealt with before significant progress can be made. Too often, presentations are made to senior management and reports are written but little fundamental change takes place. The result is numerous and costly change initiatives that do not solve underlying problems.

Because feedback is from key people who speak directly to senior management, and not from consultants, HR professionals, or employee surveys, leadership teams *cannot ignore* the feedback. Consider what Steve Fossi, a general manager at Agilent Technologies, said about his experience with the Strategic Fitness Process: "[It] is set up in a way that makes it basically impossible to ignore the feedback. You are compelled to do something about it. It comes from inside the company vs. from outside consultants, gathered by trusted middle managers who invested so much time and energy to get the data. It's almost impossible to not act on the data once you've got it."[11]

In every one of Merck's Latin American country organizations, as well as in dozens of other organizations where the SFP has been implemented and studied, senior teams were motivated by the truth, delivered by their own people, to agree on the broad outlines of a plan for systemwide change—one that targeted several relevant change levers, including their own leadership role and behavior.

Honest, collective, and public conversations speed change; contrary to conventional assumptions that participation slows change. Top-down solutions that appear to be decisive and quick usually undermine the quality of the solution and commitment. They often have unintended consequences, make people feel underutilized and underappreciated, damage their identification with the firm, and ultimately slow change. Well-designed learning and governance systems

TABLE 7.1. THE RELATIONSHIP BETWEEN SPEED
AND PARTICIPATION.

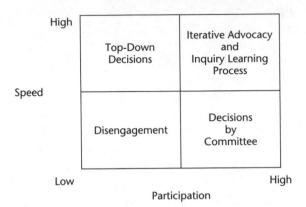

actually enable *rapid change while also enabling high participation*. This is because they integrate top-down and bottom-up change. Implementing the SFP takes only six to eight weeks and only five days of senior management's time, which is time well spent on important business problems. In a safe environment that enables truth to speak to power, issues are confronted rapidly (see Table 7.1) and long, multiple, politically correct meetings where everyone talks indirectly or around the problem are avoided.

Speed and participation, as we have found in our work with the SFP, are made possible by an *iterative process of advocacy* by senior management *and inquiry* by a task force of key people (see Figure 7.2). Such an interactive process enables leaders to articulate a direction and a solution, if they have one, while also enabling employees to confront otherwise unspoken concerns and doubts. Authority for proposed solutions is left in the hands of senior teams, but that authority is legitimated when key people on the data-gathering task force are provided a forum to challenge senior management's thinking and participate with the senior team to modify solutions. When the process, as well as challenges by lower levels, is made transparent to the larger organization, senior management's legitimacy and moral authority are enhanced in the eyes of all employees.

Ed Ludwig, now the CEO of Becton Dickinson (BD), felt that the SFP, implemented six months after he took charge of a failing business unit in 1990, "saved him 24 months." He reports why:

It [Strategic Fitness Process] allowed us to discuss the undiscussable: it got things on the table that would have taken me years. Getting feedback from the employees is indispensable, and putting it into a strategic context is important.

FIGURE 7.2. GOVERNANCE AND LEARNING AS AN ITERATIVE PROCESS OF ADVOCACY AND INQUIRY.

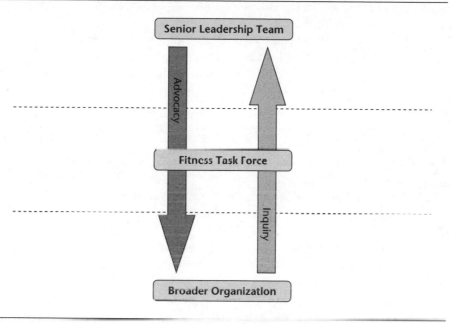

We were there to discuss behaviors that were consequential; it wasn't personal. We discovered things that would help us succeed or that were preventing us from succeeding. There were strategic issues, such as delivering the goods and services to our customers better than our competitors. Once we decided it was strategic, we had to fix it [quickly] or suffer the consequences; no one is willing to suffer the consequences of gradual loss of competitive position.[12]

Organization-wide conversations, in my own experience, give general managers with ineffective senior teams an *opportunity to improve their team's readiness to change.* Upon hearing feedback from lower levels, senior team members realize that what they thought was unknown to lower levels is not only known but widely discussed. The truth motivates leadership teams to take responsibility for issues that they may have known existed but that were difficult to deal with. Their sense of duty, the emotional impact of honest feedback, and their new clarity about the link between reported barriers and performance all produce a sense of urgency to deal with difficult strategic issues. A mandate for change is developed. "I was taking a lot of notes," recalled Steve Fossi, a senior team member in

Hewlett-Packard's Santa Rosa Systems Division, "but all I could think of the whole time, was 'how did it get this bad? The whole thing was easily the worst day in my HP career.... It hit me that we were up to our necks now and there was no turning back."[13]

The truth, when conveyed constructively, also improves trust between top team members and increases their commitment to act. Consider the report of a senior executive at a well-known technology company following an honest and collective conversation designed by the company's internal organization development staff in 1991: "It was an important turning point—behavior changed as people began to trust each other in talking through the issues. There was a collective sigh of relief that the problem had been brought out."[14]

Governance and learning systems are *an important means for developing psychological alignment and a community of purpose.* The barriers to creating such a community, Charles Heckscher and Nathaniel Foote argue, is the *norm of deference,* the unwillingness and inability of lower levels to challenge ideas from the top, and the *norm of autonomy,* the mythical expectation that with responsibility should come complete authority and control of one's own organizational subunit. These norms undermine collaboration and community, but are overturned by honest, collective, and public conversations.[15] Employees at Merck Mexico, as in the other nine country organizations, became increasingly committed as they learned that others shared their concerns and that the senior team was listening and acting on the barriers that had been made public. Hope for real change increased, as did a sense of community. The same was true at countless other organizations with which we have worked. Here is how one top team member assessed the community effects of enabling truth to speak to power: "The task force feedback really served several important roles. Not only did it function as a powerful tool to communicate difficult issues, but it also showed that the top team cared about what employees thought and that we would not institute a change process without asking for their input. Also I believe that by asking for their 'unvarnished' opinions, the employees realized just how serious we were about improving [our organization's] effectiveness."[16]

Evident in our findings was that leadership did not continue to be a major barrier to effectiveness a year or two later *if* the leader took seriously the feedback obtained from the learning and governance process. Employees felt better about their leaders because they took action that employees understood to be connected to their feedback, and leaders came to appreciate the capabilities and earnest concern of their people.

Governance and learning systems can *reduce the organization's dependence on consultants.* Although no one employee may know all the problems or have all the solutions, obtaining views from many parts of the organization allows a remarkable amount of important and usable information to surface—the same information that senior leaders often pay management consultants a substantial amount of money to collect. Consultants are handicapped by knowing little about the organization. Their intervention often undermines commitment. The opposite is true when management creates a means for employees to have a voice. A senior team member spoke about an employee task force's contribution as follows: "The work that the employee task force did was extremely impressive. They operated much like a professional consulting firm, except unlike consultants they were a part of the organization and knew it inside and out. I think they worked so well together because they believed in what they were doing."[17]

Governance systems enable leaders to *integrate the interests of multiple stakeholders* with different identities and interests. They mobilize open conversations about organizational performance issues that matter to the parties. They make stakeholders' goals and interests transparent. Leaders help employees understand the expectations of financial stakeholders to whom they are accountable; employees help management understand their interests and the everyday needs of customers. When multiple stakeholders can converse constructively about their seemingly divergent expectations, leaders are able to create solutions that meet the interests of all parties even when tensions have been high. A "cold war" between two key managers and their functional departments in one business unit we studied was resolved when the senior team heard about its effects on commitment and performance. This happened because rich feedback about the effects of the conflict reframed the issues for these managers. It was no longer about what each one thought was best; now it was about what was best for the business.

Governance and learning systems can ensure *continuous improvements in the quality of management and leadership*, as I contend in the introduction to this chapter. A CEO or business unit manager whose pattern of management was successful at one stage of the organization's life may no longer fit the next stage in the organization's development.[18] Executives are naturally reluctant to expose their own weaknesses, even though doing so will enable them to discover problems well before they threaten the business and their careers. Indeed, the history of business failures, as I've previously stated, teaches us that blindness fed by arrogance and denial is very often the root cause of failure.[19]

If senior managers at higher levels ask general managers of subunits to lead a learning process and then share the findings, the management quality in each of the reporting subunits becomes discussable. This is essentially what Merck's Grey Warner did with each of his ten country managers. Indeed, he framed his request to country managers that they lead the Strategic Fitness Process as a professional development opportunity. Transparency made it possible from him to become a coach. A valid agenda for organizational and leadership change was mutually developed.

Without such a transparent learning process, management will lack knowledge about the most important qualities of leadership—the will and skill of the manager to learn and grow. Time and money will be lost before needed change occurs. Of course all this depends on a trust-based collaborative learning relationship in which higher levels adopt a coaching stance rather than a punitive one. Multi-unit managers like Grey Warner are more likely to develop that trust-based relationship if they themselves are open to learning from the very managers whom they are asking to learn and change.

Empirical Support for Voice and Participation

At the heart of a learning and governance process such as the one employed by Merck Latin America is the assumption that giving employees a voice and enabling their participation contribute to effectiveness. Most of us intuitively believe that. These conclusions are not just a matter of opinion, however. Many studies, too many to cite here, have proven that participation improves quality of decisions, performance, employee satisfaction, and commitment, as well as cohesion and community.[20] Here I want to illustrate how this research and our own studies relate to the type of learning and governance process I propose as an essential lever.

True participation in learning and governance proposed in this chapter involves conflict. Considerable evidence exists that when corporations operate in uncertain and dynamic environments, where rapid processing of divergent information is essential for success, organizations that foster constructive conflict perform better than those that do not.[21] An important precondition is the degree to which the leader believes and accepts constructive conflict, and has the capability to deal with it. I find that this is not the case with many general managers. My own studies suggest that even exceptional CEOs and general managers, who are naturally open, find a structured learning and governance process—like that employed in Merck's Latin American region—helpful in their quest to build an HCHP organization.

Another important precondition for productive conflict is a work climate of psychological and career safety. Psychological safety, the freedom to voice concerns, make mistakes, and suggest change, has been proven to have a direct bearing on team efficacy. My colleague Amy Edmondson has demonstrated, for example, that hospital teams where members feel psychologically safe enough to admit and identify errors ultimately have higher performance levels and fewer errors than teams where team behavior is ruled by fear. Psychologically safe climates have also been shown to be associated with firm-level performance.[22] Learning and governance processes must therefore ensure safety.

Participation in decisions has been shown to contribute to perceptions that leaders and their decisions are *just and fair*. Academics call this procedural justice. They find that when management is open about future plans, invites reactions, and takes these into account when making decisions, the results are positive, even when that decision has negative effects, such as layoffs. Joel Brockner, prominent researcher in this field, reports that "study after study shows that employees' productivity and morale depend on both the fairness of their outcomes (what happened) and the fairness of the decision-making processes accompanying those outcomes (how things happened)."[23] Giving people a voice is also the most cost-effective intervention that management can make to improve commitment. Increasing employee perceptions of fairness is far cheaper, Brockner argues, than increasing wages, bonuses, and other costly benefits. One of the purposes of learning and governance systems is to ensure procedural justice and fairness in the process of organization adaptation.

Victor Vroom and his colleagues have helped us understand the conditions under which voice and participation are appropriate, and when employee participation can improve quality of decisions and commitment. These conditions are:[24]

1. The quality of the decision matters.
2. Leaders do not have the requisite knowledge to make such a high-quality decision.
3. The problem to be solved is unstructured, requiring reciprocal interaction among people with different information and perspectives.
4. Commitment to the decision by employees is important because they must implement it.
5. There is sufficient time to involve others.
6. People share the organizational goals to be attained in solving the problem.
7. Management desires to develop employees.

Conditions 1 through 4 and 7 are true of most corporations that aspire to HCHP in a competitive environment. Leaders who aspire to transform an underperforming organization may not start with condition 6, shared goals. But unless they engage managers and front-line workers they will never be able to develop shared goals or be able to assess their managers' readiness to become committed to the larger purpose of the enterprise. Condition 5, sufficient time, is invariably in short supply in most organizations where we have worked. Urgent problems too often drive out work on important long-range issues such as building an effective HCHP system.

Our findings are that a disciplined learning and governance system like SFP provides a "container" that enables senior teams to orchestrate a participative organizational learning process that otherwise would not occur due to fears that conflict will erupt and not be constructively resolved. Our evaluation is that people involved in the learning and governance process emerge with shared goals. Managers become less parochial and more committed to mission and purpose.

Vroom and his colleagues note that participation is appropriate when management desires to develop people. We find that participation in the Strategic Fitness Process has that effect. For example, a task force member in one company reported that participating in SFP "was the most developmental experience he had in his fifteen years in the company."[25] Managers saw participation with the senior team in solving business and organizational problems as a valued opportunity to make a difference, and as way to learn how the business and various parts of the organization worked in concert to achieve performance goals. Senior management in this organization supported their view. They believed that the experience of some fifty managers on SFP task forces over a six-year period contributed significantly to the development of their managers.

Validation for giving people a voice in business and organizational matters comes from the practices of HCHP companies. Though they vary in formality and scope, companies such as Johnson & Johnson, Southwest Airlines, and Hewlett-Packard all have employed a variety of methods designed to give people a voice in the affairs of the business. Southwest Airlines has its culture committee, and Johnson and Johnson asks its people to participate in honest discussions about their "code of conduct" that the company founders developed. Is it being applied? Does it need alteration to make it relevant to new realities? For many years Hewlett-Packard's senior executives brought in groups of employees to meet with them, without their supervisors. They were asked to voice their concerns and ideas for change. Consequently, HP's employees were far more committed than those of other comparable companies, employee attitude surveys revealed. This process was an invention of cofounder Bill Hewlett, who saw HP's means for giving employees voice as essential. He wrote:

> The people at the top of an organization may have the best of intentions in the world. . . . But there are a lot of layers between the top and bottom and, in transmitting them from layer to layer, sometimes ideas inadvertently become distorted.

It always amazes me at our communication lunches to find out how much concepts had changed in the transmission process. Feedback such as this is necessary if you wish to determine what is really happening in the organization.[26]

Can managers below the top provide value if asked to participate in organization design decisions, normally the prerogative of senior management? Consistent with our findings regarding the value of the Strategic Fitness Process as a learning and governance process, Susan Mohrman and Tom Cummings found that involving middle managers in reorganizing the business and in ongoing evaluation of the new organization's efficacy resulted in organizational solutions that had fewer unintended consequences and garnered more commitment.[27] General Electric's Work-Out, which gave employees a voice in improving organizational effectiveness and required managers to act on this feedback on the spot, played an important role in the company's transformation.[28] Our own study of twelve organizations that implemented SFP showed that when leaders fully embraced this governance and learning system, the "silent killers" discussed in chapter 5 turned into positive management capabilities.[29]

Do learning and governance systems apply only at the management level or can they be applied in operating units? The answer is yes. Asda's successful transformation (chapter 11) was enabled by customer and employee listening groups in every one of the company's two hundred stores. A restaurant chain, in which turnover of front-line employees was very high, successfully employed a downsized version of our Strategic Fitness Process in a number of its restaurants, forming task forces from part-time workers, many between eighteen and twenty-two years old. Significant improvement in employee attitudes and operating measures occurred. After just one quarter, improvements such as the following were noted in one restaurant:[30]

- "Managers develop and support associates through constructive feedback and coaching." (from 34 to 66 percent)
- "I am valued and recognized for my contributions." (from 34 to 66 percent)
- Associates support and maintain the financial health of our store." (from 29 to 53 percent)
- "I have trust in management." (from 64 to 81 percent)
- "My job allows me to use my personal initiative and judgment." (from 54 to 66 percent)

Performance in this restaurant improved on a variety of operating measures, including turnover (32 percent improvement), guest satisfaction (8 percent improvement), and labor cost (1.3 percent improvement). The restaurant was able to operate with fewer managers as employees became more committed and took more responsibility. What's more, the improvements were sustained over time.

Challenges That Learning and Governance Systems Must Overcome

If governance and learning systems have so much promise, why have they not been widely adopted? CEOs have concerns. Some of these are articulated openly; others are rooted in deeply held assumptions and beliefs of which leaders may not be aware. Consider the following:

Organizations Are Prone to Defensive Routines[31]

Leaders are human and do not want problems in their organization exposed. Rather than taking the risk involved in an open-ended learning process like SFP or GE's Work-Out, they prefer to limit inquiry to narrowly defined problems. And they prefer to keep what they learn from becoming known to too many people. This approach makes it highly unlikely that hidden barriers having to do with their own efficacy as leaders will be exposed or acted on.

Cost

The cost, *measured in time and money*, can be a source of concern. "We already have too many initiatives and our employees are overloaded," or "Our best people are too busy to take part in this process" are typical refrains we have heard from senior management. Although it is true that learning processes take time, they do not cost a lot of money, and they deliver huge value, especially if they are focused on strategy and performance rather than employee relations issues. Recall from our earlier discussion that Ludwig, BD's CEO, felt that the SFP learning and governance process saved him twenty-four months and handled critical strategic issues.

Threat

Senior executives may see learning and governance systems as *threats to formal management authority*, though the exceptional HCHP leaders are not so threatened, at least in my experience. To some leaders, allowing employees to participate is viewed as an abdication of authority. This concern is not justified in our experience and flies in the face of the assumptions underlying governance systems. On the contrary, by making themselves vulnerable and following through with solutions, leaders with whom I have worked enhanced perceptions that the organization was being led well. Consequently their power and influence actually increased.

Fear of Politics

Managers fear that *the process will be politicized;* that individual managers will raise concerns that reflect their own political agendas. Managers sometimes raise concerns that the task forces, whom they have commissioned to interview one hundred others, will slant findings to suit their own agenda. Quite the contrary actually occurs. Our findings show that, when designed effectively, senior teams and the task forces they have commissioned shed their parochial views and became committed to the "once-in-a-lifetime opportunity" to help the organization confront long-standing issues. Consider a manager in R&D, assigned to a Strategic Fitness task force, who, after interviewing employees in marketing, concluded that, "I thought they [marketing] were the problem but now that I have completed my interviews I think my own R&D function is probably the problem."[32] A task force member at Whitbread PLC noted that "We felt we had been handed an important responsibility and we wanted to do it justice. The process and the group seemed to be very good at encapsulating the essence of what we learned rather than getting caught up in any individual's hobbyhorse."[33]

Lack of Skills

Conflict can only be constructive if leaders and organizational members have the skills to hold an *open learning-oriented dialogue.* These skills require individuals and groups to "suspend their assumptions and communicate them freely."[34] If defensiveness, particularly on the part of management, enters the dialogue, it shuts down openness to learning. Learning and governance processes must prevent these breakdowns in honest conversations if they are to be effective and credible. My research into the effectiveness of the SFP process finds that by creating simple rules and a structure for the dialogue between leadership teams and lower levels, nondefensive dialogue will occur consistently.

◆ ◆ ◆

Fears, concerns, and barriers associated with learning and governance processes will cause managers to avoid them altogether or to try to design them in ways that limit learning. For these reasons, leaders of HCHP companies are well advised to institutionalize a rigorous process that overcomes these challenges.

Governance and Learning Design Guidelines

Below are design guidelines that emerged from Russell Eisenstat's and my research in dozens of organizations that have adopted SFP.[35] They emerged from encounters with many of the challenges discussed above. These are high-level guidelines and must be translated by each organization into specific operating steps of the kind reflected for the Strategic Fitness Process depicted in Figure 7.1. They provide managers and internal human resource professionals a road map for implementation. Availability of a detailed manual we developed for SFP enabled internal staff, who may not have had extensive consulting experience or skills, to implement SFP.[36]

Senior Team Should Be at the Center of the Process

Too often senior management delegates the process of change to staff groups or lower levels. They collect the data, analyze it, and make recommendations. This distances the senior team from the change and causes lower levels to doubt senior management's commitment. Senior teams should not only articulate a compelling direction but be directly involved in listening to what employees have to say and in redesigning policies and practices, at least at a high level. This conveys to the organization that they are serious in their intention to lead, learn, and change. Support for change, our research finds, is strongest when people see the senior team owning up to problems and working hard to overcome them.[37]

Focus Inquiry on Strategy and Performance

Many companies give people a voice about, for example, employee relations matters, their satisfaction with pay, with their sense of engagement, or with their supervisor. This kind of input does not provide rich information about why such problems exist, nor about their relationship to managerial and organizational effectiveness. Performance and organizational effectiveness should be made the focus of the inquiry. We have learned that this can be done by presenting interviewees with a brief two-page strategic direction statement developed by the senior team. Because lower-level managers understand that performance is the game, this focus prevents politicization of the process. Our experience is that a learning process thus focused energizes those involved and recommits them to the organization and its goals. It is an important first step in the development of a partnership between senior teams and the larger organization.

Data Must Be Valid and Lead to a Comprehensive Diagnosis

Senior teams cannot learn the *whole truth* by conducting an inquiry themselves, though they should always motivate it. We have found that a task force appointed by the senior team, and properly trained to conduct confidential interviews, learns the whole truth. Each of Merck's Latin American country organizations, managed by Merck's majority partners for years, had been autocratically managed and consequently had punitive cultures. Yet task forces were able to learn the whole truth, deliver that message to their managing director, even when in some cases he had created the very culture that needed change. Because feedback comes from a task force that senior teams themselves have appointed, they accept the feedback. To reject it, senior teams understand, would irreparably damage their legitimacy and credibility.

Broad questions should be employed in interviews. Does the strategy make sense? What are our strengths and barriers to implementing our strategy? (Strengths should always be part of the inquiry.) This enables managers or front-line employees to define issues based on their own experience and in their own language, in contrast to more superficial information gained when a predefined framework and closed-ended survey are the means of inquiry. Broad, open-ended questions and the resulting rich information paint a picture of the organization's culture, enable a rich diagnosis, and discourage senior teams from prematurely focusing on narrow "technical issues," such as compensation or specific management practices, before they understand the systemic nature of the issues.[38]

The Dialogue Must Be Honest Yet Safe

Unless conversations between the senior team and lower levels are honest, the senior team will not learn the whole truth. If the senior team does not have valid data to address problems, employees become cynical and lose trust in senior management. Without trust, effective problem solving is not possible and commitment cannot be built.[39]

To have an honest dialogue, managers providing the feedback must be assured psychological and career safety. Neither those delivering the feedback nor the senior team that is receiving it can feel that an open dialogue threatens their dignity or careers. "Don't shoot the messenger" is often the way task forces begin their conversations to senior teams, indicating their anxiety and the need to assure safety.

In our experience, safety can be provided through several design features. Interviewees must be assured that their names will not be associated with the issues they raise. Ground rules for communication control the dialogue between the task force and the senior team. They prevent senior management from questioning the validity of feedback, and employees from making unconstructive responses. That validity is assured by prescribed steps in the analysis of the data and development of themes. Both senior management's dignity and employee safety are preserved if lower levels deliver feedback in a non-evaluative manner. This means the feedback is about both strengths and weaknesses, is descriptive, and illustrates consequences of problems for commitment and performance.

We have learned that it's best if the senior team selects task force members with high performance and potential whom they see as objective and credible to collect data. These are employees whom they will believe. Employees' sense of safety derives from knowing that they are reporters and from speaking as a group rather than as individuals. One way we have found for doing this is to use the "fishbowl" method for feedback (see Figure 7.3). The task force sits at a table talking about their findings theme by theme; the senior team has been instructed to ask only questions for clarification at the end of each theme.

With the aid of this structure and process for the conversation, we have never seen a task force fail to deliver the unvarnished truth. Nor have we have found senior teams challenging task forces composed of their best employees. Quite the contrary, senior teams come away impressed by the comprehensive and professional character of the feedback. "As good as or better than consultants," said one general manager.

FIGURE 7.3. THE "FISHBOWL"—A STRUCTURE THAT ENABLES TRUTH TO SPEAK TO POWER.

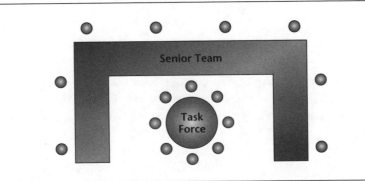

The Conversation Must Iterate Between Advocacy and Inquiry

Both advocacy and inquiry are essential if the parties to a dialogue are to learn.[40] Advocacy, the *assertion of one's viewpoint*, is typically overused, causing others, particularly lower-level people, to shut down. Inquiry, the willingness to *open oneself to questions and challenge others*, is underused, particularly in hierarchical organizations. Because most managers do not generally employ inquiry nor are skilled in enacting it in real time, the learning and governance system should be designed to ensure iteration between these two modes of communication. Senior teams begin with advocacy about the mission, strategy, and values for the organization, followed by an inquiry phase into perceptions held by lower-level people about the quality of the direction as well as barriers to achieving it. After this phase comes the senior team's advocacy of changes that they believe are responsive to the feedback, and this is followed in turn by the senior team's inquiry into the quality of their plans for change (see Figure 7.2). This iterative process must continue over time for the organization to learn and be adaptive.

My experience with the Strategic Fitness Process, which divides each of these iterations into a separate and distinctive phase, is that an honest conversation can develop without any previous training in dialogue skills, though clearly such training would help in the long run. People in the organization emerge from SFP feeling that the truth has been represented to top management, just as senior management teams accept the data as the truth and act on it.

Senior Team Is Accountable to Lower Levels

A community of purpose, one in which employees and management have a shared purpose, can only be built if people feel they are able to make a difference. For this reason, senior teams must report to lower levels what they heard, what they plan to change, and why. By making themselves accountable to lower levels, senior teams legitimize the demands that they as leaders will have to place on the lower-level people in order to implement change. In this way commitment and community are built. Without this, employees will come to see the process of engagement as a waste of time, or even worse—a sham. In our experience senior teams do not have to respond to every problem to retain their legitimacy so long as they explain why. Accountability to lower levels is what makes the process a governance system.

The Conversation Must Be Collective and Public

By *collective* I mean that key people responsible for major value-creating activities in the target organizational unit (corporate, business, or operating unit) are engaged directly, as interviewees, or indirectly, by being informed about feedback given to top management and action taken. By *public* I mean that everyone in the organization understands that senior management is engaged in a learning process. Senior teams will communicate what they heard, what they plan to change, and invite feedback about the quality of their plans. The collective and public nature of the process further reinforces the sense of partnership and community.

The Conversation Must Be Structured

The most important problems facing a business are those that give rise to emotions. We have found that feedback by task forces often conveys the emotions and frustrations of lower levels and arouses understandable emotions in senior teams. A "container" is needed to guide people through this emotionally charged conversation. As noted earlier, it is too easy for managers to make mistakes that send unintended signals. It is too easy for lower-level groups to err in the data collection and feedback process by smoothing over or avoiding feedback about difficult issues. It is also too easy for honest conversations to become destructive rather than constructive and productive.

A well-thought-out structure and process for learning and governance that adheres to these guidelines is a way to reduce the chances that top management's position of power and their human desire to avoid disconfirming information will cause the firm to fall prey to the "Icarus Paradox," the decline that seems to follow success.[41] It is an important mechanism for enabling learning and change and ensuing *sustained* commitment and performance.

Conditions for Governance and Learning Systems

For governance and learning systems to become a regular means for improving the quality of organization and management in all major subunits of a large company, several interrelated conditions must exist or be developed.

Top management must believe in employee participation and partnership. They must model this by adopting a learning and governance process to help them lead the corporation's journey to HCHP. And they must hold managers in every part of the organization accountable for engaging their business or operating unit in learning. Managers who believe they have all the answers or who are overly egocentric are unlikely to embrace learning processes or have the ability to implement and sustain them over time. Those who will and can lead organizational learning are likely to be *egalitarian, open to feedback, and interested in developing a partnership with their employees*. These should therefore be the criteria for selecting and promoting leaders in HCHP organizations. These criteria must certainly be employed by the board of directors in selecting the CEO.

Learning and governance systems make transparent the behavior and effectiveness of leaders and their organizations. Senior management can utilize these systems to evaluate and develop leaders and their organizations if they do this carefully and in the right sequence. Because HCHP organizations seek to create sustained commitment and performance, learning and governance systems *should be employed first and foremost for leadership and organization development and not to identify and replace ineffective managers*. Leaders should only be replaced after the developmental process has failed. If senior management does not establish this principle clearly, they risk loss of trust. Lower levels will become more protective of their leaders and leaders will grow resistant to the learning system if they believe its purpose is evaluation rather than development.

Countries whose cultures legitimize inequality in power (power distance) or individualism are probably less likely to embrace learning and governance systems, because values of egalitarianism and partnership are embedded in the design of such systems. Nevertheless, our research and experience with SFP suggest that its successful adoption is much *more a function of the leader's will and skill than it is a function of national culture*. How else are we to explain Grey Warner's success in introducing the SFP in Latin America, a culture with high power distance; the successful application of General Electric's Work-Out in its varied country organizations; Becton Dickinson's success on applying the SFP in countries as diverse as Mexico and Japan; or Alan Parker's successful implementation of SFP in Whitbread PLC, a U.K. firm? Each cultural setting will present different challenges and will require some adjustments in the process, but our research suggests that only minor adaptations are necessary.

Why Institutionalize Learning and Governance?

Learning and governance processes are to management quality as quality improvement processes are to product quality (see Figure 7.4). They can help management to learn how their stewardship is affecting performance alignment, psychological alignment, and capacity for learning and change. This learning process should ideally exist at multiple levels—corporate, business unit, and major operating units. It will encourage greater innovation and diversity in management practice, thus allowing the best leaders to develop leading units that

FIGURE 7.4. GOVERNANCE AND LEARNING AS CONTINUOUS IMPROVEMENT IN QUALITY OF MANAGEMENT AT MULTIPLE LEVELS.

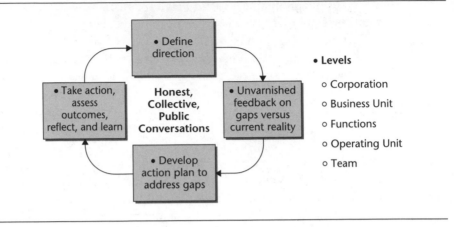

model best practices for lagging units. This means senior management has to see differences as an opportunity to promote cross-unit learning. This is superior to using rules and procedures to enforce standardized practices, something I see a lot of corporations doing. Rules reduce variability but limit innovation and progress.

Although HCHP organizations possess a greater capacity to learn and change than average firms, it is my observation that in many HCHP firms the capacity to learn and change is the weakest of the three pillars. While HCHP firms typically have multiple mechanisms for employee participation and voice, these often do not meet the criteria for the honest, collective, and public conversation discussed in this chapter. Consider Hewlett-Packard's fall from grace in the late 1990s, after having managed to stay on the HCHP path for nearly six decades. The company had institutionalized management by walking around (MBWA) and employee surveys. Neither was powerful enough, however, to help senior management and the board to learn the source of underperformance—the silent killers that existed at the corporate level—and make appropriate changes.[42]

Most HCHP firms institutionalize quality assessment and improvement processes for almost every aspect of the firm's operations—manufacturing, customer service, and product development, for example. But with the exception of Jack Welch, who insisted that all GE leaders apply Work-Out, most HCHP firms have not institutionalized a learning and governance process. Its importance, compared to other quality-improvement processes, is evident in what Jody Edwards, the HR manager of the Santa Rosa Systems Division of Hewlett-Packard (SRSD), said about the learning and governance process institutionalized by her business unit: "In most engineering companies like HP, if you ask people what is the most important process, they will say, New Product Innovation/Introduction. For us, that is not true. For us, everyone would say the Organizational Alignment Process (SRSD's learning and governance process)."[43]

Unless CEOs insist that all key business and operating unit leaders adopt a learning and governance process, they cannot be certain that lower-level leaders are learning continuously about their leadership and organization. It is simply too easy for managers and their organizations to stray from the HCHP path.

Though it is not yet a practice in most HCHP firms, exceptional CEOs whom we have worked with and studied have applied some form of organizational learning process and encouraged lower levels to do the same. It explains in part Becton Dickinson's successful transformation across three CEO eras. In the first several years of its journey to HCHP, approximately thirty-five subunits (the corporate center, business units, country organizations, and some key functions) utilized the SFP to learn about their effectiveness, and make changes that fit their circumstances and stages of development. More importantly, it set a new standard for how leaders should engage their employees in their efforts to improve alignment and performance. When Ed Ludwig became CEO in 2000, one of his first acts was to apply the principles for learning and governance that he had learned as a division manager to cope with serious performance problems. In 2006 he again employed the same process to assess progress and focus change on a whole new and much more subtle set of corporate issues.

Boards of directors are an essential ingredient in institutionalizing an organizational and leadership learning process. They have an interest in transparency; asking the CEO to adopt a learning and governance process could help fulfill their responsibilities and prevent corporate scandals and failures. Unless they do, they will not only fail to enable the development of an HCHP company, but they will also fail to avert the type of catastrophic failures we have seen in financial service institutions during 2008. Unfortunately, as the economic meltdown of 2008 illustrates, most boards of directors do not want to know what is really going on inside the organization. This may explain why they don't learn about serious ethical and effectiveness problems until there is a crisis.

An example of opportunities for learning lost by a board of directors was illustrated to me some years ago. I was a consultant to a CEO who employed SFP to learn about and eliminate numerous problems in his company. Though the decision to implement SFP was the CEO's alone, he wanted me to present findings and plans for change to the board after the process was completed. His motivation was to show the board that he was making changes. The process did indeed surface effectiveness and commitment problems, and as expected, developed trust and produced an action plan for change; nevertheless, the CEO cancelled our presentation that he had planned, fearing to expose the truth about the conditions in his organization to the board, despite the positive climate and a promising action plan he had put in place.

Nine months later I received a call from a board member. What had been the outcome of the SFP? Key managers had complained to board members that there was no follow-up to what they considered a positive learning and change process. The board wanted me to tell them what I had learned about the organization and what changes had been planned, something I could not do because the board had no hand in commissioning SFP, nor had they contracted with the CEO for a review of findings and his plans for change. Consider the positive learning and change outcomes the board and the CEO could have had if both parties had agreed in advance to initiate this governance and learning process and to discuss results afterwards.

Exceptional HCHP CEOs we have been studying develop such trust-based learning relationships with their boards.[44] They engage their boards in honest and open discussions about strategy and organizational issues. They possess the confidence and courage to learn despite the risks because they are concerned about the greater good.

Summary

Corporations can achieve continuous improvements in the quality of management and leadership if they institutionalize honest, collective, and public conversations. CEOs aspiring to build an HCHP organization can employ this leadership and learning platform to activate and manage change in each of the three design levers discussed in the next three chapters.

Although there are various means to give employees voice and foster organizational learning and community, most mechanisms employed by corporations fall far short of the design criteria discussed in this chapter. Only those systems that are designed to encourage honest, collective, and public conversations will enable real and fundamental change. These conversations create trust, commitment, and community. Enabling truth to speak to power allows senior management to tap vital knowledge that employees have about firm effectiveness and commitment. And when senior teams are at the center of the process, as opposed to delegating it to staff functions or consultants, they learn the truth about how their assumptions and behavior have shaped the system they are leading.

If each major subunit of the larger corporation engages its employees in a learning process, each comes to understand its own culture and pattern of management and embarks on a continuous process of improvement. This is far superior to top-down initiatives that ignore local circumstance and circumvent local leaders. Top-down programs are in fact the reason so many corporations lack the leaders they need. Given ready-made solutions and marching orders, leadership teams do not learn to think for themselves or lead.

Top management cannot encourage or require that senior leadership teams engage in honest conversations without submitting themselves and the corporate center to such a conversation. It is only by enabling truth to speak to power that they avoid the potential pitfall of power—arrogance and blindness.

Senior teams who wish to evaluate whether truth can speak to power in their organizations will want to discuss the following questions:

1. Do we want to hear the unvarnished truth about the effectiveness of our leadership and organization?
2. Are we regularly challenged by lower-level managers about important business and organizational issues?
3. Do we actively solicit the view and opinions of lower-level managers about potential barriers to our effectiveness?
4. Are we getting adequate feedback about our leadership of this organization?
5. Do the formal methods that we now employ to solicit feedback from our employees enable us to learn the unvarnished truth about our organization and leadership?
6. Are we prepared to adopt and institutionalize a learning and governance system? If not, why not?

PART FOUR

ORGANIZATION DESIGN CHANGE LEVERS

CHAPTER EIGHT

MANAGE ORGANIZATIONAL PERFORMANCE STRATEGICALLY

Change Lever 3: The Strategic Performance Management System

HCHP organizations could not deliver sustained exceptional results if they did not develop a high-performance culture and have a well-designed strategic performance management system (SPMS). Unfortunately, in most companies strategic performance management is a ritual—a series of meetings and motions that people go through—not the disciplined, demanding, and systemic learning process found in HCHP companies.

To achieve sustained high-performance results, exceptional leaders like General Electric's Chris Richmond developed *a disciplined process* for formulating strategy, setting ambitious goals, aligning the organization and its people, evaluating performance rigorously, and learning from experience through honest conversations. They then adapt strategy and goals to ever-changing realities. This is not an abstract planning process. Most effective strategies emerge from capabilities already inside the firm and they extend those capabilities as the firm reaches into new market segments, new product lines, and new geographies.

An effective strategic performance management process involves matching capabilities with external opportunities and developing high-priority strategic initiatives that will extend those capabilities.[1] A truly disciplined strategic performance management process then enables alignment of behavior and capabilities with top management priorities. It involves top-down direction and communication about priorities and bottom-up participation in execution. And it requires honest communication from lower levels about problems with the strategy or organizational barriers to its implementation. This is the very capability that our research has shown is weakened in underperforming organizations by the silent killers discussed in chapter 5.

General Electric's well-known success is a function of a performance culture that is devoid of silent killers and proud of its disciplined strategic organizational performance management system. Consider the view expressed below by Kevin Sharer, a former senior executive at GE, now CEO of Amgen:[2]

> [GE] has set a standard in candor—that is, dealing with reality and rigor in communicating around the company. Everybody has a real chance to know exactly where they are. There is no puffery. That is buttressed by rigorous, fact based, honest assessment of the business situation. There isn't an ounce of denial in the place.

> In addition, there is real pride in being part of GE—a common sense of purpose. It's well known but still worth noting that the operations and financial promises are not "we'll give it our best shot" kind of promises. They're really sacrosanct. Finally, GE is aggressive. They think big and they take risks.

Why Companies Fail to Manage Performance Strategically

The number one reason many firms fail to achieve sustained high performance is that management systems and their underlying cultures are based on an increasingly outdated view of performance; namely, that performance is best measured by short-term financial results. As Figure 8.1 illustrates, performance management in companies that harbor this perspective focus on the budget. Performance reviews are largely a discussion of past financial performance, and little attention is paid to other stakeholders and objectives. Ironically, failing firms often give incentives for achieving financial targets only. Although management may believe that this is the path to sustained high performance, the opposite is true. The shocking meltdown on Wall Street of investment banks in 2008 is the most recent example of this error. An obsession with profits went unchecked by objectives and measures regarding customers and employees, not to speak of the long-term interests of investors. Nor could there have been the kind of strategic conversation that a robust SPMS would foster.

Historically, focusing only on financial performance measurements made sense. As Robert Kaplan and David Norton conclude, "In the early decades of

FIGURE 8.1. SHORT-TERM FINANCIALLY ORIENTED STRATEGIC ORGANIZATIONAL PERFORMANCE SYSTEM.

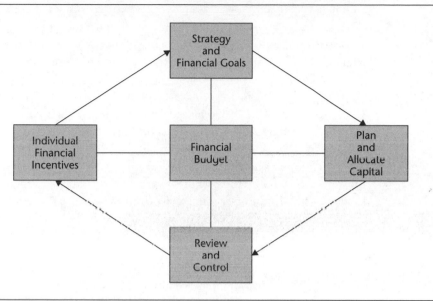

Source: Adapted from Kaplan & Norton, 2001.

the twentieth century, DuPont Corporation and General Motors Corporation developed the return-on-investment metric as an integrating device for the multidivisional firm. By the mid-twentieth century, multidivisional firms were using the budget as the centerpiece of their management systems. In the 1990s companies had extended this financial framework to embrace financial metrics that correlate better with shareholder value, leading to economic value added (EVA) and value-based management metrics."[3]

Kaplan and Norton go on to explain: "In the 1980s and 1990s many companies added quality improvements and customer satisfaction to their strategic goals. Still others adopted human resource objectives such as employee satisfaction, motivation and skills to their focus. While each of these goals plays an important role in sustained organizational performance, the goals remained un-integrated and meeting the financial targets remained the primary measure of success."[4] The operative word from Kaplan and Norton is "un-integrated." HCHP firms learn to integrate financial targets with other, equally compelling goals.

Below are the three major reasons why a performance strategy based solely on meeting financial goals is bound to fail.

1. *Financial goals dominate management's attention.* As a result, even key people often do not have a clear idea of the strategy or the values that animate the strategy. When we showed employees a written statement of the strategic direction developed by the top team, we found that employees were often surprised by its content or questioned whether the direction makes sense.[5] Managers often attribute this to poor communication when in fact this problem has deeper roots.

2. *Financial goals fail to inspire commitment.* People want to attach meaning to their goals. They want to feel that they are making a difference not only for shareholders, but also for valued customers, fellow employees, community, and society. Financial goals do not create meaning. Employees coming out of a presentation in one low-performing company we studied talked about how unexciting they found the goal of 18 percent return on investment articulated by the CEO.[6] Employees come away from these types of presentations convinced that management cares only about the shareholder. Just as important, they were left without an inspiring goal or higher purpose.

3. *Financial goals result in underperformance.* The politics of power and pay can cause managers to set unambitious financial goals to ensure their bonuses and promotions. "Lowballing," as this process is called, was reported by a surprisingly large percentage of executives attending Harvard Business School's Advanced Management Program.[7] Alternatively, an exclusive focus on financial goals and incentives can result in setting unrealistic and unachievable goals and an unsustainable business model. Both threaten sustained high performance.

Symptoms of Failure

In chapter 2 I suggested that sustained HCHP depends on achieving performance alignment, psychological alignment, and the capacity to learn and change. An inadequate strategic performance management system undermines these outcomes.

Poor Performance Alignment

A Bain Consulting study discovered that seven out of eight companies in a global sample of 1,854 large corporations failed to achieve profitable growth, though more than 90 percent had detailed strategic plans intended to achieve their high-performance targets.[8] *Senior management had not developed a good strategy or translated the strategy into operational and actionable terms.* Consider the following symptoms of poor performance alignment:

Pendulum Swings in Strategic Direction. *Senior teams who focus only on financial performance are less likely to have a deep commitment to a focused strategic direction.*[9] That focus takes their attention away from the firm's core capabilities, defining a mission consistent with the firm's capabilities and their values, or developing a focused strategy aligned with their animating beliefs. Without these anchors, senior teams are *too easily swayed to change course by emerging threats and opportunities.*

Conflicting Priorities and Poor Coordination. Performance management systems *driven by financial budgets* result in each activity along the value-creation chain defining priorities in terms of its own unit's task as opposed to the firm's strategic tasks. Competition demands speed and integrated solutions responsive to customer needs. Yet in organization after organization, we found that key people perceived that other departments do not share their priorities.

Senior teams do not translate an overarching conception into a prioritized list of *strategic tasks.* Nor do they ask each function, business, or geographic unit to define their goals in the context of those strategic tasks. Consequently, different parts of the organization allocate varying amounts of financial and human resources to strategic tasks that require interdependent planning and execution. A second-order effect is that cynicism and distrust in turn erode teamwork, and psychological alignment and commitment.

Weak Execution. Financially driven firms are less likely to invest time and effort in *linking strategy to implementation.*[10] They are also more likely to be managed in a top-down manner. Consequently, they fall prey to the following errors.

- *Strategic priorities are not linked with budget and plans.* Some 60 percent of companies do not link strategic priorities to budgets, thus ensuring that key initiatives are not allocated the financial and human resources required. Two-thirds of functional departments such as HR and IT do not link their plans to the organization's strategy.[11]
- The planning process does not discipline managers to *work backwards from the desired end result* and due date to the many intermediate milestones that must be achieved on the path to final completion. It fails to require managers to define capabilities and resources required (time, people, and money) and to confront shortfalls. Moreover, plans do not examine how the multiple goals and

supporting work streams conflict with each other. Nick Craig, who has worked with many companies to help them improve their execution through "back planning"—a process of working backwards from goals to what is needed to achieve them—finds that the path to successful implementation of strategic initiatives is often unclear. Departments have not integrated their plans, the sequences of required tasks have not been clearly specified, and resources—people, time, and money—have not been clearly defined.[12]

- Commitment to implement a strategic initiative is undermined when *initiatives are "pushed" from the top by corporate staff* as opposed to "pulled" by leaders of business and operating units.[13] Unless the leadership team of each of these value-creating subunits sees the value of the corporate initiative, they will comply with the corporate initiative but will not ensure commitment by their people.

- *Employees at middle to lower levels have not been made into strategic actors.* They do not understand the strategy, how their role and goals are linked to the strategy, and have not been empowered to make decisions. Consequently, it should not be a surprise that they do not behave in a way that supports the strategy.

Poor Psychological Alignment

The inability of financially driven bureaucratic organizations to execute their strategy and adapt to changing circumstances is often a function of low commitment on the part of managers and front-line employees.

- *Emotionally compelling mission or values have not been developed* by senior management. Consequently, people and departments are not motivated to cooperate.

- *Top management articulates goals but fails to establish their legitimacy* in the eyes of down-the-line managers. When managers feel pushed to attain goals they do not believe in, they find ways to explain away failures by pointing to circumstances beyond their control; for example, a bad economy, or other activities on the value-creation chain that did not live up to their commitments. Goals are modified or abandoned and a culture of blame erodes commitment and performance.

- *Managers come to believe that initiative is not recognized and rewarded.* Teresa Amabile has found that tight deadlines, a climate of fear and competition rather than collaboration, and motivation based on monetary incentives depress creativity, an outcome essential for sustained high performance.[14] The barriers to creativity, and I might add initiative, that she finds are predictable outcomes of a hierarchical and financially driven strategic performance management system. A bureaucratic performance management system also creates a culture in which mediocre performance is accepted rather than challenged. Facts give way to political considerations in discussions about the business. Relationships, and even worse, cronyism, become an important factor in promotions. Results and adherence to corporate values are not factored in.

- *Winning is not valued*. People are not committed to achieving ambitious goals and do not feel accountable for producing them. They do not strive to make the firm the best at what it does, nor do they strive to grow and develop themselves to be the best they can be.

Low Capacity for Learning and Change

Continuous changes in markets, technology, and the competitive landscape require continuous organizational learning and change.

- Research shows that most companies do not have a strategic management process that enables learning.[15] Most senior teams spend less than one hour per month discussing strategy, Kaplan and Norton report. Our research and that of others show that the conversations within the senior team or between the senior team and lower levels are often not honest or searching, and fail to close rapidly on an action plan. Organizations with these behaviors experience costly performance surprises. Managers are fired, making others afraid to speak up about performance problems, thus reinforcing a culture of nonlearning. The result is an unadaptive organization.
- Challenging the status quo is not rewarded. Individuals who bring fresh ideas that will shake up the direction of the business or the way things are done are not given more responsibility or promoted.

GE's Commercial Equipment Finance Business

Jack Welch appointed Chris Richmond in 1994 to head the Commercial Equipment Finance (CEF) business, the fourteenth largest business in GE.[16] With sales that year of $8 billion, CEF was larger than most Fortune 500 companies. Shortly after taking charge of CEF, Richmond was handed an envelope by Welch. Inside, he found a new demanding goal for his business—to grow profits 25 percent annually, a dramatic departure from its historic growth rate of 10–12 percent. Welch had decided that GE had the potential to become a growth stock; each of its financial services companies should double its net income over the next four years. Richmond recalled the distinctive way GE set targets and the effect it had on him and his management team:

> Communicating targets in GE is different from any other company. Welch developed this frame—GE has to grow this much—he didn't look at the capacity of his companies to set their growth target. He just announced a straightforward and easy to understand challenge.
>
> What all of us realized immediately was you couldn't waste any time talking about whether or not the target was right. There was no alternative. We had to focus, given the targets, on what would it take to get there. What must be in place to make this attainable? We began to focus on the drivers of success, rather than the constraints of the past.

When Richmond took charge, CEF was a long-standing successful business without a strong case for change. The company focused on leasing equipment that "could hurt you if it fell on you" (airplanes, for example), as Richmond was fond of saying. The common wisdom about the business was that it would not exceed its historical growth rates. It was not viewed as a glamorous business. CEF had knowledgeable, if not particularly creative personnel, many with long tenure, who were known to be good at execution. Yet between 1994 and 2000, the period of Richmond's tenure, CEF met Welch's demanding challenge (see Table 8.1). It moved from GE's fourteenth largest company to its eighth largest company. CEF's revenues grew from $8 billion to $40 billion, net income grew from $130 million to $455 million, its annual growth rate was between 22 and

TABLE 8.1. COMMERCIAL EQUIPMENT FINANCING: BEFORE AND AFTER.

	1994	2000
Served Assets	$8 billion	$42 billion
Net Income	$130 million	$455 million
Growth Rate	12–14% per year	20–24% per year
ROE	18%	20%
Geographic Scope	North America: United States, Canada, Mexico	14 countries in addition to North America
Relative Size Within GE	14th largest business	8th largest business (largest commercial business in GE Capital)

Source: Adapted from Chris Richmond.

24 percent, return on equity grew from 20 to 24 percent, and it evolved from a North American company to a global one, establishing a footprint in fourteen new countries. Even discounting for the growth in financial services in the 1990s, these are impressive results.

Strategic Performance Management Principles

The story of CEF is one of transforming a good business into a superior one, not a turnaround of a bad business into a good business. This distinction is important. Sustained high performance requires not a one-time turnaround, but continuous improvements to levels of performance often thought to be unattainable. How then did CEF manage to meet Welch's change? Richmond, like other leaders of HCHP companies, developed a high-performance culture and followed a set of principles for managing organizational performance strategically discussed below. By following these principles, Richmond's Commercial Equipment Finance business achieved remarkable growth in revenue, earnings, scale, and scope.

Develop a High Performance Culture

Embed Organization with a Desire to Win. Leaders must have the *desire to achieve extraordinary results* or they will be unable to demand high performance of executives below them. Early on in his tenure, Welch demanded that each business be number one or two within its product or market domain. He demonstrated this desire again when he asked Chris Richmond to achieve a 25 percent growth rate, double the historic growth rate of CEF. Richmond did the same with his own team. There is considerable evidence that ambitious and often risky goals, what Jim Collins and Gerry Porras call "big hairy audacious goals," are a characteristic of HCHP companies. Collins and Porras call them "visionary companies" in their seminal book *Built to Last*, "because they outperformed their peers by an extraordinary margin over a long period of time."[17] Gary Hamel and C. K. Prahalad argue that "the real function of a company's strategy is not to match its resources with its opportunities, as many executives assume, but rather to set goals which 'stretch' a company beyond what most managers believe is possible."[18] Setting "big hairy audacious goals" stretches managers in the organization to develop capabilities the company does not yet have. And capability building is important for enabling the organization to learn new things.

How much participation should leaders allow in setting goals? GE would not have achieved high-performance targets if Welch and Richmond had allowed a debate about the overarching goal to grow at 25 percent. GE executives would not, however, have achieved their high ambitions unless they could find a way to *legitimate* their goals.[19]

Solving this paradox—ambitious goals driven from the top and commitment of key managers to them—is one of the keys to creating a high-performance culture. This can only be done when management creates fact-based conversation about the reality of the competitive environment—the performance of best-in-class companies. Of course, if such discussions yield convincing new facts that raise questions about the validity of the goals, senior managers risk failure unless they reevaluate the goal. The balance between asserting a new, demanding objective and listening to concerns is a difficult one to achieve. Chris Richmond talked about the GE Way: "Goal setting was not a discussion, but it wasn't Neanderthal either. They [Welch and corporate executives] explained how they got the number—they didn't just make it up. It was based on what the stock value needed to be, what 'best-in-class' financial services companies were achieving and the huge potential of globalization."

Offering managers help and resources to reach ambitious goals is another way in which leaders can legitimate goals and ensure commitment. As Richmond observed: "You were not going to do it alone—we committed to give you [business heads] whatever resources you need to get there as long as you managed them well—so business reviews were not about beating you up—it was about both pushing and helping you—how you're thinking about the problems, how we were thinking about the problems." Many companies fail to grasp this principle. They make demands but offer no help or resources. If managers are fired when they fail, employees will question the legitimacy of the goal-setting process.

Imbuing high targets with meaning legitimizes goals and creates commitment. Another method is to articulate the value of the goals for employees—for example, the survival of the firm, long-term job security, or the value being created for customers, community, and society. Understanding the context in which Welch was articulating the goal of 25 percent growth made a difference to Chris Richmond. "At the time," Richmond observed, "Jack was under pressure to bust up GE, but wanted to prove the value of an integrated company."

What stops most leaders from building such a demanding organizational environment? Quite simply, it's easier *not* to be demanding. Demanding leaders have to be equally demanding of themselves. High expectations at the top lead to equally high expectations from below for help, resources, and management time to discuss and resolve new challenges created by high aspirations. Unless leaders are willing to discipline themselves and work as hard as their people, leaders cannot sustain such a system. That is why most don't try. Jack Welch and his key people, including Chris Richmond, made that commitment. Richmond understood each part of his business, traveled extensively to stay connected, confronted difficult issues, reviewed his businesses and its people continuously and rigorously, and met new threats and opportunities head on.

Create a Meritocracy Without Eroding Collaboration.
The desire to achieve high standards, not once but on an ongoing basis, requires that leaders create a collective perception that merit, not relationships or politics, is the basis for recognition and rewards. This is achieved in several ways. Richmond consistently reached deep down in his organization to promote younger high-performance managers into positions of responsibility that were considerably higher than anyone might have expected. In fact, one quarterly strategic performance review meeting a year was devoted to discussing these high potentials and how they could be employed to lead key strategic initiatives.

Managers who miss targets consistently or who do not live the firm's values must be replaced. Top management often fails to make these difficult decisions because in retrospect they are uncertain about the legitimacy of the goals they set or because they lack conviction about their values. This gives the wrong signal; namely, that missing goals or failing to live the values is acceptable, further undermining management's capacity to create a high-performance culture. Leaders of HCHP companies I have interviewed have typically concluded that they should have moved faster to replace underperforming managers. Interestingly, when these managers are removed, lower-level people often confide that they don't know what took senior management so long.

Jack Welch powerfully communicated the connection between values and merit at GE when, at a top management meeting, he publicly named five senior executives whom he had recently asked to leave the company because their management and leadership approach was not consistent with GE's values. (The five executives had been informed in advance and were not at the meeting.) Chris Richmond remembers that "you could have heard a pin drop." It was never again necessary, according to Richmond, for Welch to do the same thing again. Everyone "got it."[20] Chris Richmond also made similar replacements.

HCHP organizations rigorously evaluate their employees, often using a comparative ranking system. GE under Welch went further than most companies by insisting that the bottom 10 percent of the workforce be terminated annually. Although it was never implemented mindlessly or in the same way in all parts of GE, the rigor and discipline of this exercise created an ethos in the company that performance mattered. Some might think that such a hard-edged method would undermine people's self-worth and their commitment. Not necessarily so. For decades, Hewlett-Packard, with a more supportive and relationship-oriented culture than GE's, had an employee ranking system that compared employees across divisions. In 1995, HP management modified the system to limit ranking to the top and bottom 20 percent. In retrospect, I wonder if this indicated a "softening" of the performance culture that HP's founders, David Packard and Bill Hewlett, had created in the 1940s.[21]

Tough and rigorous individual evaluation systems pose a danger, however. Managers begin to focus on their own results at the expense of others. Leaders must, therefore, be clear that they expect collaboration and reinforce that expectation through policies, practices, and rewards. When I first learned in 1980 that Hewlett-Packard used an employee ranking system to compare people in similar types of jobs, it seemed to me inconsistent with its team-based culture. I came to appreciate how much of HP's success can be attributable to managing this paradox. Though GE never articulated collaboration as a value per se, it introduced a number of practices that specified how managers ought to operate. For example, the "boundaryless organization" asked managers to work cooperatively across organizational lines.

Commitment to excellence must be developed. Making employees feel they are part of a special, even elite organization, one unmatched by any other, does this. The New England Patriots developed a commitment to excellence in this way, as did the Celtics basketball team in the 1970s and 1980s. Chris Richmond created this feeling by communicating clearly how CEF compared to other benchmark companies and by letting people know they were part of a high-performance team. "It was clear if you signed up, you would be playing on the Varsity not the JV [Junior Varsity] where the stakes and the rewards were high," Richmond commented. Richmond told managers that if they were not prepared to live in such a culture, GE and CEF were not the place for them. Enabling employees to make an *informed choice* and providing support in the search for alternative employment are important ingredients in assembling managers who are ready and able to work in a demanding performance environment.

Winning is an ethos that must permeate the culture of an HCHP firm. Such a culture not only causes everyone to strive—to be the best they can be—but attracts people who want to work in a company that allows them to be the best they can be. CEF's success was in large measure due to Richmond's success in attracting and retaining people who wanted to play on the "varsity."

Create a Compelling and Focused Direction

Vision. To provide direction and meaning as well as to inspire commitment, senior teams should develop a vision. It must answer questions about purpose that are uppermost in employees' mind, but too often missing from the top management's directions.

- Who are we and why do we exist?
- What do we want to become and why?

Discussing and coming to agreement about these questions not only answers important questions about the firm's vision and capabilities, but energizes the team and provides a compelling direction for lower levels. In my experience and research I have found that the strategic direction of the business often does not make sense to employees, because the questions above have not been discussed and a broader vision has not been articulated.

Mission. Vision articulates management's beliefs about the firm's ultimate purpose and how they want to organize and lead the business given the challenges the organization faces. Johnson & Johnson (J&J), one of the HCHP companies listed in chapter 2, was founded with the idealistic aim "to alleviate pain and disease." Later, it was translated into a mission that put customers and concerns for employees ahead of shareholders. You may think this naive and impractical. Yet studies of HCHP organizations show that firms with mundane products or services can frame their mission in a higher-order way. These studies also show that making mission rather than profits the first objective works so long as the firm is concerned about and measures outcomes for all stakeholders.[22]

A higher calling can help an organization navigate difficult circumstances and avoid self-destructing through irresponsible or unethical behavior. Consider J&J's response to the Tylenol crisis in 1982. After it was found that several people had died from taking Tylenol, J&J's CEO, James Burke, followed the company's multiple stakeholder credo and pulled Tylenol off all shelves—at great cost to the company's short-term profits—to prevent further harm.[23] This enabled J&J to retain customer commitment, and for that matter, employee commitment. It continued J&J's long tradition of multistakeholder mission and values and enabled the company to save the brand, one that continues to be a major profit source.

Strategy. The organization's *game plan* to achieve its mission and vision, *strategy* is often thought of as an elegant and sophisticated master plan, one that relies on sophisticated analysis by the very smartest strategists—executive or consultants. This way of thinking has been shown to be counterproductive.[24] One reason is that it requires a lot of resources. Ford Motor, a failing company, spent $1.2 billion per year on strategic planning in past years.[25] More important, managers easily become captivated by the intellectual excitement of thinking abstractly about the future instead of focusing on solving basic problems presented by customers and employees.[26] Knowing becomes disconnected from doing, when in fact doing is essential for knowing.[27] Instead, it is best to think about strategy formulation and reformulation as a *process of action learning*. Consider that Nucor, one of the HCHP companies listed in chapter 2, has no written strategic plan. The same is true of most Japanese companies, including Toyota.[28]

Sustained high performance can only be achieved through pursuing an and/also stance—exploitation of one's current products and services for profit through incremental change and exploration of new opportunities by proactive "probes," as Chris Richmond calls them, into new domains. These thrusts must be connected in some way to the organization's customers, core technologies, or organizational capabilities. In effect, what the firm intends to do—its over-arching mission, vision, and strategy—remains constant over time, although its products, customers, and footprint may change. "Strategies from the consulting office. . . even the executive suite," Ahlstrand and Mintzberg remind us, "often prove sterile because real strategies are about living customers and dynamic markets and evolving technologies, not about abstract strengths, weaknesses, threats and opportunities." Instead, strategies are about conversations with customers—those the firm has and those it would like to have—conversations from which managers decide what to exploit and what to explore.[29]

HCHP firms *evolve their strategy gradually* into new markets, products, or geographic regions as they learn from success and failure, what James Bryant Quinn called "*logical incrementalism*."[30] Hewlett-Packard evolved its instrument business into a computer and printing business because the original business developed capabilities in computing and printing that its instrument customers required. There are many converging strands of research that support this view of a winning strategy.[31] Making a dramatic shift is simply too risky in most instances, given the time and financial resources required to build a totally new market identity or brand. Second, execution requires organization design, culture, and capabilities that fit the strategy. At Asda, a U.K. grocery chain, losing focus—veering away from a historic low-price value proposition into a high-end business that seemed more attractive to its management—created misalignment and caused its decline. Copying someone else is not the way of HCHP companies. Asda's turnaround, which I revisit in chapter 11, corrected the misalignment by returning the firm to its core strategy and capabilities, and then building new capabilities to compete much more effectively in the low price and value niche it had chosen long ago. Inconsistency in strategy—continuously reacting to other competitors—makes alignment virtually impossible.

Often, the vision is bold and audacious, such as Southwest's vision of creating an airline that would compete with cars and buses; but the strategy, particularly for companies with established businesses, is paradoxically conservative with regard to its evolution, thereby limiting risk. Chris Richmond utilized this strategy development process to transform CEF into a high-performing business.

This is how he described the process: "[It was a] very tactically based strategy. [We] didn't do a lot of market studies. [We] did a lot of stuff close to what we [already] did and then built platforms to transfer skills to the next level so they (lower levels and acquired companies) could do it themselves.... We started with what we knew how to do, drove it well and then got bigger.... It was about avoiding the most risky thing—losing money."

Richmond's "stair step" or "viral growth strategy" was ambitious, but very much evolutionary, not revolutionary (Figure 8.2). Aware that he needed short-term performance to fund long-term growth, he hit performance targets with an early acquisition, building the sales force and focusing on productivity between 1994 and 1995. In 1995–96 he then began to extend his existing products to new markets and to build capabilities in acquisition, developing high potentials, and developing a new risk-management model. In 1996–97 new products were developed and sold into existing regions and markets, and more acquisitions were made utilizing new acquisition skills that CEF had developed the previous year. In 1997–98 CEF aggressively expanded globally, adding fourteen new countries to CEF's portfolio. In the last period of Richmond's tenure, expansion occurred in all three dimensions—markets, products, and

FIGURE 8.2. CEF's "VIRAL GROWTH STRATEGY" ACROSS SEGMENTS, PRODUCTS, AND GEOGRAPHIES.

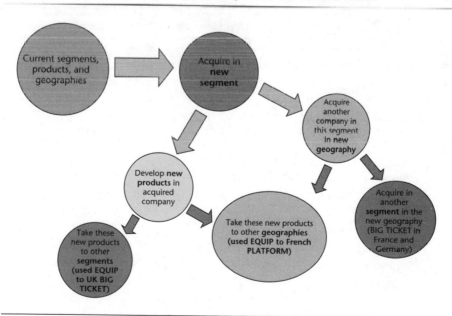

Source: Adapted from Chris Richmond.

geography. Throughout this time period, CEF focused on building strategic capabilities in acquiring companies and pricing, and organizational capabilities such as leadership and teamwork.

Executing a simultaneous exploration and exploitation strategy is challenging. It is very easy for the primary business of a firm to draw all the attention of senior management and use all available resources. Fear that new opportunities will cannibalize existing businesses undermines commitment to potential new businesses. Firms that succeed in being serial explorers while effectively exploiting their existing business develop a disciplined process. This process starts with identifying potential opportunities that match internal capabilities. These are then prioritized and the best pursued. Once identified, teams are organized and resourced to develop each opportunity. Business development opportunities are then reviewed by senior management and reprioritized, based on progress and promise, with resources cut and resources reallocated accordingly.

Chris Richmond's successful viral growth strategy succeeded because of such a disciplined process. Hewlett-Packard's incredible growth record in the 1960s and 70s can be similarly attributed to the founders' concerted efforts to talk to engineers to find opportunities and then organize to explore these opportunities.[32] Recent research finds that IBM's continued growth since its turnaround in the 1990s is due to top management's focus on identifying and sorting opportunities, organizing to develop each opportunity into a business, and then assigning senior executives responsibility for overseeing each business development.[33] A disciplined process such as this makes it less likely that firms will experience what Clay Christensen has called the innovator's dilemma, the consistent tendency of large, well-established businesses to not take advantage of new innovations.[34]

Manage for the Long Term, Focus on the Short Term

Firms must hit short-term performance targets in today's capital markets, but HCHP companies do so while managing for the long term. Their top management does not make decisions that will increase short-term financial results and stock price while undermining the integrity of the firm and its long-term value to all stakeholders. Their goal is long-term *economic value creation*. This means looking to maintain a constant positive trend in profits, not necessarily revenues, over a long period and not succumbing to actions that will undermine this in any given quarter or two. And it means finding ways to continue to invest in developing products, as well as building customer and employee commitment, regardless of short-term declines in revenues and profits. Moreover, leaders of these firms do not look to short-term stock price performance as the measure of success, as discussed in chapter 3.

This perspective is not common in today's economy. Recent surveys show that a lot of executive time is focused on capital markets and stock price.[35] A CEO attending an HCHP leaders' conference I conducted in 2007 recounted how the failing company of which he took charge years earlier had responded to competitive pressures. To keep stock price rising they tried to raise profits by raising prices. When they realized they were losing market share, they cut people and investments, thus undermining long-term performance. This CEO then described the long-term philosophy he employed to run the company:

> Every year—and we report on it—every year we measure our total share-owner returns relative to our peer group and our employee engagement relative to the Gallup database. . . . Our goal is to [be the best] over a decade; [to] have the best total shareowner returns in our industry. All the math we've done says if we can stay above average on a rolling three-year basis, over that decade we will be the best. Because inevitably [other companies] reach too high [and] fall down. And our goal is to be on a rolling three-year basis, above average every year.

The Wall Street meltdown and economic crisis of 2008 are in large measure a function of this short-term profit perspective, one not held by HCHP companies such as Southwest Airlines, discussed in chapter 2, or Warren Buffett's National Indemnity Company (NICO), discussed in chapter 3. The top management of failed Wall Street firms like Bear Stearns and Merrill Lynch loaded up on risky mortgage-backed securities because they saw a lucrative market that would and did boost their profits and their compensation. "They had found this huge profit potential, and everybody wanted a piece of it. But they were pigs about it," noted an industry insider.[36]

GE and CEF utilized return on equity and net income over a longer time frame as two of its principal performance measures. In addition to an annual bonus opportunity (cash and stock options), GE rewarded managers on the basis of a three-year rolling average of their own results and corporate results, not results for just one year. A long-term perspective is essential to developing *an economic surplus that the firm can reinvest* in developing and maintaining the commitment of customers, employees, and communities. Moreover, if a firm is able to develop a reputation for consistent economic value creation it can attract long-term investors, who in turn will support the longer-term perspective required to build an HCHP organization.

There is ample evidence that managing for the long term pays off. Danny and Isabelle Le Breton-Miller report in their book *Managing for the Long Term* (see chapter 3 of this book for a brief description of their findings) that private, family-owned or family-managed companies outperform public companies.[37]

These companies are not subjected to the short-term pressures of financial markets. But equally important is family members' focus on building an institution that will last beyond their lifetimes.

Can public companies manage for the long term? It is certainly more difficult, but the stories of GE, Southwest, Johnson & Johnson, and Nucor Steel, among others, suggest that they can. Though the time frame of GE's Chris Richmond was relatively short (six years), he focused on a long-term growth strategy from the outset. His decisions in the first year to acquire another company and launch a capability-building initiative in his sales force were made in the context of a long-term plan that he and his team had developed. These moves enabled him to accumulate resources—money, capabilities, and knowledge—needed to implement the long-term plan. They were not intended to create the illusion of progress. The long-term effect of Richmond's efforts to build a high-performance culture is evident in the sustained performance of CEF, which maintained the same growth for many years after Richmond left.

New CEOs taking charge of an underperforming company cannot, of course, focus immediately on the long term. Jack Gabarro has shown that new leaders must first attend to fixing obvious problems that undermine performance before they attend to the longer-term agenda for change.[38] However, by exploring gaps in performance with the involvement of key people, new leaders increase *dissatisfaction with the status quo*. When the gap between reality and desired outcomes is discussed honestly, and the consequences are assessed, the energy needed for change is released.[39] Closing the gap becomes an urgent matter.[40] And it sets the stage for the second wave of change for developing an HCHP firm. When Mark Hurd, appointed in 2005 to turn around the fortunes of Hewlett-Packard—once an HCHP company—he utilized his first year to attack HP's serious performance deficiencies, and the company's performance improved significantly.[41] Starting with a long-term perspective would have been the wrong place to start. That developmental perspective will, however, be critical if Hurd is to succeed in transforming HP into the HCHP company it once was.

Long-term declines in performance and commitment are often caused by the tendency for CEOs to cling to a mind-set that led to past success and to defend themselves from unwelcome information by failing to actively seek the truth and failing to create organizational mechanisms that will deliver the truth. They succumb to the erroneous conclusion that long-term profitable growth is unattainable due to industry trends, government regulations, and other external forces beyond their control.[42] This in turn leads them to peg performance aspirations to the lowest common denominator of the industry.

The long-term perspective in HCHP companies is motivated by the multiple stakeholder philosophy discussed in chapter 3. CEOs of HCHP companies create a performance management system, as I will discuss below, that measures the commitment of customers, employees, shareholders, communities, and suppliers; they confront openly the inevitable conflicts; and find, as much as possible, solutions that satisfy the interests of all. By assessing a "balanced scorecard" of performance measures, CEOs can resist short-term actions that will take their companies off the HCHP path.[43]

Build an Organization That Executes

Strategic performance management is much more than strategy formulation. It is all about execution and learning from execution. Percy Barnevick, former CEO of ABB, a global power and electric equipment company that he transformed in the 1980s, believes that strategy development, which is a "cognitive process"—in other words, thinking—should occupy 10 percent of management's attention, whereas implementation should occupy 90 percent of management's attention.[44]

The importance of execution in achieving sustained high performance is supported by a major study conducted by Nitin Nohria and his colleagues. The study examined why companies outperform peers in the same industry.[45] It concluded that strategy was *only one of four primary factors* that made a difference. The second was *execution*, the capacity of the organization to consistently meet expectations of customers and to create efficient operations. The third and fourth factors were *organization structure* and *culture*—also the means by which flawless execution is achieved (discussed below). Ram Charan and Larry Bossidy have also advocated the importance of execution. Charan, a well-known consultant, collaborated with Larry Bossidy, a former GE executive who became CEO of Allied Signal, to transform that company into a high-performance company.[46] How is this done?

***Translate Strategy into Operational Terms.**[47]* *Strategic tasks, also known as key success factors, reflect what management believes the firm must do to succeed.* They enable strategy execution because they translate an abstract statement into operational terms. They allow value-creating departments to set individual goals in the context of corporate-wide strategic initiatives, and therefore facilitate coordination and collaboration. This is diametrically opposite to how goals and planning occur in underperforming organizations, where each department is given financial targets and then creates its own individual goals.

To articulate firmwide strategic tasks, all members of the senior team must come into the conversation with a general management perspective, not that of their own departments. If top team members do not agree on strategy, are

TABLE 8.2. COMMERCIAL EQUIPMENT FINANCE'S STRATEGIC TASKS.

Extend current market segments with existing products
Extend geographic reach with current products
Develop new products for current and emerging markets and regions
Develop strong customer relationships and loyalty
Improve productivity through process improvement
Identify and develop leaders
Develop capability to integrate acquisitions quickly and effectively
Develop a risk-management model and process that will prevent major losses and
    improve returns

Source: Adapted from Chris Richmond.

solely concerned about their own departments and careers, and are unable to subjugate their own interests to that of the larger organization, it is unlikely that departmental goals will integrate with those of other departments. That is why we found an ineffective top team a consistent silent killer of strategy implementation (see chapter 5).

Strategic tasks are "the business drivers." Table 8.2 shows the strategic tasks developed by CEF's Richmond and his senior team early in the transformation process. The first three reflect what had to be done to execute CEF's "viral growth strategy." The others reflect key success factors—what the business had to do to build customer loyalty and improve productivity, and the capabilities CEF had to develop to succeed; for example, leadership development and skills for integrating acquisitions. The senior team became touchstones for every business unit, function, and region; they set goals and made resource allocation decisions to achieve their strategic tasks.

Note that capability building has to be a corporate-wide goal. Because the organization is a system—more than the sum of its parts—simply developing a capability in one part of the organization will not create value. Imagine if a cooperative attitude and skills in teamwork were created among Southwest Airlines' flight attendants, but not among its pilots and station personnel and management. It would do nothing to speed up airplane turnaround time. Imagine that CEF's human resource function had leadership development as its goal and that line managers did not.

Top teams' ability to work together in developing strategy and strategic tasks is rooted first and foremost in the leader's decision to create a team, her capacity to create a compelling purpose and to focus on getting the right people on the team.[48] But the capacity to translate strategy into strategic tasks also requires that top teams have the capacity to think logically about how business goals regarding profit and growth translate into tasks. My colleagues Robert Kaplan and David Norton have developed a tool for doing this—they call it the strategy map—to help managers with this process.[49]

Simply articulating strategic tasks will not translate into execution unless a comprehensive system of goals and measures is created that goes well beyond the financial goals that most companies have historically employed. Attaining high commitment and performance requires firms to set goals and measures with regard to intangible assets such as customer commitment as well as employee commitment and capabilities. They must be able to assess the effectiveness and efficiency of internal business processes that deliver these valued outcomes as well as their capacity to learn, improve, and change. Kaplan and Norton have developed a framework and tool they call the Balanced Scorecard. They offer extensive case-based evidence that effective implementation of the balanced scorecard improves company effectiveness and performance.[50] The balanced scorecard, or the "Win Card" as CEO Alan Parker calls it, played a very important role in the successful transformation of Whitbread PLC, a U.K. company that I have worked with and observed for many years. It shifted the focus away from operating margin and labor costs, a focus that had undermined customer and employee commitment outcomes.

The overarching goal for developing the balanced scorecard is firm profitability. Improvements in customer and employee commitment are valued because they are instrumental to profit. It is important, however, that top teams apply their values to the task of designing the balanced scorecard to ensure that goals in all of its domains are not chosen solely for their contribution to profit, that they reflect the firm's genuine commitment to all stakeholders. For this reason a balanced scorecard must emerge from a strategic dialogue by the senior team in which they discuss the linkage between the scorecard and their strategic tasks *and* values. They create the framework and outlines of goals to be incorporated into the scorecard. But they cannot dictate specific measures without incurring concerns and resistance. That is what happened when a CEO and his corporate staff introduced a balanced scorecard without consultation. It is best that senior teams in business and operating subunits be involved in the developing measures that they think best reflect performance in each of the scorecard's domains. Unless they have a stake in developing the scorecard it will be merely another "technical system" imposed by top management.

Align the Organization and Its People. To implement organization-wide strategic tasks successfully, business units, operating units, corporate staff groups, and geographically dispersed organizational units will have to learn how to play the "game" together. That game is defined by the organization's *formal organizing* *system—the roles, responsibilities, decision rights, and relationships—*needed for seamless coordination along the value-creation chain. GE's CEF had to be reorganized to support Richmond's "viral growth strategy." A "matrix" decentralized authority to regional, market, and product organizations while maintaining centralized functional oversight for developing essential capabilities.

Senior teams must be willing and able to make changes in roles and responsibilities that some will see as losses in influence and threats to their historic role in the organization. Chris Richmond and his CEF senior team recognized that to grow through innovation in new financial products and services, they had to take day-to-day risk-management decisions away from the corporate risk-management function and delegate much greater authority to the regions, in effect decentralizing the organization for the rapid response required for innovation and growth.

Formal arrangements are not enough. Human resource policies and practices must be designed and managed to produce the skills, capabilities, and attitudes needed to play the game as defined by the organizing system.[51] At CEF, developing and deploying leaders who had the will and skill to achieve ambitious targets was a key building block of their growth strategy. When growth goals outstretched the organization's talent pool, Richmond reached down several levels to promote high-potential managers who had been identified at regular talent reviews. These assignments were used to test and develop managers.

Because an aligned organizing system and supporting people and culture are change levers critical to successful transformations to HCHP, they will be treated in depth in chapters 9 and 10.

Enable Every Employee to Be a Strategic Actor

If you have ever called a corporate call center and wanted a problem resolved that requires more than a routine response, you will have experienced what I have. Front-line employees simply do not know enough, nor do they feel empowered, to deal with customer problems. When asked to bring problems to their manager, they seem reluctant or even afraid to do so. Passivity, lack of empowerment, and ignorance do not an HCHP organization make.

For every employee to become a strategic actor, managers and front-line employees must be empowered and trained to take actions in support of the company's strategy with regard to customers, employees, and investors. Empowerment enables everyone to think proactively about improvement in every aspect of the business that he or she touches. No company does this better than Toyota, and it is one reason why they now dominate the worldwide automobile industry. Southwest Airlines empowers their front-line employees to do whatever is necessary to solve customer problems, even if it breaks normal routines.

To enable strategic behavior at all levels, a balanced scorecard of goals aligned with strategy has to be cascaded down the organization. The specific goals and measures of success must be developed by subunit managers in conjunction with their immediate higher manager. Investing in making every employee a strategic actor through a cascading set of goals and the power to act enables management's strategic intent to be translated into action at organizational levels far removed from their personal scrutiny and control. Brian Baker of Mobil Oil, who introduced a balanced scorecard that aligned goals from top to bottom, talked about the importance of employee understanding and commitment to the strategy and relevant goals:

> I am accountable for a large organization spread over a large geographic area. At the end of the day, success comes from individuals at the front line of operations. You've got an operator at a refinery, sitting in front of a computer screen controlling a process unit at 3 AM on Sunday. Frankly, management is not around. My fate, in a very real sense, is determined by that person's attitude, whether that person is paying attention. Thirty seconds of inattention at the wrong time can shut down that refinery, stopping production. If you are going to drive the business you have to drive down to that individual who is at the front line, making the decision.[52]

Even if lower levels are empowered to achieve aligned goals, they will run into corporate policies that block them from satisfying customers. They must therefore be able to challenge higher levels about the validity of the policy, and higher levels will have to be responsive if they want every employee to be a strategic actor. Top management's intent to make employees strategic actors will not succeed unless employees are specifically told to advocate changes in corporate policies, processes, and practices; including the very role, responsibilities, and accountabilities they have been assigned.

HCHP companies create a high-stakes psychological contract. Goals are "sacrosanct." Missing the goals will have consequences. For "Jack [Welch] a stretch target was the target," according to Chris Richmond. "You have to make it possible." The contract is about results, and not about the means by which managers will achieve them. HCHP companies give maximum freedom regarding the means. Chris Richmond at CEF referred to this as a "loose-tight system; tight about metrics but very loose about how you hit them." This loose-tight system of goal setting allows managers to hold employees accountable. Equally important, senior management in HCHP companies provide support.

Chris Richmond recalls that when he went to Welch to obtain stock options for a sales force that was performing particularly well, there was no delay; "in three days we had it."

To avoid a self-serving, short-term focus detrimental to execution of the strategic tasks, rewards such as stock options and bonuses are based on a multiyear performance horizon. As noted earlier, at GE, a portion of a manager's financial reward was based on a three-year rolling average of performance outcomes. Hewlett-Packard employed a different practice. It had no executive bonuses and used goal setting, its commitment culture, and corporate profit sharing to motivate cooperation and stock options to recognize outstanding performance.

Make Strategic Management a Disciplined Continuous Learning Process

For an organization to achieve sustained high performance it must be disciplined and adaptive. Discipline requires that managers create business goals and stick to them. Adaptability requires innovation and diversity. Jim Collins found that "great" companies managed to integrate this paradoxical state of consistency *and* adaptability through a culture of responsibility and learning, the same capacity for learning and change that, as I argued earlier in this book, is one of three essential pillars of HCHP organizations. Managing this paradox requires a disciplined strategic performance management process that defines and redefines as appropriate the following elements in the strategic performance system discussed above (see Figure 8.3):

- A compelling direction—"who are we and why do we exist?" and "what do we want to become?"
- Strategy and strategic tasks
- Multistakeholder goals, balanced scorecard to measure progress, and an aligned organization
- Change strategic initiatives, goals, measures, organization, and people as required

A high-performance culture and honest fact-based conversations are the underpinnings of an HCHP strategic organizational performance management system, as Figure 8.3 shows. They enable continuous learning and adaptation. Without honest conversations, the value of sophisticated principles discussed in this section, as well as the value of sophisticated tools such as the balanced scorecard and strategy maps, become meaningless and ineffectual.

To enable continuous learning, HCHP companies create regular and disciplined meetings. These meetings are designed to enable managers to review results and make necessary midcourse corrections in strategy, organizational arrangements, and people. They include review and discussion of more than financial results. CEF's SPMS was organized around quarterly meetings, each with a different focus (see Table 8.3) and an annual management meeting that

FIGURE 8.3. HIGH-PERFORMANCE, STRATEGIC PERFORMANCE MANAGEMENT SYSTEM.

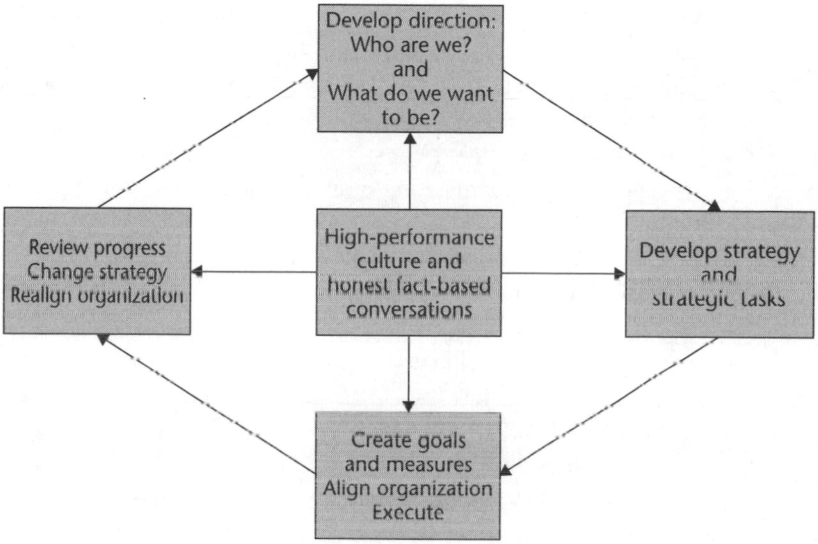

TABLE 8.3. THE ANNUAL CYCLE FOR STRATEGIC PLANNING AT GE'S COMMERCIAL EQUIPMENT FINANCE.

Meeting	Timing	Summary Description
Strategic review (four year plan)	Summer	Focus on how to make targets
Third quarter operating review	Fall	Focus on current year, best practices
Annual meeting	Winter	Look backward and forward
First quarter operating review	Winter	Focus on resource allocation, new initiative launch
Second quarter operating review	Spring	Focus on review of high potentials

Source: Adapted from Chris Richmond.

included a larger group of key managers. Only one quarterly meeting focused on detailed financial targets. The other meetings focused on best practices, a review of the leadership pipeline, and resource allocation. Richmond felt that creating this strategic management rhythm was essential to his success.

The quality of meetings in HCHP organizations is very different from that of underperforming companies. The transformation in the strategic performance management system and the conversations that it fostered accounts, in part for CEF's successful journey to high commitment and high performance, according to Chris Richmond (see Table 8.4 for Richmond's views of what changed). His meetings focused on business drivers rather than targets and outcomes; they focused on diagnosing problems and coming to consensus on what the company needed to fix and change, as opposed to dispensing blame. The meetings were characterized by honest conversations that confronted barriers and did not evade discussing root causes.

Leading-edge companies employ an *office of strategic management* (OSM) to coordinate and facilitate the strategic performance management steps in Figure 8.3. The OSM can support senior management in answering the following questions: Do we have a clearly articulated strategy? Have we defined the right goals and strategic tasks to support the strategy? Does our scorecard embody the right measures? Are we allocating resources correctly to support our strategy? Do our people understand the strategy? Do we have honest discussions about performance? Are best practices spreading to all parts of the organization? Are new emergent strategic ideas bubbling to the top?[53]

Ideally, the OSM ought to include both strategy and strategic human resource or organization development professionals. Historically, expertise in

TABLE 8.4. WHAT'S DIFFERENT ABOUT HCHP REVIEWS?

FROM:	TO:
Focus on rearview mirror	Focus on what needs to change going forward
Finding out who was responsible	Finding out who can fix the problem
Interpreting results to avoid responsibility	Putting the whole story on the table
Focus on outcomes, not drivers	Focus on drivers of successful strategy
Pushing blame/success around the room	Hold everyone accountable for success
Dictating solutions from the top	Collaborate on solutions
Not discussing root cause	Discuss barriers to success
Focus on the quarter, not the plan	Focus on short *and* long term.

Source: Adapted from Chris Richmond.

these matters has been embedded in different functional departments and has not been properly integrated. For example, strategic HR has been blocked by being part of an administrative and transactional HR function. Strategy embedded in finance can be blocked from developing the balanced multiple stakeholder perspective. Effective strategic management calls for splitting the strategic human resource and organization development activities from the HR function and integrating them with a strategic management department.[54] Becton Dickinson's early steps in the journey to HCHP began when the vice president of strategic management was given responsibility for human resources. This led the company to engage many of the questions listed above and motivated development of the type of strategic performance management system I have outlined in this chapter.

♣ ♣ ♣

Becoming an HCHP company requires a substantial change in the psychological contract; for example, the high-investment, high-return value proposition which is at the heart of these firms. Senior management's expectation of managers and employees is far higher than is common in most firms: higher goal attainment, a stronger work ethic, a faster pace, more proactive strategic decisions and actions at the lowest possible level, greater capacity to deal with feedback, and very rapid response to that feedback. But as top management's expectations rise, so do midlevel managers' expectations of senior management. They expect clear and timely communication of direction, greater delegation of responsibility and decision rights, more attention and time to resolve issues, as well as openness to honest feedback from lower levels about changes in leadership behavior and organization design. In short, HCHP organizations are as demanding of leaders as they are of lower levels and much more disciplined than most firms in pursuit of their goals at every level.

The Challenge: Overcome the Silent Killers

Stimulated by groundbreaking research by Robert Kaplan and David Norton, many companies are adopting a variety of emerging strategic performance management practices and tools: the "technical tools" of strategic management, such as mission and value statements, strategy maps, a balanced multistakeholder scorecard, and an office of strategic management as the integrating department for all strategic performance management.[55]

Despite the increasing use of these sophisticated "technical tools," there is evidence that simply adopting the latest and best, as helpful as they may be, does not necessarily create an HCHP organization. Consider how managers heading the office of strategic management in several different companies responded when asked to characterize the reason why their "technically" sophisticated strategic management system and office were *not* living up to their expectations.[56] When these findings were discussed at a conference attended by the managers it became clear that they were silent and undermined the efficacy of the SPMS.

- "My executive peers are concerned about whether they are losing control over their operations, or are nervous about the increased level of transparency over the management of their functions."
- "Having honest and open dialogue. *Executive teams* willing to take risks, make mistakes, establish priorities, communicate to teams, and engage in real performance analysis and understanding of root causes. We don't have all these attributes yet."
- "There is a *natural resistance* on the part of some individuals to not want to be measured or held accountable. Therefore barriers are put up to stop a program whose goal is measurement and accountability."
- "Weak track record with cross-functional process consistency. *Getting all groups to agree* to and actually follow one consistent process."
- "We have a culture that combines manufacturing, scientific inquiry and medical decision-making. Often, the professional backgrounds of these groups make alignment a challenge. For me the struggle is: *everyone recognizes alignment is an issue, it is not known how to correct the problem.*"
- "Organization must *change the culture* and learn to accept that [numbers] that do not meet targets are not inherently bad; the issue may be that the organization needs to reallocate resources to reach a desirable performance level (Red is not the enemy). Senior management needs to ensure that their staffs understand the importance of presenting accurate information, regardless of low performance scores."

Adopting new and sophisticated "technical systems" is clearly not enough. The social or cultural system must be developed as well. The barriers voiced above reflect the very same *silent killers* discussed in chapter 5. Table 8.5 shows the behaviors that my colleagues at TruePoint and I have found block strategic performance management. It is a framework that senior teams may use to diagnose barriers to strategic management and plan change.

TABLE 8.5. SILENT KILLER BEHAVIORS THAT BLOCK STRATEGIC PERFORMANCE MANAGEMENT.

		Undiscussable Behaviors That Block Strategic Performance Management
Quality of Direction	Top-down or laissez-faire senior management style	• Top-down—Personally takes control of initiatives, rather than enabling others on senior team and below to take charge • Laissez-faire—Does not engage senior team and organization in identifying problems and solving them • Reluctant to advocate point of view • Does not inquire (seek challenge and disagreement) into quality of direction or the organization's effectiveness and own leadership effectiveness
	Ineffective senior management team	• Team does not spend time discussing strategic issues and reformulating strategy • Team does not possess the capacity to confront differences or conflict and resolve them through problem solving • Team does not challenge its underlying assumptions about how the organization should be designed and managed • Team does not review regularly progress in implementing strategy • Team does not review regularly alignment of their behavior and that of subunits with values
	Unclear strategies and conflicting priorities	• Senior team or lower levels do not understand or agree with strategy • Mission and values not clear or widely embraced • Different parts of the organization all along the value chain have different priorities (assign time, people, and money to projects or business initiatives inconsistently)
Quality of Learning	Poor vertical communication	• Lower levels do not know or understand the strategy or values of the business • Senior team does not seek or receive feedback from lower levels about barriers to strategy implementation (the silent killers) and alignment with values • No formal mechanisms exist for ensuring a safe and productive dialogue about silent killers and other barriers to leadership and organizational effectiveness
Quality of Implement-ation	Poor coordination across functions, businesses, or borders	• Organization is not designed to enable good coordination • Structure and its embedded roles, responsibilities, and accountabilities are not aligned with strategy • Planning and budgeting formulation and review processes do not facilitate timely and integrated management process • Leadership team does not function or act in a way that promotes coordination
	Inadequate down-the-line leadership skills and development	• Leaders of key functions and subunits do not behave in a way that is consistent with strategy (the freelance) • Leaders are not effective • Leaders behavior is not consistent with values

Integrating Learning and Governance with Strategic Management

Business leaders I have worked with and studied were able to ensure the wider organization's commitment to the strategic plan by integrating a learning and governance system with their strategic performance management system. These companies develop honest, collective, and public conversations, as discussed in chapter 7, about the validity of their strategic plans and goals and the silent barriers to achieving them. Such a conversation would also identify the barriers to strategic performance management and behaviors listed in Table 8.5.

Consider the Component Test (CT) division of Agilent Technologies, which employed our Strategic Fitness Process (they called it the Organizational Alignment Process) as their learning and governance system. (Figure 8.4). Following

FIGURE 8.4. STRATEGIC PLANNING AND ORGANIZATION ALIGNMENT PROCESS.

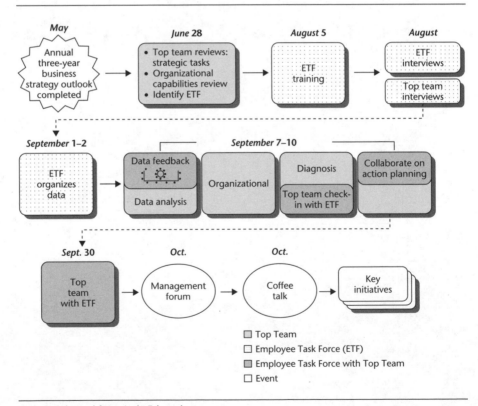

Source: Adapted from Jody Edwards.

the development of their three-year strategic plan and the establishment of key strategic tasks, the senior team appointed an employee task force of high-potential employees to interview key people about their reactions to the plan itself and about organizational strengths and barriers to implementation. Senior management then used feedback from the task force to modify their plan and to realign the organization and its processes with the strategy as necessary. A large management forum and coffee talks followed to communicate and discuss the final strategy and goals. They found that this level of involvement increased employee understanding and commitment to the strategy and provided early discovery of problems that might have prevented them from meeting their performance targets. And at the same time it served as their annual assessment of the progress on their journey to high commitment and high performance.

The Financial Group Insurance division of Sun Life, a Canadian insurance company, developed somewhat different means for engaging its stakeholders in the strategic planning process and broadened the process to include customers and shareholders.[57] The process had three stages (see Figure 8.5). The first stage, information gathering, involved listening to the voices of customers, employees, and shareholders through a variety of mechanisms, including focus groups, in which honest opinions about the effectiveness of management and operating processes — not people — were solicited. Stage two, strategy formulation, involved a senior team of managers in developing a strategic and operating plan as well as specifications of key projects and initiatives (strategic tasks) based on feedback from customers and employees. Following the development of the division's

FIGURE 8.5. STRATEGIC PLANNING PROCESS AT SUN LIFE.

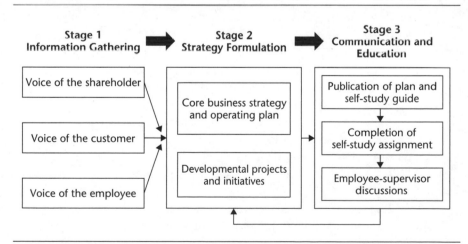

Source: Roberto, M., *Strategic Planning at Sun Life*, 2001, Harvard Business School Press.

overall plan, each line of business was invited to develop its own plan. The third stage, communication and education, engaged employees throughout the business to discuss the plan, and provided further feedback. To prepare for these discussions, employees were given a copy of the plan, a self-study guide, and study assignments.

These levels of involvement may seem extraordinary to many managers, but HCHP organizations achieve better and faster alignment, execution, and commitment. The Japanese, who have traditionally employed comparable high levels of involvement, implement their strategies much faster and with fewer problems than most Western firms. Jody Edwards, Component Test's human resource executive quoted earlier in this book, believed that the learning and governance system they adopted was the most important process at CT, even more important than the many processes that high-technology businesses like CT typically employ.

Learning and governance processes such as these do not replace the honest and fact-based strategic performance quarterly reviews that Chris Richmond employed so successfully at General Electric. The latter enable quick quarterly corrections—but may not identify hidden organizational and leadership barriers that can undermine achievement of strategic intent. Nor do they build commitment in the large group of managers and front-line employees who are not involved in strategic reviews. That is the role of the learning and governance process when integrated into the strategic management process.

Summary

HCHP firms manage organizational performance strategically in the following ways.

- They move from a financial and budget review process to a strategic performance management process that focuses on customer, employee, and operational outcomes.
- They develop a high-performance culture where people want to win; new recruits are selected based on their desire to be on a team composed of the best. Merit is the basis of promotion; people are empowered to be strategic actors at their level; and collaboration is the means of decision making and implementation.
- They develop a strategic performance management system characterized by:
  1. A strategic and emotionally compelling direction composed of mission, values, vision

2. An inside-out evolutionary and incremental strategy, deeply rooted in their distinctive capabilities; they are less likely to use or require the services of strategy consultants to define their strategy

3. Strategy is translated into operational terms through the definition of strategic tasks, a balanced multistakeholder scorecard that incorporates customer, employee, operational improvement, and capability-building goals and measures, as well as financial outcomes

4. A means for aligning the organization and people capabilities with strategic intent

5. Empowering employees to be strategic actors by providing them with a balanced scorecard of goals and measures

6. A disciplined set of meetings that enable managers to review results, learn and take appropriate actions

- Research suggests that strategic performance management tools and practices are undermined by undiscussable silent barriers. To overcome these and build commitment to strategy, senior teams will want to integrate a learning and governance system with their strategic management process. It enables them to align their organization, management practices, and people with their strategy.

Senior teams that wish to assess their organization's strategic performance management system and culture will want to answer the following questions:

1. Are we continuously surprised by late projects and lower-than-expected results?

2. Do we have people who want to be challenged and work with the best people?

3. Do we know who we are, why we exist, and what we want to be as a business?

4. Have we articulated an inspiring direction, a clear strategy, and stretch targets?

5. Do we have a "balanced scorecard" that measures the commitment of our customers, employees, and community to the firm—and not just shareholders? And does that scorecard include an assessment of operational and organizational effectiveness?

6. Do we have a disciplined strategic management process—periodic meetings that cover not just financial results but talent management, best-practices sharing, and searching strategic discussions? And do these meetings encourage honest conversations that matter?

7. Have we established a learning and governance process that identifies hidden barriers to our strategic intent, enables change, and at the same time builds commitment to our strategy and goals?

CHAPTER NINE

ORGANIZE FOR PERFORMANCE AND COMMITMENT

Change Lever 4: The Organizing System

Historically there has been a reorganization of the sales department every six months. Every time they are in trouble they reorganize. The solution is always reorganization for whatever the hell the problem is. And the reorganizations are never thought out. They [seem to think] God damn, that bunch didn't work, we'll try a new organization. They just don't know how to conceptualize in that end of the business and they are going to have to.

—AN EXECUTIVE VICE PRESIDENT,
FORTUNE 500 COMPANY

Reorganization is a continuing task for companies in the twenty-first century. As yesterday's opportunities and threats subside, new ones emerge. The frequency with which a firm will have to reorganize depends on the intensity of competitive rivalry in the industry.[1] High intensity can cause whole industries to reorganize through acquisitions and mergers, and in turn challenge firms to reorganize themselves. In some industries changes in the competitive landscape occur over decades; in others they occur over only a few years. But for all firms the average number of years between strategic shifts is declining rapidly, making reorganizations an ever-present reality. Not only do strategic tasks shift as the competitive landscape changes, but as organizational behaviorist Larry Greiner has observed, firms go through periods of evolution, followed by more dramatic episodes of revolution; gradual evolutionary change in how the firm is organized is no longer adequate given changes in the firm's scale and scope.[2]

If senior management aspire to build an organization capable of sustained performance and commitment, they will have to evolve their design through various stages and periodically navigate frame-breaking revolutions to move to the next level in the organization's development. Figure 9.1 shows the evolution that most firms have historically followed from inception to maturity. As I

FIGURE 9.1. EVOLUTION AND REVOLUTION AS ORGANIZATIONS GROW AND ADAPT.

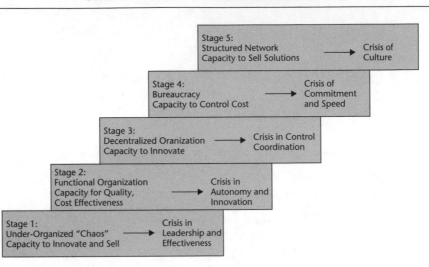

Source: Adapted from Greiner, L., "Evolution and revolution as organizations grow." *Harvard Business Review*, July-August, 1972.

will show later, the organizing model at each stage of the firm's evolution possesses strengths but also weaknesses that ultimately require frame-breaking reorganization.[3] I do not intend to suggest that every company goes through or should go through every stage in exactly the order shown in Figure 9.1, just that evolution in how the firm is organized is necessary and that revolution may be required periodically.

Leaders who build an HCHP organization would be well advised, for example, to avoid bureaucracy; to develop from inception the collaborative capabilities and culture required to overcome differentiated functions at stage 2, or decentralized divisions in stage 3; and to ready the organization for the multidimensional structured network in store for successful and growing HCHP firms. At the same time, it is important to note that achieving the mature state of a collaborative structured network beyond one's years is just as difficult for firms as it is for human beings, despite the fact that HCHP aspirations demand it. But early development is possible. Recall the seminal Stanford study cited in chapter 3 which showed that about a third of start-up founders developed at the outset a commitment and collaborative culture.

This way of conceiving the path to sustained HCHP suggests that the first challenge for senior teams is to recognize clues—conflict, turf battles, low commitment, and poor coordination—that signal that the current organizing model is no longer functioning. If they do not recognize that the firm's organizational design is not working, performance and commitment will decline as people become disillusioned with the firm's ineffectiveness. The senior team's second challenge is to find an organizing model that fits the organization's competitive and strategic circumstances, as well as its scale and scope. Leadership teams will have to manage, better than their competitors, the natural evolutions and revolutions in organizing if they want to sustain HCHP. If unable to emerge from periods of reorganization as a community of purpose, the firm will have forfeited its status as an HCHP community.

Success and Failure in Navigating Organizational Revolution

For its first four decades Hewlett-Packard (HP), an HCHP company, achieved a compounded annual growth rate in revenues of 25 percent and 27 percent in profits, far better than its competitors.[4] HP achieved these results in part because its leaders were able to organize for success and develop a supporting culture, human resources policies, and management processes. A decentralized divisional structure enabled the company to pursue a strategy of exploration and innovation, first in instruments, and later in computers and printers. Each time a new opportunity emerged, the company formed a new division to build the new business. By 1995 Hewlett-Packard had sixty divisions that were clustered into instrument, computer, and printer business groups, and sold its products through three group-level sales forces in over sixty countries.

Two changes in the competitive landscape—commoditization and price pressures—as well as customer needs for solutions and supporting services, rather then products, called into question HP's decades-long organizing logic. Its decentralized divisional organization (stage 3 in Figure 8.1) began to be unresponsive to customer needs, despite its collaborative high-commitment culture. Customers of both the computer and instrument business complained that HP had great technology and products, but that its many product divisions made it difficult to receive integrated solutions. They pointed to the large number of business cards they had received from sales people in different parts of HP. The very form of organization that had given HP performance alignment and decades of outstanding performance and commitment had become a potential liability.

This story illustrates that a high-commitment collaborative culture is not enough. When the organizing model ceases to be effective, performance alignment is not the only casualty. Psychological alignment begins to erode as a result of frustration with the organization's effectiveness. Despite the substantial psychological alignment and commitment that HP still possessed in the late 1990s and the understanding by many that decentralization had become a liability, the firm was unable to mobilize this understanding into the necessary reorganization—which would require top and middle managers to abandon the firm's legacy assumptions about the best way to organize and manage the business. Letting go of legacy assumptions is complicated by the potential losses in autonomy, power, relationships, and identity that all frame-breaking reorganizations bring. At HP, the autonomy and power of division managers, indeed their very identity, would be threatened by a reorganization that modified their historic role. Successful change, therefore, requires that senior management understand organization design logic and lead a collaborative high-involvement change process that minimizes perceived losses by key people.

In response to a decline in HP's performance, HP's board of directors, which in retrospect did not understand the value of HP's collaborative culture, brought in Carly Fiorina, a senior executive from Lucent.[5] The instrument business had by then been spun off as Agilent Technologies. Though Fiorina gave lip service to the "HP Way," early decisions clearly signaled that she intended to change HP's culture. To make HP's computer and printer organizations more responsive to customer needs, one of Fiorina's first decisions was to reorganize HP into a "front-back" structure, a particular type of structured network discussed later, characterized by formal and informal mechanisms intended to achieve coordination, collaboration, and teamwork around customer needs. Front-facing customer marketing units assumed the responsibility for interfacing with customers to identify new opportunities and had responsibility for seeing to it that "back-end" functions of product engineering, manufacturing, and distribution were focusing on the opportunities they identified. This complex matrix-like organization eliminated the decentralized structure that had led to six decades of success—and altered roles, responsibilities, and relationships throughout HP. Most significant, it reduced the role of the once powerful and high-status division general manager who had full responsibility for all facets of the business, including marketing.

Though in theory this new way of organizing the firm made sense, it was developed in a matter of only months by Fiorina and her expert organization design consultants, and without much participation from key managers. Though many understood HP's need to be more responsive to solution-seeking customers, key executives did not necessarily agree with this radical departure. "I don't know anyone who was in favor of it [the new front-back organization] other than Carly," said one executive. "She came in with a recipe," said another, "and come hell or high water, she was going to use it." Carolyn Ticknor, head of laser printers, remembered, "I was like a deer caught in the headlights when she [Fiorina] described the front and back end."[6] Two years after she announced the reorganization, Fiorina quietly abandoned it.[7] Six years after Fiorina's appointment as CEO, HP's performance, morale, and commitment were at an all-time low. Failure to navigate an organizational revolution had failed to restore performance and had caused a precipitous decline in psychological alignment. Fiorina's approach to change had also reduced HP's capacity to learn and change.

A very different outcome occurred about a decade earlier at IBM, another failing computer and information processing company. Like Bill Hewlett and Dave Packard, Thomas Watson Jr., the founder's son, had developed IBM into an HCHP company. By the early 1980s, IBM held a dominant position in mainframe computers, its technical innovation and superior customer service unrivaled by others in the industry.[8] It was a mammoth company with independent product divisions, a global presence through IBM World Trade, a regional organization with powerful heads, and strong and talented corporate staff groups at the leading edge of their respective professional specialties. But in the early 1990s, IBM was failing. Like HP, IBM had been unable to meet the increasing demand by customers for solutions products. Much like HP, IBM's strong product divisions and geographic regions had become fiefdoms, each concerned with maximizing its own revenues and profits, making it impossible for the company to integrate its offerings into the solutions its customers required. In the late 1980s and early 1990s, IBM's financial fortunes declined rapidly enough that some feared bankruptcy.

CEO John Akers correctly understood that IBM, like all corporations, had to create coordination between its diverse parts in order to deliver solutions to its customers and value for its shareholders. Unable to conceive or implement a needed reorganization that would improve coordination and deliver solutions, Akers considered breaking up the company so that each business unit could succeed.

Before he could break up the company, though, Akers was forced to resign. Lou Gerstner, a former McKinsey consultant, senior executive at American Express's Travel Services, and CEO of RJR Nabisco, was appointed to replace Akers in 1992. Gerstner recognized that tailored solutions and service were the future, and that a front-back organization—similar to the structured network that Fiorina adopted at HP a decade later—with a strong customer-facing unit would best coordinate IBM's resources around emerging opportunities in the solutions space. In contrast to HP, IBM succeeded in adopting this complex organization. In the decade that followed, IBM became the preeminent provider of information technology solutions and services, a business Carly Fiorina wanted HP to dominate.

How did this happen? Unlike Fiorina, Gerstner recognized that making IBM responsive to customer requirements for solutions would take time. It was not just a matter of designing the right structure, important as that was. He evolved the organization over several years; he viewed reorganization as a learning process requiring support for changes in people, rewards, and culture. Under Gerstner's leadership, the change at IBM led to performance alignment, and over time, to psychological alignment.

The Organizing Challenge

HCHP companies must continuously adapt their organizing model to new market realities. They anticipate necessary revolutions in how the firm is organized and negotiate them without destroying their high commitment culture. To this end, leadership teams must be able to:

- Identify tensions in the organization before a decline in performance alignment materially affects customer commitment and financial results. Enabling truth to speak to power can help in this regard.
- Design a new organization that fits new strategic realities. This requires an understanding of organization design logic and alternative organizing models.
- Change the other change levers discussed in the book to support the reorganization. Without these complementary changes, top management's intention does not become a reality.
- Lead change in a way that minimizes perceived losses by key managers and maintains commitment of as many affected parties as possible. Given that all reorganizations create winners and losers with respect to influence, decision rights, and resources, this is a difficult challenge.
- Invest for the long term by developing adaptive attitudes, skills, and culture that will make the firm "change ready" for inevitable organizational transitions in its future. HCHP organizations are advantaged because they possess these adaptive qualities.

If higher management follows these principles, leaders will be able to transition their organizations through periods of organizational evolution and revolution as the firm grows, without significant declines in commitment and performance.

The Santa Rosa Systems Division[9]

When I began to work with and study the Santa Rosa Systems Division of Hewlett-Packard in 1994, its general manager, Scott Wright, faced daunting challenges. Two years earlier Wright had been charged with leading a new test and measurement systems business unit. Slowing demand from the defense and aerospace industry for HP's sophisticated single-purpose instruments, designed primarily for engineers, led to a top management decision to enter the emerging telecommunications market with systems that offered solutions to complex measurement problems faced by equipment manufacturers. Becoming a solutions business confronted Wright and his senior team with the very same challenges faced by Fiorina five years later, though on a smaller scale. SRSD had the same HCHP culture that characterized HP as a whole, and they were imbued with the same legacy assumptions about how to organize—decentralize the business—that played a role in Fiorina's failure to install a front-back structured network.

The new division inherited systems products developed in the previous decade by HP's multiple instrument divisions in the test and measurement group. These systems had been developed in response to customer requests, as opposed to a coordinated and concerted strategy. As in most businesses operating in dynamic and often turbulent market environments, Wright and his senior team were confronted with the challenge of *exploring* and developing new business opportunities using HP's superior technology while at the same time *exploiting* the legacy product lines they had inherited. Revenues and profits from these legacy products were needed to support SRSD's investment in R&D.

SRSD's senior team had to manage an unusually complex and wide array of product lines. These served different markets and customers, varied considerably in their underlying technology, and ranged from mature to developing products still in R&D. Due to variation in maturity, some product lines required a heavy investment in R&D (exploration strategy) and were assigned to the R&D department, whereas others could do with far lower investment but were a source of immediate profits. The latter product lines relied on the support of a custom systems engineering group to build systems from existing instruments for customers who required them immediately (exploitation strategy).

Shortly after the formation of SRSD, Wright and his senior team conducted a strategic assessment of the business that identified three new systems business opportunities. Recognizing that they could not manage the complex array of new and legacy products from the top, management created three business teams composed of representatives from R&D, custom systems, marketing, and finance, each responsible for managing new and legacy products. But HP's organizational legacy of decentralized functionally organized divisions led them to create teams in name only.

With the creation of three business teams, SRSD's senior team had created a matrix-like structured network, but without fully understanding all the design features required. Roles and responsibilities assigned to key managers still conformed to those of a functional structure, as did skills of key players, thus limiting the new organization's effectiveness. Section heads in R&D, with no business management experience, were responsible for coordinating R&D, custom systems engineering, and marketing (a legacy of HP's historic practice of giving R&D the lead in business development), but they did not have profit responsibility or authority over team members. Functional managers still retained their full authority over their domains. Given their R&D orientation, team leaders focused team meetings on new product development, but failed to give time and focus to mature product lines that were the source of SRSD's revenue and profits. Consequently, custom systems engineers, who resented the fact that their increasingly successful efforts to bring in much-needed revenues were being ignored, failed to attend meetings. Because custom systems engineering required support from R&D's engineers and R&D required support from custom systems engineers, conflict between the two functional departments was continuous, with both sides claiming that their requirements had priority, leading at least one engineer to call the struggle "a cold war." Marketing, a key function in the solutions businesses that SRSD wanted to enter, had little influence and was underresourced. A poorly designed organization was to blame. It reflected management's assumptions about organizing that were rooted in HP's history of making and selling single-purpose instruments.

Two years after the reorganization, SRSD was struggling. Morale was at an all-time low, eroding SRSD's high-commitment culture. SRSD had missed, by a wide margin, top management's expectations for growth in revenue and profits. Managers and engineers described SRSD's problems as follows:[10]

- "We have two competing strategies that are battling each other for the same resources. The resultant factions around these strategies are tearing the organization apart."
- "The members of the top team operate within their own functional silos. They are like a group of fiefdoms that refuse to cooperate effectively for fear that they will lose their power."
- "SRSD is still not sure what kind of a business it wants to be."

To rescue the business from its impending failure, SRSD's senior management had to reorganize. Like all senior teams who lead an unsuccessful organization with inadequate performance and psychological alignment, SRSD's senior management had to confront tensions in their organization that they had ignored, diagnose their root causes, and then reorganize.

Unlike HP's corporate efforts to become a solutions business a few years later, however, Wright and his team succeeded in reorganizing the business as a structured network suited to the solutions business. Despite the revolution in roles, responsibilities, and decision rights that this reorganization brought about, SRSD was able to achieve dramatic improvements in effectiveness, performance, and commitment. Several years after SRSD initiated its reorganization, Ned Barnholt, senior executive vice president of HP's test and measurement sector, of which SRSD was a division, described the results he saw:

> They have done a terrific job after a year or so of struggling to figure out what the business was and how to get it going. . . . Today I see them as one of our star divisions. In results, they have achieved and exceeded my and Dick's [Wright's immediate boss] expectations [not only] in terms of level of business and speed with which they have made progress in achieving business results, but also in terms of the magnitude of the turnaround. Today SRSD represents best practices in a lot of areas. It is one of the best, if not the best, in software. The best in project management. They have really turned around weakness into strengths. A marvelous success. They now have the infrastructure and skills to really grow.[11]

SRSD's successful revolution in organizing can be attributed in part to the knowledge about organizing brought to the design task, as well as the honest, collective, and public conversation they employed to lead learning and change.

Organization Design Logic

The essence of the organizing challenge is to develop *differentiated subunits* with the specialized tasks, goals, capabilities, and culture needed to innovate, and at the same time *coordinate* these differentiated resources to respond in a timely and efficient manner to opportunities and threats presented in the marketplace. HCHP organizations manage the paradox of differentiation and coordination better than their competitors. They are able to do this thanks to their design and commitment culture, and consequently are able to achieve the strategic advantage of exploration and exploitation so essential for sustained performance.

Differentiation

The resources of the firm are its horizontally differentiated subunits—functional departments, business units, geographic regions or staff groups inside the firm, as well as supply chain and business partners outside the firm.[12] These are the building blocks of the organization. Differentiation is essential if the organization is to formulate and implement its product-market strategies. The more uncertain and turbulent the environment in which firms operate, the more differentiation is required. Such differentiation allows each activity in the value chain to develop its distinctive pattern of behavior, culture, and capabilities.[13] Failing to differentiate research from development, for example, may prevent a company's basic researchers from innovating, because tight product development schedules pull them away from more speculative research work. Failing to separate strategic planning from finance can lead to strategic blindness as financial goals become paramount. Inadequate differentiation of geographic regions can prevent effective response to local customer needs. Failing to separate an emerging business in the exploration stage from a more mature business in the exploitation stage will prevent the focus and attention needed for the business to succeed. That is why HP's top management chose to establish SRSD as a systems division. This, they thought, would enable it to focus on the development of a business that served a very different market and customers.

Organizations also face the problem of vertical differentiation—how many levels the organization will have and what the roles and responsibilities of these levels will be. Too many levels will create a top-down decision-making process, slow decisions, erode commitment, and increase cost. Too few levels will pull senior management into operating details that should be managed below them and away from their strategic management role.

The more uncertain or turbulent the environment, and the larger the scope and size of the organization, the more differentiated the organization becomes. Management is faced with the ever more complex challenge of defining:[14]

1. Roles and responsibilities of differentiated subunits and levels.
2. Accountability of differentiated unit and levels—how performance will be measured and evaluated.

Coordination

Integration of differentiated subunits is the second major challenge facing all organization. Management must enable coordination between functional departments, business units, geographic regions, and other value-creating activities outside the boundary of the organization to allow cost-effective and timely implementation of its strategic tasks. These tasks are the firm's key opportunities for economic value creation and high performance.[15] In the case of both IBM and HP, this meant reorienting multiple product divisions, geographic regions, and functions to respond to customer needs for solutions. In the case of SRSD, this meant developing stronger coordination between R&D, marketing, and the custom systems group to deliver solutions that customers needed. The "cold war" between these functional departments prevented this. To be fully exploited, each strategic task requires a *coordinating mechanism*.

Several different mechanisms from which senior teams can choose are illustrated in Figure 9.2. They range from a relatively weak liaison person with no formal authority; cross-functional teams led by a functional manager with little or no formal authority (such as SRSD had designed); fully functioning business teams composed of representatives from different functional departments who report to a business team leader with responsibility for strategy and profits; or a separately organized business unit led by a general manager with authority over all functions and resources required to manage the business. More formal lines of authority are typically required when the measure of task accomplishment has an important business outcome, such as profitability.

The coordination challenges of larger and more complex organizations are both vertical and horizontal. Management must make or facilitate the following design decisions:

1. *What lateral and vertical relationships are required to coordinate subunits?* Management must identify the key functions, business units, or geographic regions that must be coordinated for effective execution of businesses or strategic tasks. And they must answer the question of who will lead these efforts.

FIGURE 9.2. COORDINATING MECHANISMS "LADDER."

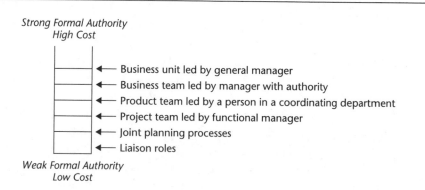

Strong Formal Authority
High Cost

← Business unit led by general manager
← Business team led by manager with authority
← Product team led by a person in a coordinating department
← Project team led by functional manager
← Joint planning processes
← Liaison roles

Weak Formal Authority
Low Cost

2. *What decision rights will each subunit and the person representing them have?* Who will have responsibility and authority, who has approval rights (to veto), who must be consulted to obtain their support, and who will be merely informed? These decisions are particularly critical in structured networks (discussed below) such as matrix or front-back organizations where multiple parties are involved and the traditional single boss source of coordination and control does not exist.[16]

3. *Management processes to be employed in vertical and horizontal coordination.* This is the question of *how* vertical and horizontal conversations should be executed (meetings, topics to be discussed, and process) to enable good decisions. For example, how will the senior team review the business (vertical coordination)? How will cross-functional or cross-business teams work together to produce the best decisions? What behavioral norms are to govern conversations? Of course, senior management can only set the parameters; the actors involved must develop the details.

HCHP organizations are more innovative and execute more effectively than their competitors because they excel in their capacity to integrate across highly differentiated value-creating activities. They do this through superior organizational design and a supporting collaborative high-commitment culture. They can employ flatter structures (fewer levels) because they delegate more responsibility to lower levels and because their high-commitment culture requires less oversight.

Internal Motivation and Commitment

Senior teams who wish to develop an HCHP organization must ask: Does the organizational design we are contemplating create jobs/roles that foster internal motivation?

We know from seminal research conducted by Richard Hackman and Greg Oldham that jobs must provide three psychological states in order to develop high internal work motivation.[17] Individuals must see their work as meaningful, they must feel responsible for the outcomes of their work, and they must have knowledge of the results of their work. You might think that only lower-level, front-line workers experience deficiencies in these psychological states, and of course they frequently do (though less so in HCHP organizations), but my own observation is that managers, sometimes high-level managers, do not always find their jobs meaningful or feel they are responsible for the results of their business, given the amount of top-down control over their decisions.

For this reason, solving the coordination problem with large central staffs (a bureaucratic organizational solution shown as stage 4 in Figure 9.1) will undermine commitment. HCHP leaders avoid this by designing a flat (fewer levels) organization with larger spans of control than most and delegate decision making to the lowest possible level. High psychological alignment in an HCHP firm motivates managers and front-line employees to take responsibility with far less top-down control than in other firms. It is this cultural context that enables HCHP organizations to be flat and effective.

This was the strength of Hewlett-Packard's nonbureaucratic decentralized divisional organization for many decades. Spans of control were larger than those found in most companies, making it difficult for group-level executives to closely control their division managers. Corporate staffs were small and had little authority over division managers. Staff work was often accomplished by task forces of managers from line divisions. And division managers had considerable authority and autonomy to achieve performance goals set mutually with their higher-level management. In effect, they were given freedom to fail. The role of higher-level management was to coach, not control.

When I began working with the struggling Santa Rosa Systems Division there was no evidence of heavy-handed supervision by Scott Wright's boss. You might think, as many of my students often do when I teach the SRSD case, that Wright's boss must not have been doing his job given the difficulties SRSD faced when I first arrived on the scene. An interview with Wright's boss a few years later indicated that he was doing his job. He understood very well the challenges Wright faced, suggesting that he chose to restrict his supervision of Wright to coaching and offering help. Had he intervened more, I doubt that Wright and his senior team would have had the opportunity to learn, grow as managers, and ultimately develop an organizing model that contrasted sharply with HP's decentralized organizing model. Of course, the "HP Way" philosophy of management was the cultural context that enabled all this.

Choosing How to Organize

Developing an HCHP organization requires senior teams to be directly involved in choosing between three fundamental organizing archetypes and avoiding one—bureaucracy. That did not happen at HP when Carly Fiorina reorganized into a structured network without involvement of her senior team. That accounts for the resistance she encountered and the ultimate failure of HP to become a structured network. Each organizing model represents a distinct way to solve the differentiation and coordination problem; each has its own costs and benefits. By being involved in the design process, senior teams come to understand these costs and benefits. This enables them to let go of their biases and to adapt the organizing model they choose to their particular situation.

Five *criteria* ought to be considered in making a design choice.[18] It is unlikely that all criteria can be satisfied, thus usually making tradeoffs necessary.

1. Fit with strategy
2. Availability of scarce managerial talent and functional specialists
3. Differential cost incurred in managing each archetype
4. Differential difficulty of leading and managing each organizational type
5. Internal motivation and commitment achieved by the design

Though few companies employ a pure form of each archetype—most organizations are hybrids—the organizational design of each enterprise is primarily patterned after one. For example, Hewlett-Packard was principally a decentralized divisional organization, but it incorporated elements of the structured network in coordinating across decentralized divisions. SRSD was principally a functional organization, but its business teams incorporated aspects of the matrix—one type of structured network.

Managing a business involves four fundamental decisions listed below. Each organization type described below allocates *rights to decide* these questions differently. And senior teams are well advised to understand how these decision rights will be distributed in the organizational model they choose.

a. *What* are our goals and our strategies for achieving them? What customers will we serve? What performance levels must we achieve? What strategic initiatives will we have to launch to achieve these results?
b. *When* must activities supporting these goals and strategies be completed? By when must a new product be developed? By when must we achieve a certain level of performance?
c. *Who*—which people should be assigned to key jobs?
d. *How* should the functional activities supporting our goals and strategies be accomplished? What are the best and most efficient practices that should be employed?

Senior teams who choose an organizational design without understanding the implications for the five criteria (strategy, cost, and so on) or the allocation of decision rights (what, when, who, and how) set up the organization for failure.

TABLE 9.1. STRENGTHS AND WEAKNESSES OF ALTERNATIVE ORGANIZING MODELS.

	Functional Organization	Decentralized Divisional Organization	Structured Network
Strategy	Exploitation through cost and quality effectiveness	Exploration through organic growth and acquisition	Exploitation and exploration Customer-centric customer solutions
Strengths	• Enables focus on single business • Enables strong functional capabilities • Facilitates operational effectiveness • Relatively easy to manage	• Enables focus on multiple businesses, services, or geographic regions • Enables sale and acquisitions of businesses • Clear accountability for profit • Develops general managers • Relatively easy to manage	• Enables focus on multiple businesses, functions, and regions • High coordination and collaboration • Responsive to environmental changes • Knowledge sharing and learning • Flexibility in refocusing business and allocating resources accordingly • High conflict
Weaknesses	• Poor coordination between functions • Innovations do not receive attention and resources • Decisions made at top • Does not develop general managers	• Duplication of resources makes it a high-cost structure • Does not enable strong functional capabilities • Poor coordination between divisions • Hard to reallocate people and money resources across divisions • Little knowledge sharing and learning between divisions	• Costly to design and difficult to manage • High conflict • Requires strong, collaborative, high commitment culture • High transaction costs—meetings • Difficult to assess performance and hold people accountable

The three fundamental archetypes and their strengths and weaknesses are discussed below and are shown in Table 9.1. It is important to remember that each enterprise will have to adapt its choice based on its own circumstances.

Archetype I: Functional Organization

The functional structure is often the first organizational form a business evolves to as it emerges from the chaos of a start-up (see Figure 9.1). It is the appropriate structure for a business with a single-product market focus. Best at enabling low cost or product or service quality, the functional structure is the choice for businesses whose strategy is growing and "defending" their single-product market domain.[19] Low coordination costs—principally hierarchy—enable it to be cost-effective. Coordination between differentiated functional departments is largely accomplished through the general manager; this is the most conventional and traditional mechanism in the coordination ladder shown in Figure 9.2.

Because of the relative simplicity and stability of the business, senior teams can develop a plan and oversee its execution relatively easily. They have most of the information and knowledge needed to make the four fundamental business decisions (what, when, who, and how), and the general manager can exercise his or her positional power to enforce them.

The functional organization's weakness is innovation. With focus and attention on one core product or service, new product or service ideas do not get the attention and resources they require. All of senior management's attention and the organization's resources are focused on the primary business line. SRSD was formed as a separate business unit by HP's top management for this reason. Systems solutions that were germinating in multiple single-purpose instrument divisions organized functionally were not getting the attention, resources, and investment required to grow them into full-fledged businesses.

Even if senior management were to attend to and resource new and emerging business lines, senior teams would begin to experience information overload. They would not have the specialized customer and "technical" knowledge and information to make effective decisions at their level.[20] Under these circumstances, the functional organizational form leads to a crisis of autonomy and innovation (stage 2 in Figure 9.1). Leaders of new business lines become frustrated with their inability to acquire the resources and get decisions they need from their senior team to achieve their goals. This is the problem that SRSD's senior team faced. Senior team members did not have the time and expertise to run multiple legacy product lines and three new systems solutions on which they were betting the future. Growth and profit goals were not met. Management faced a choice as to which of the remaining organizational models might serve them best.

Archetype II: Decentralized Divisional Organization

The crisis in autonomy and innovation that is inevitably associated with the growth of a successful and thriving business (Figure 9.1) leads to the creation of new divisions, each focused on developing and growing new business lines that were previously stifled. This decentralized divisional structure is best suited for corporations that wish to "prospect" for new opportunities.[21] Each business unit is focused on a single-product market domain. In its pure form, the decentralized divisional structure enables senior management to explore new opportunities through organic growth—innovation in its focused business units—or acquisition. Hewlett-Packard employed a process they called cellular division. When a new product was developed by a business unit, it was split off into a new business unit when its scale became large enough.

Responsibility for strategy (what and when) and execution (how and who) are invested in each division's senior team. Each division can focus its resources on one key business opportunity. A strength of this organization is that accountability for performance is unambiguous. Corporate top management can reward divisional managers if they are successful, and remove them if they are not, without any concerns about fairness. The decentralized divisional organization also enables companies to develop a cadre of general managers through experience, the best way to test their capabilities and enable learning.

Vertical coordination is a challenge in decentralized organizations as they grow. Top management must oversee an ever-larger number of divisions. Clear measures of performance, such as revenue and profit, make this task relatively easy, but as an increasing number of divisions stretch senior management capacities, divisions are clustered into groups or sectors headed by a senior executive. This solves senior management's "span of control" problem. A disadvantage of decentralized corporations is the cost. A large number of general managers and a complement of experienced functional managers have to be deployed in each business.

The very success of the decentralized form will eventually make it difficult to gain the necessary cooperation from autonomous divisions needed to develop solutions for customers—the problem faced by Hewlett-Packard in 1999—or to share resources in an effort to reduce cost (it is an expensive organizing model). The result is a crisis in coordination and control to which the company must respond if it is to continue profitable growth (stage 3 in Figure 9.1). IBM and Hewlett-Packard each faced this crisis.

Firms have historically responded to this crisis with a false step, although some might argue it is a necessary learning stage. They strip decentralized divisions of some decision rights and activities and assign them to strong corporate staff groups. The result is better control and coordination, but also a bureaucracy that ultimately leads to a crisis of commitment and market responsiveness (Figure 9.1). Focus, speed, flexibility, and innovation of business units are sharply reduced, not to mention commitment of managers. This is the bureaucracy that General Electric's Jack Welch dismantled as a first step in GE's journey to HCHP. For these reasons the organizing model is an alternative to be avoided by senior teams who aspire to build an HCHP firm.

HCHP companies that have developed a collaborative high commitment culture are able to sidestep the bureaucratic phase and can move much more quickly than their competitors to the structured network—the organizing form that HCHP corporations will have to adopt as they grow in scale and scope.

Archetype III: Structured Network

Writing about complex organizations, Michael Goold and Andrew Campbell conjure up the following image.[22] When one thinks about an ideal complex organization, it is "seductive" to imagine multiple value-adding activities—product units, functional staff groups, and geographic regions, for instance—voluntarily interacting with each other to coordinate their activities to meet customer needs. In such an ideal world, every unit knows its role, takes responsibility for making decisions that are in the best interest of the larger organization, as opposed to their own unit, and relationships along every axis of interaction are positive and collaborative. The result is a unified and purposeful enterprise with little need for hierarchy or top-down authority. It is a "self-managed network," a boundaryless organization.

Such an ideal is of course far from reality in most complex corporations. For a variety of management and leadership reasons (see discussion of silent killers in chapter 5), subunits in a complex organization find it hard to coordinate their efforts. They do not always understand or accept their roles and responsibilities, nor do they always link up with the right subunits or people, or establish collaborative relationships. Bureaucracy is the way many companies ensure that the right units and people work together.

The alternative that HCHP firms must adopt is the *structured network* (stage 5), a term Goold and Campbell coined to describe an organization designed to achieve integration and coordination without heavy-handed hierarchy. Structured networks are designed to bust silos and to encourage a network of relationships—along multiple axes. They unify subunits around business opportunities, particularly customer solutions. Research by Jay Galbraith and my colleague Ranjay Gulati finds that structured networks enable organizations to become customer-centric.[23] Gulati finds that they outperform organizations not so organized.

Structured networks provide the benefits of the decentralized organization—focus on opportunities and innovation—and, simultaneously, the advantage of shared resources—functional capabilities or regional organizations with local knowledge. Units with relevant resources and capabilities are linked (networked) with market-facing business leaders through the types of coordinating mechanisms listed in Figure 9.2. I include in this broad class of designs cross-functional program or project organizations, matrix organizations (two-boss or dotted-line variations), and the front-back organization adopted by HP in 2000. In all these forms, front-end marketing or customer-facing strategic business units have responsibility for what and when decisions. Supporting units have responsibility for who and how decisions. The structured network, in whatever form, requires

FIGURE 9.3. SIMPLE STRUCTURED NETWORK AS "DIAMOND."

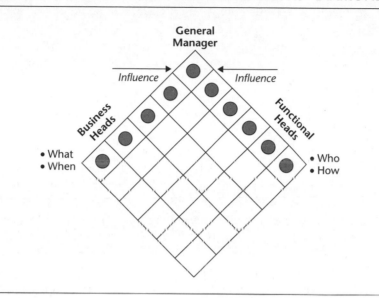

high levels of coordination and collaboration. It is characterized by multiple solid or dotted-line relationships.

In its simplest form, employed here as an illustration, the structured network is a two-sided matrix—functions on one side and strategic business initiatives on the other—as shown in Figure 9.3. Cross-functional teams charged with managing strategic initiatives or businesses overlay functional departments—the organization's resources. The "diamond" illustrates that the allocation of responsibilities for managing each business is split between business heads on the left side of the diamond and functional heads on the right side; the power of each side is intended to be approximately equal. Business heads are assigned responsibility for making what and when decisions, and functional heads are assigned responsibility for who and how decisions. If the structured network is organized as a full matrix structure, team members will report to two bosses. They are each responsible for seeing that their functional department's perspective is represented to the business head and team, and then for ensuring that their functional activity meets their commitments.

Structured networks are intended to surface conflicts, often hidden in more hierarchical organizations, between different axes of the network. This should enhance the quality of decisions so long as the conflict is dealt with constructively. For this reason an effective structured network organization requires managers with interpersonal skills and a collaborative culture. None of this is possible without a senior team, composed of key managers from all sides of the network who are able to work together in a highly effective manner. That team must define roles and responsibilities clearly, continuously define priorities and allocate resources accordingly, be capable of constructive conflict required to sort out differences, form a consensus about the values and behavior they expect, advocate them strongly, and model these in their own functioning as a team. This softer dimension of structured network organizations is often shortchanged by companies. Leaders install a matrix or front-back organization without developing their top team or the necessary culture.

The structured network is the most difficult of the three alternative organizations to lead and manage because it requires collaborative attitudes, skills, and behavior that do not exist in many organizations. They require leaders at the top who are committed to developing a culture that will encourage collaborative behavior. In short, it requires an HCHP leader who will lead a collective learning process (chapter 6) such as that employed by SRSD and which I will describe below. Such a learning process is essential to the development of the very collaborative skills and attitudes the structured network requires.

Self-Designing the Organization

If a new organization design is to be implemented effectively, senior teams ought to "self-design" the organization; that is, involve themselves and lower levels in the design process, particularly if their goal is to build an HCHP organization. This conclusion is supported by the work of Tom Cummings and Sue Mohrman, who coined the term self-design.[24] A self-designing senior team engages lower levels in the design process, discusses alternative designs, and makes a choice, as opposed to relying on consultants or internal staff groups to recommend a new design. By being deeply involved in designing the organization, typically with the help of a consultant as a resource, the senior team is better prepared to lead the new organization. Without a diagnosis by the senior team of current organizational failures, and deep involvement in the redesign, inevitable resistance from some quarters will weaken commitment to the structure and reignite political debates about how to organize. Self-design by senior teams is rare and may explain many reorganization failures like that at HP under Carly Fiorina in 1999. This high-involvement process is essential for senior teams who want to develop performance alignment and psychological alignment, as well as the capacity of the organization to learn and change in the future. The process of involvement leads to understanding and commitment; in effect, it allows a dress rehearsal that clarifies how the organization will work and thereby changes attitudes.

The SRSD story illustrates the self-design process. The senior team changed its fortunes by spending the better part of a three-day off-site meeting choosing an organization design—after involving lower levels to understand why their current organization was not effective. After receiving feedback from a task force that they had commissioned to learn the unvarnished truth, they used what they learned to conduct a diagnosis. They had to answer the question of why their people perceived two conflicting strategies and why there was a "cold war" between R&D and custom systems. Finance manager George Mosby began the diagnostic discussion by observing that SRSD's "legacy" assumptions were the reason for the flawed organizing model:

> SRSD suffers from the legacy of HP. We are not a box [instrument] division yet we manage and have structured SRSD as though we are. Although [we] have taken on a more expansive role in creating systems than we ever did in past divisions.... Although test and measurement systems have to be heavily market oriented, we still have R&D calling most of the shots. Although our product lines need to be grown and managed as businesses, we still treat them as projects. The systems market is [so] vastly different than anything HP has done in the past with test and measurement, that we need to start thinking of ourselves as a unique entity operating in circumstances that require a different strategy and structure than has been traditionally utilized by [Hewlett-Packard in] the past.[25]

After concluding that their current functional organization with poorly designed business teams (really project teams as Mosby saw it) led by R&D would not work in the solutions business, the senior team began to evaluate alternative organizing models. For this part of the discussion they employed the design logic discussed earlier. Consultants can serve as a resource to this discussion, as I did in the case of SRSD, not as an advocate for one alternative. By exploring organizational design options, SRSD's senior team came away with a deep understanding of the matrix organization that they chose reluctantly; it was very important that they formed an understanding of what it would take to lead and manage the new organization.

The diamond model (Figure 9.3) was employed by SRSD's senior team to choose which of three organizational archetypes was right for their strategy and situation. By rotating it to the left and right we were able to discuss the strengths and weaknesses of each organizational archetypes. We started by rotating to the left, putting the functional side of the matrix in the superior position (at the top) with decision rights for what, when, who, and how. This was their current ineffective state. Advantages and disadvantages of this alternative were then discussed, confirming the diagnosis that the current organizing model was not suited to their strategy and situation.

The diamond was then rotated to the right, putting the business side of the matrix in the superior position (at the top) with rights to decide what, when, who, and how. The advantages and disadvantages of this decentralized divisional organization were then discussed. Because this organization model would require four new general managers, the senior team concluded that it was not practical for SRSD. The senior team could not identify four managers with general management experience to head the divisions, and given the cost of additional senior positions and complementary staffs, this alternative, although the most familiar and comfortable to these HP managers, was not an option.

The model was then rotated back into the starting diamond position as shown in Figure 9.3. This position represents the matrix form, with equal power for both sides of the matrix. A discussion of the advantages and disadvantages of the matrix organizing model followed. Considering SRSD's customer-centric solutions strategy and the disadvantages of the decentralized divisional organization, and given SRSD's circumstances, the senior team chose the two-boss matrix (business team members would have a solid-line reporting relationship with functional as well as business heads). They chose this organizing model despite considerable initial discomfort with matrix management. They feared that HP's higher management, committed to the decentralized divisional organization, would regard their choice with skepticism. And they had heard many negative stories about matrix.

What motivated SRSD's senior team to embrace an unfamiliar organizational model they regarded with skepticism? The discussion of advantages and disadvantages using the design logic discussed in this chapter helped enormously. As one senior team manager said, "We finally had to suck it up and do it because it was the only option." The power of self-design in a much larger organization is illustrated by the following example.

In the early 1980s, Peter Lewis, CEO of Progressive Insurance, brought together his top twenty managers and announced his belief that a reorganization would be needed if the firm were to continue on its highly successful path.[26] The company's growth and changes in the competitive landscape required it. He asked each manager to submit a letter of resignation from his or her current position to signal that he expected all of their roles to change, though their jobs were secure. He then assigned them responsibility for redesign. After a year-long process of data collection, meetings in subgroups, and whole-group meetings with Lewis, a new design emerged, one that profoundly changed the roles and responsibilities of all senior executives and was launched successfully. This began a sustained period of HCHP at Progressive, a company that retains its preeminence in the auto insurance industry as of 2008.

Structure Is Not Organization

Consistent with the systems perspective discussed in chapter 4, redesigning the structure of the organization is not enough, although it is an important frame-breaking first step. Organization change requires changes in assumptions, attitudes, skills, and behavior; that is, changes in the culture.

Consider what Ned Barnholt, executive vice president of Hewlett-Packard's Test and Measurement Organization (TMO), discovered in his successful effort to reorganize TMO in 1993. TMO had experienced a decline in its traditional defense businesses and Barnholt saw opportunities in the emerging telecommunication sector (SRSD was a division in TMO and followed a year later with the reorganization discussed in this chapter). Barnholt observed:

> It became clear that we had to step back from the structural changes and begin to address the cultural changes that were needed. That's what led to project TMO. The easy part is the structural changes. One can create divisions in the stroke of a pen. The problem was how to get the businesses [divisions] to see what it takes to be successful to put a business model in place. A lot of the divisions struggle with that. We had the General Managers of the divisions in for an unspeakable meeting and to address the barriers to change. We realize that many of the changes in TMO and the divisions had to be deeply rooted cultural changes about how we approached our businesses.[27]

The root cause of TMO's struggles to reorganize, and of the struggles in virtually all organizations I have worked with and studied, is a pattern of ineffective management behavior, bolstered by a set of assumptions and beliefs about how to organize and manage, that is borne from past success of the organizing model. Because structure is not organization, reorganizing the business confronts leaders with the culture barrier that Barnholt discovered. Enabling truth to speak to power about barriers to effectiveness—Barnholt's "unspeakables"—is in my experience a powerful first step in motivating and creating a mandate for change. That is why the learning and governance process is one of five critical levers for change. SRSD's senior team employed the Strategic Fitness Process as its learning and governance platform, and it played an important role in motivating them to embrace change.

Confronting the truth is only a first step. It readies senior teams for next steps, changing the pattern of management behavior and, consequently, the culture. To accomplish this, the total system for organizing and managing must be changed over time (see chapter 4). Complementary hard and soft facets of the organizing system must be realigned to fit the new organizing model. Reorganizations falter when the following facets of the organization are not confronted and redesigned:

- Senior team effectiveness—membership, role, responsibilities, relationships, and process
- Roles, responsibilities, and relationships of major value-adding activities or departments
- Performance evaluation measures
- Strategic performance management system and process
- People—who will fill key positions in the new organization and what must be done to close short falls?
- Culture—values and behavior that senior management expects of lower levels

All of the issues above were dealt with by SRSD's senior team in their three-day off-site meeting and more detailed work that followed later. I will discuss these issues briefly and illustrate them with a short description of how they were handled by SRSD.

Senior Team Effectiveness

Each organizational type discussed above makes different demands of the senior team. It is therefore essential that senior teams define their role in the new organization and examine the implications for membership as well as for team process and behavior. SRSD's senior team significantly changed how they would function—how often they would meet, what agenda they would pursue in different meetings, and the process they would employ to run meetings efficiently and effectively.

One of the issues typically not confronted in reorganizations is the effectiveness of the senior team itself. Having heard from lower levels that they were ineffective. and having rarely met as a group (general manager Scott Wright had dealt with team members in one-to-one meetings), the senior team spent time diagnosing the reasons. This led to a decision to discuss strategic issues in the future as a team. Because fear of extended debate and conflict was the reason that Wright resorted to one-to-one meetings, the senior team set ground rules for resolving conflicting views and reaching decisions, and posted these ground rules in their conference room. Wright would put a key issue on the table: a time period would be set for discussion and a consensus decision, and if a decision could not be made by the end of that period, Wright was to make the decision there or at a later date. He would then inform the senior team of his decision and allow a much shorter period to test for agreement; if there was none, and an acceptable alternative could not be developed, his decision was final. One top team member reported that, as simple and obvious as these ground rules were, visiting managers from other divisions often commented about their value and took them back to their own organizations. They helped Scott Wright and his senior team to put difficult issues on the table without fear.

Roles, Responsibilities, and Relationships

Discussing and defining roles in the new organization is a powerful way to clarify how the new organization will work and obtain commitment to it. This is particularly important for successful transformations to a structured network. SRSD's senior team spent a portion of the three-day off-site meeting defining the roles of functional and business heads as well as the role of the senior team and Scott Wright himself. The results were recorded, posted, and communicated to the larger organization; the role clarification process then continued within business teams. It is not only the final definition of roles, responsibilities, and relationships that matters, but the discussion of roles and responsibilities, and the airing of concerns about how the new organization will work. Responsibility charts, such as the one in Figure 9.4, have been found to be helpful in organizing these discussions. Defining roles in this way was useful to a global logistics company that had adopted a global matrix. Key people around the world were engaged in discussions about who had responsibility for key decisions and activities, who had approval or veto rights, who had to be consulted, and who simply needed to be informed.

Strategic Performance Management Process

The strategic management process required by each organizing model is different. The most challenging is the structured network with multiple axes and strategic businesses. SRSD's senior teams redefined the process by which they would develop their three-year plan and how they would review progress, reprioritize the potential of each of their businesses and product lines, and allocate resources accordingly. This was essential because they did not know in advance which of their new systems solutions would begin to succeed first and thus require additional resources and attention. One of the major benefits of the matrix organization they adopted is the relative ease with which people can

FIGURE 9.4. RESPONSIBILITY CHART.

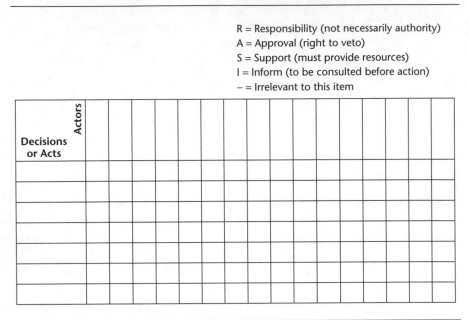

R = Responsibility (not necessarily authority)
A = Approval (right to veto)
S = Support (must provide resources)
I = Inform (to be consulted before action)
– = Irrelevant to this item

Source: Beckhard, R., & Harris, R. T. *Organizational Transitions: Managing Complex Change.* (2nd ed.) Reading, MA: Addison-Wesley, 1987.

be moved from one strategic business initiative to another (they stay in their functional department but are assigned to a different business).

People

One might think that discussion of alternative organizing models might cause senior team members to advocate the organizational model that is most favorable to them. Not if the leader announces in advance that no managers should assume they will occupy their current roles after the reorganization. When Scott Wright made that announcement, it enabled a free discussion of alternative designs and the ultimate choice of the matrix organization.

The question of who would fill the business manager's role forced SRSD's senior team to confront reality; they did not have managers with the general management experience or potential to lead the four business teams which they planned. Their solution was to assign functional heads a second role as leader of one of the businesses, at least until that business grew large enough to allow the expense of a full-time business line manager. This turned out to be a brilliant stroke. By occupying a dual role, each functional manager gained immediate appreciation for the business side and thereby fostered collaboration between the business and functional heads. In the late 1980s, ABB, then led by Percy Barnevick, also employed dual assignments to foster collaboration in their worldwide matrix.

The selection of senior team members for a role in the new organization occurs in one-to-one meetings with the CEO or general manager following agreement about the new design. Scott Wright met with members of the senior team to ascertain their interest in a role and then assigned his key managers to new jobs. Once senior team roles have been assigned, lower-level positions can be filled.

Culture

Culture cannot be changed directly. It emerges over time from planned change in each aspect of the organizing system. It was the virtual simultaneous changes—structure, senior team effectiveness, roles and responsibilities, strategic management process, and people—that were partly responsible for rapid change in SRSD's effectiveness and performance. SRSD's "cold war" dissipated and was replaced by the collaborative culture needed to operate in a matrix. Revenues and profits improved dramatically at the end of the year, and that trajectory was maintained in the outyears. When I contrast successful reorganizations from less successful ones, it is the nearly simultaneous change of structure with the supporting facets of the organizing system that made a difference (see the Corning EPD case in chapter 5).

SRSD's culture change was made easier by HP's collaborative corporate high-commitment culture, in which SRSD managers had worked for years, an advantage that HCHP cultures bestow. The ineffectiveness of its organizing model and the conflicts that it created were what eroded trust and commitment. The redesign of the total system allowed that collaborative culture to reemerge. And as SRSD's human resource manager observed, the total systems change and the collective learning process that SRSD employed, to which I turn next, enabled "SRSD to gain its culture back and then some."

Organizing as Continuous Learning

Organizing for commitment is a continuous learning process, not a one-time affair. Unintended consequences are a by-product of all reorganizations. The initial choice of the organizing model has to be followed by implementation and

FIGURE 9.5. THE ITERATIVE REDESIGN PROCESS.

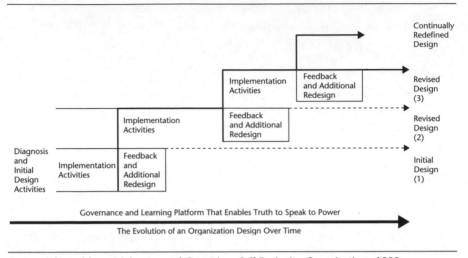

Source: Adapted from Mohrman and Cumming, *Self-Designing Organizations*, 1989.

then learning from the implementation. The experience of living and working in the new organization reveals unanticipated problems that require adaptation of the organizing model, for reorganization is a process of successive approximation. Figure 9.5 shows how a continuous learning process unfolds, over time, from the initial organizational design through several redesigns. At each successive redesign phase, senior teams obtain feedback about the effectiveness of the organization's design; based on what they learn, they revise the design and then implement the redesigned organization.

The learning process must be collective, must enable honest conversations, and must be public in the sense that everyone knows it is going on and that the larger organization is informed about what was learned and what will change (see chapters 6 and 7). Lower levels know how the new organization is actually working and can help senior teams reinvent the organization. Because the learning process will go on for years—senior teams must continually evolve their organizing model and be alert to revolutionary changes that might be required—a disciplined learning and governance process that becomes institutionalized is beneficial. This finding is supported by a cross-sectional analysis, conducted by my colleagues and myself, of more successful and less successful reorganizations.[28] All employed the SFP, but those that did not recycle this honest, collective, and public organizational learning process were less successful than those that did.

SRSD's successful reorganization as a matrix stands in stark contrast to Carly Fiorina's failure to move the corporation to a structured network. The SFP, their collective learning process, created an initial mandate for change. It delivered valid data that enabled a diagnosis and initial revolutionary change to which people became committed. By recycling SFP annually they were able to learn the unvarnished truth about what was and was not working. It served as a durable platform for continuous learning and self-design. For example, in the second year the senior team realized that their organization's design did not deal with their broken order-fulfillment process. In the third year they discovered that the two-boss appraisal system they had created in the first year had eroded. A member of SRSD's senior team provides insight into the contrast between the first and second iterations of SFP:

> Honestly, I did not think that we could get that much out of this [second] iteration. The first time we knew very clearly that there were things that needed to get done because we felt the strain that they placed on us. The strains and tensions within the organization were almost palpable. Well this time the issues and tensions were much less apparent, comparatively. But even so, in this second [SFP], we dug into the complexities of the system like we had never done before and really understood how the different levers affect the process and culture. The first iteration was about how we wanted to set ourselves up as an organization. This time it was about how we wanted the organization to operate.[29]

Because organizing is an action learning process, companies that employ management consultants to design the organization are at a disadvantage. The design process is just beginning when the consultants walk out the door! This all too frequently used approach to reorganization assumes that arriving at the "right" structure and systems is enough. But it does not lead to the deep learning by the senior team or by lower levels necessary for commitment and sustained change.

The consultant's and top management's choice may actually be valid, as was Carly Fiorina's reorganization of HP into a structured network (front-back organization), but management attitudes, skills, and behavior at the top and lower levels may lag far behind. After a period of time, problems implementing the new design embolden opponents and make it hard for the CEO to persevere. The design is abandoned, as in the case of HP, or the CEO pushes harder from the top. This only reinforces the perception by lower levels that top management does not want to hear about managerial barriers or about unanticipated and unintended consequences of the reorganization. Moreover, this approach undermines the development of a high-commitment culture and does not develop the capability that senior and lower-level managers need to engage in self-design, an essential capability in the constantly changing environment of the twenty-first century.

What would have happened had Carly Fiorina employed a self-designing process motivated by an honest, collective, and public conversation such as that which SRSD utilized or Peter Lewis employed at Progressive? We don't know, of course. But the difference that ongoing learning can make may be inferred from SRSD's and Progressive's successes with the high-involvement learning process that enabled their revolutionary reorganizations. Though a comparison between successful change in a business unit like SRSD and the more complex problem of transforming the much larger Hewlett-Packard corporation is somewhat problematic, it is nevertheless instructive. SRSD's senior team orchestrated the very same organizational revolution Fiorina failed to make at the corporate level—a transformation to a solution-oriented structured network. It had the same culture and its managers reflected the same commitment and collaborative instincts. SRSD's managers harbored the same assumptions about how to organize a business—that the decentralized divisional organization is best and the matrix form is not the model of choice. SRSD's honest, collective, and public learning process and the iterative self-designing process that this conversation enabled was, in my view, a major contributor to the success of the structured network (matrix) and the solutions strategy it enabled. When asked in my Harvard Business School executive education class what accounted for the success of the matrix organization, Steve Fossi, a member of the senior team, said, "It was the process."[30]

Summary

Organizations go through periods of evolution and revolution in their organization's design as they face strategic inflections and grow in scale and scope. Firms unable to respond to obsolescence in their organization design risk decline in performance and commitment and endanger their survival. Leadership teams who aspire to build an HCHP organization must be prepared to take responsibility for redesigning the organizing system that best fits their competitive circumstance. And they must know how to engage lower levels in the design process, rather than delegating it to consultants or staff groups, something that reduces the quality of learning and commitment. Senior teams should therefore be familiar with the following organizational design principles.

- Reorganizations should be based on the following fundamental design logic:
  - Appropriate levels of *differentiation* between functions, businesses, and regions are needed to enable each to develop distinctive focus, capabilities, and culture. This enables innovation.
  - *Coordination* must be developed between differentiated activities by designing integrating roles, structures, and processes. This ensures the integration needed for efficiency and responsiveness to customer needs.
  - A flat nonbureaucratic organization creates roles or jobs that foster internal motivation and commitment, an essential feature of HCHP organizations.
  - HCHP firms are resilient—able to adapt and cope to ever-changing circumstances—because, better than competitors' organizations, their collaborative cultures can navigate the paradox of high differentiation and high coordination.
- There are three archetypal organizational models from which senior teams must choose—the functional organization, the decentralized divisional organization, and the structured network. Once a fundamental choice is made, the design must be adapted to individual business circumstances. Each alternative has advantages and disadvantages that senior teams must understand if they are to manage the problems inherent in each choice.
- Structure is not organization. Superior organizational design involves a number of complementary design decisions. What will be the senior team's role? The roles and responsibilities of differentiated departments and integrating teams? What strategic performance process best fits the design? Which people best fit key roles and what reward systems are needed to enable the design to work effectively?
- A self-design process for reorganization rather than the typical consultant-driven reorganization achieves deeper learning and commitment within the senior team and at lower levels. Top teams who involve themselves in diagnosis and design decisions and engage others as needed arrive at the most durable design.
- Reorganization is an iterative and continuous learning process that enables evolution and alerts senior teams to the potential need for an organizational revolution—a frame-breaking change in structure and management process. In effect, reorganization is a process of successive approximations; sequential periods of design, implementation, assessment, and redesign.
- Continuous learning requires a disciplined learning and governance system. Honest, collective, and public conversation enables senior teams to redesign the organization based on valid data. And the collective and public conversation builds organization-wide commitment to the reorganization and capability to learn and change.

Senior teams who want to explore their readiness to manage the evolution of their current organizing system and the revolution that is in their future will want to ask the following questions:

1. Are there palpable tensions in our business that suggest a change is needed in our organizing system?
2. Are we learning the truth about the effectiveness of our organization?
3. Do we have agreement about the strategy and values to which we must fit our organizing system?
4. Do we possess the knowledge about organizational design that will enable us to self-design?
5. Have we been overly reliant on expert consultants to recommend a new organizational design?
6. Are we committed to a high-involvement process of learning and self-design?
7. Have we institutionalized a well-designed learning and governance process that allows us to have an honest, collective (organization-wide), and public conversation about the efficacy of our organization—its performance alignment?

CHAPTER TEN

DEVELOP HUMAN AND SOCIAL CAPITAL

Change Lever 5: The Human Resource System

Many times two teams playing for a championship each have equally good players. In this case teamwork becomes very important, especially in the split-second plays: Given equally good players and good team work, the team with the strongest will to win will prevail. I have remembered that advice, and it has been a guiding principle in developing and managing [Hewlett-Packard]. Get the best people, stress the importance of teamwork, and get them fired up to win the game.[1]

—DAVID PACKARD,
FOUNDER, HEWLETT-PACKARD

If you ask CEOs, human resource executives, or consultants what is the most important source of long-term advantage, they will undoubtedly tell you talent. How to win at the game of talent management—recruiting, selecting, and developing the best and brightest—occupies 90 percent of human resource (HR) conferences, journals, and magazines. McKinsey & Company has dubbed this game the "war on talent." The argument is that in a fast-moving, knowledge-driven economy, advantage goes to companies with the best and the brightest employees. The logical extension of this argument, one that many companies apply, is that firms should do whatever it takes—money, titles, perks, benefits, and red-carpet treatment—to attract and retain talent.

There is validity to the talent argument. Getting the best talent matters, as David Packard suggests in the quote above. We live in a time of explosive knowledge growth in almost every field. It follows that without smart people with the best skills and knowledge—*human capital*—companies are disadvantaged. Companies that develop the best products and services will win in the twenty-first century, the talent argument goes. And there is evidence that talent makes a difference. Intelligence, Frank Schmidt has found, is a predictor of success in virtually every job category.[2] Wide gaps in performance exist between individuals in similar jobs, suggesting that capabilities matter.

Shouldn't a company then try to recruit and select the best talent? Of course it should. But that argument is too simplistic. There is evidence that *overemphasis* on hiring the best and brightest individuals can lead to unintended outcomes. Stars can be hard to retain and their performance will not necessarily live up to their reputation.

Consider Pennsylvania Pharmaceuticals (a pseudonym). Attempting to improve performance, the company made a specially constructed effort to hire only talented MBAs from the best business schools.[3] Within three years of being hired, all the MBAs left for greener pastures, despite the fact that they were told by top management they were the "new breed" the company needed, and top management went out of their way to meet with them regularly to make them feel special.

Boris Groysberg, Ashish Nanda, and Nitin Nohria, my colleagues at the Harvard Business School, found that hiring stars is a losing strategy. They followed 1,052 "star" financial analysts as they moved from company to company—seventy-eight investment banks in all. Their conclusion: "When a company hires an individual star, the star's performance *plunges*, there is a sharp decline in the functioning of the group or team the person works with, and the company's market value falls."[4] Moreover, the star analysts' performance remained below their previous level for *five years*.[5] Groysberg has found similar effects in other occupational groups, including CEOs.

These findings suggest that high performance also requires *social capital*, a collaborative high-commitment culture. An essential facilitator of interactions, social capital translates individual capabilities into organizational capabilities. Supporting this view, Groysberg and his colleagues found that when a star moved with his or her entire team, the star's performance did not decline. Individual performance is a function of the system—the team and other organizational supports—in which the person works. We can conclude, therefore, that an organization is far more than the sum of its talented individuals.

Human capital and social capital are of course both important strategic assets.[6] But social capital is often overlooked, even damaged, when HR policies are designed exclusively to attract, motivate, and keep the best and brightest individuals.[7] As the transformational story of Becton Dickinson will illustrate, the journey to HCHP begins with changing the management system and developing a team culture, not with attracting and motivating individual talent. Talent must be hired and developed to fit the system and culture.

Social Capital: The Underemphasized HR Dimension

Winning soccer teams have a team culture that encourages players to *forgo* kicking a goal if another player is in a better position to do so. Italy defeated an equally talented Brazilian team to win the 2006 World Cup because "the Italian team was more than the sum of its parts."[8] Similarly, the New England Patriots achieved three Super Bowl wins in five years by building a team of players committed to executing their assigned role in the "system" and taking on other roles as needed. Offensive players play defense on certain plays and vice versa. The Patriots develop this collaborative attitude in their players by selecting on much more than football talent, though talent is clearly important. Scott Pioli, vice president of player personnel, says, "We're going after players who fit *our system* [emphasis mine] and our overall [team] philosophy."[9] Coach Bill Belichick and owner Robert Kraft focus on creating a cultural context that enables players and employees to meet high standards and win the game. They do not tolerate players who insist on promoting themselves, nor do they motivate by extraordinary individual incentives. The red-carpet treatment most football teams extend to talented players is not used by the Patriots. Belichick and Kraft will trade players, no matter how outstanding, who want too much money or cannot control their egos.

The human resource management principles successfully employed by winning sports teams are the same principles required to build an HCHP organization. McKinsey, Goldman Sachs, SAS Institute, and the Harvard Business School, among other HCHP organizations listed in chapter 2, are not star systems (see chapter 3). They have human resource management practices that prevent their talented people from developing hubris and behaving like stars. For example, at Goldman Sachs, individuals who proudly announce that "I" just closed a deal are corrected that "we" closed the deal. But these companies are not just high-commitment cultures focused on building a team (social capital). They find a way to hire talented high-performance individuals and develop them into team players. Teamwork (social capital) and individual talent and performance (human capital) are both valued and nurtured (Table 10.1).

What does a corporate team culture feel and look like? *Fast Company* magazine described the SAS Institute as follows: "In an era of relentless pressure, this place is an oasis of calm. In an era of frantic competition, this place is methodical and clearheaded. In a world of free agency, signing bonuses, and stock options, this is a place where loyalty matters more than money."[10] Not surprisingly, *Fortune* magazine has consistently ranked SAS Institute one of the top ten on its list

TABLE 10.1. THE AND/ALSO OF HCHP COMPANIES.

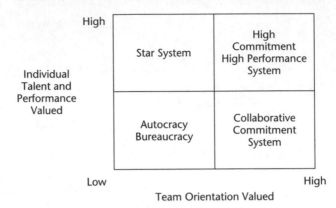

of one hundred best companies to work for, and *Working Mother* has selected SAS Institute as one of its one hundred best companies for working mothers. Its turnover is less than 4 percent, compared to 20 percent in the software industry, where it is customary for people to move from one company to another for more money and a promotion.[11]

How do HCHP companies like SAS Institute attract, retain, and motivate employees without offering rich signing bonuses and stock options? They offer opportunities for meaningful professional and leadership development. Managers spend a lot of time building networks of relationships and developing people because they see these activities as central to achieving results. People at McKinsey are paid well (though not as highly as these talented individuals could get elsewhere) but compensation is not the primary focus of recruitment or firm management. As a former McKinsey partner explained, compensation is pushed into the background once you are hired, and team performance becomes the foreground. Employees in HCHP companies like McKinsey value the organization's capacity to bring out and develop their best working selves.

Edward Deming, the father of total quality management, argued that the system—the organization's culture, processes, and practices—are the determining factor in individual and organizational performance. He even believed that companies should abolish individual performance appraisals because they focus management on the wrong things.[12] The organizational climate in which people work—level of trust, collaboration, knowledge exchange, training, caring, and support—can have a profound effect on organizational capabilities and performance, as well as on individual development.

Deming's view of the system's power is borne out by a study of 2,086 mutual fund managers between 1992 and 1998. Researchers "found that [only] 30% of the fund's performance could be attributed to the individual manager [his performance in the previous fund he/she managed] while 70% was due to the manager's institution, presumably its system of management and culture."[13] If this is true in a knowledge industry such as financial services, in which one could logically argue that individual talent really matters, it has to be even more true in most other industries, where coordination and teamwork are essential.

These findings are consistent with action research conducted by Russ Eisenstat that I discussed in chapter 5. People interviewed about strengths and weaknesses of their organization almost always said that the system of management and culture   the silent killers—were barriers to performance and commitment. They consistently listed "people" as the organization's strength. We can infer from this that people were blocked from achieving their potential by the organizational context in which they were operating, one in which social capital was low. Validation for this conclusion comes from the effects of our interventions to change the system toward more teamwork. They often succeeded in improving commitment and performance without large-scale replacement of the people. Recall that NUMMI, the joint venture between General Motors and Toyota (see chapter 2), was turned around using Japanese management principles introduced to largely the same unproductive employee body that caused GM to shut down the plant.

How Social and Human Capital Interact

Developing both human and social capital presents a challenge. An exclusive focus on attracting and keeping the best talent at all cost can undermine the development of social capital. A sole focus on social capital can be injurious to attracting talented people.

Striving to attract and retain talented, ambitious people that fit *only* the current strategic imperative and immediate job function is a recipe for failure because it often leads to HR policies and practices that undermine *social capital*—relationships built on trust and norms of reciprocity—that sense of mutual obligation born of strong identity with mission and values.[14] Inducing people to join the organization with money, titles, and promises of promotion can easily result in an influx of the "wrong" people—talented people more concerned about themselves than the team. It makes it virtually impossible to develop what management scholars call "citizenship behavior"—unselfish behavior that supports the mission and strategy of the firm as a whole.[15]

Employees who see the firm recruiting talented outsiders to fill positions for which they feel they are qualified will come to resent that practice. Long-term employees at Becton Dickinson, the company I describe next, resented seeing outsiders and consultants brought in to fill the company's needs. Their self-worth, morale, and commitment to the company were damaged. Stars recruited into an HCHP-aspiring company do not understand its culture, nor do they have the relationships with people in their new company that they would need to be effective. They are likely to display hubris and assume that they were brought in to fix the company. Resistance develops, particularly if their compensation and perks are out of line with corporate standards. Soon their efficacy declines. It does not take long before they become disillusioned and leave for greener pastures, as did the pedigreed MBAs recruited by Pennsylvania Pharmaceutical.

An exclusive concern with building social capital can lead to an internal focus and not enough infusion of new ideas. Social capital is built and maintained, but the firm becomes less diverse, innovative, and adaptive. This is one reason that HCHP firms that promote primarily from within recruit *some* external talent. But they work very hard to socialize new high-level recruits and don't keep them if they don't learn to fit in. Leaders of these HCHP firms understand the role that social capital plays in giving their firm an inimitable advantage.

Knowledge and skills that people possess are only valuable when shared with others and converted through teamwork into new products and services. Moreover, without an emotional connection to the firm to hold them, talented individuals will respond to the highest bidder for their services. Turnover and knowledge loss will be high. Labor costs will be high as firms spend more for recruitment and meet demands for higher salaries, bonuses, and stock options. Some of this is inevitable as global labor markets become more competitive, but HCHP companies with a strong team-based culture will avoid this as much as possible. An important outcome of positive social capital is what scholars call *embeddedness;* when people are embedded in a network of positive relationships with peers and management, they do not want to disrupt their connections by leaving and are motivated to stay, learn, and perform.[16] An illustration of the phenomenon was brought to my attention by a partner in a search firm who tried but failed to induce a senior executive to leave Hewlett-Packard for three times his total compensation.

A strong team culture enables firms to recruit the talent they need. A strong community of purpose will give the firm a reputation as a great place to work. This increases the labor pool from which the company can draw like-minded employees and improves the organization's capacity to be selective. That in turn enables the company to hire only those who fit the culture and creates a virtuous cycle. In contrast, weak or negative social capital damages the firm not only through the recruitment costs that high turnover and financial incentives impose, but also by the more subtle and expensive cost of the time needed—perhaps years—for replacements to perform at the same level as their predecessors.

In sum, social capital is valuable. It is relatively easy to buy talent, but much harder to achieve organizational performance that is greater than the sum of talented recruits without social capital. Organizations with high social capital are better at developing and enhancing the talents of their members (human capital) because individuals can draw on team support and because strong norms place pressures to contribute and improve performance. Moreover, developing talent internally creates company-specific capabilities—skills unique to the firm—and offers an advantage. It makes talent more valuable to the firm than to its competitors and reduces the likelihood that others will be willing to offer higher compensation for capabilities that are not useful to them, thus reducing turnover for the firm with high social capital. At the same time, companies that entice high performers—the stars—to work for them pay too much for the performance they get, as the Groysberg research shows, thus disadvantaging them.

A team culture is needed to foster career mobility across functions, businesses, and geographic regions. A task force of employees commissioned by the CEO to ascertain barriers to management development at Health Technology (a pseudonym)—a company they described as lacking a teamwork culture (social capital)—reported that managers across the company perceived heads of key business units as unwilling to transfer the best and highest potential people for fear of losing their least dispensable managers. Instead, they transferred the least talented and most dispensable managers. Management development requires cross-boundary and challenging experiences, a claim supported by a seminal study conducted by Morgan McCall, Michael Lombardo, and Ann Morrison of the Center for Creative Leadership.[17] Without social capital that will not happen.

Becton Dickinson: A Company in Need of Transformation[18]

In 1990, when I began to work with and study Becton Dickinson (BD), a global medical technology company with a long history dating back to its founding in 1897, the company was rated by Wall Street analysts as a "hold" and very definitely not a "buy." The company faced numerous challenges after a successful defense against a takeover and a period of major restructuring and cost reduction that repositioned the company in the increasingly price-sensitive global health care sector. BD's newly appointed CEO, Ray Gilmartin, described the challenges: "There are certain skills that we require as an organization to pull off our strategy. We are trying to achieve multidivisional selling and supply chain management, which have to involve all of our divisions. The transnational balance between global scale economies and national responsiveness require an organizational philosophy and a way of operating that is not traditional. We also need organizational mechanisms, commitment, and skills to manage technology."[19]

Becton Dickinson was a long way from being the company Gilmartin sensed it should be in order to compete. Managers saw a strong and appropriate emphasis on strategy, but saw no evidence or articulation of "human" values. The company lacked the collaborative culture and structures to integrate multiple divisions, geographic regions, and functions into a coherent whole. BD's innovation strategy was threatened by an isolated corporate R&D center and the deeply functional structure and culture within the business units.

This state of affairs had multiple causes. Business unit managers complained about the gap between top management's espoused management philosophy of participative and collegial decision making and the reality of micromanagement. Managers thought they were overloaded and pointed to too much emphasis on budgets and financial controls, detailed and time-consuming oversight by the corporate finance function, as well as a top-down strategic planning process that disempowered sector and division managers.

One reason for many of these problems was a paucity of managers who had the collaborative values and skills that Gilmartin perceived as essential—managers who had the will and skill to participate effectively in worldwide strategy teams or cross-functional product development teams. This problem was due to a lack of several human resource policies and practices. Though top management had created a committee to review management talent, it did not meet regularly. No such review process existed at the business unit level. Nor were there any existing corporate standards of managerial effectiveness. With little cross-functional and cross-business mobility that might develop managers, the company filled positions with external hires selected for their fit with the immediate job. Managers complained about the company's frequent use of consultants to solve problems. To them this indicated a lack of faith in their problem-solving capacities. They also felt the company was slow to identify poor performers and take appropriate action.

Unsurprisingly, there was widespread dissatisfaction with the HR function. Senior line executives, including Gilmartin, were dissatisfied with HR's inability to support business strategy at the corporate and business unit level. A frustrated corporate human resource manager described the situation as follows: "People hate HR. Nobody feels there is any career development. . . . It's all without direction. I've been here seventeen years, and have been promoted, but if I'm going anyplace in the company no one ever told me. It was just never discussed."

BD's insufficient supply of social and human capital could be traced to top management's background and orientation. Its key executives were very smart, well-intentioned, and strategically oriented managers whose primary focus on strategy had prevented them from aspiring to and developing an HCHP human resource management system and culture.

Could BD's leaders transform their managerial philosophy and develop its human and social capital? What changes in its human resource system and function would be required? More specifically, what shape should the company's human resource policies and practices take? What should be the path—sequence of leadership interventions—to develop a high-commitment human resource system and a team culture? How long would such a transformation take? As a researcher and consultant who saw many of BD's problems firsthand, I had my doubts about whether BD could ever achieve HCHP status.

My doubts were not warranted. Between 1998 and 2007 Becton Dickinson's return on revenues grew from 7.6 to 13.5 percent, its return on total assets grew from 11.7 to 17.7 percent, its return on equity from 15.8 to 20.9 percent, and its stock price increased dramatically. What is particularly impressive is that BD, the bureaucratic, top-down company whose key people saw no guiding human values in 1990, is now ranked by a Hay Group study, sponsored by *Human Resource Executive* magazine, as among the top fifty companies in human resource management; in another study, BD was listed among the most admired companies with respect to its people management, innovation, product and service quality, and quality of management. And in 2007, ASTD, the world's largest human resource professional association, recognized BD with a "BEST" Award and ranked BD in the top five submissions among one hundred companies from eight countries for its accomplishments in management development and learning.

I will return to the question of transformation and BD's successful journey at the end of the chapter.

The HCHP Human Resource Management System

What type of human resource policies and practices develop human and social capital? Despite the many different industries in which HCHP firms are found, policies and practices of the most progressive companies bear remarkable similarities.

One reason is management's assumptions about people. They are positive and optimistic. They believe most people are capable of learning, are motivated intrinsically, want to contribute and make a difference, and prefer not to be controlled through monitoring and incentives. At SAS Institute, an HCHP company that makes software, "the emphasis is on coaching and mentoring rather than monitoring and controlling. Trust and respect—it's amazing how far you can go with it," says a senior executive at SAS Institute.[20]

No single HR policy or practice can by itself change a company—all of them must work in concert; together, they must enable performance and psychological alignment as well as the organization's capacity for learning and change. Because the HR policies discussed below are deeply connected to management philosophy, they cannot be copied from others.[21] They must evolve, over time, from a process of leadership and organizational learning.

Long-Term Employment

HCHP companies believe in hiring for the long term—even for life. They see the *development of people who fit the culture as an investment they do not plan to liquidate* unless absolutely forced by circumstances. They strive to keep their employees as long as they possibly can—for their whole career, if possible—because they regard the development *of human and social capital* as an investment. And they work extremely hard to avoid circumstances that might force liquidation of human assets.

Contrary to those who assume employment security is a do-good policy that has no place in today's competitive marketplace, leaders of HCHP companies like SAS Institute and Southwest Airlines *avoid layoffs for business reasons*. These companies do let low-performing and low-potential people go, but they do so humanely and only after due process (performance discussions and coaching). Indeed, HCHP companies are aggressive about letting low performers go and are cautious about hiring precisely because they know they will not lay off in bad times. Although long-term employment, let alone employment security, may seem like a policy destined to lead to low performance, the evidence is quite the opposite. Companies as varied in their business model and industry as Lincoln Electric (welding and electrical equipment), Nucor Steel (mini-mills), Hewlett-Packard (technology), New United Motors (automobiles), and Southwest Airlines (airline) have outperformed their competitors for long periods during which they offered employment security; that is, they did not lay off employees in economic recessions. Southwest's Herb Kelleher believes that such a policy means giving up some profits but in return gaining partnership with employees (social capital). "Our most important tools for building employee partnership are job security and a stimulating environment.... Certainly there are times when we could have made substantially more profits in the short term if we had furloughed people, but we didn't."[22]

Evidence shows that striving to avoid layoffs makes economic sense. In a recent study, Wayne Cascio "found no significant, consistent evidence that employment downsizing led to improved financial performance (stock price and return on assets)."[23] His conclusion: stabilizing employment will improve performance as well as commitment. We do not know from this study if firms with long-term employment policies were able to implement such a policy because they had a winning business model and good performance in the first place or whether avoiding layoffs enhanced their performance. What is clear is that profits and a long-term employment policy go together. Interestingly, even in successful performance turnarounds studied by Jim Collins, companies "rarely used head-count lopping as a tactic and almost never used it as a primary strategy."[24]

How does a long-term employment policy lead to high performance? Losing people to layoffs or turnover means losing commitment and capabilities that have been developed over many years. Discontinuities that arise from frequent or large "in and out employee flows" weaken relationships with other employees and customers. These relationships lead to lower customer loyalty and productivity. Layoffs increase recruitment and hiring costs, and these often outweigh payroll savings obtained from layoffs. In a study of manufacturing plant layoff practices at Corning in the 1970s, Jim Thurber, at the time my colleague at Corning, demonstrated this very effect.[25] Plant gross margin would have been approximately the same without layoffs, and the plant would not have damaged its social capital.

Long-term employment develops a long-term perspective among employees and managers, and this enables employees to improve efficiency without fear that they are jeopardizing their job security. Employees become more flexible and innovative. Leaving a successful legacy becomes the ethos driving management's strategic decisions. Danny Miller found that family-owned or family-dominated companies with this ethos outperformed publicly traded companies on average. But publicly traded HCHP companies can also reap the benefits of the long-term perspective if they think clearly through, as discussed in chapter 3, business policies and strategies regarding debt, growth, and acquisitions. The objective is to minimize risk and avoid placing the firm into a position where layoffs are the only way the firm can survive. As Herb Kelleher points out, this may mean forgoing some short-term profits.

Employment security has one other very important benefit; it "forces" management to be careful about who they hire, and how many. Kelleher argues as follows: "It turns out, providing job security imposes additional discipline, because if your goal is to avoid layoffs, then you hire very sparingly. So our commitment to job security has actually helped us keep our labor force smaller and more productive than our competitors."[26]

Is it realistic for firms in today's turbulent markets to have a long-term employment policy, even an employment security policy? Yes, but only if senior management possesses the values and philosophy that must underlie such a policy. Those values clearly did not guide CEOs in the years leading up to the Wall Street meltdown and massive layoffs of 2008. If senior management does aspire to adopt a long-term employment policy, then its feasibility requires careful study of the business and of the *fully burdened costs* of the current hiring and firing policies. Questions such as the following are useful. Just how volatile has the revenue stream been historically? How much is this volatility a function of market forces over which there is little control, and to what extent can it be reduced with more conservative business policies? (In its first few decades, Hewlett-Packard's management decided to forgo defense contract business because they did not want to expose themselves to its rather dramatic cycles.) How would recruiting, selection, customer dissatisfaction, and training costs, to name only a few, be reduced with a long-term employment policy? What are the anticipated benefits of long-term employment in terms of added flexibility, commitment, and other benefits discussed earlier?

A long-term employment perspective is not possible unless business policies discussed in chapter 3 are adopted to limit financial and cultural risk. There is little question that firms aspiring to adopt a long-term employment policy would also be helped significantly by capital markets with a longer time horizon. This requires changes in national policy; for example, regarding short- and long-term capital gains, beyond the scope of this book.

Selective Recruitment and Hiring

The type of people brought into the firm matters. HCHP companies stand out from average firms in their insistence on hiring talented people who fit the values and principles that underlie their culture. They select on the basis of attitudes, values, and potential to grow and develop, although there may be exceptions in the case of essential specialists hired to fill niche roles. Of course, those selected must be highly competent in their field, but their "technical" competence is not the only or even the primary criterion. Jenny Chatman shows how selecting to fit the company results in a strong culture, faster adjustment to the firm, and more satisfied employees who stay longer.[27] These outcomes probably boost performance of the individuals and the organization as well. Hewlett-Packard recruited the best engineers from Stanford, but they were not hired unless they fit the HP Way. Leaders in HCHP firms understand that except for some technical specialties, coaching and training can develop ability, whereas attitude and values are more difficult to develop and are critical to developing social capital.

To hire only people who *fit*, high-commitment firms have to be very selective. Southwest Airlines selects one out of a hundred recruits. One way in which firms improve their selection ratio is by recruiting from alternative labor markets not typically accessed by their competitors. For example, social workers may be a good fit for jobs in the service industry.

The interview process in HCHP firms focuses on who the person is, in addition to what he or she has achieved. These firms typically rely on multiple interviews conducted by tenured employees—often in high management positions. In an HCHP hotel I studied, the general manager insisted on interviewing all prospective employees including the lowest-level cooks and doormen, for example. In other HCHP companies, senior people conduct interviews because they have passed the firm's cultural screen and are therefore able to detect those who do and do not fit. Interviewers ask prospective employees to describe how they would handle certain situations or they ask directly about their values. Questions focus on learning experiences that illuminate the person's motivation, capacity to learn, and whether the person sees himself or herself as a team-oriented person or an individual achiever. They ask, "Do you have a personal mission statement? If you don't, what would it be if you were to write it today?"[28] When HCHP companies offer employment security, they do not grant this status until the employee has proven himself or herself during a trial period. At Southwest Airlines it is two years. Others do not hire until the prospective employee has been through a training program that allows the company to assess the applicant's fit with the culture.

To launch a policy of selective hiring, senior teams must themselves design their recruitment and selection strategy, particularly with regard to professional and management employees. That policy is simply too important to delegate to the HR function. Senior teams must agree on the personal qualities that fit their strategy and values as well as whom they don't want to hire—that is, what attitudes and values are a knockout punch in the selection process. Potential is far more important than previous experience when selecting someone to fill a position. I am continually amazed at how many companies look for job-specific experience and knowledge and pass up individuals who have personal qualities that indicate high potential.

Importantly, senior teams will have to examine how the firm's historic growth rate, if continued, will impact the probability of achieving a favorable selection ratio. Recall that Southwest's and Hewlett-Packard's success in maintaining the "Southwest and HP Way" was enabled by managing growth with an eye to its impact on the selection ratio and the capacity of the firms to socialize new people.

Socialize People to Fit the Culture

Identifying with a company is a profoundly personal and emotional process. Each individual employee must find ways to say to him- or herself, "I want to fit in" or "I want to become like the others." Just as important, employees must decide that "I do not fit" and leave. This occurs naturally in all organizations, but if top management wants to develop identity and commitment with its values, they must create emotionally powerful occasions that transmit the values and norms they want to instill. Again, Jenny Chatman's research shows that those who receive the most intense socialization fit the firm's values better than those who do not.[29]

There is considerable evidence from the field of anthropology, notably Joseph Campbell's research and writing, that culture is created and transmitted through myths. Campbell's studies demonstrate that mythological archetypes are anchored in each person's unconscious, yet shared by all people in the community. It is through myths that people give up their individuality and become capable of experiencing community.[30] HCHP companies must find various ways to transmit myths that exemplify their values and norms. This can occur through carefully constructed orientations for new employees, management training, company meetings and social events, as well as celebrations, often for long-tenured employees.

Designating heroes is one way that companies make their norms and values concrete and emotionally relevant. Employees can then identify with real people who they will want to emulate in the hope of one day achieving the same hero status. When I visited the U.K. grocery chain Asda, I found a wall of heroes in its headquarters building. There for all to see and admire were pictures of employees who had achieved results or behaved in a way that reflected the culture Asda was developing. These heroes were also celebrated in company newsletters and meetings.

Storytelling is another way to convey myth and culture. Stories paint pictures symbolizing the firm's vision. They convey an understanding that is "logical, intuitive, and emotional."[31] On my first case-writing visit to Hewlett-Packard in 1980, I learned about several stories that were being told in orientation sessions for new employees, various management training programs, and at social events. These exemplified HP's character at that time—innovation and achievement, quality, common sacrifice:

- How Bill Hewlett challenged HP Labs to build a scientific calculator he could put in his shirt pocket, which led to the introduction of the world's first small scientific calculator and one of HP's most important business segments.

- How Dave Packard physically smashed up an instrument in a laboratory one day because he thought it was poorly designed, unreliable, and generally a "hunk of junk."
- How during the 1970 business downturn when electronic companies across the United States were laying off employees, every employee at HP took a 10 percent pay cut and worked nine out of ten days—taking every other Friday off.

Rituals are another means of transmitting underlying values of the firm and reinforcing its myths. In its heyday, Hewlett-Packard held annual employee picnics at which top management did the cooking and served employees. This transmitted the egalitarian community of purpose the company had created and sent the message that with position comes no special status.

The ritual used at Mary Kay, a company that relies on the internal motivation of its geographically distributed female sales force, offers an especially elaborate example. A journalist described reward ceremonies as follows:

> [G]old and diamond pins, fur stoles, and the use of pink Cadillacs (Buicks in China) are presented to salespeople who achieve their sales quota. Music tends to arouse and express emotions, and all participants sing the Mary Kay song, "I've got that Mary Kay enthusiasm," which was written by a salesperson to the tune of "I've got that old time religion." This song, a direct expression of the mission statement and values of Mary Kay, is fervently sung numerous times during the awards ceremonies. The ceremonies are reminiscent of a Miss America pageant, with all salespeople dressed in glamorous evening clothes. The setting is typically an auditorium in front of a large, cheering audience. During the ceremony, when Mary Kay was introduced, she would levitate on billows of smoke to the stage. The illusion of her rising and being kept in the air with little physical support symbolized how women could rise up and enrich their lives. During the ceremonies, bumblebee–shaped diamond pins are given to women who reached certain sales levels. The pin presents a myth that bumblebees should not be able to fly because of their aerodynamics. However, with their will power and self-determination, they can fly. The use of the bumblebee reflects Mark Kay Ash's vision for women that with help and encouragement everyone can find their wings and fly.[32]

Engaging long-tenured leaders as teachers is yet another way to convey the culture and socialize employees. Because these leaders possess the company's DNA, they are the best people—much more so than HR managers or professional educators—to convey human resource management practices and the culture and values they intend to represent. When I first encountered Becton Dickinson in the late 1980s, and through the early 1990s, the company prided itself on bringing in professors (myself among them) from prestigious business schools to teach. But this has changed. The company's transformation has been aided by BD Corporate University, where hundreds of long-tenured managers, not professors, transmit the company's values by teaching how managers are expected to embrace management practices such as coaching, selection, ethics, performance excellence, and managing a diverse workforce.

Develop Talent to Fit the Strategic Task and Culture

Leaders of HCHP companies view employee development, particularly leadership and management development, as a source of competitive advantage. Without effective down-the-line leaders there is little hope that even the smartest top managers can develop a high-performing company with a high-commitment culture. Recall that inadequate leadership development and a paucity of down-the-line leaders were barriers to effectiveness consistently mentioned by key people in underperforming organizations. Senior leaders in HCHP firms would agree with one of Goldman Sachs' former CEOs:

> Our people have driven Goldman Sachs' success for 130 years through sustained, superb execution across a range of markets and products. The best way to maintain that advantage is by recruiting, training, and mentoring people as we always have—one at a time, with great care. We want Goldman Sachs to be a magnet for the very best people in the world—from new graduates to senior hires. At the same time, we are focusing on developing our very deep bench of talented people and improving and extending our skills. We are, for instance, placing young leaders in demanding positions that stretch their abilities. We are also devoting more time and attention to the formal training and development of leaders, particularly senior leaders.[33]

Ample evidence demonstrates that employees value personal development more than their paycheck. Research also finds that seminal experiences lead to attachment and commitment. Moreover, setting high expectations and providing stretch assignments enable personal and leadership development as well as performance. No company has done this better than GE. Chris Richmond (see chapter 8) was able to achieve extraordinary growth in revenue and earnings by fast tracking young, high-potential managers and assigning them to strategically critical jobs. Jim McNerney, now CEO of Boeing, describes his assignment to be GE's Asian leader as a seminal experience. "Jack Welch gave me no blueprint, just said Asia is the biggest opportunity we've got, and we are not doing much—go figure it out."[34]

The development of people, and particularly leaders, is essential for companies to sustain high performance. A shortage of leaders prevents companies from responding to new opportunities. There simply are not enough effective and culturally aligned leaders to lead initiatives, emerging businesses opportunities, or acquisitions. For every effective and aligned leader a company requires, it must develop several potential candidates in order to compensate for attrition as managers either do not develop as planned or leave. (There are fewer instances of this in HCHP companies, given their lower turnover rate.) When growth outruns the supply of leaders, corporate growth strategies are imperiled.

To grow internationally, Becton Dickinson needed leaders who could work in teams across boundaries and who were committed to the mission of the company more than to their own country organization. They also needed a pool of leaders to draw on to lead new businesses that are an inevitable by-product of growth. These leaders were simply not available. Managers had been selected for their skills to fill their immediate jobs, as opposed to their potential or fit with HCHP values, which had not yet been developed. The company had also not focused attention and resources on the development task. Change in these policies was central to the dramatic changes in commitment and performance that the company achieved by 2006.

Managers in HCHP companies such as GE and McKinsey spend a lot of time inspiring people to achieve, mentoring and coaching, reviewing, and planning assignments to broaden and develop their high-potential people. Jack Welch spent better than 50 percent of his time on people. Archie Norman told me that he spent 75 percent of his time at Asda on human resource issues in the first three years of the company's turnaround.[35] Nucor Steel's CEO, Dan DiMicco, believes that, "Every person is capable of endless growth on a trail that leads we don't know where. If we'd put the holds on Cro-Magnon man, where would we be today?"[36] Boeing's CEO, Jim McNerney, says: "I don't start with the company's strategy or products. I start with people's growth because I believe that if the people who are running and participating in a company grow, then the company's growth will in many respects take care of itself. I have this idea in mind that—all of us get 15% better every year."[37] Of course, conviction has to be translated into concrete policies and practices.

Most HCHP companies have a *policy of promoting primarily from within*. This enables them to offer developmental assignments to high potentials and ensures that those promoted reflect the company's values, its DNA. At McKinsey, this DNA is analytic skills, the capacity to build client relationships and to develop teamwork between talented people across the globe in support of a client engagement. At Southwest Airlines, DNA is a friendly and cooperative attitude that is essential for the good internal coordination required for fast airplane turnarounds and customer loyalty, capabilities that give Southwest a distinctive advantage. Note that despite being in very different industries, both companies hire for the capacity of the person to work with others—their capacity to add to the company's social capital.

Of course, an internal promotion policy can present challenges when new technology, markets, and administrative practices require skills that are not extant in the firm. HCHP firms handle that by hiring the smallest possible number of outsiders necessary to avoid diluting the culture and to minimize the risk that outsiders will not fit in. In the early days of computers, Lincoln Electric sent its staff elsewhere to learn about computers, to avoid hiring outsiders. They quickly realized, however, that this was not enough to keep up with the fast pace of changing technology and began to hire outsiders with computer data processing capability.

Career paths in high-commitment companies take high-potential people across functional and business unit boundaries, often laterally. Their skills to motivate and lead are tested and developed when they cannot rely on substantive knowledge alone to solve problems. At Hewlett-Packard, employees called this process the "career maze," to reference its lack of predictability. My research with colleagues Russell Eisenstat and Bert Spector found that in companies failing to compete successfully, such as Bethlehem Steel in the 1980s, senior executives had risen vertically through the function they had entered.[38] Cross-boundary experiences are a test, and they also develop leadership skills; they develop in managers the general management perspective so essential in leading businesses.

Seminal research conducted in the 1980s by Morgan McCall and his associates at the Center for Creative Leadership found that characteristics that led to managers' derailment were as much a function of the company's human resource practices as a function of personal characteristics (Figure 10.1).[39] Intelligent and technically superb managers derailed when the company's policy was to move managers rapidly through narrow vertical functional channels. Managers with impressive results and strong track records derailed if the company did not evaluate and consider personal flaws in their development and promotion decisions. Managers who were intelligent and achieved great results also derailed if the company focused entirely on short-term objectives. These findings explain why human resource practices such as cross-boundary career paths, long-term goals, and evaluation of interpersonal capabilities enable HCHP firms to develop a deep bench of leaders.

High-performance companies evaluate their people, particularly their managers, differently. They are *evaluated on both results and fit* with values and culture. People who behave

FIGURE 10.1. DERAILMENT PATTERNS OF HIGH POTENTIALS AND HR POLICIES.

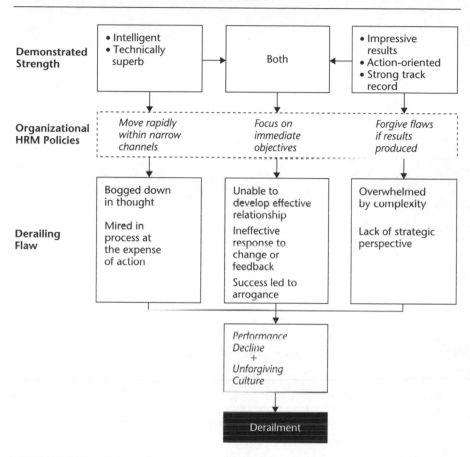

Source: Adapted from: McCall, M. W. *High Flyers*. (1988). Boston: Harvard Business School Press, p. 56.

in ways that violate cultural norms are weeded out (Table 10.2). To create a team-based culture at Morgan Stanley in the early 1990s, John Mack introduced 360-degree evaluations (self, peer, and boss) that for the first time put the firm's investment professionals on notice that negative assessments by peers would affect their pay and promotions. This was a radical step in the investment banking industry. When Mack heard that a senior leader in London had tried to take his people to another firm, clearly demonstrating that they were not committed to Morgan Stanley, he personally flew to London on an overnight flight, fired the uncommitted leaders, and made it public in subsequent speeches to employees.

TABLE 10.2. CRITERIA FOR PROMOTION IN HCHP COMPANIES.

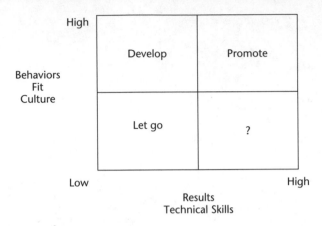

To succeed, leadership development must be motivated and managed by the corporate center and must involve senior teams at every level. The first task is for senior teams to define the capabilities they believe are essential to implement their business model and the values they want to guide behavior. The HR function can then develop the detailed practices required and support managers in their implementation.

At Becton Dickinson, three successive CEOs and their senior teams transformed its selection, promotion, and development policies and practices. In 1990, the CEO, Ray Gilmartin, and his senior team, whose management review committee had previously met irregularly, sat down to define essential capabilities and values. Each senior executive identified managers they considered to fit the strategy and high-commitment values. They discussed and ranked these managers, and from this discussion created a list of personal qualities they thought critical to improving the company's effectiveness, performance, and commitment. The criteria and the practices defined in 1990 have undergone continual redefinition in the years that followed; they have become better and richer under Gilmartin's successors as CEO, Clateo Castellini and Ed Ludwig.

Becton Dickinson also developed an elaborate system of bottom-up talent review meetings that culminated at the very top, where Ludwig and his team review the firm's key managers and high potentials. Business unit managers are required to have a specified minimum number of replacements for themselves. To ensure that this process is carried out at all levels, BD does not pay out a bonus unless the evaluations and development plans have been submitted. At GE, talent review meetings in each major business in the company were attended personally by Jack Welch. This was his opportunity to get a feel for the best people.

Specific developmental practices may differ from company to company, but in all HCHP organizations management makes the time to discuss and develop people. That process has a subtle beneficial effect. It reminds the managers conducting reviews about the company's performance standards and values. At the Harvard Business School, an HCHP organization for a hundred years, the reinforcement of standards and values is particularly powerful. All senior faculty (around ninety) read each promotion "case" (a twenty-page report written by a committee about the candidate's achievements) and gather in one room to discuss the person's qualifications and then vote on the promotion. No faculty member can sit through this process without being reminded of the school standards, feeling humbled by the standards, evaluating one's own accomplishments, and recommitting to high performance in one's work. This extensive review process is particularly valuable in a situation where promotions to full professor are for life, but it suggests that HCHP firms can use such in-depth reviews not only to evaluate and develop high potential managers, but also to reconnect and recommit senior managers.

Though stretch assignments and boundaryless career paths are the primary means that HCHP firms employ to develop managers, they also offer extensive education and training to *supplement* on-the-job development. When managers are used to teach and coach in these programs, as Becton Dickinson has done, the firm's culture is transmitted and reinforced in those who deliver the training. Learning experiences should include not only classroom work, but *action learning*, the assignment to high-potential managers (individually or in teams) the assessment of a business or organizational problem, recommendations for solutions to senior management, and if at all possible, involvement in implementing the solution.

Rewards

People are motivated by extrinsic rewards, such as money and status, as well as by intrinsic rewards, such as challenging work and meaningful purpose. HCHP companies employ both types of rewards to motivate. They are distinctive, however, in their concerted effort to organize and manage people in a way that appeals primarily to intrinsic and higher-order needs such as challenging work, self-actualization, and participation in a community of purpose (see chapter 5). The result is employees who are more internally controlled—the essence of commitment—rather than externally controlled. Nucor's former CEO, the late Ken Iverson, believed that if you give people responsibility and get out of their way they will achieve extraordinary results. He designed the firm to give mill managers and front-line workers full responsibility for achieving results with as little interference from corporate as possible. Consider this example:

> "It was 2 PM on March 9 [2006] when three Nucor Corp. electricians got the call from their colleagues at the Hickman (Ark.) plant. It was bad news: Hickman's electrical grid had failed. For a minimill . . . there's little that could be worse. The trio immediately dropped what they were doing and headed out to the plant. Malcolm McDonald, and electrician from the Decatur (Ala.) mill, was in Indiana visiting another facility. He drove down, arriving at 9 o'clock that night. Les Hart and Byson Trumble, from Nucor's facility in Hertford County, N.C., boarded a plane that landed in Memphis at 11 PM. Then they drove two hours to the troubled plant.

> No supervisor had asked them to make the trip, and no one had to. They went on their own. Camping out in the electrical substation with the Hickman staff, the team worked 20-hour shifts to get the plant up and running again in three days instead of the anticipated full week."[40]

There was *no direct financial incentive* for managers and employees at Nucor for this type of outstanding performance, no extra money in their paycheck or special bonus. Indeed, Nucor's steel workers make substantially less per hour than workers in other companies. Managers and workers do take part in a profit-sharing plan that has paid off handsomely for managers, workers, and investors. Nucor's return of 387 percent to shareholders between 2000 and 2005 beat all other companies in the Standard & Poor's 500-stock index.[41] Profit sharing, as I will explain later, is not what motivated Nucor's employees; having more responsibility and authority provided their motivation. The same approach to motivation contributed to the success of Hewlett-Packard, AES Corporation, and Southwest Airlines. Asda's turnaround was a result of shifting control from the corporate center to store managers.

The relative power of intrinsic as compared to extrinsic rewards in shaping behavior is borne out by many studies, too many to cite here. Consider the results of a "Quality of Employment Survey" that found:

- 76.3 percent disagreed with the statement, "I'd be happier if I didn't have to work at all."
- 72 percent responded that they would continue to work even if they were financially set for life.

- Approximately half agreed with the statement "What I do at work is more important to me than the money I earn."
- More than half said they disagreed with the statement that they worked to get money in order to do other things.
- 58 percent reported that they put in "*a lot* of extra physical and mental effort into their jobs beyond that which is required."

Though compensation systems vary, the goal of HCHP pay systems should be to do no harm, to avoid destroying meaning and the value of the work itself as the primary motivators while at the same time recognizing differences in individual performance with compensation, and paying well, usually above average. HCHP firms do this by making their meaningful, challenging HCHP climate—*not* compensation—the primary basis for recruiting and motivating employees. Though this philosophy is intuitively obvious to HCHP leaders, it is supported by research that finds that a focus on money can actually *undermine* intrinsic motivation. People come to see money as the reason for their effort.[42] This in turn leads to an erosion of meaning, lowered commitment to mission and purpose, heightened self interest, and more focus on pay—the very opposite state of heart and mind that HCHP organizations want to develop.

Though all HCHP companies' total compensation—salary, bonuses, profit sharing, and stock options—is often above the median, leaders understand that individual pay-for-performance systems can breed self-serving dysfunctional behavior. They avoid tying money too tightly to *individual* goal accomplishment. Managers are aware that except for simple jobs, in stable situations and in circumstances where performance outcomes are not dependent on others (a rare circumstance), it is virtually impossible to develop measures of performance that reflect completely an individual manager's efforts and abilities.

Tightly coupling pay to individual results is understood to lead to narrow self-serving behavior and invidious comparisons that cause people to feel that they are not being recognized, and will lead them to feel they're being unfairly treated. This results in lowered trust and commitment as well as disproportionate amounts of time spent by management in administering pay and redesigning pay systems to deal with complaints. Moreover, pay-for-individual-performance systems signal to people that management is in control, not a condition that is likely to breed internal commitment. For these reasons HCHP companies are very careful about how they design and use pay systems for individual results, if they use them at all. Such systems are understood to have the potential to undermine social capital—the high-commitment, team-based culture. HCHP leaders understand that incentive systems are best thought of as an exercise in damage control. John Clarkson, former CEO of the Boston Consulting Group, explained that he views his compensation system as an exercise in justice. Design your compensation system to achieve fair outcomes, he argued, as opposed to designing it to induce motivated behavior.[43]

This perspective is supported by a body of research too extensive to cite here.[44] In one noteworthy study, Alan Binder, a Princeton economist and former vice chairman of the Federal Reserve Board, reviewed many studies about pay and motivation of lower-level workers (not managers) and found, to his surprise, that employee treatment and involvement were associated with productivity more than pay based on individual performance. He found the best systems were stock ownership by all employees, and profit- or gains-sharing plans like Nucor's combined with worker participation. These systems do not use rewards to motivate, but enable employees to feel part of a community engaged in a collective effort to achieve the organization's mission and results.[45]

My own research and that of others suggest that skepticism about the role of compensation in motivation should also be applied to executive compensation. When I received resistance from senior executives (particularly U.S. executives; less so from European or Japanese executives) in Harvard Business School's Advanced Management Program to assertions about the potential detrimental effects of individual financial incentives, I asked executives to participate in a survey study of their companies' compensation system and its effects. In the survey, I found *no* relationship between the percent of compensation (bonuses and stock options) at risk, the reported motivation of managers in the firm, effectiveness of the firm's organization, and the firm's actual financial performance.[46] Like Binder, I found that the most effective reward systems were those that tied pay to firmwide performance—the success of the team. Most interesting, the only factor in this study that predicted firm performance was the extent to which executives reported a *participative and team-based culture*.

Not surprisingly, I found that executives of firms with a higher percentage of pay at risk reported more dysfunctional outcomes. Unproductive managerial behavior—such as setting low achievable targets, lack of cooperation, and excessive focus on achieving one's own goals rather than corporate goals—was higher in firms that put a greater percentage of individual compensation at risk. In these companies the percentage of time spent administering and redesigning compensation systems in response to executive complaints was perceived to be excessive. In my experience, any executive compensation system that does not pay off is seen as a bad system, leading to high administrative and redesign costs and less focus on fixing problems and performance. Such systems were also associated with much larger multiples between CEO pay and that of the lowest-level employee (500 to 1 compared to much lower multiples in HCHP companies), making it much harder to create an egalitarian culture and a mission-driven community of purpose. This deleterious effect of inequities in pay within senior teams has been well documented. Large inequality between the compensation of the CEO and the rest of the top team has been found to be associated with lower firm performance.[47]

Reviewing a large body of literature, Baron and Kreps conclude, "Pay for performance schemes are too blunt an instrument, resulting in misalignment of incentives; they load uneconomically large amounts of risk on the worker; they often have problems with perceived legitimacy; they can breed inflexibility; and they can dull intrinsic motivation.[48]

Why then do so many companies pursue compensation policies that undermine effectiveness, commitment, and performance? My Harvard study provided some insights. Executives' responses revealed that they themselves were actually uncertain about whether compensation motivates, but reported that their top management firmly believed it did. Top management was apparently unaware of or ignored the dysfunctional effects of executive incentives reported by the key executives in my study. The meltdown of Wall Street financial institutions in 2008 illustrates this phenomenon. The top management of these low commitment and performance companies also held to the strong belief in incentives and failed to understand its potentially disastrous effects.

But couldn't an HCHP firm with a strong culture improve its commitment and performance by creating an equally strong incentive system contingent on financial results? Surely two powerful levers are better than one? I have found that incentive systems introduced into high-commitment cultures—even those based on team performance—undermine that culture. Under competitive pressures in the late 1980s and early 90s, a number of business unit general managers at Hewlett-Packard convinced senior management to let them introduce monetary incentive systems for achieving specific results (mostly group incentives in manufacturing plants), something that HP had historically eschewed. Within three years the very same executives who had lobbied for these systems decided to discontinue them.[49] Perceived inequities by employees lowered employee trust, something HP managers cared about. They also found they were spending too much time on pay system issues and not enough time on improving effectiveness and performance.

Collaboration between Stanford researchers and McKinsey confirms the idea that pay systems must fit cultural objectives.[50] The study found that firms that employ "soft" motivation levers—relationships and culture—did not employ "hard" levers such as incentive systems. The only exception in their sample was Enron, where we know now that executive hubris and greed, undoubtedly stimulated by their compensation system, caused its downfall. This study and the Hewlett-Packard experience suggest that HCHP companies that adopt conventional pay-for-results incentive systems risk stimulating self-serving, dysfunctional, and even unethical behavior that will ultimately erode their high-commitment culture.

◆ ◆ ◆

In a world where competitors recruit talent using money as the carrot, leaders of HCHP companies must find a way to differentiate rewards based on performance while avoiding the erosion of the high-commitment culture that individual pay-for-performance systems can cause. The following compensation principles enable HCHP firms to manage this paradox, the *and/also*.

Non-Monetary Rewards. Instead of seeing monetary rewards as the key to motivation, HCHP firms emphasize rewards such as more responsibility and freedom, challenging work, fun, private and public recognition, and symbolic awards. Compensation is seen as recognition for good work and not as an inducement to do it.

Compensation Level. Ensure that *total compensation* is well above the median. This ensures the company's capacity to attract and keep talented people. Costco, an HCHP firm, pays its employees approximately 40 percent above the market and still they achieve extraordinary firm performance. Senior management has to continually rebuff calls from Wall Street analysts to reduce wages to industry levels. Wall Street does not appear to understand the difference between cost and productivity per employee. The latter is the key to high performance.

Symbolic Egalitarianism. HCHP firms generally make a concerted effort to reduce the trappings of hierarchy. They eschew outrageous gaps in compensation and compensation practice between top management and lower levels. They create broad pay ranges to deemphasize hierarchy and facilitate transfer of employees to where they are most needed and will best develop. Symbolic rewards that differentiate positions at varying levels are reduced, and in some HCHP companies eliminated entirely. Everyone, including senior management, is generally subject to the same compensation and benefit plans as lower levels, and distinctions are minimized with regard to perks such as offices, titles, and health care policies. At Toyota everyone receives the same percent of his or her wages as a performance bonus (based on overall business performance). Within a year of taking over Asda, Archie Norman abolished all offices, including his own. HCHP companies that think private offices are necessary see to it that all offices are the same.

To leaders of firms who want to develop a community of purpose, these are intuitively obvious practices. But they are actually supported by research in cognitive psychology. Humans tend to use cues around them to make sense of their social experience. These become anchors that shape their judgments. Similarly, expectations communicated by others, particularly those in high-status positions, shape our attitudes. Survey research in actual work situations supports the implications of these basic research findings. For example, firms with "more generous" employment policies and well-defined career ladders often exhibit high levels of employee dissatisfaction."[51] Employees use these symbols to define their progress and to define how easy or difficult it may be to share their views with senior management.

Pay for Performance. Given the potential damage of incentives to a high-commitment culture, HCHP firms must find ways to recognize differences in performance between individuals, something that is essential for compensation to be seen as fair and to minimize turnover. One way this is done is to make compensation contingent on multiple factors—individual business unit performance as well as corporate performance, individual goal achievement, and behavior consistent with firm values. Lincoln Electric was able to employ effectively a piece-rate incentive system (individuals paid for number of units produced) that constituted 100 percent of production workers' pay—a huge incentive that can spur self-serving behavior—by making payouts contingent on collaboration with others.

The Lincoln Electric example of a shop floor pay system notwithstanding, HCHP companies generally avoid tightly coupling incentives to financial results or production. Instead, managers judge overall performance by incorporating hard and soft performance outcomes. Multiple people are asked to offer judgments about how team-oriented a worker or manager is and how broadly they approach their jobs. Becton Dickinson incorporates several factors in evaluating managers; compensation decisions are made through informed judgment that integrates these factors.

HCHP firms, like Nucor, use profit- or gains-sharing systems and distribute stock options to all employees. When specific incentives are employed, they are based on individual and subunit as well as firm performance, another way to encourage team behavior. Gains sharing is meant to signal the shared fate of all employees, including senior executives, and is not assumed to motivate. When economic performance declines, everyone—managers and workers—shares in the pain. Nucor has met the economic crisis of 2008 by cutting compensation for *everyone*—managers and workers—by 50 percent, rather than lay off employees.

Pay, Justice, and Employee Voice. HCHP organizations create *formal mechanisms* by which employees can voice their concerns about their rewards.

Involving employees in the redesign of pay systems is another way to foster perceptions that pay is fair. Cummins Engine's Jamestown, New York, manufacturing plant did this with success in the 1970s. Fear that the pay system proposal would be unreasonable proved to be unwarranted. Proposals made by a team of employees were reasonable and effective.[52] Ed Lawler and Richard Hackman have showed in a field experiment that involvement in the design of pay systems has a salutary effect.[53] These findings are consistent with the literature on what academics call "procedural justice." Giving employees a voice in decisions increases perceived fairness and acceptance of the decision.

Senior Executive Pay. There is no more controversial symbol attended to by employees, and in recent years, by shareholders, than the pay of senior executives. It should come as no surprise that most senior executives in HCHP firms, though paid consistent with their responsibilities, enjoy less generous compensation packages and perquisites when compared to other senior executives. A recent study of 2,275 U.S. companies, for example, found that CEOs at twenty-five companies with the worst performance (with regard to increasing shareholder wealth) had an average pay package of $16.7 million, whereas CEOs of the twenty-five best companies received $4.4 million on average.[54] This contradicts the conventional wisdom that CEO pay is the key to firm performance.

Employee Voice

Commitment and trust cannot develop unless employees are given voice. HCHP companies develop extensive mechanisms that enable lower levels to overcome the hierarchy's barrier to voicing grievances and concerns to higher management. Hewlett-Packard was the gold standard in this regard. Because the founders cared about people and wanted to foster loyalty, they created the following policies:

- Open office layout that made managers more approachable.
- Managers were expected to "manage by walking around" (MBWA), a policy that was firmly institutionalized at HP. Managers who did not were removed.
- An open-door policy gave employees the right to go to their boss with their concerns. They had the right to go to successive next levels, all the way to the CEO, if they were not satisfied that their problem had been resolved.
- Senior executives led meetings with employees at lower levels, without their bosses, to hear about concerns and ideas.
- In later years, regular employee surveys were used to give people voice, and survey results were used to evaluate managers.

Becton Dickinson institutionalized several voice mechanisms during their transformation. Associates have the right to post comments on their performance evaluation that go to the next level. An anonymous ethics hot line allows voice about unethical behavior. Employee surveys are used fairly extensively and regular surveys are being contemplated. The Strategic Fitness Process has been employed over the years to enable Ludwig and other senior managers to learn the unvarnished truth.

Managing the Inevitable Crisis

The journey to HCHP is not a straight line up. At various stages of the journey the company will face a crisis in performance. How that crisis is dealt with will determine the organization's future HCHP trajectory. Will the company liquidate its investment in high-commitment culture and the talented people it took years to develop and infuse with the company's DNA? Or will the crisis be negotiated without liquidating the company's social and human capital? These moments of truth define the organization's future much more powerfully than speeches, or mission or value statements.

Consider the case of Dreyer's Grand Ice Cream, a $1 billion company.[55] In June 1988, unexpected events coincided to make it the most difficult period in the company's history. Investments in the company's expansion took longer, cost more than anticipated, and expected profits were delayed. The price of butterfat, the key ingredient in ice cream, rose to a record level. The company could not raise prices because of aggressive discounting by its chief competitor. Revenue in one of Dreyer's new product lines began to drop. And one of its customers threatened to terminate its long-term distribution contract.

Under these pressures from capital markets, most executives would begin restructuring and cutting costs immediately. Dryer's senior management began with honest and open communication. Gary Rogers and Richard Cronk had spent many years building an open, team-based culture, one in which they had made themselves accessible, so employees believed them. When they were prepared to announce their restructuring to the financial community, executive committee members were on airplanes to talk with every one of their four hundred employees. Cronk observed, "We know our limits and understand the law, but we tend to be very open with our employees, we communicate a lot." "They reassured us," said an account executive, "by calling it straight . . . they informed us of their game plan and that they needed us . . . you looked at these [senior managers] and thought, you'd run through a wall for this guy."[56]

The story does not end there. An 800 number was set up so employees could call to hear CEO Rogers' prerecorded speech about the situation and his plans.

The speech was honest and owned up to problems, but also was upbeat. Senior management continued to invest in the Dreyer Leadership University (DLU), demonstrating that they cared about employee development. Cronk and others in senior management thought this was an investment in the future that would pay off. "When people heard that we were investing another million dollars into the [culture] and DLU it created a high degree of comfort and confidence that we're focused on what really matters," observed the VP of sales."[57]

The company' revenue, profits, and stock price rebounded from this dire situation. By 2001 Dreyer's stock had risen from 9.88 in 1988 to 36. In January 2003 the stock price rose to 71.23. Reflecting on how they handled the crisis, Cronk said, "It was a common trust and of sharing the facts openly. We weren't sugarcoating anything, putting a Hollywood spin on anything . . . we were honest and clear . . . people believed the story and they understood . . . there was an enormous amount of pride and optimism."[58]

In addition to open and honest communication and continued investment in HCHP management practices, corporations need to develop an a priori set of policies in advance of the crisis that will minimize damage from restructuring and downsizing and maintain employee dignity and commitment. Wayne Cascio, who has studied companies with a record of stable long-term employment contracts, lists the following policies to preserve the dignity and relationship with survivors and departing employees.[59]

- "Use downsizing as a last resort; at the same time, reinvent your business." There are several ways companies have done this.
  - Rely on attrition to downsize the organization.
  - Use redeployment and make layoffs a last resort. Hewlett-Packard used this strategy extensively throughout the 1980s as it faced intensified competition. Employees were given three months to find a job in HP and helped to do so. If they could not find an equivalent level job they were offered a lower-level job. If they preferred not to take that job they were given generous severance packages.
  - Ask for volunteers who want to take extended vacations, a sabbatical, leaves of absence, or a shorter work week.
  - Ask everyone to share the pain by taking a pay cut. Senior management should take a larger one. Hewlett-Packard used this approach several times in its early history. Nucor's decision to avoid layoffs and cut compensation by 50 percent in 2008 not only avoided liquidating commitment—it increased it. Shorten work weeks and offer stock options in return.
  - Lend employees to not-for-profit firms and pay the difference in their wages.
- "Do everything you can to manage survivors well." Tell survivors exactly how departed employees are being treated.

- "Generate goodwill, even loyalty, among departing employees" by taking great care with how they are separated. Generous severance packages, outplacement services, and retraining are typical strategies.

A profit-sharing compensation policy increases the capability of an HCHP company to retain its employees in a time of crisis. Because 25 percent of employee pay in Japanese companies is based on company profits, a crisis in performance automatically reduces their cost structure and allows them to avoid layoffs. The global economic crisis of 2008, the worst since the Great Depression, may make such policies more attractive to employees as job security becomes more salient for a generation of workers, just it did after the Great Depression.

Unions

Though only 10 to 11 percent of the United States is unionized, in Europe and Asia that percentage is much larger. HCHP practices can and have been implemented in unionized settings. Some of the earliest experiments in high-commitment manufacturing plants at Procter & Gamble and General Motors occurred in these unionized settings. Recall the HCHP practices introduced at NUMMI (see chapter 2). Although not all HCHP HR policies and practices can be implemented in a unionized operation, the management philosophy can and has been successfully applied. The key in all of these experiments was to develop a partnership between union and management. That means recognizing the legitimacy of unions, involving the union in strategy discussion and plans, respecting voice and governance mechanisms, and involving workers at all levels in solving problems.

Southwest Airlines is unionized and has managed sustained high performance not in spite of the unions, but because they see and treat them as partners. It complicates the management task, but it also provides some protections. Unions are an excellent check on management, can prevent management from making mistakes, and can help mobilize workers. A comparative study of unionized and nonunionized manufacturing plants, for example, found that productivity in unionized plants was actually higher than in that of nonunionized plants.[60] However, to achieve partnership, leaders on both sides must want to make it work.

Transforming Human Resource Management

How should a company go about transforming its human resource management (HRM) system? The first inclination of CEOs is to delegate this task to the chief human resource officer. HR executives' first instinct is to copy the HR policies and practices of HCHP companies, and the first place they are inclined to start is with HRM practices: recruiting, selecting, training, evaluating, compensating, and developing people.

This may, however, be a false start. The human resource policies discussed in this chapter will only work if embedded in a positive social or organizational context. Developing innovative practices does not change how people are actually managed. Becton Dickinson is an excellent illustration of this point. Its human resource department had received an award from the Society of Personnel Administration for its development of several innovative human resource practices. But the company did not possess social or human capital. Indeed, the HR function was widely thought of as ineffective.

Human resource policies and practices do not in themselves change the way people are organized and managed. Neither can the human resource function drive change. The transformation of a company, as I argued in chapter 4, requires a systemic approach that must focus on changing how the aspiring firm is organized and managed. The human resource function can help the CEO, but he or she must develop the foundation for a transformation in organizing and managing people along with the senior team.

Essential Ingredients for HRM Change

Although there is no fixed sequence, the following ingredients must be in place in order to transform human resource management. The discussion of BD's transformation will illustrate how these ingredients interacted.

Focus on Strategy and Performance. One cannot start a human resource management transformation until strategy is clarified and a general vision and its implications for human and social capital are developed. Ray Gilmartin began transforming Becton Dickinson in 1990 when he articulated his diagnosis and vision of the company just after he became CEO: "There are certain skills that we require as an organization to pull off our strategy. We are trying to achieve multidivisional selling and supply chain management, which have to involve all of our divisions. The transnational balance between global scale economies and national responsiveness requires an organizational philosophy and a way of operating that is not traditional. We also need organizational mechanisms, commitment, and skills to manage technology."[61] Note how much BD's strategy required social capital and human capital, with social capital being most important. Gilmartin, as the case below will illustrate, took some first steps to creating better coordination between interdependent activities, a new "nontraditional" approach and a "new philosophy" of management before his unexpected departure to lead much larger Merck & Company.

Leadership and Values. Without a CEO who has an HCHP set of values and management philosophy, no amount of effort by the human resource function to introduce HCHP human resource policies and practices will work. Though first steps were taken by Gilmartin, his successor, Clateo Castellini, motivated by his deep belief in people's capabilities and the need to empower them, began the cultural transformation of BD. Ed Ludwig, Castellini's successor, accelerated, enriched, and institutionalized the cultural transformation.

A Collective Learning Process. A collective learning process that enables truth to speak to power, as discussed in chapters 6 and 7, enables senior teams at all levels to learn about how the organization and their leadership are aligned with strategy and values. And the collective learning process itself builds social and human capital.

A Human Resource Function That Is a Change Agent. Successful HRM transformations require an HR function that can evolve from its traditional transactional and administrative role into a strategic change role. In this capacity HR facilitates leadership and organizational learning.[62] Its leaders must have the courage to raise important questions, collect data that may not always be welcome, help leaders understand where they are in the journey, and help senior management redesigning the system. To be change agents, organization and management development functions typically housed in the HR function may have to be differentiated from the administrative role, perhaps even organized as a separate unit reporting directly to the CEO or to the top strategy officer.[63] And its manager should have a deep knowledge of the business as well as the instincts, knowledge, and skills of a strategic change agent. BD's transformation did not take off until Gilmartin asked Ralph Biggadike, the company's highly competent VP of strategy, to also head human resources. That assignment and that of a line executive in later years brought a business perspective to the function it lacked.

Becton Dickinson's Human Resource Management Transformation[61]

Becton Dickinson's twenty-year transformation to HCHP began in 1988. I was invited to an annual management meeting of the top eighty executives, where I talked about strategic alignment and the kind of learning and change process needed for realignment—gathering valid data, conducting a diagnosis, and planning change. Gilmartin, then COO, asked business unit leaders to employ this process in their organization and report back what they had learned and what changes they planned. Though a few leaders had the will and skill to do this, most did not. Some leaders never started. Others began but did not complete the process successfully. Still others did not learn the truth about their organization's and leadership effectiveness.

Failure led to the development and adoption of a formal learning and governance process, then called Strategic Human Resource Management (SHRM) Profiling, an early version of the Strategic Fitness Process described in chapter 7. That process enabled honest collective and public conversations and allowed senior teams, including Gilmartin and his top team, to diagnose their organization, learn, and plan change. In the next four years, the HR function helped implement this process in multiple business units, country organizations, corporate functions, and a few operating units.

Senior management learned that BD was hierarchal and bureaucratic. A top-down strategic planning process disempowered sector presidents, succession planning was erratic, worldwide business teams were ineffective, the corporate finance function requests for information interfered with business unit effectiveness, and BD's employees felt BD was devoid of "human values." Change began in all of these areas. For example, BD's first value statement was developed and the management succession and development process was strengthened. So were worldwide teams. Key executives at several levels developed new insights about leading and managing. This stage led to more profound changes later.

In 1994, Gilmartin's successor, Clateo Castellini, began a cultural transformation in earnest. He described his aspirations as follows:[64]

> When I first became CEO I had a vision of creating a very different culture at BD. The culture I envisioned was upside down from the command and control culture that we were known for; where people at the front lines were free to act, to take initiative, take risks, to think about new products and new ways of doing work, be more entrepreneurial, and where they were much more empowered. I felt this change was necessary to make BD better able to respond to changing conditions in our industry.

In 1996 Castellini described the sequence of steps he took in 1994 to change the company and its culture:

> Since I became CEO I have spoken about this vision wherever I met with investors and with employees. At the time, I knew that a cultural transformation was not something that would happen overnight, so we first set some financial goals and worked on our strategy and organizational structure. When this was completed in mid-1995, I decided it was time to begin a more formalized process of transforming culture. My executive team and I agreed that random talks and memos about culture were not enough. I felt that if

we did not transform our culture, we would fall into the old trap of having the perfect strategy, but not the organizational capabilities [and culture] to implement it.

Castellini and his top team recycled the process of learning and change in 1995 that Ray Gilmartin began in 1990. This began with learning about the state of BD's organization and culture using BD's learning and governance process. It was followed by a top team workshop, led by my colleague Russ Eisenstat and me, to discuss *Built to Last*, the Collins and Porras book about companies that had demonstrated sustained performance and commitment over a period of decades, followed by a discussion and an analysis of Hewlett-Packard's HCHP human resource system. From this workshop emerged a mission with which BD's employees could identify emotionally, as well as a set of values and core ideology. To engage their employees about the values and to obtain feedback, the top management held town meetings around the world. These led to various working groups that defined ambitious goals for the company and revised BD's mission to "Helping All People Live Healthy Lives." Working groups then followed to review and define how BD would be organized and managed as a global company, and how BD's new human resource system should go about hiring, assessing, and developing people to fit the new values, culture, and organization.

Building on the first two eras of change, Ed Ludwig, BD's current CEO, has led the most profound changes in the company to date.[65] When he took over as president in 1999, he met BD's performance crisis with a willingness to get to the underlying problems facing the corporation. Making himself vulnerable to critique for decisions that he and the top team had made, he began yet another cycle of learning by enabling truth to speak to power by employing BD's learning and governance process, one that he had successfully used earlier as a division manager.

Seven years later, reflecting about that personal and organizational crisis in 2000, Ludwig said that what he learned about the company's strengths and barriers "made his job easy." It enabled him and his leadership team to develop a systemic diagnosis and action plan. As he said, "It told me exactly what I had to do."[66] For example, he learned that his effort as CFO to introduce an SAP information system was failing. By owning up "publicly" to this failure and his role in it, Ludwig developed immediate trust, hope, and commitment. He also decided to terminate certain incentive programs in order to improve supply chain and manufacturing efficiencies, reduce costs, and establish closer links with customers, all changes suggested by the feedback from the learning and governance process. Although personally difficult, honest conversations freed Ludwig to lead the next era of change and gave him the moral authority to do so.

According to Ludwig, the governance and learning process helped him and his senior team to develop the systemic blueprint for change that is still in progress today.

Mission, vision, and value, as well as strategy, were redefined and then communicated widely. The new company goals illustrate BD's evolution to a multistakeholder philosophy:

- To make a contribution to society
- Achieve great performance
- Become a great place to work

The worldwide organization again came under scrutiny, and roles and responsibilities were clarified. The largest and most concentrated changes occurred in human resource policies and practices (some described in the previous section). How people managed became as important as what they accomplished. Manager evaluation evolved from financial results only to informed judgment based on multiple factors. Several mechanisms for employee voice were introduced. To sustain BD's transformation, Ludwig once again employed BD's learning governance process in 2006, this time to learn the truth about progress made and new emerging problems.

Despite impressive changes in performance alignment, psychological alignment (commitment), and its capacity to learn and change, Ludwig believes BD has a long way to go in its never-ending journey to HCHP. In 2008 BD is turning its attention to a next-generation leadership program. Its purpose is to deepen leaders' understanding of how to design, develop, and lead an HCHP company. And this will involve managers who are expected to lead the corporation in the next five to ten years in corporate change initiatives identified through yet another iteration of BD's learning and governance process (the Strategic Fitness Process) that was instrumental in launching BD's journey to HCHP in 1990.

Summary

The transformation to an HCHP company requires the development of human and social capital. An overemphasis on talent management (human capital) can cause companies to underinvest in the development of social capital (the development of a high-fit, team-based culture) necessary for a community of purpose. Vertical and horizontal relationships are an essential context for the implementation of HCHP human resource policies and practices. And these policies and practices must be designed to enable the company to select talented individuals who fit the company's high-commitment culture. Managing the paradox of hiring and retaining best-in-class talent, while molding them into an effective community of purpose, is the central human resource management dilemma that HCHP firms face. These firms distinguish themselves by avoiding the trap of offering red-carpet treatment and monetary incentives that is often necessary to hire the most talented people.

HCHP human resource policies and practices must be internally consistent and support the development of a community of talented individuals. To this end, HCHP companies start with a long-term employment policy aimed at retaining talent for as long as they contribute. To support this strategy, HCHP firms hire selectively for fit, socialize people to help them fit into their team culture, and grow leaders internally. They do not source promotions to key management positions with outsiders, except when unique capabilities that the firm does not have are essential. Intrinsic rewards such as responsible, challenging, and meaningful work as well as participation are used to motivate. HCHP firms avoid individual pay-for-performance schemes or augment them with group and organizational performance. And they minimize hierarchical differences to enable an egalitarian community of purpose. When HCHP firms face inevitable crises in firm performance, they do everything they can to avoid layoffs.

A human resource transformation cannot begin with policies and practices developed by the HR function. It starts with a collective organizational learning process that aligns the organization and its people with strategy and values. Human resource policies and practices emerge from this process as opposed to being imported from other companies, though models are helpful. The following ingredients are essential for a successful HRM transformation:

- Focus on strategy and performance
- Leaders with HCHP values
- A learning and governance process
- An HR function that is a change agent

A senior team that wants to pursue the development of an HCHP HR system should consider the following questions:

1. What is the purpose of the firm and what are our values?
2. Are we prepared to begin a long journey to create a strong high-commitment, team-based culture?
3. Is our business organized and managed in a way that is consistent with our values and strategy? If not, how do we begin to align it with values and strategy?

4. Who are the people currently in our organization who best fit the values we want to live by? Who in our organization clearly does not fit?

5. Are we prepared to develop a set of internally consistent HR policies and practices that simultaneously develop human and social capital?

6. Are we developing the next generation of HCHP leaders who will sustain our HCHP legacy?

7. Are we prepared to adopt the long-term employment perspective needed to create a community of purpose and the HR policies to support it?

8. Are we prepared to be demanding about performance and to ask underperformers to leave?

9. Will we lay off people at the first sign of a performance crisis or are we prepared to adopt practices that will delay this eventuality as long as possible?

10. Have we put in place business policies with regard to growth rates, debt, and mergers and acquisitions to reduce risk and the potential for a crisis that might force liquidation of our human assets?

PART FIVE

TRANSFORMING THE ORGANIZATION

CHAPTER ELEVEN

EMBRACE E AND O CHANGE STRATEGIES[1]

There is nothing more difficult to take in hand, more perilous to conduct, or more uncertain in its success, than to take the lead in the introduction of a new order of things.

—NICCOLO MACHIAVELLI[2]

To transform an underperforming company with low commitment requires dramatic change. Unfortunately, few companies manage change well enough to achieve sustained improvements in performance, commitment, and adaptability. Only eleven companies out of 1,435 managed sustained extraordinary improvements in financial performance over a fifteen-year period in Jim Collins's "Good to Great" study.[3] Many sources, including our own research, suggest that top-down change strategies employed by many companies—introduction of information technology, downsizing, restructuring, education and training programs, and culture programs—do not succeed.[4]

If there is one thing that my study of organization change has convinced me, it is that whether an organization develops all three pillars of HCHP companies—performance alignment, psychological alignment, and the capacity for learning and change—is determined by *how leaders manage change;* the goals they have and the choices they make about speed, people, focus, process, and motivation; as well as by their choice of consultants. Indeed, how organizational change is brought about will have a profound effect on the ultimate character and culture of the organization. Wrong choices will undermine aspirations to develop the three pillars of HCHP.

Theory E or O: The Conventional Choice

CEOs' decisions about change appear to cluster into two archetypal *theories and strategies of change,* neither of which is sufficient to achieve both commitment and timely and sustainable performance improvements. *Theory E focuses on creating economic value.* Its strategies occupy the headlines in the business press and general news coverage and employ "hard" measures to improve financial performance. Key executives are given huge financial incentives and they go about managing rapid change through restructuring the company—selling off poorly performing businesses, downsizing, and layoffs.

E strategies are common in the United States where capital markets are strong and viewed as the primary, even the only way, to improve company performance, especially given the pressure from investors who can easily sell one company's stock on Monday and buy another company's stock on Tuesday.[5] Europe and Asia, cultures with a strong sense of community, employ Theory E strategies less frequently, though the increasingly global financial system is eroding that resistance. The story of change at Scott Paper illustrates the Theory E strategy for change and its results.

Scott Paper embarked on a journey of change in 1994 when Al Dunlap took over as CEO. Scott had participated profitably in the forest products and paper industry since 1879, but ran into profitability problems in the early 1990s. International expansion had stretched resources at a time when the industry was again entering a period of over-capacity, a pattern that had repeated itself many times. Performance and shareholder returns dropped at an alarming rate. Bowing to pressure from capital markets, the board of directors recruited Dunlap, a turnaround manager with a success record in restructuring companies. Dunlap immediately ordered a layoff of eleven thousand employees, about 42 percent of Scott Paper's workforce. He sold a number of businesses and closed down a number of its less-profitable plants. In the remainder he imposed a strict regime of efficiency measures with the help of external consultants. And within months he fired most of Scott's top management, often after chastising them in public.

At the end of two-and-a-half years Dunlap sold Scott's remaining core business, the consumer packaging business, to competitor Kimberly Clark at three times Scott's market capitalization at the time he took charge ($9 billion compared to $3 billion). The financial community applauded Dunlap's efforts and pointed to Scott Paper's approach to change as a model to be emulated by others. Dunlap's total compensation was over $100 million, and many of the company's shareholders, including the senior executives he had fired, became much wealthier in just twenty months. A proud company, however, ceased to exist. According to informal reports, Kimberly Clark's management was surprised by the condition of the company it had acquired. To be sure, Scott Paper's many tangible assets were there, but its organizational capability and human assets had been depleted.

The second archetype, *Theory O, focuses on developing organization capabilities and culture.* The goal of this apparently "softer" strategy is to develop corporate culture and human capability through employee and organization development. CEOs employ O strategies because they want to build a commitment-based psychological contract. This strategy is illustrated by the story of Champion International.[6]

Champion International, a company also operating since 1893 in the forest products and paper industry, embarked on a journey of change in the early 1980s. Like Scott Paper, it found competing in an industry with frequent cycles of under- and over-capacity extremely challenging. The company had operated for many years as a functional and hierarchical organization and had poor relations with its unions. Its shareholder returns lagged the average for companies in the Fortune 500 as well as among its peers in the industry. CEO Andrew Sigler had resisted the revolution in capital markets that demanded underperforming companies improve shareholder returns by restructuring. He spoke about this publicly. He did, however, pursue an O strategy to build an effective high-commitment organization.

Sigler began the transformation journey by articulating a new set of Champion Way values, but despite the autocratic management style he had exhibited over the years, he did not drive organization change from the top. Instead, organization change began with low-profile changes at the company's periphery. A new manufacturing plant was designed around principles of cross-functional self-managed teams organized along horizontal processes. With the help of a handful of change consultants, managers and employees were involved in designing the plant. This experiment led to similar change efforts in an ever-larger circle of new and old manufacturing facilities. Over more than a decade, change that started at the periphery spread to the corporate center. At the corporate level, what had been at one time a deeply functional corporation evolved into a matrix structure organized around product groups. All corporate functional activities were oriented through the matrix toward markets, businesses, and customers. Few financial incentives were used to move change, and no reengineering efforts or layoffs were implemented, although key plant and functional managers who did not adhere to the new philosophy of management were asked to leave.

The transformation was remarkable. Productivity, union-management relationships, and customer and employee satisfaction all improved. A long march, facilitated by a small number of OD [organization development] consultants, in cooperation with the human resource function, had succeeded in managing a change in culture and operating performance, particularly in productivity and customer satisfaction. But these changes did not improve Champion's return to shareholders. "Champion's share price had failed to keep pace with the S&P 500 Index and it did not keep pace with companies in its own industry. Return on assets, return on equity, return on sales, and sales per employee were all below those of comparison companies in the paper industry."[7] In 1997 Sigler's successor stated that shareholder returns had to be the objective going forward. Two years later the company was sold at only one-and-a-half times its market capitalization in 1981.

Embrace Contradictions of E and O

Each change theory has validity and can help senior executives achieve some important goals. An E strategy ensures the economic viability of the enterprise. This is an essential first step in change and may have to be repeated if future crises endanger the survival of the business. But E strategies do not build the organizational capabilities and culture needed for sustained high commitment and performance, the main focus of this book. For these reasons, change leaders must become knowledgeable and skilled in embracing the paradox E and O strategies represent—the third strategic change choice. Embracing the paradox means more than simply implementing both E and O. It requires an integrative strategy. If this strategy is implemented properly, the corporation can obtain the benefit of rapid change in financial performance required to survive short-term pressures and gain the long-term benefits of sustained change in all three HCHP outcomes.

To implement E and O in an integrated manner requires, however, that managers enter uncomfortable emotional and demanding interpersonal territory.[8] They have to stay in a positive relationship with managers they may ultimately replace and workers they plan to lay off. E/O strategies require that leaders explain why downsizing and restructuring are necessary and respond to human concerns. If this is not done, the legitimacy of harsh E strategies will be questioned, trust will decline, and commitment will be impossible.

Senior executives who plan to integrate E and soft O strategies will want to approach their affected employees to communicate sympathy and explain why their decision is necessary, despite the fact that their natural instincts will be to avoid these employees. Asda's CEO, Archie Norman, recalled the discomfort inherent in the integrated E/O strategy he pursued.

> In the space of the first five years, basically 90 percent of the top team, the top 200 people changed. Most of them left the business and that's something that's very difficult to cope with. And it gives you the initial problem that a lot of the people you've got to work with and you've got to rely on, and actually you know in your heart, aren't going to be there. And yet you're dependent on them for their performance which means that you've got to convince them

to give their best even though you're working on the knowledge that probably they're not going to be part of your team in a year or two's time. It is a very uncomfortable situation.[9]

Discomfort must be engaged and overcome by top managers if they are to perform "necessary evils," according to Andy Molinsky and my colleague at Harvard, Joshua Margolis.[10] They argue that for leaders to enact necessarily evils in a positive manner, they first need an internal narrative that makes sense of their conflicting goals and the consequent emotions aroused. Doing this psychological work will help leaders involve the very managers who, as Norman describes, may have to be replaced in the future. In the case of layoffs it will enable leaders to acknowledge the harm caused to people and the organization, an act that signals to employees that top management is fully aware of the human toll their E strategy is taking.

The difficulty of enacting and explaining conflicting change strategies as well as resolving conflicting emotions may be one reason that many companies do it so poorly. Pendulum swings of hard E strategies are followed by softer O strategies, followed again by harder E strategies when the company again faces difficult times. This destabilizes the organization and its people and prevents the development of an HCHP organization.

Consider the implicit psychological and economic "contract" when people are hired during the E phase of the change and how different it is likely to be from a new "contract" when the company is in its O phase. E strategies attract managers who are interested in the big incentives offered for enacting emotionally difficult things such as restructuring and downsizing. They are likely to have less-empathic personalities and to have learned how to distance themselves from lower levels. It is not hard to understand why these managers are not likely to embrace O strategies easily when they are called for, just as managers and advisers hired to enact O strategies will be uncomfortable with restructuring and downsizing and are thus likely to avoid it.

How might E and O be integrated to achieve the benefits of both? The most obvious way to avoid pendulum swings is to sequence E and O in a much longer time frame. This will prevent the uncertainties about direction and lead to better implementation. And it will be less demanding emotionally. Managers do not have to confront tension between E and O in their interactions with employees.

The transformation of General Electric (GE) by Jack Welch began with E and was followed by O some six years later. Welch started with the top-down demand that each business be first or second in their market position. If a business was not in that position, it had to be fixed; if it was not fixed it would be closed or sold. This phase also featured efforts to streamline GE's bureaucracy through massive downsizing. Between 1981 and 1985, GE's employment dropped from

412,000 to 299,000 while revenues increased by 19.7 percent and income by 37.8 percent. The number of organizational levels was reduced from nine to six. The corporate planning and finance functions, among others, were downsized by 60 percent. A climate of fear and intimidation prevailed and Welch began to be referred to as "Neutron Jack" inside the company and in the business press.

Unlike other CEOs who employ Theory E strategies and stop there, Welch came to realize, with advice from consultants and internal staff, that this approach would not create psychological alignment and commitment or capacity for learning and change. Though Welch's personality did not change, his perspective on what it takes to create a sustained transformation did. Between 1985 and his retirement as CEO in 2001, Welch turned to Theory O strategies of change. He and his top team articulated a set of values and began to use values as part of the evaluation and promotion process. And Welch focused on making GE a values-driven organization by incorporating values like teamwork to achieve global coordination. A disciplined application of Theory O strategies increased commitment and enabled a long period of sustained performance. Not all managers who were asked to enact E change became committed to O; those who could not were asked to leave. Most managers will commit to O change because it humanizes the organization. It appeals to their higher-order needs for challenging work, meaning, and community.

The GE story suggests that a sequence of E followed by O can work. But most CEOs do not enjoy the tenure of twenty-plus years that Welch had. Even more problematic, most leaders are unable to change employee perceptions created by E strategies and therefore find it hard to establish the trust and communication necessary to lead a collective learning process. Welch's story is clearly the exception that proves the rule.

It is unlikely that the reverse sequence—O followed by E—can lead to an HCHP company. This sequence will create a sense of betrayal followed by cynicism and low trust. Consider Hewlett-Packard from 1999 to 2005 under Carly Fiorina. Thousands of employees were laid off and most of the policies that had created an exceptional firm were abandoned. This was followed by voluntary departures of managers, and with this the company lost its culture. Whether it can regain that culture under CEO Mark Herd, HP's CEO since 2005, will depend on whether he aspires to rebuild an HCHP culture and on his will and skills to employ a concerted O strategy.

Truly integrating E and O strategies requires that they be enacted simultaneously. This enables CEOs to achieve rapid improvements in financial performance while simultaneously developing trust and commitment. Though these goals may appear paradoxical, our research shows that it is possible to apply E and O together. The transformation of Asda, a major grocery chain in the United Kingdom, is an example of simultaneous use of E and O change strategies, one that I advocate for leaders who aspire to successfully develop HCHP companies.

ASDA: A Remarkable Transformation to HCHP

When Archie Norman took charge of Asda in December of 1991, the company was 1.5 billion pounds in debt and near bankruptcy. Asda, like Scott Paper and Champion International, had a long and venerable past. It had sprung from a dairy farmers association into one of Britain's leading grocery chains. It was the first to build superstores and one of the most successful in broadening its offerings to include clothing and other nonfood items. Though Asda offered value, and therefore had lower profit margins than its high-end competitors, it had been consistently profitable. Due to over-capacity in the industry, however, Asda experienced intense pressures on margins and experienced the slow growth characteristic of the industry, though it continued to be the grocer of choice for working-class shoppers. In the 1980s, in an effort to improve margins and grow the business more rapidly, management decided to change strategy and compete with high-end grocery chains. They changed the product mix, began to raise prices, and acquired a number of nongrocery retail businesses. By borrowing money to purchase sixty stores instead of capitalizing the purchase, management caused the company to incur an unsustainable debt burden when interest rates increased in the inflationary environment of the late 1980s.

When Norman arrived, he found a hierarchical and bureaucratic organization running out of cash. Top management's autocratic style had prevented store managers from voicing their views about buying practices and policies that were eroding customer loyalty. Store managers felt they had no influence on a trading (purchasing) group at headquarters who bought high-end products that Asda's working-class customers did not want. Morale was extremely low.

Norman quickly moved to stem off bankruptcy. He fired the chief financial officer within hours of his arrival, stopped all capital expenditures, sold unrelated businesses and unprofitable stores, imposed a wage freeze, and laid off 10 percent of the workforce. Declaring to the financial community that it would take three years to see results, Norman also visited stores in the first two weeks to talk with and listen to employees and store managers. He immediately reconfigured his top team by removing a layer of management and recruited two new senior executives. One of them, Allen Leighton, later to become his deputy and partner in leading change, complemented Norman's strategic and intellectual capabilities with his down-to-earth style and personal leadership skills, though both shared similar values.

Simultaneous with the restructuring initiatives, Norman articulated a back-to-roots strategy and O-like values that would govern the business in the years ahead. He authorized radical experimentation in one and then two other "renewal" stores, and declared them "risk-free zones." Renewal store managers would not be held accountable for short-term financial results like other store managers. A cross-functional task force was commissioned to work with store management in reinventing the concept of an Asda store—its design, retail proposition, and approach to organizing and managing people. This began a renewal strategy that in over eight years transformed Asda's two hundred stores. During this period a system for continuous improvement—improvement teams, cross-stores knowledge sharing teams, and various task forces—was institutionalized. Throughout, Norman and Allen Leighton spent enormous amounts of time in conversations with various groups of employees in the company, all the time articulating their strategic goals and values, surfacing barriers to progress, and engaging people in developing solutions. During eight years of change a large number of managers who were unable to adopt the "Asda Way" were replaced.

Asda's financial performance turned around by 1994 and was followed by a long string of quarters in which it outperformed the industry in like-for-like sales improvement. The company soon began to be regarded as a leader in the retail industry, with profits and share price improving steadily. The culture was transformed completely from a hierarchical, bureaucratic organization with low morale to one in which employees and customers were given voice through a variety of institutionalized learning and governance mechanisms for two-way dialogue. Asda developed organizational capabilities such as coordination, commitment, competence, creativity, open communication, and the ability to manage conflict in a productive way that is typically found in companies with sustainable competitive advantage.

In 1999 Asda was sold to Wal-Mart at eight times what its market capitalization had been at the time Norman took charge. Wal-Mart managers were quoted as saying that "Asda is more like Wal-Mart than Wal-Mart is like Wal-Mart." Whether this was in fact true—there are many reasons to doubt it—what's important is that Wal-Mart was paying for Asda's cultural transformation and not just greater efficiency brought about by early cost cutting. Norman had successfully led a financial *and* cultural transformation that Wal-Mart executives recognized as the source of sustained performance. Indeed, in subsequent years Wal-Mart adopted many of Asda's approaches to organizing and managing their business.

Asda's performance since Norman's and Leighton's departure has continued to be outstanding in all but two years—years marked by structural changes in the industry. And its high-commitment culture has been sustained despite the departure of Norman and Leighton and some other senior executives. In 2008 it was outperforming sector competitors in growth rate by 3 percent and had hit its profit targets. It was listed in the "Top 50 Best Places to Work Survey" conducted by the United Kingdom's *Sunday Times* newspaper for five years running, and *Fortune* Europe named it as the Best Employer in the U.K. Wal-Mart views Asda as one of the jewels in its crown. According to Asda's management, the company has been very successful in paying back the financial targets set at the time of its acquisition in 1999. There is little question that the organizational transformation of Asda to an HCHP company was, without question, fundamental and enduring.

Integrating E and O Change Strategies

The successful embrace of and/also—an integrated E and O strategy for change—must occur in each of eight key strategic change dimensions in Table 11.1. Without integration in most of the change dimensions discussed below, it is unlikely that the organizational transformation will develop all three pillars of high commitment and performance. In each of the next eight sections I describe how the paradox of E and O can be embraced, and I will use the Asda story to illustrate it.

Goals: Drive for Results and Develop the Organization

Embracing E and O at the outset is essential, given the rapid improvements in shareholder value needed to survive in the short run, while simultaneously building the organizational capabilities and culture needed for long-term success. Norman's speech to Asda's executive team on the first day made clear that he was not ambivalent about embracing the paradox of E and O. He said:

> Today is Day Zero in our recovery program. This business is in poor shape and must change sharply in order to survive. Incremental change is not enough. There are no sacred cows and nothing that can't be examined. Our number one objective is to secure value for our shareholders and secure the trading future of the business. I am not coming in with any magical solutions. I intend to spend the next few weeks listening and forming ideas for our precise direction. We need a culture built around common ideas and goals that include listening, learning, and speed of response, from the stores upwards. There will be management reorganization. My objective is to establish clear lines of communication, and build one team.[11]

TABLE 11.1. E AND O STRATEGIES FOR CHANGE AND THEIR INTEGRATION.

Strategic Dimensions of Change	Theory E	Theory O	Integrated E and O Strategies
Goals	Maximize shareholder value	Develop organizational capabilities	Explicitly embrace restructuring to improve shareholder value, and organization development to change culture.
People	Replace	Develop	Replace and develop
Focus	Change structure, systems, and technology	Change corporate culture: employees' behavior and attitudes	Change the total system—focus simultaneously on the hard (structures and systems) and the soft (corporate culture)
Process	Plan and establish change programs driven from the top	Learn from spontaneous subunit innovations	Plan for innovation in model subunits and plan to spread them systematically
Motivation	Motivate change through financial incentives	Motivate change through involvement—use pay as fair exchange	Motivate through shared goals and involvement/use money to recognize and affirm
Use of Consultants	Outside experts who analyze problems and make recommendations	Process consultants who facilitate problem-solving conversations	Outside expert resources who partner with managers in solving problems
Pace	Rapid	Slow	Deliberate speed and sustainable change
Leadership	Top-down	Bottom-up	Collective learning that is both top-down and bottom-up

Norman's unsentimental focus on shareholder value and at the same time Asda's culture—shared goals, openness, teamwork, and participation—is a model for leaders aspiring to build HCHP organizations. Norman's description of what key executives can expect from him makes his appeal authentic and clarifies what embracing E and O means at the interpersonal level. Most important, Norman's opening speech illustrates the way in which leaders must think and act—integrating E and O—from the very start.

For leaders to embrace the tension between E and O successfully, they must harbor a commitment to building an *institution*—an organization that will last. That requires going beyond the *relatively quick-and-easy E strategies* and building a culture for the future. Here's how Norman later talked about his E and O goals for Asda:

> If you're running out of money you know you've got to raise cash. If stores are losing money . . . you . . . work to close them. If you can't afford a wage and salary increase, which we couldn't, then you don't have one so those are the easy decisions. . . . They may sound tough but actually they're the easy decisions . . . but a culture takes 5 years to forge. . . . The real acid test . . . is what will be the character of this business in 10, 20 years' time. Creating a high commitment business out of a shipwreck means having a clear and very deliberate programme to transform the culture.[12]

Norman's simultaneous short- and long-term perspective is characteristic of an integrated E/O change strategy. While undertaking restructuring he had his eye on creating an institution with sustainable advantage. That perspective is what enables the embrace of O strategies at the very same time that E strategies are being implemented. Aspirations and goals are not enough, however. The ultimate success of a transformation to HCHP depends on integrated strategies with respect to a number of other change dimensions that I discuss below.

People: Replace and Develop

An integrated E and O strategy actively incorporates replacement and development. Avoiding the either-or choice is the most effective way forward. Why?

Replacing key managers who do not fit the new vision speeds the pace of change significantly. Leaders do not have to cope with resistance to changing the old habits of mind and heart often held by long-time employees. Moreover, removing low-performing managers and workers who do not fit the new cultural direction of the firm is quite often met with applause from employees who have known for years that these individuals were ineffective and managed autocratically.

New managers, conversely, accept the urgent need for change. If these new managers are hired to fit HCHP values, "culture drag" is reduced. Getting the "right people on the bus," as Jim Collins found, is associated with successful transformations.[13] Asda's rapid and successful transformation supports this general conclusion. Norman had replaced 90 percent of the top two hundred executives by the end of five years. This can have a salutary effect; as Asda's Allan Leighton noted: "I think that in a strange way the toil and the turmoil helped because people did know that we were all about performance."

The fact that replacement of most key managers is associated with successful transformations does not prove, however, that a less drastic replacement intervention might not be equally effective. Massive firing of key managers has potentially huge costs. It increases fear and distrust among survivors; in effect, the breakdown of community. Surviving managers at Scott came to hate Dunlap and presumably were not eager to help. Memory, skills, and knowledge are lost, putting the firm at potential risk. And massive replacements send a message that learning and development—important for developing the organization's capabilities and capacity to learn and change—are not valued. I recently observed the disastrous effects of rapid and massive replacement of managers and staff in a not-for-profit organization. Though financial performance improved, customer and employee satisfaction declined, as did the reputation of the organization in the community, thus threatening the viability of the enterprise. Without the years of experience and tradition to guide them, the new leaders made many mistakes.

An integrated replacement and development change strategy is based on the premise that the first step is to engage managers and help them improve, unless there is clear evidence that they cannot or will not change. This principle may be more difficult to enact with regard to the most senior executives because they are important role models on whom the CEO will rely to change the culture. Moreover, CEOs who do not move quickly to replace underperforming senior managers who do not fit the new way will raise questions about top management's determination to transform the organization. Several years ago I worked with a company whose senior executives espoused high commitment and participative values. They asked me to hold several workshops around the world about leading in the new participative culture. When I arrived in the lobby of a Singapore hotel to lead a workshop, I was greeted by a distraught country manager who insisted on seeing me immediately. His message: if senior management does not remove the autocratic and abusive corporate VP of manufacturing to whom he reported, he and other managers would not believe a word of what senior management and I said in the workshop. Symbolism matters and may dictate a violation of the "develop first and replace second" principle.

But with regard to middle and upper-middle managers, "develop first and replace second" is certainly valid. These managers are often wrongly assumed to be resistant to change, research by Quy Nguyen Huy shows. He finds that middle managers "make valuable contributions to the realization of radical change . . . contributions that go largely unrecognized by most senior executives." Consistent with our findings that lower levels know what is wrong in the organization and are motivated to change if properly led, Huy finds that middle managers add value with entrepreneurial ideas, are better than senior executives at leveraging informal networks, understand employees' moods and emotional needs, and help in managing the paradox of continuity and change.[14]

The exact mix of replacement and development is contingent on the situation—urgency of the crisis, how dependent leaders are on the knowledge and skills of current managers, and the time frame for selecting new managers who fit. As Norman noted, he had to rely on some key executives who, he knew, might have to be replaced later because he could not possibly recruit two hundred replacement managers who fit his values and vision at the pace that wholesale replacement of managers would warrant. The five years that it took Asda to replace 90 percent of its management cadre provided ample time for those who were capable of changing to demonstrate it. Moreover, hiring to fit values, as I noted in chapter 10, requires careful selection, and that takes time.

Because replacement is an inevitable part of an integrated E and O change strategy, the perception that replacement and layoffs are fair is crucial. To the extent that the survivors perceive actions taken by senior management to be self-serving, as inconsistent with the newly espoused ethic of performance and commitment, and to the extent that they remain unconvinced that massive firing and downsizing are warranted, it will be very hard to build an HCHP organization. A deep literature on organizational justice tell us that perceived fairness is a function of both the outcomes of decisions (what happens and to whom) and the process by which the decisions are made.

Equality of Outcomes. Perceived equality of outcomes can be enhanced if people perceive the following:

- *Visible sacrifices by top management*, such as lowering their own salaries and eliminating excessive stock payouts, enhance perceptions of fairness. At Delphi, the auto parts company bought in 2006 by private equity interests, top management awarded themselves outlandish pay packages and stock options worth millions. The negative reactions of employees, unions, and community suggest that already low levels of commitment were further decimated. Norman and his top managers were paid well for their efforts and stood to gain from improvements in long-term performance. However, their compensation package was never an issue, and therefore did not undermine trust and their ability to lead the transformation of Asda.

- *Survivors should be given opportunities to develop and grow.* Though Norman replaced 90 percent of the top two hundred managers, a significant number of positions were filled by high-potential and high-performance managers hidden several levels below the top. Allan Leighton noted: "[In] bad businesses there are always some good people if you can find them, and half the time they're . . . pretty good. It's the business that stifles."

Fair Process. Explaining why change is necessary and how organization change is led affects commitment to the change.[15] Necessary evils may be painful, but explaining decisions in the *context* of changes in the competitive environment and the requirements it imposes on how the firm must be organized and managed will increase a perception of fairness. Communicating the struggles that management went through to arrive at decisions and conveying empathy is also essential. The CEO of Continental Airlines had the courage to visit every facility affected by downsizing and addressed employees, including those who would lose their jobs, to explain why downsizing was necessary—a stellar example of transparency and empathy. The organization that emerged is an HCHP one.

How people are treated after they are fired or replaced also matters. Are they escorted out of the building by a security guard on Friday afternoon or are they allowed to leave with dignity? Are resources such as outplacement services provided? The goal should be to ensure that every downsized employee feels positively about the company despite losing a job.

Companies should take both performance and length of service into account. A financial service company recently downsized one-third of its workforce by cutting everyone in new businesses threatened by the credit crisis in financial markets, regardless of performance or length of service. This approach will not build long-term commitment to the company. In contrast, in the mid-1980s Hewlett-Packard used length of service and performance to restructure the company in advance of anticipated competitive pressures. Downsized employees were given an opportunity to look for equivalent-level jobs in the company. If they could not find one, they were offered a lower-level job. If they decided not to take the jobs, they received a severance package. This process conveyed a concern for the well-being and commitment of employees appropriate for an HCHP company. This process grew out of the pain that David Packard and Bill Hewlett felt when, early in the company's history, they had to let an underperforming loyal employee go. "The impact of that decision," Packard reflected in later years, "is still with us, and in subsequent years has led us to make every effort to find an appropriate niche for loyal employees. Interestingly enough, we have had good success through the years in relocating such employees within the company."[16]

Focus: The Total System—Hard and Soft Facets

CEOs who implement E change strategies focus primarily on restructuring, incentives, and IT systems. These changes in the organization's "hardware" are often recommended by consultants unconcerned with building the organization's HCHP culture. Although such changes are essential, the idea that changes in the "hardware" alone will make the ultimate difference is false. In my own experience, changing hardware without first thinking through the core business model, and before engaging people in the redesign, will fail. Consider Jim Collins's conclusions with regard to the role of information technology in successful journeys from good to great. "When used right, technology becomes an *accelerator* of momentum, not a creator of it. The good-to-great companies never began their transitions with pioneering technology."[17] Hardware innovations should proceed only after the business model has been clarified or changed and after some progress has been made in overcoming silent management barriers to effectiveness. This facilitates a diagnosis of the business and involves relevant groups and individuals—the users of the hardware—in the change.

Pure Theory O change could not be more different from E change. Top management typically articulates a set of values or principles intended to inform employees about expected behavior and future culture. Employees are then involved in a variety of ways to discuss, amend, and reinforce the new norms. At the extreme, the assumption is that commitment and dedication will produce performance improvements. Though Champion did not employ a pure O strategy by any means, an emphasis on involvement and commitment dominated the first years of change, and needed restructuring lagged. The first phase, which took place at the plant level, was actually a good example of how a high-involvement process can be used to change an organization's hardware. Managers and workers participated in redesigning manufacturing processes and technology. However, major changes in corporate structure and systems did not occur until relatively late in the journey. Restructuring the portfolio of businesses did not take place at all in the first decade.

The most rapid and successful transformations are systemic, focusing on both hard and soft aspects of the organizational system and integrating them wherever possible, as Champion did with plant-level change. Structure is changed with the involvement of relevant parties and treated as a process of continuous and successive approximation and learning discussed in chapter 9. Diagnosis is an essential part of the change effort at all stages. Management is keenly aware that they must clarify the business model and begin to tackle problems in organizational and managerial effectiveness before launching major change in the hard aspects of the organization. They also understand that involving relevant stakeholders is about more than gaining stakeholder commitment. It is about learning from people what changes in hard facets of the organization should be made and involving them in the change process. Learning and governance systems can be helpful as a platform for making such systemic changes. As noted in chapter 7, honest, collective, and public conversations enable all parties to see the whole system. And the high-engagement process itself changes the software—attitudes, skills, and behavior—while changing the hardware.

Using the *five levers* for change discussed in this book, I illustrate below how CEO Norman and his deputy Allan Leighton embraced theory E and O change. Asda's successful transformation can be directly linked to their total systems approach.

Leadership. Norman's and Leighton's *combined* values and skills permitted them to focus on hard E and soft O aspects of the business. Norman brought business and financial savvy. Leighton, a former executive at Mars, a high-commitment company, brought people skills as well as an engaging and energizing down-to-earth personality. Common values around listening and participation enabled them to combine their E and O skills.

Learning and Governance. Within two weeks of his arrival, Norman began to visit stores, unannounced and without entourage, to ask people what they saw as major problems. This immediately signaled a change in philosophy of management—bureaucracy was out and engagement was in. Communicating with and engaging employees and customers was later institutionalized in multiple ways, too many to discuss here. For example, store managers were required to establish colleague and customer listening groups. Allan Leighton periodically held "confrontation meetings" that brought together store managers and representatives from corporate to address difficult issues that might not otherwise be discussed. Norman established a "Tell Archie" upward communication and suggestion system that enabled him to hear directly and quickly about new ideas and problems. A corporate learning and governance process brought employee representatives from all parts of the company together annually to discuss the effectiveness of Asda and provide feedback to Norman and Leighton.

Strategic Performance Management. Changes in strategy, goals, and values were accompanied by changes in measures; revenue became the primary goal and the emphasis on cost was abandoned to stimulate innovation and change. Managers became accountable for customer and employee commitment. Norman and Leighton institutionalized a wholly new process for managing business performance. Instead of the old bureaucratic process, they met with store managers quarterly in multiple regional meetings to review performance and to jointly realign business and organizational practices. (Previously the review process occurred at multiple levels and store managers never saw top management.)

Organizing Model. How Asda was organized and managed changed at the corporate, regional, and store levels—resulting in fewer organizational levels, new structures and processes to promote coordination, solve business problems, and exchange best practices. Stores began to have a voice in business decisions; the central trading group, which had previously made all purchasing decisions, became less powerful. In sum, Asda moved from a bureaucratic organization to a structured network.

Human Resources. Asda began a concerted effort to recruit and select managers who fit the new performance orientation and values (90 percent of managers turned over in the first five years). Policies changed with regard to performance evaluation, compensation and incentives, and fair treatment of employees.

◆ ◆ ◆

Asda is the best corporate example of total system change that I know of, particularly when one considers the relatively short period of time in which this was accomplished.

Process: Change Is Planned at the Top But Led in Subunits

To what extent must corporate transformations be planned and driven from the top to achieve speed and consistency? To what extent is such a top-down strategy a fool's errand, especially given the complexity of corporate transformations and the commitment generated by delegating the task of leading change to business and operating unit leaders?

E strategies are characterized by top-down change—initiatives are planned at the top and driven by consultants and staff groups. Educational programs, total quality programs such as Six Sigma, information systems, incentive programs, economic value creation programs, and culture programs are among the many initiatives typically driven by corporate staff groups. This approach is based on the view that change must be planned like a military invasion; the CEO is like a general with a centrally developed battle plan who is heroically fighting for the firm's survival. Underlying Theory E change is the expectation that capital markets must be met on their terms. There is, of course, some truth in these assumptions. CEOs who fail to meet financial targets in a timely manner lose credibility and ultimately their jobs.

Our own research and that of others shows, however, that top-down programs undermine sustained transformation.[18] They can result in compliance and cynicism rather than real learning and commitment to change. Our work with task forces commissioned by senior teams to identify barriers to strategic change shows how people experience overload from too many top-down change initiatives. A recent study finds that a plethora of change initiatives reduces commitment to change in all but the most self-efficacious and determined individuals.[19] CEOs and their corporate staff groups cannot roll out change initiative after change initiative and expect people to embrace each one with the same enthusiasm that they and their consultants do.

Top-down initiatives also fail because they are applied to all parts of the organization at roughly the same time, with the same content, and in the same way. Our research has shown that one size does not always fit all.[20] Centrally driven programs may not always fit the strategy of the unit or the unit's cultural readiness to implement it. Programmatic E change undermines experimentation—the essence of successful change. It also undermines leadership development as subunit managers comply and are precluded from thinking, leading, and learning from their own decisions and actions.

Pure O strategies unfold very differently. There is no master blueprint for change. Innovation and change begin spontaneously at the periphery and spread haphazardly through emulation and unplanned transfer of innovative leaders to other subunits; if the firm is lucky, innovative leaders eventually rise to the top and foster change in the total corporation. In effect, top management "lets a thousand flowers bloom" but does not take much responsibility for ensuring cross-pollination by, for example, noticing innovations in subunits, offering political support, and then actively diffusing these changes to other subunits.

The strength of theory O change is that it enables spontaneous experimentation and learning close to the front lines. This makes change more relevant, valid, and feasible. Importantly, experimentation in subunits also prevents costly mistakes that frequently occur when top-down programs are employed. Such mistakes negatively affect performance and motivation. Asda's Norman described the potential dangers of top-down change and his countertheory:

> I think it's very dangerous to come into any failing business with a clear pre-scription as to what has to happen, so you start with some basic principles and then you listen and give yourself some time. The art is to provide sufficient directions, to give proper confidence. They know there is new leadership and momentum, while buying yourself some time to listen to what is really going on at the ground.[21]

O strategies enable self-managed experimentation, learning, and change and are consistent with the widely accepted principle that real understanding and learning come only from self-directed change; self-managed change develops self-efficacy and greater commitment.[22] O strategies develop capabilities to respond to unplanned events and contingencies because learning occurs in the situation where it will be required. Capabilities develop from the experience of managers and workers in their organizational role within the subunit system. Action learning creates knowledge in action, provides continual feedback about efficacy of actions, and enables refinement and internalization of the knowledge.[23]

However, this decentralized approach to change can be too slow, especially given investor expectations. The emergent nature of the pure O change process will create isolated islands of change, leading subunits to regress. Top management, distanced from subunit innovations, fails to protect subunits from group pressure to revert to the norm, or replaces innovative subunit managers with ones who do not understand or are unsympathetic to the new cultural values and vision embedded in the new management model that their predecessor has developed.

The most effective change process, our research shows, is one in which vision, values, and change architecture are developed at the top, but actual changes are led locally by top teams in the corporation's many subunits—divisions, geographic regions, and operating units.[24] This change strategy is superior to standardizing processes and practices across subunits. Standardization driven from the top may increase reliability but reduces diversity in subunits, thus preventing the corporation from capitalizing on innovations in leading-edge subunits. Capacity for learning and change is reduced.

Top management contemplating a centrally conceived but locally led change strategy should consider the following strategy. Commission the development of innovative new models for organizing and managing the business. Then actively plan and orchestrate the spread of the "new way" to all of the corporation's many subunits. In changing its two hundred stores, Asda used this strategy, thus enabling each subunit to be transformed as a total system. Change is managed by each subunit's senior team; they are accountable to higher management for progress. Corporate staff groups and consultants assist as needed but do not drive change (Figure 11.1).

A top management engaged in managing such a unit-by-unit change process might consider a simple tool for tracking multi-unit change. Using the corporate organization chart, they can assign a color code to each subunit based on its progress toward their vision (green for leading-edge units, yellow for units in transition, and red for lagging subunits). They can then diagnose why change has not progressed in lagging subunits and take needed action. Subunit leadership is obviously one reason, as might be the leadership and culture of the division in which the subunit is nested. Corporate policies and practices or lack of consulting resources may also be involved. Top management's role is to create the conditions for local innovation and change. Asda's Norman recognized this potential barrier to innovation when he declared that the early experimental stores he commissioned would operate in a "risk-free zone," meaning that the general managers of experimental stores would not be evaluated on traditional performance measures and would not report to regional managers who might block change.

A governance and learning process that enables each subunit to self-manage its improvements can be an *essential component of a multi-unit change strategy*. Such a process will create transparency. It enables each subunit to assess its readiness to absorb change and develop the effectiveness required for continuous change.

FIGURE 11.1. THE MULTI-UNIT AND LEVEL PERSPECTIVE OF CHANGE.

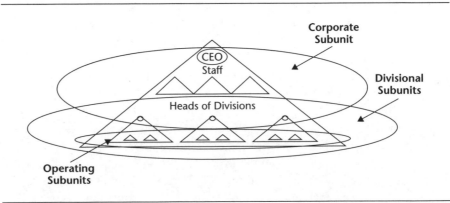

Source: Adapted from Beer et al. *The Critical Path to Corporate Renewal*, 1990.

And if senior management requires subunit leaders to report what was learned and what they plan to change, it enables a fact-based conversation between the corporate center and each subunit's leaders about readiness for change and progress. That was the essence of Grey Warner's strategy for change in Merck's Latin American region (chapter 7), as it was at Asda.

By designating leading-edge subunits and asking them to innovate and push the frontier of performance and commitment, and then asking lagging units to catch up, the unit-by-unit change strategy increases the mean or average performance of its multiple subunits and potentially reduces the sigma or dispersion in the distribution of subunit performance (see Figure 11.2). Developing subunit leaders who share the vision and values of leading-edge units is a key to this strategy. These may be recruited from the outside or developed internally by promoting promising managers in leading-edge subunits who have demonstrated alignment with the new way, and moving them to lagging sub-units where they can apply what they learned. In effect, leading-edge units become engines for developing the next generation of leaders. An executive president overseeing a successful large-scale transformation captured the essence of this change process when he referred his one hundred worldwide manufacturing plants as a team of dogs pulling a dog sled. His job, he quipped, was to push the lead dogs to ever-higher effectiveness and performance and help the lag dogs catch up.[25]

FIGURE 11.2. MULTI-UNIT CHANGE STRATEGY.

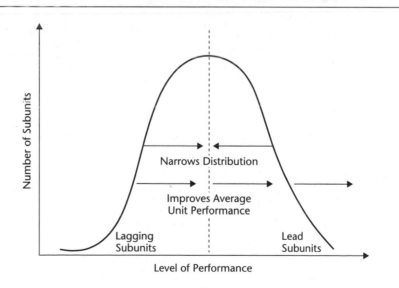

Considerable research shows that such a multi-unit strategy leads to more learning, commitment, and improvements in performance than top-down programmatic change.[26] We know that continuous improvement occurs through experimentation that is tightly connected to problems and challenges faced by front-line managers and workers. The multi-unit strategy enables each local subunit to adhere to the total system change principle articulated earlier. Multiple complementary changes are orchestrated in a coordinated manner by the subunit's leadership team consistent with their diagnosis of the subunit's effectiveness, as opposed to being driven by disconnected corporate initiatives at different times.

There are two ways to employ a centrally planned but locally self-managed change strategy. The first is most applicable to multiple subunits with the same or very similar business and operating model; for example, manufacturing plants, stores, restaurants, country organizations, hospitals, call centers, schools, or health care micro-systems with similar patient care and safety objectives. The second is more applicable to multibusiness corporations with different business and operating models. Both alternatives ideally rely on a learning and governance process that promotes honest conversations within the subunits, and between each subunit and higher management.

Alternative I: Subunits with Similar Businesses and Operating Models. Top management commissions the development of an innovative HCHP management model in one or more subunits. This creates a new and integrated system for managing the business at the frontier of effectiveness, performance, and commitment. After proving the new concept, senior management asks all of its multiple subunits to employ a centrally developed and standardized learning and governance process to self-assess their leadership and organizational effectiveness and to determine readiness to absorb the new model. A conversation follows between senior management and each subunit about their readiness to change. If managers are unable over time to change the leadership and culture of their unit to a state of readiness, they are replaced.

Asda's "renewal program" illustrates these principles and was a key ingredient in the company's rapid transformation. In the first nine months, a corporate multifunctional task force appointed by Norman, working collaboratively with management of a targeted subunit, developed a successful leading-edge model store that incorporated new retail, organizational, and management approaches to the business. The new store model was then replicated in two additional stores with similar performance and cultural improvements. Having proven the new store concept, management focused on spreading the innovative model to all two hundred stores. Before ultimately succeeding, however, Asda made a potentially fatal error that validates the unit-by-unit change strategy. Responding to their felt need to improve Asda's performance quickly, management pushed the new model into twenty additional stores without regard to their leadership and cultural readiness. Allan Leighton, responsible for transforming Asda's stores, recalled: "I crashed the program through and renewed the 20 stores in three months, but messed it up. The stores looked nice, but did not work.... The physical piece was done, but the cultural piece did not take hold.... We did the renewals but the sales did not improve."[27]

In response to this setback, Asda's management developed what they called a "driving test"—surveys and interviews by corporate human resource professionals to assess the leadership and organizational effectiveness of each store. Asda's driving test became the basis for an honest conversation between the corporate center and store managers about their organization's readiness for change. Investments in store renewal were focused only on stores that passed the driving test. Managers of stores assessed as not ready for change were provided assistance to pass the driving test. Store managers who could not pass the driving test were ultimately replaced.

Alternative II: Multiple Subunits with Different Business or Operating Models.
This change strategy differs from the first in that it requires the adoption of a learning and governance system but not a common solution. Each subunit's senior team is expected to learn, reinvent its approach to organizing and managing, and thereby improve commitment and performance. The learning and governance system can be piloted in a few subunits and then spread to all others. That can be done rapidly by requiring each subunit manager to adopt the learning system, or the learning system can be diffused more gradually through the following means:[28]

a. Publicize and lend political support to subunit leaders who employ the learning and governance system by calling attention to innovations and change in effectiveness that resulted from it
b. Arrange for visits by lagging subunit managers and key people to emerging leading-edge models
c. Transfer leading subunit leaders to lagging subunits so they can embed the learning and change process

Capability Development.
Both unit-by-unit change strategies will require new knowledge and skills that subunits probably don't possess. For example, new leadership capabilities will be required in every subunit; middle managers working in new team structures will require collaborative team attitudes and skills; technical knowledge will have to be imparted. Because the financial

and professional resources to develop these capabilities are not available in the subunits, a centrally planned strategy is essential. How shall this be done? To avoid the fallacy of driving change from the top, as discussed earlier, training and development programs can be created with the participation of subunit managers. And they can be made available to subunit managers when they and their senior team think they are ready and need it, as opposed to being offered to everyone at the same time—the one-size-fits-all approach—ready or not.

Motivation: Use Goals and Involvement to Motivate, Rewards to Recognize

E transformations are based on the assumption that rich financial incentives—stock options and bonuses—are essential motivators. Incentives are used to drive change. Proponents of this system believe that incentives are essential to attract senior executives who will put shareholder interests first.[29] There is no better example than Scott Paper where the CEO, Dunlap, developed rich incentives for senior executives and netted more than $100 million himself.

O transformations motivate people through shared goals, involvement, and meaningful work. The power of this philosophy is illustrated by the commitment generated in well-managed not-for-profit firms and causes, or school systems, for example, where rich incentives are not available. These organizations also find that they must differentiate between strong and weak performers to ensure fairness and find ways to attract and keep talented people. Charter school experiments suggest, for example, that merit pay can be an important change ingredient if embedded in a changing culture.

HCHP change strategies integrate E and O by putting the new mission, and high performance standards and culture in the foreground, and compensation changes in the background. Jim Collins concluded from his research into corporate transformations: "We found *no* [emphasis mine] systematic pattern linking executive compensation to the process of going from good to great. The evidence simply does not support the idea that the specific structure of executive compensation acts as a key lever in taking a company from good to great."[30] This finding is consistent with the compensation philosophy and practices of HCHP companies discussed in chapter 10. Asda's Norman echoes Collins's findings when he described the role of monetary incentives in Asda's transformation:

> I think they [monetary incentives] were really very, very subordinate. It was a happy side effect of the transformation that a lot of people made money out of Asda and of course, Allan, and I and others came in partly because we felt here was a chance to make some capital. We weren't interested in just having an income. We wanted to make some capital but once the team [was] on board, I

don't think the financial incentives actually crossed our minds day to day, nor do I think that they affected the behavior down the organization very greatly. I think—it was psychologically useful to be able to offer all these store managers share options at an early stage, but the important point was not the financial incentive. It was the statement that you are on board, that you are a part of this with the top management. And again, after four years when we were able to offer the share options to shop [level] colleagues, it was a way of saying, this is really single status. You can have a bit of what the chief executives got. You're all entitled to the same type of benefits. So [they were] psychologically important, but in terms of altering behavior, I don't think very greatly. In fact, you find in the Asda culture that people don't respond very greatly to money incentives as such. They want to feel they're well paid, of course . . . There's a much stronger take in the stores which is about equality, i.e., fair pay, and very strong resentment if they feel some people are paid unreasonably or some people get a bonus for work that was actually done by somebody else.[31]

Consulting Resources: Experts Who Partner with Clients to Solve Problems

Virtually all corporate transformations involve external consultants. They bring new ideas, perspectives, and methods. CEOs could not make fundamental changes in the five levers discussed in this book without substantive expertise. Yet the impact of different choices about the type of consultants and their role is not well understood.

In their haste to satisfy investors, E leaders rely heavily on large consulting firms with armies of very smart MBAs who bring strong substantive expertise and solutions—*the what of change*. Firms that employ this top-down expert consulting model may create frustration, fear, and anger among key middle and upper-middle managers. Although emotional responses to strategic change are inevitable and essential for real change to occur, negative emotional responses are known to hinder "collective receptivity to change, collective mobilization, and learning," which undermine quality of change and commitment to it.[32]

Concerned about building trust and commitment, O-style change leaders employ a handful of organization development consultants whose expertise is in the process of change—*the how of change*, the approach employed by Champion International. They work with leaders and employees in identifying and solving problems. Consultants may bring substantive expertise but choose to subtly and skillfully bring that knowledge into the conversation rather than make formal recommendations.[33] Facilitated self-managed change undoubtedly produces positive emotions such as sympathy, comfort, and hope, and enables real but slower cultural change.

Successful transformations find ways to integrate the benefits of both consulting models. Experts are brought into the firm, but instead of bringing solutions and driving them, they partner with employees to analyze problems and develop solutions; in the process they teach internal staff. Asda's Norman saw great value in external consultants *if* they could become part of the firm:

> There's one other thing that I think is a vital tip which is to use outsiders. Now, organizations that use outsiders will have a huge advantage and some organizations are very defensive about it, struggling organizations as Asda was, tend to be very defensive. But we brought with us a sort of entourage of everything from McKinsey through Crisp . . . who is a creative [retail] guru, to Julian Richard who is an entrepreneur, really, to Peter Samuel who was an HR guy. And we managed to create an atmosphere within which the organization welcomed them and was very open about it and enjoyed having them around. And I think that created enormous power for us because it meant that we were able to pick up creative ideas from outside and to use outsiders to make internal people who were having a bit of a struggle much more effective.[34]

The danger is that firms can become dependent on outside expert consultants. Motivated to increase their billings, consultants will always want to lengthen their engagement. Concerned about Asda managers' potential dependency on the consultants he brought with him early in the transformation, Norman later reduced their involvement.

To achieve HCHP, leaders will have to integrate the expert consultation model with the process consultation model (Figure 11.3). To accomplish these results, outsiders will have to become trusted thought partners, participating in the conversation that insiders are having about problems and solutions—as opposed to acting as powerful agents of the CEO or simply facilitating conversation without being thought partners. Asda's Norman observed: "If you can translate the outsider to insiders, then that's when it works because the difference is between the ideas and the delivery."[35] To implement Norman's recommendation, management must learn to see consultants as partners in the change process as opposed to vendors.

Pace of Change: Deliberate Pace for Rapid Sustainable Change

CEOs who make E choices unleash rapid change on multiple fronts only to learn later that solutions imposed on the organization meet resistance. Effective change requires a much more deliberate pace in order to develop real learning and commitment. It is a process of discovery and successive approximation. HCHP

FIGURE 11.3. THE EFFECTS OF EXPERT AND PROCESS CONSULTATION.

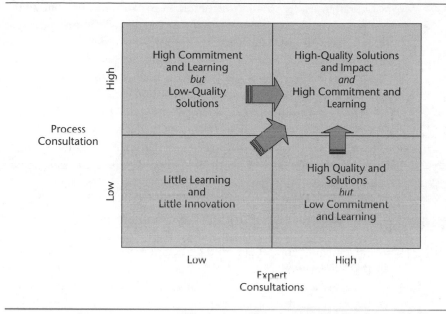

Source: Adapted from Miles, R. In M. Beer & N. Nohria, *Breaking the Code of Change*, p. 385.

leaders know that new organizational and management models rarely work as anticipated and must be adapted. They sacrifice speed for commitment and development of capabilities, a by-product of deeply engaging people in solving problems. They understand that a deliberate pace leads to deeper understanding of the organization and discovery of new problems that must be solved. An integrated E and O transformation is an emergent phenomenon—a fast-paced but deliberate building process that enables progress over multiple years.

In 1997, just as he was taking charge from Norman, Allan Leighton elaborated on the cost of a rapid pace:

> Because we were changing so many things we didn't have much chance to say, oh, no, they're not really working.... And I know we are still doing things now wrong that we were doing wrong three, four years ago that we at some stage would have found the way of doing it right, and we just missed it. But I think that's what you pay for pace. Because we did things so fast sometimes we screwed some things up, too, and I think we wouldn't do that again because we know what to do. But I think how you can institutionalize some of the learning is a bit of the trick we've missed.[36]

Very rapid top-down E change is based on CEOs' assumptions that they must respond immediately to pressure from financial institutions. Successful transformation leaders avoid this pitfall. Norman told financial analysts in the City that it would take three years to see significant improvement in results. No matter how dire the short-term circumstances—deregulation in the case of Wells Fargo, looming bankruptcy in the case of Nucor, potential takeover threats in the case of Kroger—Jim Collins found that good-to-great "transformations follow the same basic pattern; they accumulate momentum, turn by turn of the flywheel, until buildup transformed into breakthroughs."[37] Nucor's CEO observed, "We did not make a decision that this was what we stood for at any specific moment. It evolved through many agonizing arguments and fights."[38] Clearly, transformation is not a magic bullet; it requires a deliberate pace from which solutions emerge.

Leadership: Top-Down Early and Bottom-Up Later

The integrated E and O strategy for change requires CEOs to lead change from the top early on in the transformation and slowly increase the degree of lower-level involvement in decision making. The change direction and strategy must be advocated by top management even if their long-term intention is to create a participative high-commitment culture. Asda's spectacularly successful transformation is evident in Norman's deep understanding of how to meld top-down leadership with bottom-up participation:

> In the [first] year or so this was top driven and it has [to be]—it doesn't mean that the people at the bottom in the stores didn't have an influence. Of course, they did. But it was our job to listen to them. Interpret what they were saying in the context—the direction one takes in the business and then make decisions and to drive it. And there was no two ways about it. The first two years were leadership driven. Subsequently, our task then became to engineer to create an organization where change—and improvement—became part of the way of life, part of the habit of the business and in that stage, you start to change gears and encourage people to get involved.[39]

This view of change is completely consistent with the situational view of leadership long held by behavioral scientists. CEOs who aspire to build an HCHP organization must use the power of their position and the mandate they are given by the crisis at hand to break the strategic frame responsible for low performance and commitment. As leaders change the situation, however, so too they can begin to change their leadership role. But top-down leadership does not mean dictatorial or unilateral. Leaders must begin by advocating a new general direction, but as Norman observes, they also inquire and listen so that they can modify their view and shape their general direction to the specific situation. This is the collective learning process that I argue is the way to build an HCHP community of purpose capable of learning and change (see chapter 6). By inquiring and listening, the leader's mandate for change is strengthened. As the transformation unfolds, however, advocacy of new ideas can and will come from lower levels. The organization is now capable of learning and change, or continuous improvement, as Norman puts it.

Sustaining High Commitment and Performance

A transformation to HCHP is a never-ending journey of continuous improvement. In the early stages there is excitement. If the transformation begins, as it often does, with a crisis, the early stages are motivated by the desire to prevent corporate failure. The challenge is how to sustain energy for continuous improvement over time. At various stages in the journey leaders must reframe the purpose of the transformation to reenergize the organization.

Companies like Nucor have been able to sustain continuous improvements by decentralizing authority and responsibility to the lowest level possible and sharing rewards of performance with their managers and workers. These are basic building blocks for performance and psychological alignment. They are the antitheses of bureaucracy, which must be avoided at all cost if the journey is to be sustained. The difficulty comes when companies grow in scale and scope. That change cannot be allowed to undermine delegating responsibility to the lowest possible level.

Sustainability also depends on the capacity to learn from customers and from employees. This requires an institutionalized internal learning and governance mechanism such as the one Asda adopted and for which I argued earlier in the book (chapter 7). Enabling customers and employees to speak truth to power can prevent derailing the journey to HCHP. If institutionalized with the board of director's imprimatur it will ensure that CEOs, their top teams, and the board of directors continue to learn and change as circumstances shift. Even HCHP leaders can lose perspective and vision. They too can become insulated from the truth about their business and organization. They too can become stuck in a mental model and habits that require change.

No factor is more important, however, than leadership. That is why leadership succession is the deciding factor in sustaining the journey to HCHP. Asda's remarkable journey continued after Archie Norman transferred its leadership to

Allan Leighton, an executive who had been part of the transformation journey. Though different in their skills and predispositions, Norman's and Leighton's understanding of the transformations they were leading—strategy, values, and vision—evolved through their common experience. By developing Leighton to succeed him, Norman ensured continuity on the journey to HCHP. There is considerable evidence that companies with sustained records of high performance and commitment do so by promoting insiders who have demonstrated over many years their fit with emerging culture.[40] Leadership at the top is not enough; CEOs and their top teams have to commit to developing the next generation of leaders.

The importance of this was unanimously endorsed at a 2007 Harvard Business School conference of CEOs who were involved in or had led successful HCHP transformations. They felt that developing the next generation of leaders was essential to reinvigorating their company's transformation and building an enduring legacy.

Summary and Conclusion

Shortly after turning over the reins of the company to Allan Leighton, Norman reflected on his experience:

> You have to remember in '91 and '92 this was pretty grim, and there's nothing more character forming than coming into a situation where you don't know whether you're going to get out of it. I mean when I first came up here I was living in the Holiday Inn and my wife and daughter stayed in London. And they said, well, we'll kind of come up later in the year. And every evening Vanessa would ring up and say, how are things going? And I'd say, well, don't move up just yet. Just give it a bit longer and we'll see. And so it was—it was tough and depressing at times. And the fact that it's come right—it's more than come right, and we've managed to create a company and survived, and then it went beyond surviving and became quite a good company and now is, I think in some respects, an outstanding company. It's been an incredibly rewarding experience, and I think we've all gained enormously out of that and gained as individuals. And I know if I were going to do it again, I could do it better. Of course I could.[41]

The feelings of satisfaction and pride expressed by Norman stem from the great HCHP company he was instrumental in building and the positive legacy he undoubtedly felt he had left. This would not have been possible had he not had the will and skill to integrate E and O into a highly effective change strategy. Corporate leaders who want to emulate Norman's success will have to embrace the paradox of E and O in the following areas:

- *Goals:* Embrace the psychologically difficult paradox presented by short-term pressures for quarterly earnings and the long-term goal of building organizational capabilities and commitment.
- *People:* Replace longtime managers who do not fit the vision of HCHP and lay off employees while building a culture of trust and employee development.
- *Focus:* Change the system—hard elements such as structure, business processes, and the information system, and softer dimensions, such as capabilities, relationships of trust, empowerment, and culture.
- *Process:* Develop a strategy for change at the top that enables experimentation and learning in multiple subunits and groups of the larger organization.
- *Motivation:* Use compensation to recognize contribution as opposed to inducements. Motivate behavior through inspirational leadership, employee involvement, career development opportunities, and the creation of challenging work.
- *Consulting Resources:* Partner with consultants in a variety of fields who will work with the firm's managers in analyzing and solving problems as opposed to bringing in solutions.
- *Pace of Change:* Avoid the temptation to set such a fast pace of change that there is no time for deep sustainable learning.
- *Leadership:* Exert strong leadership from the top in the early stages of the transformation, but inquire and listen in order to understand the situation and develop commitment. Delegate responsibility to lead change to lower-level managers as the transformation unfolds and they display a readiness to lead.

Sustaining the transformation requires active attention to the development of all five change levers discussed in this book. Most important, it requires the development of the next generation of leaders who understand how to design and lead an HCHP company.

CHAPTER TWELVE

EPILOGUE

The Future of High Commitment, High Performance Organizations

Do HCHP organizations have a future? As I complete this book in October 2008 we are experiencing the worst economic and financial crisis since the Great Depression. Billions in capital assets have been lost, real estate defaults are rising rapidly to near-historic levels, and unemployment is projected to climb to highs not seen in decades. American automobile companies face extinction after years of mismanagement. We stand on the precipice of deflation and economic disaster. There is little question that many economic policies and regulatory practices (the lack of them) are to blame. But what we are seeing can just as easily be attributed to organizational and management barriers to high commitment and high performance discussed in this book, and to the lack of HCHP design features intended to overcome them. Put another way, had financial institutions implicated in the economic crisis been led and organized as HCHP firms, we would have avoided the crisis we face today.

The investment banks and brokerage houses of Bear Stearns, Lehman Brothers, and Merrill Lynch, or mortgage companies such as Country Mutual and Washington Mutual bore little resemblance to HCHP companies. Indeed, they were the very antithesis of the organizations discussed in the book. Their leaders—CEOs and boards of directors—did not have the aspirations, the higher moral purpose, or the savvy to build a resilient organization capable of sustained advantage. Instead, their appetite for big profits and payoffs guided CEOs in these companies.

Leadership teams of HCHP organizations, I argued in chapter 3, make principled choices. These choices begin with their definition of firm purpose—a desire to make a positive contribution to customers, employees, and society, as much as to turn a profit for investors. That was certainly not the case at Washington Mutual, where a loan officer, fired for her reluctance to issue bad mortgages, reported of the company: "It wasn't about the quality of the loan; it was about the numbers. They didn't care if we were giving loans to people that didn't qualify. Instead it was about how many loans did you guys close and fund."[1] Nor were the top management teams of these companies open to learning the unvarnished truth. Why else were employees fired for speaking up? After turning down an unwise loan, the fired loan officer reported, "You were like a bad person if you declined the loan."[2]

Financial institutions lacked the long-term focused strategy tied to firm purpose and capabilities typical of HCHP firms. "The mortgage business at Merrill Lynch was an afterthought—they didn't really have a strategy," said one industry observer. Underscoring the short-term and material purpose of Wall Street firms was the fact that all of them piled on to the mortgage business because they saw short-term profits. "They had found this huge profit potential, and everybody wanted a piece of it. But they were pigs about it,"[3] said the same knowledgeable industry observer. HCHP companies manage for the long term and regard profit as necessary to enable contributions to customers, employees, and society—not as an end in itself. Nor are HCHP leaders motivated to become enormously rich, the apparent motivation of leaders of financial institutions and banks in the mortgage business.

Unlike HCHP companies, top-down and autocratic leadership was also rampant in many firms at the center of the financial crisis. Stanley O'Neal of Merrill Lynch was reportedly an autocratic leader who urged his key executives to increase sales of risky mortgage-backed securities. It is not hard to see why no one challenged this directive. Former executives reported that O'Neal's lieutenant, who oversaw mortgage operations, "played the role of tough guy, silencing critics who warned about the risks the firm was taking." That is hardly a prescription for the honest, fact-based communications that are so essential for an organization's capacity to learn and change.[4]

Limiting financial and cultural risk, the policy stance needed to build HCHP companies, was clearly not part of the ethos in failed financial institutions. The head of Merrill's mortgage business was "always carrying a notebook with his operations' daily profit-and-loss statement," and "would chastise traders and other moneymakers who told risk management officials exactly what they were doing,"[5] a Merrill executive said. This same mortgage business head "was described as intimidating by employees,"[6] not a prescription for a searching, fact-based discussion about whether the firm was taking on too much risk. The consequence was exactly that which HCHP firms avoid with their more conservative approach: liquidation of human assets and, in many cases, the very demise of the firm itself.

Unlike the leaders of HCHP firms, CEOs of financial service firms implicated in the economic crisis brought to the task of leadership flawed assumptions about human motivation. At the heart of all failures was a "me" not "we" culture. This culture was bolstered by huge financial incentives tied to short-term profits and not to the long-term health of the firm. These assumptions created a culture that encouraged leaders to put their own interests ahead of customers, employees, investors, and society. With the exception of a few courageous individuals, that culture made it impossible for managers to evaluate their actions in the light of a larger purpose, let alone express openly to high management their innermost doubts about the company's course of action or the role they played.

One Wall Street firm, Goldman Sachs, which was listed in chapter 2 as an HCHP company, managed to do better than its competitors, though it too ran into difficulties. A 2006 report by an observer explains: "Goldman's good fortune cannot be explained by luck alone. Late in the year as the markets roared along, David A. Viniar, Goldman's chief financial officer, called a meeting . . . . At that point, the holdings of Goldman's mortgage desk were down somewhat . . . . After reviewing the full portfolio with other executives, [Mr. Viniar's] message was clear: the bank should reduce the stockpile of mortgage and mortgage-related securities and buy expensive insurance as protection against further losses."[7] If it's not luck, what is it about Goldman Sachs that is different? Over the years its leaders have built an HCHP firm that has a strong team culture, and they have encouraged humility, though this may not always be apparent to others. The company has invested in leadership development, has a flat hierarchy, and encourages executives to challenge each other, a characteristic that allows good ideas to rise to the top and is responsible for its early identification of the credit crisis that took down most of its competitors.

Although the most glaring errors can be found in the financial sector of the economy, the very same lack of larger purpose and failure to organize and manage for high performance, psychological alignment, and continuous learning and change can be found in too many firms in all sectors of the economy. How else are we to explain the failure of the automobile companies to see beyond the short-term profits that gas-guzzling SUVs brought? Or their inability to reverse a three-decade decline in their fortunes? Consider that General Motors' top management ignored and later oversaw partial dismantling of its Saturn division, an innovative and successful HCHP organization that achieved high commitment from its customers (to its low-cost fuel-efficient cars and its friendly service), employees, and union.

As I survey the rubble of poorly designed and led organizations, I am drawn to reflect back on my first visit to Hewlett-Packard in 1980, a great company led and managed by HCHP principles that many investment analysts and CEOs might have until recently thought obsolete. I found a performance-oriented company driven not by financial incentives, but by a larger purpose, a long-term perspective, and collaboration. From studying that firm I learned what was possible. Like Herb Kelleher at Southwest Airlines and leaders of HCHP firms listed in chapter 2, Bill and Dave led from a deep commitment to solving business and management problems for positive performance, people, and social outcomes. They saw their task as building a resilient company that would last. Profit was the first objective, but not the only one. In the 1940s David Packard confronted a group of CEOs who believed that businesses had a responsibility only to shareholders. His exact words were: "We [have] important responsibilities to our employees, customers, to our suppliers, and to the larger welfare of society at large."[8]

We need more healthy HCHP firms if we are to avoid future economic and social costs of the kind we observe today; and more important, to obtain the long-term economic and human benefits to society that HCHP firms offer. This requires leadership by top management and government.

The Hewlett-Packard story is doubly instructive today because Bill and Dave's success in building an HCHP company started in the depths of the Depression, and was inspired in part by the lessons of a massive economic contraction similar to the one we are experiencing today. Their experience suggests that now, while the lessons of failure are clear, is the time for corporate leaders to take stock of their purpose and their assumptions about how to organize and manage their businesses. This is the time to apply the lessons of Southwest Airlines, Hewlett-Packard, Nucor, Johnson & Johnson, Costco, and other HCHP companies.

The first step that aspiring CEOs, their senior teams, and boards of directors should take is to learn from successfully sustained HCHP companies, as well as from the ample existing management literature that details their core policies and practices. A second step is for CEOs and their top teams to engage their hearts to redefine their and their firm's purpose. What contribution do they want to make? To whom do they want to make it? What are the best measures of progress on the journey to HCHP? Third, CEOs will have to engage their heads and define a distinctive strategy that leverages the firm's human assets and unique capabilities.

Fourth, CEOs and their top teams will have to engage their hands to design very different management practices, particularly with regard to the firms' performance management and compensation systems. The former must enable hard-hitting, fact-based reviews of the business to achieve essential short-term profits in a way that does not compromise the firm's larger purpose and its long-term performance. With regard to the latter, surely a shift away from incentives for annual profits to incentives tied to long-term performance (five to seven years) is in order. Fifth, to prevent the kind of arrogance and blindness that derails so many firms, boards and directors should demand that CEOs hold periodic honest, collective, and public conversations in their organizations. This will require the design of the kind of learning and governance system discussed in chapters 6 and 7. This system will enable CEOs and their leadership teams to confront difficult issues together and do what is necessary to ensure sustained commitment from all stakeholders. It is hard to imagine a time when employees, customers, and investors would be more responsive than now.

Government, too, has a role to play in encouraging the development of HCHP firms. This is not the place to enter into a detailed discussion of that role, a subject that is beyond the scope of this book. Nevertheless, there are a few instructive points that I feel compelled to make, particularly given the change in administration in Washington. Business leaders have long argued for unfettered markets and resisted a role for government in regulating capital markets or intervening in labor markets. But as Jeff Pfeffer so eloquently argued in *The Human Equation*, there is no real evidence for this view and there is some evidence to the contrary.[9] What more evidence do we need that unfettered capital markets can fail badly than the disastrous consequences we are experiencing in 2008? Consider how regulation might have played a role in averting the behavior of mortgage-issuing companies or the irresponsible risk-management practices by major Wall Street institutions. Surely the time has come to find the appropriate role for government in preventing market failures.

Government can also reduce the headwinds experienced by CEOs who aspire to build an HCHP company. For example, what tax policies with respect to capital gains might rebalance the pressures for short- and long-term profits? Companies can too easily be acquired by those with deep pockets willing to pay a premium to gain what is often a very short-term competitive advantage, despite the fact that we know that approximately 70 percent of acquisitions fail to deliver anticipated value to investors. It is very hard for CEOs to resist making these offers or acquiescing to them. CEOs and boards of directors can often boost stock price in the short run through acquisitions. They can also trigger a decline in shareholder value and increase the chances of investor legal suits if they resist acquisitions. When the company being sold is an HCHP company, its culture is almost certain to erode unless the top management of the acquiring company shares HCHP values. Active capital markets are a powerful and important force that motivates CEOs to attend to performance and investor returns. But they are a double-edged sword. Unchecked, they encourage a merely transactional approach to business. Deal making takes precedence over business and organization building.

Using examples as varied as Europe, Singapore, and Japan, Jeff Pfeffer has illustrated how government policies can facilitate high commitment and performance.[10] For example, encouraging long-term employment by requiring that employers provide warning and issue a social plan when layoffs are coming can have positive effects without the negative consequences that free market economists and financial analysts often claim will come of government regulation. Similarly, mandated employee participation through workers' councils and industrial democracy in Europe (supervisory boards in Germany) facilitate trust and promote decisions that benefit all stakeholders. These types of policies, Pfeffer shows, have not eroded the competitiveness of most European economies; in particular, Sweden and Germany. Government can also encourage and fund research about HCHP organizations and the diffusion of effective HCHP practices. And local and state government involvement in creating labor-management forums for developing mutual understanding, resolving conflicts, and planning innovative work practices has contributed to high commitment and performance in the United States and other countries. The importance of these public policies in shaping the mental models of CEOs has become quite clear to me and my U.S. and Swedish colleagues at TruePoint. We find leaders in Sweden much more receptive to high-commitment values and practices than CEOs in the United States, for example.

To date, only extraordinary leaders who have had the vision and courage to go against the grain have succeeded in building HCHP organizations in the current unfettered market environment. The erosion of public trust in corporate leaders and business provides a unique window for CEOs to begin their company's journey to high commitment and high performance, and for government to craft policies that encourage them to build HCHP companies.

END NOTES

Preface

1. McGregor, D. (1960). *The human side of enterprise*. New York: McGraw-Hill.
2. Khurana, R., & Nohria, N. (2008). "It's time to make management a true profession," *Harvard Business Review,* Oct., pp. 70–77.
3. Schneider, B. (1980). "The service organization climate: Climate is crucial," *Organizational Dynamics, 9,* Summer; Schneider, B., & Bowen, D. (1995). *Winning the service game.* Boston: Harvard Business School Press; Heskett, J. L., Sasser, E. W., & Hart, C.W.L. (1990). *Service breakthroughs: Changing the rules of the game.* New York: The Free Press.

1. Introduction

1. McGregor, D. (1960). *The human side of enterprise*. New York: McGraw-Hill.
2. Maslow, H. (1954). *Motivation and personality*. New York: Harper; Beer, M. (1966). *Leadership, employee needs and motivation*. Bureau of Business Research Monograph, No. 129. Columbus: Ohio State University.
3. See Weisbord, M. (1991). *Productive workplaces: Organizing and managing with dignity, meaning, and community*. San Francisco: Jossey-Bass, p. 10.

4. The late Ed Huse, then a professor at Boston College, partnered with me in the development of the Medfield plant into a high commitment and performance organization.

5. See the following for description and analysis of the transformation at Medfield. Huse, E., & Beer, M., (1971). "An eclectic approach to organization development," *Harvard Business Review,* Sept–Oct.; Beer, M., & Huse, E. (1972). "A systems approach to organization development," *Journal of Applied Behavioral Science,* Jan.–Feb.

6. Hertzberg, F., Mausner, B., & Snyderman, B. (1959). *The motivation to work.* New York: Wiley.

7. See, for example, Beer, M., & Spector, B. (1984). "Sedalia Engine Plant (A) (B)." Case. Boston: Harvard Business School Press.

8. Richard Walton was a pioneer in the development of high commitment and performance manufacturing plants in a number of companies. He played a key role in many of these early experiments and in the development of the theory that underlies them. See Walton, R. E. (1979). "Work innovations in the United States," *Harvard Business Review,* July–Aug.

9. Walton, R. E. (1982). "The Topeka work system: optimistic vision, pessimistic hypotheses, and reality." In R. Zager & M. P. Rosow (Eds.) *The innovative organization.* New York: Pergamon Press; Walton, R. E. (1975). "The diffusions of work structures: Explaining why success didn't take," *Organizational Dynamics,* *3*(3), pp. 2–22.

10. For more detail see three cases on Corning's Electronic Products Division. Beer, M. (1976). "Corning Glass Works (A) (B) (C): The electronic products division." Case. Boston: Harvard Business School Press.

11. Beer, M., Spector, B., Lawrence, P., Mills, D. Q., & Walton, R. (1985). *Managing human assets.* New York: Free Press.

12. O'Reilly, C., & Pfeffer, J. *Hidden value: How companies achieve extraordinary results with ordinary people.* Boston: Harvard Business School Press.

13. See Beer, M., Spector, B., & Eisenstat, R. (1990). *The critical path to corporate renewal.* Boston: Harvard Business School Press; Collins, J. (2002). *Good to great.* New York: Harper Business.

14. That a researcher can contribute to knowledge through making a difference in human affairs was first demonstrated by Kurt Lewin, whose seminal work legitimized this form of research, mostly performed by scholar-consultants in the field of organization development. See Lewin, K. (1948). *Resolving social conflict: Selected papers on group dynamics.* G. W. Lewin (Ed.). New York: Harper & Row. For a wonderful history of organization development, see Weisbord, M. R. (1991). *Productive work places: Organizing and managing for dignity, meaning, and community.* San Francisco: Jossey-Bass.

15. Beer, M., & Eisenstat, R. (1996). "Developing an organization capable of implementing strategy and learning," *Human Relations, 49*(5).

16. Beer, M., Eisenstat, R. A., & Spector, B. (1990). *The critical path to corporate renewal.* Boston: Harvard Business School Press.

17. Eisenstat, R., Beer, M., Foote, N., Fredberg, T., & Norrgren, F. (2008). "The uncompromising leader," *Harvard Business Review,* July–Aug.

18. The observation that high-commitment organizations unconsciously embrace some eastern philosophies was first made by William Ouchi. See Ouchi, W. (1981). *Theory Z management.* Reading, MA: Addison-Wesley.

19. Beer, M., & Nohria, N. (2000). *Breaking the code of change.* Boston: Harvard Business School Press, p. 127.

20. Haidt, J. (2006). *The happiness hypothesis: Finding modern truth in ancient wisdom.* New York: Basic Books. This view is also supported by Lawrence, P. R., & Nohria, N. (2002). *Driven: Human nature shapes our choices.* San Francisco: Jossey-Bass.

21. Beer, M., & Nohria, N. (2000). "Cracking the code of change," *Harvard Business Review,* May.

22. Personal communication from Archie Norman.

23. Lawrence, P. R., & Nohria, N. (2002). *Driven: Human nature shapes our choices.* San Francisco: Jossey-Bass.

24. Nohria, N., Groysberg, B., & Lee, L. (2008). "Employee motivation: A powerful new model," *Harvard Business Review,* July–Aug.

2. Pillars of High Commitment, High Performance Organizations

1. Hornstein, H. A. (2002). *The haves and the have nots: The abuse of power and privilege in the workplace and how to control it.* New York: Financial Times Prentice Hall.

2. Gittell, J. (2003). *The Southwest Airlines way: Using the power of relationships to achieve high performance.* New York: McGraw-Hill.

3. Analysis of these companies confirmed that their annual compounded growth in revenues, profits, and market capitalization is above average. Cases, books, and articles were used to evaluate each company's culture.

4. The discussion of Southwest Airlines is based on several sources: Gittell, J., *The Southwest Airlines way*; Hallowell, R. H., & Heskett, J. L. (1993). "Southwest Airlines: 1993 (A)." Case. Boston: Harvard Business School Publishing; O'Reilly, C., & Pfeffer, J. (1995). "Southwest Airlines: Using human resources for competitive advantage (A)." Case. Graduate School of Business Administration, Stanford University.

5. Birger, J. (2002). "The 30 best stocks from 1972 to 2002," *Money, 31*(11), p. 88.

6. These statistics were gathered by my colleagues Tom DeLong and Boris Groysberg for the purpose of teaching the Southwest Airline Case.

7. Hallowell, R. H., & Heskett, J. L. (1993). "Southwest Airlines: 1993 (A)." Case. Boston: Harvard Business School Press, p. 5.

8. O'Reilly & Pfeffer, *Southwest Airlines*, p. 3.

9. Heskett & Hallowell, "Southwest Airlines: 1993 (A)," p. 6.

10. Labich, K. (1994). "Is Herb Kelleher America's best CEO?" *Fortune*, May 2.

11. Ibid.

12. Heskett & Hallowell, "Southwest Airlines: 1993 (A)," p. 9

13. The idea that various aspects of the organizational system must be configured to align or fit each other and the environment or strategy has a long history in the organizational studies literature. It has been shown in many diverse studies as an essential ingredient for effective performance and survival. See, for example, Miller, D. (1986). "Configurations of strategy and structure: Towards a synthesis," *Strategic Management Journal, 7*, pp. 233–249; Miller, D. (1987). "The genesis of configuration," *Academy of Management Review, 12*, pp. 686–701; Miller, D. (1990). "Organizational configurations: Cohesion, change and prediction," *Human Relations, 43*, pp. 771–789.

14. Interview with Gary Kelly, May 14, 2008.

15. Porter, M. (1996). "What is strategy?" *Harvard Business Review, 74*(6), pp. 61–79.

16. Eisenstat, R., Beer, M., Foote, N., Fredberg, T., & Norrgren, F. (2008). "The uncompromising leader," *Harvard Business Review,* July–Aug., pp. 50–59.

17. Gittell, *The Southwest Airlines way*.

18. Gittell, *The Southwest Airlines way*, p. 26.

19. Porter, M. "What is strategy?"

20. See Khurana, R. (2004). *In search of a savior*. Princeton, NJ: Princeton University Press.

21. Zellner, W. (1994). "This is Captain Furgeson, please hang on to your hats," *Business Week*, May 23, 1994.

22. Baron, J. N., & Hannan, M. T. (2002). "Organizational blueprints for success in high-tech start-ups: Lessons learned from the Stanford Project on emerging companies," *California Management Review, 44*(3), pp. 8–36.

23. Interview with Gary Kelly, May 14, 2008.

24. Cameron, K. (2008). *Positive leadership: Strategies for extraordinary performance*. San Francisco: Berrett-Koehler.

25. Labich, K. (1994). "Will United fly?" *Fortune*, Aug. 22, 1994, *130*(4), p. 70.

26. Ibid.

27. Bauman, R. P. (1998). "Five requisites for implementing change." In D. C. Hambrick, D. A. Nadler, & M. L. Tushman (Eds.), *Navigating change: How CEOs, top teams and boards steer transformation.* Boston: Harvard Business School Press. See also Bauman, R. P., Jackson, P., & Lawrence, J. T. (1997). *Promise to performance: A journey of transformation at SmithKline Beecham.* Boston: Harvard Business School Press.

28. Foster, R., & Kaplan, S. (2001). *Creative destruction: Why companies that are built to last underperform the market—and how to successfully transform them.* New York: Doubleday.

29. Collins, J. (2002). *Good to great.* New York: Harper Business.

30. Rosenzweig, P. *The halo effect—And the eight other business delusions that deceive managers.* New York: The Free Press, 2007.

31. Miller, D. (1990). *The Icarus paradox: How exceptional companies bring about their own downfall.* New York: Harper Business.

32. Ibid, p. 8.

33. Ben Schneider has shown that firms develop unique climates and cultures because of a pattern of attraction, selection, and attrition that creates homogeneity in personality and attitudes. See Schneider, B. (2002). "Climate strength: A new direction for climate research," *Journal of Applied Psychology, 87*(2), pp. 220–229.

34. Gittell, J., Cameron, K., & Lim, S. (2006). "Relationships, layoffs and organizational resilience: Airline industry responses to September 11th," *Journal of Applied Behavioral Science, 42*(3), pp. 300–329.

35. Ibid., p. 30.

36. Gittell, *The Southwest Airlines way.*

37. Baron & Hannan, "Organizational blueprints for success in high-tech start-ups," pp. 8–36.

38. Pfeffer, J. (1998). *The human equation: Building profits by putting people first.* Boston: Harvard Business School Press.

39. Gittell, *The Southwest Airlines way,* p. 34.

40. Ibid, p. 13.

41. Lawrence, P., & Lorsch, J. (1967). *Organization and environment: Managing differentiation and integration.* Boston: Harvard Business School Press; Walton, R., & Dutton, J. (1969). "The management of interdepartmental conflict: A model and review," *Administrative Science Quarterly, 14*(1), pp. 73–83; Eisenhardt, K. M., Kahwajy, J. L., & Bourgeois, L. J. (1997) "How management teams can have a good fight," *Harvard Business Review, 75*(4), pp. 77–85.

42. Gittell, *The Southwest Airlines way,* p. 103.

43. Ibid., p. 104.

44. For a discussion of the importance of learning and core principles for doing it see: Beer, M., & Eisenstat, R. (2004). "How to have an honest conversation about your strategy," *Harvard Business Review,* Nov.; Edmondson, A. (2008). "The competitive imperative of learning," *Harvard Business Review,* July–Aug., pp. 60–67.

45. From an interview with Gary Kelly conducted by Michael Beer in May 2008.

46. Ibid.

47. That relationships and task are two important dimensions of leadership and organizational behavior has a long history in organizational behavior and psychology. They have been presented using different nomenclature in an excellent *Harvard Business Review* article. See Goffee, R., & Jones, G. (1996). "What holds the modern company together," *Harvard Business Review, 74*(6), pp. 133–148.

48. Nocera, J. (2008). "The Sinatra of Southwest feels the love," *New York Times,* May 24.

49. O'Reilly, C. A., & Pfeffer, J. (2000). *Hidden value: How great companies achieve extraordinary results with ordinary people.* Boston: Harvard Business School Press, p. 6.

50. Baron, J. N., & Kreps, D. M. (1999). *Strategic human resource management: Frameworks for general managers.* New York: Wiley, chap. 19.

51. Douglas McGregor, in *The Human Side of Enterprise* (1960), coined the term Theory Y. In that book he suggests two managerial archetypes (Theory X and Y) with different assumptions about people. Theory Y assumes people want to contribute, are capable of it, and can be involved in decisions. Theory X assumes that people are not motivated and must be controlled. See McGregor, D. (1960). *The human side of enterprise.* New York: McGraw-Hill.

52. Baron & Kreps, *Strategic human resource management,* p. 482.

53. Pfeffer, *The human equation*; Luthans, F., & Youssef, C. (2004). "Investing in people for competitive advantage." *Organizational Dynamics, 33*(2) (in press); Hitt, M. A., & Ireland, R. D. (2002). "The essence of strategic leadership: Managing human and social capital," *Journal of Leadership and Organizational Studies, 9*(1), pp. 3–13.

54. Beer, M., & Weber, J. (1997). "Asda (A), (A1), (B), (C)." HBS No. 498–005, 498–006, 498–007, 498–008. Boston: Harvard Business School Press.

55. Bartlett, C. A., & McLean, A. N. (2003). *GE's talent machine: The making of a CEO.* HBS no. 304–049. Boston: Harvard Business School Publishing; Bartlett, C. A. "GE's growth strategy: The Immelt initiative," HBS No. 306–087. Boston: Harvard Business School Publishing; Bartlett, C. A., & Glinka, M. (2002). *GE's digital revolution: Redefining the E in GE.* HBS no. 302–001. Boston: Harvard Business School Publishing; Eckes, G. (2000). *General Electric's Six*

Sigma revolution: How General Electric and others turned process into profits. New York: Wiley; Krames, J. A. (2002). *The Welch way: 24 lessons from the world's greatest CEO.* New York: McGraw-Hill.

56. For the story of IBM's history as a high commitment and performance company see Watson, T. J., & Petre, P. (1990). *Father son & company: My life at IBM and beyond.* New York: Bantam. For the story of IBM's reemergence as a high commitment and performance company, see Gerstner, L. V. (2002). *Who says elephants can't dance? Inside IBM's historic turnaround.* New York: Harper Business.

57. O'Reilly, C., & Pfeffer, J. (2000). *Hidden value: How great companies achieve extraordinary results with ordinary people.* Boston: Harvard Business School Press, pp. 6–8; O'Reilly, C. A. (1998). "New United Motors Manufacturing, Inc. (NUMMI)," HBS no. HR11. Boston: Harvard Business School Publishing; Inkpen, A. (2005). "Learning through alliances: General Motors and NUMMI," HBS no. CMR 320. Boston: Harvard Business School Publishing.

58. Key ideas in this section were taken from Ibarra, H. (1996). "National cultures and work related values: The Hofstede study," HBS no. 496–044. Boston: Harvard Business School Publishing. Phrases in quotation come from the Ibarra note and should be credited to her. For a primary source for these ideas, see Hofstede, G. (1980). *Culture's consequences: International differences in work-related values.* Newbury Park, CA: Sage; Hofstede, G. (1992). *Culture and organizations. Software of the mind.* London: McGraw-Hill.

59. Paquin, A. R., Roch, S. G., & Sanchez-Ku, M. L. (2007). "An investigation of cross-cultural differences on the impact of productivity interventions: The example of ProMES," *Journal of Applied Behavioral Science, 43*(4), pp. 427–448.

60. House, R., Javidian, M., & Dorfman, P. (2001). "Project globe: An introduction," *Applied Psychology, 50*(4), pp. 489–505; House, R. J., et al. (1999). "Cultural influences on leadership and organizations: Project GLOBE." In W. Mobley, J. Gessner, & V. Arnold (Eds.), *Advances in global leadership*, Vol. 1, pp. 171–234.

61. Sun, L., Aryee, S., & Law, K. (2007). "High-performance human resource practices, citizenship behavior, and organizational performance: A relational perspective," *Academy of Management Journal, 50*(2), pp. 558–577.

---

3. Principled Choice and Discipline Are Essential

1. DiMaggio, P. J., & Powell, W. W. (1983). "The iron cage revisited: Insitutional isomorphism and collective rationality in organizational fields," *American Sociological Review, 48*, April, pp. 147–160.

2. The description of NICO is based on an account written for an annual report by Warren Buffett, CEO of Berkshire Hathaway. It has been confirmed by independent research conducted by Jim Weber, a research associate at the Harvard Business School.

3. Berkshire Hathaway Inc. *2004 Annual Report.* Omaha, NE.

4. Morgenstern, G. (2008). "How the thundering herd faltered and fell," *New York Times,* November 9.

5. Malone, M. (2007). *Bill and Dave: How Hewlett and Packard built the world's greatest company.* London: Penguin Books; Beer, M., & Rogers, G. (1995). "Human resources at Hewlett-Packard." Case. Harvard Business School Press. Revised November 1, 2007.

6. I am indebted to Russell Eisenstat for this framing of the multiple stakeholder perspective.

7. Malone, *Bill and Dave,* p. 59.

8. George, B. (2003). *Authentic leadership: Rediscovering the secret to creating lasting values.* San Francisco: Jossey-Bass, chap. 4.

9. Memorandum shared with the author by the chairman and CEO of the company.

10. Malone, *Bill and Dave,* p. 150.

11. Eisenstat, R., Beer, M., Foote, N., Fredberg, T., & Norrgren, F. (2008). "The uncompromising leader," *Harvard Business Review,* July–Aug.

12. Collin, J., & Porras, J. (1994). *Built to last: Successful habits of visionary companies.* New York: Harper Business.

13. Interview with Gary Kelly, May 24, 2008.

14. For an excellent discussion of why so many firms fail to achieve high performance, the role of uncertainty and risk in causing failure, and the means for dealing with risk, see Rosenzweig, P. (2007). *The halo effect.* New York: Free Press.

15. Gittell, J. H., Cameron, K., Lim, S., & Rivas, V. (2006). "Relationships, layoffs, and organizational resilience: Airline industry responses to September 11," *Journal of Applied Behavioral Science, 42*(3), pp. 300–329.

16. Ellis, C. D. (2008). *Partnership: The making of Goldman Sachs.* New York, Penguin Press.

17. Cascio, W. F. (2002). *Responsible restructuring: Creative and profitable alternatives to layoffs.* San Francisco: Berrett-Koehler.

18. Among many studies, the most systematic research was conducted by Rensis Likert. See Likert, R. (1967). *The human organization: Its management and value.* New York: McGraw-Hill; for a comprehensive review of these findings, see Pfeffer, *The human equation*; Weisbord, M. R. (1987). *Productive workplaces: Organizing and managing for dignity, meaning, and community.* San Francisco: Jossey-Bass.

19. Schneider, B., et al. (2003). "Which comes first: Employee attitudes or financial and market performance?" *Journal of Applied Psychology, 88*(5), pp. 836–851.

20. There are many case studies that show that focusing on economic performance alone does not produce sustained high commitment or performance. For example, Al Dunlap followed the financial cost-cutting strategy at Scott Paper in the early 1990s and failed. For a description of this and this general argument, see Beer, M., & Nohria, N. (2000). *Breaking the code of change.* Boston: Harvard Business School Press.

21. Latham, G. (2000). Motivate employee performance through goal-setting. In Locke, E. A. (Ed.), *Handbook of principles of organisational behaviour.* London: Blackwell Business, pp. 107–119; Lock E., & Latham, G. P. (2002). "Building a practically useful theory of goal setting and task motivation: A 35-year odyssey," *American Psychologist, 57*(9), pp. 705–717.

22. Three of the needs and corollary management practices discussed here come from Schein, E. (1965). *Organizational psychology.* London: Prentice Hall. Schein does not stipulate Achieving or Participating. These are my creation.

23. Substantial research by organizational psychologists demonstrates that goal setting develops motivation, a sense of self-efficacy, and performance. Much of this theory of motivation was developed by Ed Lock and Gary Latham. See Latham, G. P., & Budworth, M-H. "The study of work motivation in the 20th century." In Hillsdale, N. J. (Ed.), *The history of organizational psychology.* Philadelphia: Erlbaum.

24. Heckscher, C. (1995). *White collar blues: Management loyalties in an age of corporate restructuring.* New York: Basic Books; Heckscher, C., & Foote, N. (2006). "The strategic fitness process and the creation of a collaborative community." In C. Heckscher & P. S. Adler (Eds.), *The firm as a collaborative community: Restructuring trust in the knowledge economy.* New York: Oxford University Press, pp. 468–469.

25. Maslow, A. (1987). *Motivation and personality* (3rd ed.). New York: Harper Collins.

26. Lawrence, P., & Nohria, N. (2002). *Driven: How human nature shapes our choices.* San Francisco: Jossey-Bass.

27. These arguments can be found in Schein, *Organizational psychology.*

28. Ibid. Recently behavioral economists have come to the same conclusion as psychologists that needs and motives emerge from the situation. See Aieily, D. (2008). *The hidden forces that shape our decisions.* New York: Harper Collins.

29. Frost, C. F., Wakeley, J. H., & Ruh, R. A. (1974). *The Scanlon plan for organization development: Identity, participation, and equity.* East Lansing: Michigan State University Press.

30. Aieily, *Hidden forces.*

31. Some of these questions are derived from Baron, J. N., & Kreps, D. M. (1999). *Strategic human resource management: Frameworks for general managers.* New York: Wiley, pp. 474–475.

32. Baron, J. N., & Hannan, M. T. (2002). "Organizational blueprints for success in high tech start-ups: Lessons learned from the Stanford Project on emerging companies," *California Management Review, 44*(3), pp. 8–36.

33. Beer, M., & Gibbs, M. J. (1991). *Apple Computer (D): Epilogue.* HBS no. 492–013. Boston: Harvard Business School Publishing.

34. Heckscher, C., & Foote, N. (2006). "The strategic fitness process and the creation of collaborative community." In C. Heckscher & P. Adler (Eds.), *The firm as a collaborative community.* New York: Oxford University Press, pp. 482–483.

35. Ibid., p. 482.

36. Greiner, L. (1998). "Evolution and revolution as organizations grow," *Harvard Business Review, 76*(3), pp. 55–67.

37. Pisano, G., & Rossi S. (1994). *ITT Automotive: Global manufacturing strategy.* HBS no. 695–002. Boston: Harvard Business School Publishing.

38. Baron & Hannan, "Organizational blueprints for success in high-tech start-ups," pp. 9–36.

39. Ibid., p. 20.

40. Dennison, D. (1990). *Corporate culture and organizational effectiveness.* New York: Wiley.

41. Collins, J., & Porras, J. I. (1994). *Built to last: Successful habits of visionary companies.* New York: Harper Business, 1994.

42. Kotter, J. P., & Heskett, J. L. (1992). *Corporate culture and performance.* New York: The Free Press.

43. Collins, J. (2001). *Good to great: Why some companies make the leap and others don't.* New York: Harper Business.

44. Batel, A. P. (2004). "Human resource management and organizational performance: Evidence from the retail industry," *Industrial and Labor Relations Review, 57*(2), (Jan.), pp. 181–203; Zatzick, C. D., & Iverson, R. D. (2004). "High-commitment management and workforce reduction: Competitive advantage or disadvantage?" *Best Paper Proceedings,* Academy of Management Meetings, New Orleans; Godard, J. (2001). "High performance and the transformation of work: The implications of alternative work practices for the experience and outcomes of work," *Industrial and Labor Relations Review, 54*(4), (July), pp. 776–805; Appelbaum, E., Baily, T., Berg, P., & Kalleberg, A. L. (2000). *Manufacturing advantage: Why high performance work systems pay off.* Ithaca, NY: Cornell University Press; Baker, T. (1999). *Doing well by doing*

good. Washington DC: Economic Policy Institute; Becker, B. E., & Huselid, M. A. (1998). "High performance work systems and firm performance: A synthesis of research and managerial implications," *Research in Personnel and Human Resource Management, 16,* pp. 53–101.

45. Huselid, M. A. (1995). "The impact of human resource management practices on turnover, productivity, and corporate financial performance," *Academy of Management Journal, 38*(3), p. 645.

46. Cascio, W. (2006). "The new human capital equation," *The Industrial-Organizational Psychologist, 44*(2), October.

47. Zatzick & Iverson, "High-commitment management and workforce reduction," p. 3.

48. Quoted in Cascio, W. F. (2002). *Responsible restructuring: Creative and profitable alternatives to layoffs.* San Francisco: Berrett-Koehler, p. 13.

49. MacDuffie, J. P., & Krafcik, J. H. (1992). Integrating technology and human resources for high performance manufacturing: Evidence from the international automobile industry. In T. A. Kochan & M. Useem (Eds.), *Transforming organizations.* New York: Oxford University Press, pp. 209–225.

50. Schneider, B., Parkington, J. J., & Buxton, V. M. (1980). "Employee and customer perceptions of service in banks," *Administrative Science Quarterly, 25*(2), pp. 252–267; Schneider, B., & Bowen, D. E. (1985). "Employee and customer perceptions of service in banks: Replication and extension," *Journal of Applied Psychology, 70*(3), pp. 423–433; Schneider, B. (1991). "Service, quality and profits: Can you have your cake and eat it too?" *Human Resource Planning, 14*(2), pp. 151–157.

51. Heskett, J. L., Sasser, W. E. Jr., & Schlesinger, L. A. (1997). *The service profit chain: How leading companies link profit and growth to loyalty, satisfaction, and value.* New York: Free Press.

52. Miller, D., & Miller, I. (2005). *Managing for the long run: Lessons in competitive advantage from great family businesses.* Boston: Harvard Business School Press.

53. Baron & Hannan, "Organizational blueprints for success in high-tech start-ups," p. 26.

54. Beer, M., & Eisenstat R. A. (2004). "How to have an honest conversation about your business strategy," *Harvard Business Review, 82*(2), pp. 82–89.

55. Beer, M. (1988). *Leading change.* HBS no. 488–037. Boston: Harvard Business School Publishing.

56. Hamel, G., & Valikangas, L. (2003). "The quest for resilience," *Harvard Business Review, 81*(9), pp. 52–63; Miller, D. (1990). *The Icarus paradox.* New York: Harper Business.

4. Building the High Commitment, High Performance System

1. Quote taken from Dunphy, D. (2000). "Embracing paradox: Top down versus participative management of organizational change, a commentary on Conger and Bennis." In M. Beer & N. Nohria (Eds.), *Breaking the code of change.* Boston: Harvard Business School Press.

2. Barney, J. B. (1986). "Organizational culture: Can it be a source of sustainable competitive advantage?" *Academy of Management Review, 11,* pp. 656–665; This argument framed in human resource terms has also been made by Pfeffer. See Pfeffer, J. (1998). *The human equation: Building profits by putting people first.* Boston: Harvard Business School Press.

3. Personal communication from Clateo Castellini, October, 28, 2008.

4. Nadler, D., & Tushman, M. (1990). "Beyond the charismatic leader: Leadership and organizational change," *California Management Review,* Winter, pp. 77–97.

5. Gary Kelly's understanding of the system and how different he is from Herb Kelleher became evident in an interview with him in May 2008.

6. Collins, J., & Porras, J. (1994) *Built to last.* New York: Harper Business.

7. Collins, J. (2002). *Good to great.* New York: Harper Business.

8. Bebchuk, L. A., Cremers, M., & Peyer, U. (2007). "CEO centrality." *National Bureau of Economic Research,* Working paper No. 13701, December.

9. Baron, J. N., Burton, D. M., & Hannan, M. T. (1996). "The road taken: Origin and evolution of employment systems in emerging companies," *Industrial and Corporate Change, 5*(2), pp. 239–275.

10. Collins & Porras, *Built to last.*

11. Oshry, B. (2007). *Seeing systems: Unlocking the mysteries of organizational life.* San Francisco: Berrett-Koehler, p. xiv.

12. Fredberg, T., Beer, M., Eisenstat, R., Foote, N., & Norrgren, F. (2008). "Embracing commitment and performance: CEOs and practices to manage paradox." Boston: Harvard Business School Working Paper.

13. See the following sources for systemic models that could be used by senior teams. Beer, M. (1980). *Organization change and development: A systems view.* Santa Monica, CA: Goodyear Publishing; Tushman, M., & O'Reilly, C. (1997). *Winning through innovation.* Boston: Harvard Business School Press; Walton, R. E. (1986), "A vision-led approach to management restructuring," *Organizational Dynamics, 14*(4), Spring, pp. 5–16.

14. I am indebted to Peter Dunn for the idea that the strategy of high commitment and performance firms reflects their values. Gary Kelly, CEO of Southwest

Airlines, clearly supported this view with his description of the strategy formulation process by its founders.

5. Hidden Barriers to Sustained High Commitment and High Performance

1. For a description of the process utilized to identify silent barriers, see Beer, M., and Eisenstat, R. A. (2004), "How to have an honest conversation about your strategy," *Harvard Business Review, 82*(2), pp. 82–89.

2. For a discussion of psychological safety, see Cannon, M. D., & Edmondson, A. C. (2005). "Failing to learn and learning to fail (intelligently)," *Long Range Planning, 38*(3), pp. 299–319.

3. Beer, M., & Eisenstat, R. (2000). "The silent killers of strategy implementation and learning," *Sloan Management Review, 41*(4), Summer.

4. Morrison, E. W., & Milliken, F. J. (2000). "Organizational silence: A barrier to change and development in a pluralistic world," *Academy of Management Review, 25*(4), 706–725; Argyris, A., & Schon, D. (1996). *Organizational learning II: Theory, method and practice.* Reading, MA: Addison-Wesley; Senge, P. (1990). *The fifth discipline: The art and practice of the learning organization.* New York: Doubleday.

5. Moskal, B. S. (1991). "Is industry ready for adult relationships?" *Industry Week,* January 21, pp. 18–25.

6. Ryan, K. D., & Oestreich, D. K. (1998). *Driving fear out of the workplace.* (2nd ed). San Francisco: Jossey-Bass.

7. Milliken, F. J., & Morrison, E. W. (2003). "Shades of silence: Emerging themes and future directions for research on silence in organizations," *Journal of Management Studies 40*(6), pp. 1563–1568.

8. Detert, J., & Edmondson, A. C. (2007). "Everyday failures in organizational learning: Explaining the high threshold of speaking up and work." Harvard Business School Working Paper, 06–024.

9. Supporting research for each of the silent killers is found in diverse literature on senior teams, leadership, the role of integration in strategy implementation, the role of clear and common goals and values in motivation and integration, the role of open and honest communication in organizational learning and resource allocation, and the importance of developing down-the-line leaders. This research is too numerous to cite in full, but examples are cited throughout this chapter and book.

10. Interview with Gary Kelly, CEO of Southwest Airlines, in May 2008.

11. Beer, M. (1976). "Corning Glass Works: The electronic products division (A)." HBS no. 477–024. Boston: Harvard Business School Publishing.

12. Ibid., p. 1.

13. For a discussion of the empirical findings underlying this chapter, see Beer & Eisenstat, *The silent killers,* pp. 29–40.

14. Source: Interview by author in anonymous organization.

15. Beer, *Corning Glass Works,* p. 8.

16. Kaplan, R., & Norton, D. (2005). "The office of strategy management," *Harvard Business Review, 83*(10), pp. 72–80.

17. Hambrick, D. C. (1995). "Fragmentation and the other problems CEOs have with their top management teams," *California Management Review, 37*(3), pp. 110–127; Miles, R. E., & Snow, C. C. (1978). *Organizational strategy, structure and process.* New York: McGraw-Hill; Hambrick, D. C., Nadler, D. A., & Tushman, M. L. (Eds.) (1997). *Navigating change: How CEOs, top teams, and boards steer transformation.* Boston: Harvard Business School Press.

18. Eisenhardt, K. M., & Schoonhoven, C. B. (1990). "Organizational growth: Linking founding team strategy, environment, and growth among U.S. semiconductor ventures, 1978–1988," *Administrative Science Quarterly, 35,* pp. 504–529.

19. Hambrick, D. C. (1998). "Corporate coherence and the top management team." In Hambrick, Nadler, & Tushman, *Navigating change,* p. 123.

20. Beer, "Corning Glass Works," p. 4.

21. Beer, "Corning Glass Works," p. 12.

22. Beer, "Corning Glass Works," p. 12.

23. Eisenhardt, K. M., Kahwajy, J. L., & Bourgeois, L. J. (1998). "Confronting senior team conflict: CEO choices." In Hambrick, Nadler, & Tushman, *Navigating change,* p. 142.

24. Beer, "Corning Glass Works," p. 4.

25. See Beer, M., & Weber, J. (1997). "Asda (A)." HBS no.498–005, Boston: Harvard Business School Publishing.

26. Beer, "Corning Glass Works," p. 5.

27. See Beer, M., & Rogers, G. (1997). "Hewlett-Packard's Santa Rosa Systems Division (A): The trials and tribulations of a legacy." HBS no. 498–011, Boston: Harvard Business School Publishing.

28. See Burns, T. M., & Stalker, G. M. (1961). *The management of innovation.* London: Tavistock; Lawrence, P. R., & Lorsch, J. W. (1967). *Organization and environment: Managing differentiation and integration.* Boston: Division of Research, Harvard Graduate School of Business Administration; Miles & Snow, *Organizational strategy.*

29. Gittell, J. (2001). *The Southwest Airlines way: Using the power of relationships to achieve high performance.* New York: McGraw-Hill.

30. Beer & Weber, "Asda (A)."

31. Beer, M., & Williamson, A. D. (1991). "Becton Dickinson (B): Global management." Case 9–491–152. Boston: Harvard Business School.

32. For a discussion of the importance of collaboration, see Ashkenas, R., Ulrich, D., Jick, T., & Kerr, S. (2002). *The boundaryless organization: Breaking the chain of organization structure.* San Francisco: Jossey-Bass, chap. 6; Hansen, M., & Nohria, N. (2004). "How to build collaborative advantage," *MIT Sloan Management Review, 46*(1), pp. 22–30.

33. For research about the importance of union management collaboration for productivity and profitability, see chapter 6 in Baron, N., & Kreps, D. M. (1999). *Strategic human resources.* New York: Wiley; and chapter 3 in Beer, M., et al. (1985). *Managing human assets.* New York: Free Press.

34. Beer, *Corning Glass Works*, p. 10.

35. Ashkenas, Ulrich, Jick, & Kerr, *The boundaryless organization*; Adler, P. Heckscher, C. (Eds.). (2006). *The firm as a collaborative community: The reconstruction of trust in the knowledge economy.* New York: Oxford University Press.

36. The shortage of leadership skills and its importance in creating a high performance firm has been documented by Kotter, J. P. (1988). *The leadership factor.* New York: Free Press. For the importance of managers who play an integrating role that promotes teamwork between functions, see Lawrence, P. R., & Lorsch, J. W. (1967). "New management job: The integrator," *Harvard Business Review, 45*(6), pp. 142–151.

37. The lack of open and honest dialogue has been widely documented. See Argyris, C., & Schon, D. (1996). *Organizational learning II: Theory, method and practice.* Reading, MA: Addison Wesley; and Argyris, C. (1993). *Knowledge for action: A guide to overcoming barriers to organizational change.* San Francisco: Jossey-Bass. For a recent study of this problem, see Edmondson, A., & Detert, J. R. (2004). "The role of speaking up in work life balance." In E. Kossek & S. Lambert (Eds.), *Work and life integration.* Mahwah, NJ: Erlbaum.

38. Beer & Rogers, "Hewlett-Packard's Santa Rosa Systems Division."

39. Detert, J. R., & Edmondson, A. C. (2007). "Why employees are afraid to speak up," *Harvard Business Review, 85*(5), May.

40. The term "brutal facts" was coined by Jim Collins. He found that firms that were able to develop sustained improvement in performance had CEOs who insisted that their senior teams have honest conversations about business and organizational realities. See Collins, J. (2001). *Good to great: Why some companies make the leap and others don't.* New York: Harper Business. For a discussion of how the inability of CEOs to confront new business realities causes business failure, and the underlying psychological and underlying reasons, see Finkelstein, S. (2003). *Why smart executives fail.* New York: Portfolio; and Miller, *The Icarus paradox.*

41. Ed Schein was the first to my knowledge to articulate that adaptive coping capability is what makes organizations effective. Schein, E. H. (1965). *Organizational psychology.* Englewood Cliffs, NJ: Prentice Hall, pp. 99–103.

42. For a discussion of the value-chain concept and its role in creating economic value, see Porter, M. (1985). *Competitive advantage: Creating and sustaining superior performance.* New York: The Free Press.

43. Beer, "Corning Glass Works," p. 2.

44. Ibid.

---

6. Lead a Collective Learning Process

1. Longfellow, H. W. (1893). *The complete poetical works of Longfellow.* Boston: Houghton Mifflin.

2. Bynner, W. (1944). *The way of life, according to Lao Tzu.* New York: The John Day Company, pp. 34–35.

3. Beer, M., & Weber, J. (1999). Transcript of interview with Archie Norman and Allan Leighton.

4. The seminal Stanford research discussed in chapter 3 showed that founder perspective and values clearly influenced the ultimate employment model and supporting HR policies and practices extant in the company. See Baron, J. N, Burton, D. M., & Hannan, M. T. (1996). "Origins and evolution of employment systems in emerging companies," *Industrial and Corporate Change, 5*(2), pp. 239–75. Ed Schein has shown why and how leaders influence the development of the organization's culture. See Schein, E. (1985). *Organization culture and leadership.* San Francisco: Jossey-Bass. Jim Collins has shown that Level 5 leadership was essential to the extraordinary sustained improvements in returns. See Collins, J. (2001). *Good to great: Why some companies make the leap and other don't.* New York: Harper Business. Also see Beer, et al. (1990). *The critical path to corporate renewal.* Boston: Harvard Business School Press; Beer, M., & Eisenstat, R. (2000) "The silent killers of strategy implementation and learning," *Sloan Management Review,* Summer. For the important role of leadership in organizational change, also see Kotter, J. (1996). *Leading change.* Boston: Harvard Business School Press.

5. The Center for Creative Leadership has also begun to frame leadership as a collective process. See Drath, W. H., McCauley, C. D., Palus, C. J., Van Velsor, E., O'Connor, P.M.G., & McGuire, J. B. (2008). "Direction, alignment, commitment: Toward a more integrative ontology of leadership," *Leadership Quarterly, 19*(6), December.

6. Khurana, R. (2002). "The curse of the superstar CEO," *Harvard Business Review,* Sept.

7. Ibid.

8. Porter, M., Lorsch, J. W., & Nohria, N. (2008). "Seven surprises for new CEOs," *Harvard Business Review,* Oct.

9. As quoted in Fullan, M. (2001). *Leading in a culture of change,* San Francisco: Jossey-Bass, p. 3.

10. Beer, M. (1999). "Leading learning and learning to lead." In J. Conger, G. Spreitzer, & E. Lawler (Eds.), *The leader's change handbook.* San Francisco: Jossey-Bass; George, W. (2003). *Authentic leadership: Rediscovering the secret to creating lasting value.* San Francisco: Jossey-Bass.

11. Grove, A. (1996). *Only the paranoid survive.* New York: Doubleday.

12. For an in-depth discussion of why senior teams are important and what it takes to make them great, see Wageman, R., Nunes, D., Burruss, J. A., & Hackman, J. R. (2008). *Senior leadership teams: What it takes to make them great.* Boston: Harvard Business School Press.

13. Khurana, R. (2002). *Searching for a corporate savior: The irrational quest for charismatic CEOs.* Princeton, NJ: Princeton University Press.

14. Groysberg, B., McLean, A. N., & Nohria, N. (2006). "Are leaders portable?" *Harvard Business Review,* May.

15. Houghton, J. R. (1998). "Corporate transformation and senior leadership." In D. C. Hambrick, D. A. Nadler, & M. L. Tushman (Eds.), *Navigating change: How CEOs, top teams, and boards steer transformation.* Boston: Harvard Business School Press.

16. The material about Gullette and Clean Lodging comes from research conducted by Laura Morgan Roberts, Jim Weber, and myself with a firm that wants to remain anonymous.

17. I am indebted to my colleague Scott Snook at the Harvard Business School for this framework.

18. The ideas in this section are discussed by Luthans, F., Norman, S., & Hughes, L. (2005). "Authentic leadership for a new time." In R. Burke & C. Cooper (Eds.), *Inspiring leaders.* London: Routledge.

19. Gabarro, J. H. (1987). *The dynamics of taking charge.* Boston: Harvard Business School Press.

20. Readers who want to learn more about the servant leadership philosophy may do so by reading Greenleaf, R. K. (1977). *Servant leadership: A journey into the nature of legitimate power and greatness.* New York: Paulist Press.

21. Collins, *Good to great;* Bower, M. (1966). *The will to manage: Corporate success through programmed management.* New York: McGraw-Hill.

22. Heifetz, R. A. (1994). *Leadership without easy answers*. Boston: Harvard University Press, p. 21.

23. The role of stretch goals and targets in high-performance organizations has been documented by Bartlett, C., & Ghoshal, S. (1997). *The individualized corporation*. New York: Harper Business.

24. Collins, *Good to great*, p. 71.

25. Kaplan, R. E., Darth, W. H., & Kofodimos, J. R. (1985). "High hurdles: The challenge of executive self-development." *Technical Report,* no. 25, Center for Creative Leadership.

26. Ibid., pp. 21–25.

27. Cha, S. E., & Edmondson, A. C. (2006). "When values backfire: Leadership, attribution, and disenchantment in a values-driven organization," *The Leadership Quarterly*, *17*, pp. 57–78.

28. Detert, J. R., & Burris E. R. (2007). "Leadership influence on employee voice behavior: Is the door really open?" *Academy of Management Journal, 50*(4).

29. Eisenhardt, K. M., Kahwajy, J. L., & Bourgeois, L. J. III. (1997). "How management teams can have a good fight," *Harvard Business Review, 97*(402), July.

30. Hirschhorn, L. (2004). "Changing structure is not enough: The moral meaning of organization design." In M. Beer & N. Nohria (Eds.), *Breaking the code of change*. Boston: Harvard Business School Press, chap. 8, pp. 161–176.

31. Ibid., pp. 161–176; Huy, Q. N. (2005). "An emotion-based view of strategic management." In G. Szulanski, J. Porac, & Y. Doz. (Eds.), *Strategic process, advances in strategic management*. Vol. 22. Amsterdam: Elsevier B. V.

32. Huy, "An emotion-based view," p. 3; Burks, J. S., & Huy, Q. N. (2009). "Emotional aperture and strategic change: The accurate recognition of strategic change," *Organizational Science, 20*(1), Jan.–Feb.

33. Center for Creative Leadership. *Leading Effectively e-Newsletter,* July 2007. For extended discussion of what conflict competent leaders must know and be, see Runde, C. E., & Flanagan, T. A. (2007). *Becoming a conflict competent leader: How you and your organization can manage conflict effectively*. San Francisco: Jossey-Bass.

34. Huy, "An emotion-based view."

35. Hirschhorn, p. 163.

36. Ibid.

37. Deutsch, M. (1973). *The resolution of conflict*. New Haven, CT: Yale University Press.

38. For a deep understanding of the shift from bureaucratic organizations to collaborative enterprises and its implications, see Heckscher, C. (2007). *The collaborative enterprise*. New Haven, CT: Yale University Press.

39. Aiken, C. B., & Keller, S. P. (2007). "The CEO's role in leading transformation," *McKinsey Quarterly*, February.

40. Beer & Weber, Transcript of interview with Archie Norman and Allan Leighton.

41. Panchak, P. (2002). "Putting employees first pays off," *Industry Week, 251*(5), p. 14.

42. Quoted in George, W. (2007). *True north: Discover your authentic self.* San Francisco: Jossey-Bass, p. 169.

43. Ibid.

44. Collins, *Good to great*, p. 27.

45. Among others, see Collins, *Good to great*, chap. 2; Kotter, J. P., & Heskett, J. L. (1992). *Corporate culture and performance.* New York: The Free Press; George, *True north*; Bennis, W., & Nanus, B. (1985). *Leaders: Strategies for taking charge.* New York: Harper & Row.

46. Personal communication from Henry Gullette.

47. Aiken & Keller, "The CEO's role," p. 22.

48. Quote taken from Aiken & Keller, "The CEO's role."

49. Personal communication, 2006.

50. Miller, D., & LeBreton-Miller, I. (2005). *Managing for the long run: Lessons in competitive advantage from great family businesses.* Boston: Harvard Business School Press.

51. Gulati, R., & Sytch, M. (2007). "Dependence asymmetry and joint dependence in interorganizational relationship: Effects of embeddedness on a manufacturer's performance in procurement relationship," *Administrative Science Quarterly, 52*, pp. 32–69.

52. Eskew, M. (2007). "Stick with your vision," *Harvard Business Review,* July–Aug., p. 56.

53. Hambrick, D. C. (1998). "Corporate coherence and the top management team." In D. C. Hambrick, D. A. Nadler, & M. L. Tushman (Eds.), *Navigating change: How CEOs, top teams, and boards steer transformation.* Boston: Harvard Business School Press, p. 123.

54. Among these studies are: Ibid.; Eisenhardt, K., & Schoonhoven, C. B. (1990) "Organizational growth: Linking founding team strategy, environment, and growth among U.S. semiconductor ventures, 1978–1988," *Administrative Science Quarterly, 35*; and Pfeffer, J., & Davis-Blake, A. (1986). "Administrative succession and organizational performance: How administrative experience mediates the succession effect," *Academy of Management Journal, 29*, pp. 72–83; Smith, J. K., Carson, K. P., & Alexander, R. (1984). "Leadership: It can make a difference," *Academy of Management Journal, 27*, pp. 765–776.

55. Gittell, J. H. (2003). *The Southwest Airlines way: Using the power of relationships to achieve high performance.* New York: McGraw-Hill, chap. 5.

56. Ibid., p. 71.

57. Beer, M., Eisenstat, R. A., & Foote, N. Unpublished research on the effectiveness of the Strategic Fitness Process.

58. Biggadike, R. E. (1998). "How CEOS, top teams, and boards of directors make successful transformations." In D. C. Hambrick, D. A. Nadler, & M. L. Tushman (Eds.), *Navigating change: How CEOs, top teams, and boards steer transformation,* Boston: Harvard Business School Press. p. 383.

59. Beer, M., & Weber, J. (1999).

60. Biggadike, "How CEOS, top teams, and boards of directors make successful transformations."

61. Lorsch, J. W., & Colin, C. (2003). *Back to the drawing board: Designing corporate boards for a complex world.* Boston: Harvard Business School Press.

62. Quinn R. (2005). "Moments of greatness: Entering the fundamental state of leadership," *Harvard Business Review,* July–Aug.; Quinn, R. E. (2004). *Building the bridge as you walk on it: A guide for leading change.* San Francisco: Jossey-Bass.

63. For extensive discussions of these ideas, see George, W. *True north*; Quinn, "Moments of greatness."

64. Quinn, "Moments of greatness."

7. Enable Truth to Speak to Power

1. Houghton, J. (1998). "Corporate transformation and senior leadership." In D. C. Hambrick, D. A. Nadler, & M. L. Tushman (Eds.), *Navigating change: How CEOs, top teams, and boards steer transformation.* Boston: Harvard Business School Press.

2. Finkelstein, S. (2003). *Why smart executives fail.* London: Portfolio, p. 41.

3. Gerstner, L. V. Jr. (2002). *Who says elephants can't dance? Inside IBM's historic turnaround.* New York: Harper Business, pp. 25, 37–38.

4. Finkelstein, *Why smart executives fail.*

5. Senge, P. M. (1990). *The fifth discipline: The art and practice of the learning organization.* New York: Doubleday, p. 242.

6. Ibid., p. 241.

7. For a description of the Strategic Fitness Process, see Beer, M., & Eisenstat, R. A. (2004). "How to have an honest conversation about your strategy," *Harvard Business Review, 82*(2), pp. 82–89; for a discussion of the relationship between organization learning and leadership development, see Beer, M.

(1999). "Leading learning and learning to lead." In J. Conger, G. Spreitzer, & E. Lawler (Eds.), *The leader's change handbook.* San Francisco: Jossey-Bass.

8. This story is drawn from a case series by Beer, M., & Weber, J. (2001). "Merck Latin America (A & D)." HBS no. 401–029, 401–030, 401–031, 401–032. Boston: Harvard Business School Press.

9. All quotes in this section are taken from Beer, M., & Weber, J. (2001). "Merck Latin America (D): Mexico." HBS no. 401–032. Boston: Harvard Business School Press.

10. Beer & Weber, "Merck Latin America (D)," p. 2.

11. Personal communication from Steve Fossi, general manager at Agilent Technologies, 2000.

12. Beer, M., & Williamson, A. D. (1991). "Becton Dickinson (D-1): SHRM Update." Case. Boston: Harvard Business School Press.

13. Beer, M., & Rogers, G. (1997). "Hewlett-Packard's Santa Rosa Systems Division (A): The trials and tribulations of a legacy." HBS no. 498–011. Boston: Harvard Business School Press.

14. Interview conducted by the author.

15. For a discussion of how a governance and learning system can create shared purpose and collaboration, see Heckscher, C., & Foote, N. E. (2006). "The strategic fitness process and creation of collaborative community." In C. Heckscher & P. Adler (Eds.), *The firm as a collaborative community: The reconstruction of trust in the knowledge economy.* New York: Oxford University Press.

16. Beer & Rogers, "Hewlett-Packard's Santa Rosa Systems Division."

17. Ibid.

18. Ward, A. (2003). *The leadership life cycle.* New York: Palgrave McMillan.

19. Finkelstein, *Why smart executives fail;* Miller, D. (1990). *The Icarus paradox: How exceptional companies bring about their own downfall.* New York: Harper Business.

20. For a review of participation theory and research, see Miner, J. B. (2002). *Organizational behavior: Foundations, theories and analyses.* New York: Oxford University Press, pp. 359–434; for an argument about the role of participation in leading change, see Bennis, W. (2000). "Leadership of change." In M. Beer & N. Nohria (Eds.), *Breaking the code of change.* Boston: Harvard Business School Press.

21. Lawrence, P. R., & Lorsch, J. W. (1967). *Organization and environment: Managing differentiation and integration.* Boston: Harvard Business School Press; Eisenhardt, K., Pelled, L., & Xin, K. (1999). "Exploring the black box: An analysis of work group diversity, conflict, and performance," *Administrative Science Quarterly, 44*(1), pp. 1–28; Gittell., J. (2002). *The Southwest Airlines way.* New York: McGraw-Hill.

22. Edmondson, A. (1999). "Psychological safety and learning behavior in work teams," *Administrative Science Quarterly, 44*(4), pp. 350–383; Baer, M., & Frese, M. (2003). "Innovation is not enough: climate for initiative and psychological safety, process innovations, and firm performance," *Journal of Organizational Behavior, 24*(1), pp. 45–68.

23. For an extended discussion of process fairness and its efficacy, see Brockner, J. (2005). *The paradox of process fairness*. Working paper, Columbia Business School.

24. Vroom, V. H., & Yetton, P. W. (1973). *Leadership and decision making*. Pittsburgh, PA: Pittsburgh University Press; Vroom, V. H., & Jago, A. G. (1988). *The new leadership: Managing participation in organizations*. Englewood Cliffs, NJ: Prentice Hall.

25. Reported by Jody Edwards in answer to questions after a case discussion at Harvard Business School. See *The organizational alignment process at Hewlett-Packard*. Boston: Harvard Business School Publishing.

26. Quoted in Malone, M. S. (2007). *Bill & Dave: How Hewlett and Packard built the world's greatest company*. London: Penguin Books.

27. Mohrman, S. A., & Cummings, T. G. (1989). *Self designing organizations: Learning how to create high performance*. Reading, MA: Addison-Wesley.

28. Ulrich, D., Kerr, S., & Ashkenas, R. (2002). *The GE work-out*. New York: McGraw-Hill.

29. Beer, M., Eisenstat, R., & Foote, N. (2001). Unpublished findings of an evaluation of twelve applications of the strategic fitness process.

30. Schrader, D. (2005). *Steak 'n Shake in Grand Rapids, MI: "Fast 'n friendly" service through strategic fitness (A)*. Unpublished case: Burlington, MA: TruePoint.

31. For a discussion of defensive routines in organizations, their consequences and how to overcome them, see Argyris, C. (1990). *Overcoming organizational defenses: Facilitating organizational learning*. Wellesley, MA: Allyn & Bacon.

32. Personal communication to author during the implementation of the strategic fitness process, 2000.

33. Beer, M., & Weber, J. (2005). "Whitbread PLC (A)." Case. Boston: Harvard Business School Press.

34. Senge, *The fifth discipline*.

35. Beer & Eisenstat, "How to have an honest conversation," pp. 82–89.

36. More detailed description of the strategic fitness process can be found in Eisenstat, R., & Beer, M. (1998). *The strategic fitness process manual*. Unpublished document. Burlington, MA: TruePoint.

37. Beer, M., Eisenstat, R. A., & Spector, B. (1990). *The critical path to corporate renewal*. Boston: Harvard Business School Press.

38. Ed Schein has long argued that to understand and change culture requires organizational members to define issues in their own terms. Closed-end paper-and-pencil surveys do not enable that. See Schein, E. H. (1988). *Organizational culture and leadership.* San Francisco: Jossey-Bass.

39. Zand, D. E. (1972). "Trust and managerial problem solving," *Administrative Science Quarterly, 17*(2), pp. 229–239; Edmondson, A. (1996). "Learning from mistakes is easier said than done: Group and organizational influences on the detection and correction of human error," *Journal of Applied Behavioral Science, 32*(1), pp. 5–28; Edmondson, A. (1999). "Psychological safety and learning behavior in work teams," *Administrative Science Quarterly, 44*(4), pp. 350–383.

40. The notion of advocacy and inquiry as a requirement for learning is discussed in Argyris, C. (2000). *Flawed advice and the management trap: How managers can know when they're getting good advice and when they're not.* New York: Oxford University Press.

41. Miller, *The Icarus paradox.*

42. Beer, M., Khurana, R., & Weber, J. (2005). "Hewlett-Packard in changing times." Case: Harvard Business School Press; Burrows, P. (2003). *Backfire: Carly Fiorina's high-stakes battle for the soul of Hewlett-Packard.* Hoboken, NJ: Wiley.

43. Presentation to a group of senior HR executives in Harvard Business School's Strategic Human Resource Management program, circa 2002.

44. Eisenstat, R., Beer, M., Foote, N., Fredberg, T., & Norrgren, F. (2008). "The uncompromising leader," *Harvard Business Review,* July–Aug.

---

8. Manage Organizational Performance Strategically

1. Miller, D., Eisenstat, R., & Foote, N. (2002). "Strategy from the inside out: Building capability-creating organizations," *California Management Review, 44*(3), pp. 37–45.

2. Colvin, G. (2006). "What makes GE great?" *Fortune,* Mar. 6, pp. 91–104.

3. Kaplan, R., & Norton, D. P. (2001). *The strategy-focused organization.* Boston: Harvard Business School Press, p. 25.

4. Ibid.

5. Beer, M., & Eisenstat, R. A. (2000). "The silent killers of strategy implementation and learning," *Sloan Management Review, 41*(4), pp. 29–40.

6. Beer, M., Eisenstat, R., & Spector, B. (1990). *The critical path to corporate renewal.* Boston: Harvard Business School Press.

7. Executives consistently reported this phenomenon during discussions of executive compensation in organizational behavior classes I taught over several years. See Beer, M., & Katz, N. (2003). "Do incentives work? The perceptions of a worldwide sample of senior executives," *Human Resource Planning, 26*(3), pp. 30–44.

8. Kaplan, R., & Norton, D. P. (2005). "The office of strategic management," *Harvard Business Review, 83*(10), pp. 72–80.

9. Nitin Nohria and his associates identified developing and maintaining a clear and focused strategy as one of four key ingredients in companies that achieved a total return of $11 for each $1 invested. See Nohria, N., Joyce, W., & Robertson, B. (2003). "What really works," *Harvard Business Review, 81*(7), pp. 43–52. Miles and Snow have shown that a residual fourth strategic archetype that they discovered in their study of strategy, what they called the Reactor, experienced difficulty in adapting and performing. See Miles, R., & Snow, C. C. (1978). *Organizational strategy, structure, and process.* New York: McGraw-Hill.

10. Lagace, M. (2006). "The office of strategy management: Q&A with Robert Kaplan and Andrew Pateman," *Harvard Business School Working Knowledge,* March 27. Boston: Harvard Business School Press.

11. Ibid., p. 1.

12. Craig, N. (2006). "Using results-driven backplanning to improve strategic implementation," *Employment Relations Today, 32*(4), pp. 15–24.

13. Beer, Eisenstat, & Spector, *The critical path to corporate renewal,* chap. 2.

14. Amabile, T. N., Hadley, C. N., & Kramer, S. J. (2002). "Creativity under the gun," *Harvard Business Review, 80*(8), pp. 52–61.

15. Kaplan & Norton, "The office of strategic management," p. 13. The importance of organization learning has also been noted by many other organizational scholars cited in various parts of this book, among them Chris Argyris and Don Schon, Peter Senge, and Ray Miles and Charles Snow.

16. The case of GE's Commercial Equipment Finance business is based on interviews with Chris Richmond, its president from 1994 to 2000, and has been documented in a research case written by Jim Weber under the supervision of the author.

17. Collins, J., & Porras, G. (1992). *Built to last.* New York: Harper Business.

18. Mintzberg, H., Ahlstrand, B., & Lampel, J. (2005). *Strategy bites back: It is far more and less, than you ever imagined.* Upper Saddle River, NJ: Pearson/Prentice Hall, p. 19.

19. Years of psychological research by Ed Locke and Gary Latham support the central idea that goals are key to work motivation and performance.

Locke, E. A. (2002). "Building a practically useful theory of goal setting and task motivation: A 35-year odyssey," *American Psychologist, 57*, pp. 705–717.

20. Personal communication from Chris Richmond, May 2006.

21. I learned this on a case-writing trip in 1995 when I sat in on a meeting of a corporate task force assigned to reevaluate the ranking system in which this recommendation was made.

22. Pfeffer, J. (1998). *The human equation: Building profits by putting people first.* Boston: Harvard Business School Press; Collins & Porras, *Built to last*; George, W. (2003). *Authentic leadership.* San Francisco: Jossey-Bass.

23. Tedlow, R. S., & Smith, W. K. (1989). "James Burke: A career in American business." Case 389177. Boston: Harvard Business School Press.

24. Henry Mintzberg has exposed the myth of strategic planning. See Mintzberg, H. (1994). *The rise and fall of strategic planning.* New York: The Free Press.

25. Pfeffer, J., & Sutton, R. I. (2006). *Hard facts, dangerous half truths and total nonsense: Profiting from evidence-based management.* Boston: Harvard Business School Press, p. 147.

26. Ibid., chap. 6.

27. The importance of doing as a means of acting and learning has been developed by Pfeffer, J., & Sutton, R. (2003). *The knowing-doing gap: How smart companies turn knowledge into action.* Boston: Harvard Business School Press.

28. Mintzberg, Ahlstrand, & Lampel, *Strategy bites back*, p. 29.

29. Ibid., p. 33.

30. Quinn, J. B. (1980). *Strategies for change: Logical incrementalism.* Homewood, IL: Irwin.

31. See, for example, Nohria, Joyce, & Robertson, "What really works"; Collins, J., *Good to great.*

32. Malone, M. S. (2007). *Bill & Dave: How Hewlett and Packard built the world's greatest company.* London: Penguin Books.

33. O'Reilly III, C. A., Harreld, J. B., & Tushman, M. L. (2009). "Organizational ambidexterity: IBM and emerging business opportunities." Paper presented by Charles O'Reilly at the Harvard Business School in December 2008.

34. Christensen, C. (1997). *The innovator's dilemma: When new technologies cause great firms to fail.* Boston: Harvard Business School Press.

35. Pfeffer, *The human equation.*

36. Morgenson, G. (2008). "How the thundering herd faltered and fell," *New York Times*, November 9.

37. Miller, D., & Miller, I. (2005). *Managing for the long term.* Boston: Harvard Business School Press.

38. Gabarro, J. (1987). *The dynamics of taking charge.* Boston: Harvard Business School Press.

39. Beer, M. (1988). *Leading change.* HBS no. 488–037. Boston: Harvard Business School Press.

40. Kotter, J. (1996). *Leading change.* Boston: Harvard Business School Press.

41. Keefe, R. (2006). "A tech CEO about-face," *Austin American-Statesman,* April 3.

42. This conclusion is supported by a study of why executives fail. See Finkelstein, S. (2003). *Why smart executives fail.* New York: Penguin Group.

43. "Balanced Scorecard" approach to managing performance was pioneered by my colleagues Robert Kaplan and David Norton. See Kaplan, R. S., & Norton, D. P. (1996). *The balanced scorecard: Translating strategy into action.* Boston: Harvard Business School Press.

44. Morosini, P. (2000). *ABB in the new millennium: New leadership, new strategy, new organization.* HBS no. IMD128. Boston: Harvard Business School Press; Strebel, P., & Govinder, N. (2003). *ABB (A):The Barnevik era (1988–200).* HBS no. IMD172. Boston: Harvard Business School Press; *Barnevik, Percy, and ABB.* (1994). VHS video recording. Babson Park, MA: Babson College.

45. Nohria, Joyce, & Robertson, "What really works," pp. 1–12.

46. Charan, R., & Bossidy, L. (2002). *Execution: The discipline of getting things done.* New York: Crown Publishers.

47. Some of the ideas in this section, including the title of the section, are based on the pioneering work of my colleagues Robert Kaplan and David Norton. See Kaplan, R., & Norton, D. (2001). *The strategy-focused organization.* Boston: Harvard Business School Press.

48. Wagemen, R., Nunes, D. A., Burruss, J. A., & Hackman, J. R. (2008). *Senior leadership teams: What it takes to make them great.* Boston: Harvard Business School Press.

49. Kaplan & Norton, "The office of strategic management."

50. Kaplan, R., & Norton, D. (1992). "The balanced scorecard: Measures that drive performance," *Harvard Business Review, 70*(1), pp. 71–79; Kaplan & Norton, *The balanced scorecard.*

51. For example, see Nohria, Joyce, & Robertson, "What really works," p. 1–12; Hitt, M. A., & Ireland, R. D. (2002). "The essence of strategic leadership: Managing human and social capital," *The Journal of Leadership and Organizational Studies, 9*(1).

52. Kaplan & Norton, "The office of strategic management," p. 49.

53. These questions are an adaptation of similar questions Robert Kaplan and Andrew Pateman list in an interview by *Harvard Business School Working Knowledge.* See Lagace, "The office of strategy management."

54. Beer, M. (1996). "The transformation of the human resource function: Resolving the tension between a traditional administrative and a new strategic role," *Human Resource Management Journal, 36*(1), pp. 49–56.

55. For a discussion of these tools and practices, see Kaplan & Norton, *The strategy-focused organization;* and Kaplan & Norton, "The office of strategic management."

56. These views were collected in research conducted by the author in collaboration with Balanced Scorecard Collaborative. See also Beer, M., & Pateman, A. (2005). "OSM change management case: Taylor Way corporation," *Balanced Scorecard Collaborative;* Beer, M. (1999). "Organizational fitness: The context for successful balanced scorecard programs," *Balanced Scorecard Report.* Sept. 15. Boston: Harvard Business School Publishing.

57. Roberto, M. (2001). *Strategic planning at Sun Life.* HBS no. 301–084. Boston: Harvard Business School Press, p. 7.

---

9. Organize for Performance and Commitment

1. For a discussion of the forces that create competitive rivalry, see Porter, M. (1998). *Competitive strategy.* New York: Free Press.

2. Greiner, L. (1972). "Evolution and revolution as organizations grow," *Harvard Business Review, 50*(4), pp. 37–46.

3. There is substantial research evidence to support the view that changes in environment and strategy require changes in organizational form, and that each form has strengths and weaknesses. For example, see Lawrence, P., & Lorsch, J. (1967). *Organization and environment.* Boston: Harvard Business School Press; Miles, R. E., & Snow, C. C. (1978). *Organizational strategy, structure and process.* New York: McGraw-Hill.

4. Beer, M., & Rogers, G. (1997). "Human resources at Hewlett-Packard (A)." HBS no. 495–051. Boston: Harvard Business School Press.

5. Beer, M., & Khurana, R. (2004). "Hewlett-Packard in changing times." Case. No. 404–084. Boston: Harvard Business School Publishing.

6. These quotes are to be found in Spector, B. (2007). *Implementing organizational change: Theory and practice.* Upper Saddle River, NJ: Prentice Hall, p. 46. The original source is Burrows, P. (2003). *Backfire: Carly Fiorina's high-stakes battle for the soul of Hewlett-Packard.* Hoboken, NJ: Wiley.

7. See Beer, M., Khurana, R., & Weber, J. (2004). "Hewlett-Packard: Culture in changing times." HBS no. 404–087. Boston: Harvard Business School Press.

8. Watson, T., & Petre, P. (1990). *Father, son & co.: My life at IBM and beyond*. New York: Bantam Books.

9. Beer, M., & Rogers, G. (1997). "Hewlett-Packard's Santa Rosa Systems Division (A)." Case. Boston: Harvard Business School Press.

10. Beer & Rogers, "Hewlett-Packard's Santa Rosa Systems Division (A)."

11. Beer, M., & Rogers, G. (1997). "Hewlett-Packard's Santa Rosa Systems Division (B3)." Boston: Harvard Business School Press.

12. Paul Lawrence and Jay Lorsch developed the concepts of differentiation and integration employed in this section. See Lawrence, P., & Lorsch, J., *Organization and environment*.

13. Ibid.

14. The design logic discussed in this section is based on a long and rich organization design literature. For example, Goold, M., & Campbell, A. (2002). *Designing effective organizations: How to create structured networks*. San Francisco: Jossey-Bass.

15. Eisenstat, R., Foote, N., Galbraith, J., & Miller, D. (2001). "Beyond the business unit," *McKinsey Quarterly, 1*(1), pp. 54–63.

16. A tool that is useful in this regard is known as a responsibility matrix. Beckhard, R., & Harris, R. T. (1977). *Organizational transitions: Managing complex change*. Reading, MA: Addison-Wesley, p. 78.

17. Hackman, J. R., & Oldham, G. R. (1980). *Work design*. Reading, MA: Addison-Wesley, pp. 75–80.

18. Seminal research by Miles and Snow found that there are three primary types of strategy, structure, and process configurations. A fourth, which they called the Reactor, they found in firms that continuously changed strategy, structure, and processes and never achieved alignment. Miles & Snow, *Organizational strategy*.

19. The "defender" label for this strategic archetype was coined by Miles and Snow in *Organization strategy, structure and process*. Miles & Snow, *Organizational strategy*, pp. 31–49.

20. This information processing view of the firm was first articulated by Jay Galbraith. See Galbraith, J. R. (1977). *Organization design*. Reading, MA: Addison-Wesley.

21. The "Prospector" label for the decentralized multibusiness organization focused on innovation was coined by Miles and Snow. Miles & Snow, *Organizational strategy*.

22. Goold & Campbell, *Designing effective organization*.

23. See Galbraith, J. (2005). *Designing the customer-centric organization: A guide to strategy, structure and process*. San Francisco: Jossey-Bass; Gulati, R. Forthcoming.

Building customer-centric organizations: Silo busting for success. Boston: Harvard Business School Press.

24. The term *self-design* was first coined by Tom Cummings and Susan Mohrman; Cummings, T., & Mohrman, S. (1989). *Self-designing organizations: Learning how to create high performance.* Reading, MA: Addison-Wesley.

25. Beer, M., & Rogers, G. (1997). "Hewlett-Packard's Santa Rosa Systems Division (A1): The profiling process and creation of the future model." HBS no. 498–012. Boston: Harvard Business School Publishing, p. 4.

26. Eccles, R. (1980). *Progressive Corp.'s divisionalization decision (A).* HBS no. 481–067. Boston: Harvard Business School Publishing.

27. Interview with Ned Barnholt by the author in 1997.

28. Unpublished research conducted by Michael Beer, Russell Eisenstat, and Nathaniel Foote that evaluated twelve applications of the strategic fitness process.

29. Beer & Rogers, "Hewlett-Packard's Santa Rosa Systems Division," p. 1.

30. Beer, M. *Matrix organization at Hewlett-Packard's Santa Rosa Division.* Video. Boston: Harvard Business School.

10. Develop Human and Social Capital

1. Packard, D. (1995). *The HP way: How Bill Hewlett and I built our company.* New York: Harper Business, p. 12.

2. Schmidt, F. (2008). "Select on intelligence." In E. Locke, *Handbook of organizational behavior.* London: Blackwell.

3. Beer, M., & Walton, E. (1986). *Pennsylvania Pharmaceuticals Corporation.* Case. Boston: Harvard Business School Press.

4. Groysberg, B., Nanda, A., & Nohria, N. (2004). "The risky business of hiring stars," *Harvard Business Review,* May, *82*(5).

5. Ibid., p. 2.

6. Hitt, M. A., & Ireland, R. D. (2002). "The essence of strategic leadership: Managing human and social capital," *Journal of Leadership and Organizational Studies, 9*(1), pp. 3–14.

7. Pfeffer, J., & Sutton, R. I. (2006). *Hard facts, dangerous half-truths and total nonsense.* Boston: Harvard Business School Press, chap. 4.

8. Kay, J. (2006). "Football's example can help companies score," *Financial Times,* ft.com., July 10.

9. Glick, L. J. (2004). "Patriots tap top management practices," *American City Business Journals,* Jan. 30.

10. Fishman, C. (1999). "Sanity Inc.," *Fast Company,* January, p. 84.

11. Cascio, W. F. (2002). *Responsible restructuring: Creative and profitable alternatives to layoffs.* San Francisco: Berrett-Koehler.

12. Deming, W. E. (1986). *Out of the crisis.* Cambridge: Massachusetts Institute of Technology, Center for Advanced Engineering Study.

13. Baks, K. P. (2001). "On the performance of mutual fund managers." Unpublished manuscript cited in Groysberg, Nanda, & Nohria, "The risky business of hiring stars."

14. Nahapiet, J., & Ghoshal, S. (1998). "Social capital, intellectual capital, and the organizational advantage," *Academy of Management Review, 23*(2), pp. 242–266.

15. Gittell, J. H. (2003). *The Southwest Airline way: Using the power of relationships to achieve high performance.* New York: McGraw-Hill.

16. Holtom, B. C., Mitchell, T. R., & Lee, T. W. (2006). "Increasing human and social capital by applying job embeddedness theory," *Organizational Dynamics, 35*(4), pp. 316–331.

17. McCall, M., Lombardo, M., & Morrison, A. (1988) *The lessons of experience.* Lexington, MA: Lexington Books.

18. The description of BD is from Beer, M., & Williamson, A. D. (1991). "Becton Dickinson (A): Corporate strategy." Case. Boston: Harvard Business School Press.

19. Ibid., p. 13.

20. Pfeffer, J, (1998). "SAS Institute (A): A different approach to incentives and people management practices in the software industry." Case: Stanford University, p. 5.

21. Pfeffer, J., & Sutton, R. I. (2006). *Three myths of management.* Boston: Harvard Business School Press.

22. Pfeffer, "SAS Institute (A)," p. 67.

23. Cascio, *Responsible restructuring,* chap. 6.

24. Collins, J. (2001). *Good to great: Why some companies make the leap and others don't.* New York: Harper Business.

25. Thurber, J. (circa 1973). Unpublished study, Organizational Research and Development Department, Corning Glass Works.

26. Pfeffer, "SAS Institute (A)," p. 67.

27. Chatman, J. A. (1991). "Matching people and organizations: Selection and socialization in public accounting," *Administrative Science Quarterly, 36*(3).

28. Ibid., pp. 72–73.

29. Ibid.

30. For a further discussion, see Jarnagin, C., & Slocum, J. W. Jr. (2007). "Creating corporate cultures through mythopetic leadership," *Organizational Dynamics, 36*(3), pp. 288–302.

31. Ibid., p. 295.

32. Jarnagin & Slocum, "Creating corporate cultures."

33. Groysberg, B., & Snook, S. (2005). "Leadership development at Goldman Sachs." Case. Boston: Harvard Business School Press, p. 1.

34. Colvin, G. (2006). "How one CEO learned to fly," *Fortune,* October 30.

35. Beer, M., & Weber, J. (1997). "Asda." Case. Boston: Harvard Business School Press.

36. Kelly, H. *Nucor Steel's culture (draft).* Cited with permission of the author. The Working Manager Ltd., 2006/2007.

37. Colvin, "How one CEO learned to fly."

38. Beer, M., Eisenstat, R. A., & Spector, B. (1990). *The critical path to corporate renewal.* Boston: Harvard Business School Press.

39. McCall, M. W. (1998). *High flyers: Developing the next generation of leaders.* Boston: Harvard Business School Press.

40. Byrnes, N., & Arndt, M. (2006). "The art of motivation," *BusinessWeek,* May 1, p. 56.

41. Ibid, p. 56.

42. Amabile, T. (1988). "A model of creativity in innovations in organizations." In B. M. Staw & L. L. Cummings (Eds.), *Research in organizational behavior,* Vol. 10. Greenwich, CT: JAI Press.

43. Interview with John Clarkson, then CEO of Boston Consulting Group, circa 1998.

44. For a much more detailed discussion of this important subject, see Pfeffer, J. (1988). "Six myths about pay," *Harvard Business Review,* May-June; Pfeffer, J. (1998). *The human equation: Building profits by putting people first.* Boston: Harvard Business School Press; Milkovich, G., & Wigdore, A. (1991). *Pay for performance: Evaluating performance appraisal and merit pay.* Washington, DC: National Research Council; Ehrenberg, R. G. (Ed.). *Do compensation policies matter?* Ithaca, NY: Cornell University Press.

45. Binder, A. S. (Ed.). (1990). *Paying for productivity: A look at the evidence.* Washington, DC: The Brookings Institution.

46. Beer, M., & Katz, N. (2003). "Do incentives work? The perceptions of a worldwide sample of senior executives," *Human Resource Planning, 23*(3).

47. Siegel, P., & Hambrick, D. C. (2005). "Pay disparities within top management groups: Evidence of harmful effects on performance of high technology firms," *Organizational Science,* May-June, *16*(3), pp. 259–274.

48. Baron, J. N., & Kreps, D. M. (1999). *Strategic human resources: Frameworks for general managers.* New York: Wiley, pp. 96–97; p. 268.

49. Beer, M., & Canon, M. (2004). "Promise and peril in implementing pay for performance," *Human Resource Journal, 43.*

50. Barron, J. (2004). "Commentary" on Beer, M., & Canon, M. "Promise and Peril."

51. Baron & Kreps, *Strategic human resources*, pp. 96–97.

52. Beer, M., & Spector, B. (1984). Interview with plant managers at Sedalia Engine.

53. Lawler, E. E., & Hackman, J. R. (1969). "The impact of employee participation in the development of pay incentive plans: A field experiment," *Journal of Applied Psychology, 53*, pp. 467–471.

54. Morgenstern, G. (2006). "The best and the worst in executive pay," *New York Times,* September 17.

55. Chatman, J. A., & Cha, S. E. (2003). "Leading by leveraging culture," *California Management Review, 45*(4), pp. 29–31.

56. Ibid., p. 30.

57. Ibid., pp. 30–31.

58. Ibid., p. 31.

59. Cascio, *Responsible restructuring,* chap. 5, pp. 49–70. The quoted material in this section is taken directly from Cascio's book.

60. Clark, K. (1979). "Unionization and productivity: Micro-econometric evidence," *National Bureau of Economic Research,* Working paper 330; Clark, K. (1979). "Union management adjustment and productivity," *National Bureau of Economic Research,* Working paper 332.

61. Beer & Williamson, "Becton Dickinson (A): Corporate strategy."

62. Beer, M. (1996). "The transformation of the human resource function: Resolving the tension between the administrative and strategic roles," *Human Resource Management Journal, 36*(1), pp. 49–56.

63. Ibid., p. 55.

64. The description of BD in this era and the quotes are taken from Beer, M., & Weber, J. (1996). "Becton Dickinson (H) 1966: Transforming an organization." Unpublished case. Boston: Harvard Business School Press.

65. This section is based on published and unpublished cases about Becton Dickinson, interviews with Ed Ludwig and a human resource executive in 2006, and archival data obtained from Becton Dickinson.

66. The attributions made to Ed Ludwig in this paragraph come from two interviews conducted by the author in September and December, 2006. The quotes attributed to Ludwig are paraphrases of what he said.

---

11. Embrace E and O Change Strategies

1. The structure and substance of this chapter draw on my intellectual collaboration with Nitin Nohria—a joint book and article as well as an article and

chapter I authored on the same findings. See Beer, M., & Nohria, N. (Eds.) (2000). *Breaking the code of change*. Boston: Harvard Business School Press; Beer, M., & Nohria, N. (2000). "Cracking the code of change," *Harvard Business Review*, May-June; Beer, M. (2001). "How to develop an organization capable of sustained high performance: Embrace the drive for results and capability development paradox," *Organization Dynamics*, *29*(4), pp. 243–247; Beer, M. (2007). "Transforming organizations: Embrace the paradox of E and O." In T. Cummings (Ed.), *Handbook of organization development*. Thousands Oaks, CA: Sage.

2. Machiavelli, N. (2008). *The prince*. New York: The Modern Library. (Originally published 1532.)

3. Collins, J. (2001). *Good to great: Why some companies make the leap and others don't*. New York: Harper Business.

4. There are many sources for this observation, including the following: Beer, M., Eisenstat, R. A., & Spector, B. (1990). *The critical path to corporate renewal*. Boston: Harvard Business School Press; Schaffer, R. (1988). *The breakthrough strategy: Using short-term successes to build the high performance organization*. Cambridge, MA: Ballinger; Ingelgrad, A., & Norrgren, F. (2001). "Effects of change strategy and top management involvement on quality of working life and economic results," *International Journal of Industrial Ergonomics*, *27*, pp. 93–105.

5. Jensen, M. (2000). "Value maximization and the corporate objective function." In M. Beer & N. Nohria (Eds.). *Breaking the code of change*. Boston: Harvard Business School Press, chap. 1, p. 37.

6. Ault, R., Walton, R., & Childers, M. (1998). *What works: A decade of change in Champion International*. San Francisco: Jossey-Bass.

7. Beer & Nohria, *"Cracking the code of change,"* p. 13.

8. Folger, R., & Pugh, S. D. (2002). "The just world and Winston Churchill: An approach/avoidance conflict about psychological distance when harming victims." In M. Ross & D. T. Miller (Eds.), *The justice motive in everyday life*. New York: Cambridge University Press, pp. 168–186.

9. Beer, M., & Weber, J. (1998). Transcript of video interview with Archie Norman and Allan Leighton. Boston: Harvard Business School Press.

10. Molinsky, A., & Margolis, J. (2005). "Necessary evils and interpersonal sensitivity in organizations," *Academy of Management Review*, *30*(2), pp. 245–268.

11. Beer, M., & Weber, J. (1997). "Asda (A) (A1) (B) (C)." Case 9–498–005, 006 and 007. Boston: Harvard Business School Press.

12. Beer & Weber, "Asda (A1)," pp. 1–2.

13. Collins, *Good to great*.

14. Huy, Q. H. (2001). "In praise of middle managers," *Harvard Business Review*, Sept.

15. Bernerth, J. B., Armenakis, A. A., Field, H. S., & Walker, H. J. (2007). "Justice, cynicism and commitment: A study of important organizational change variables," *Journal of Applied Behavioral Science, 43*(3), pp. 303–326.

16. Malone, M. (2007). *Bill & Dave: How Hewlett and Packard built the world's greatest company*. London: Penguin Books.

17. Collins, *Good to great*, p. 152.

18. Beer, M., Eisenstat, R., & Spector, B. (1990). *The critical path to corporate renewal*. Boston: Harvard Business School Press; Beer, M., Eisenstat, R., & Spector, B. "Why change programs do not produce change," *Harvard Business Review*; Schaffer, *The breakthrough strategy*.

19. Herold, D. M., Fedor, D. B., & Caldwell, S. D. (2007). "Beyond change management: A multi-level investigation of contextual personal influences on employees' commitment to change," *Journal of Applied Psychology, 92*, pp. 942–951.

20. Beer, Eisenstat, & Spector, *The critical path*.

21. Beer, M., & Weber, J. (1999). Transcript of interview with Archie Norman and Allan Leighton. DVD. Boston: Harvard Business School Press.

22. Herold, Fedor, & Caldwell, "Beyond change management."

23. There is a long literature that supports this view of knowledge development. See, for example: Spreitzer, G. M. (1995). "Psychological empowerment in the workplace: Dimensions, measurement and validation," *Academy of Management Journal, 38*, pp. 1442–1465; Gagne, M., & Deci, E. L. (2005). "Self-determination theory and work motivation," *Journal of Organizational Behavior, 26*, pp. 331–362; Sandberg, J. (2000). "Understanding human competence at work: An interpretive approach," *Academy of Management Journal, 43*, pp. 9–25; Schon, D. A. (1983). *The reflective practitioner: How professionals think in action*. New York: Basic Books; White, R. W. (1959). "Motivation reconsidered: The concept of competence," *Psychological Bulletin, 66*, pp. 297–333; Wrzesniewski, A., & Dutton, J. E. (n.d.). "Caring as competence in organizational life." Unpublished paper delivered at Organizational Behavior Seminar, Harvard Business School.

24. Beer, Eisenstat, & Spector, *The critical path*.

25. Ibid.

26. Anders, I., & Norrgren, F. (2001). "Effects of change strategy and top management involvement on quality of working life and economic results," *International Journal of Industrial Ergonomics, 27*, pp. 93–105; Schaffer, *The breakthrough strategy*.

27. Beer, M., & Weber, J. (1998) "Asda (B)," p. 10.

28. Ibid.; Beer, Eisenstat, & Spector, *The critical path.*
29. Jensen, M. (2000). "Value maximization and the corporate objective function." In Beer & Nohria, *Breaking the code of change.*
30. Collins, *Good to great.*
31. Interview with Archie Norman and Allan Leighton. (1999). DVD. Boston: Harvard Business School.
32. Huy, Q. N. (2002). "Emotional filtering in strategic change." Paper, Academy of Management Meetings.
33. Beer & Nohria, "*Breaking the code of change,*" p. 137.
34. Interview with Archie Norman and Allan Leighton.
35. Ibid.
36. Ibid.
37. Ibid.
38. Ibid.
39. Ibid.
40. Collin & Porras, *Built to last.*
41. Interview with Archie Norman and Allan Leighton.

12. Epilogue: The Future of High Commitment, High Performance Organizations

1. Morgenson, G. (2008). "Was there a loan it didn't like?" *New York Times,* Nov. 2.
2. Ibid.
3. Morgenson, G. (2008). "How the thundering herd faltered and fell," *New York Times,* Nov. 9.
4. Ibid.
5. Ibid.
6. Ibid.
7. Anderson, J., & Thomas, L. (2007). "Goldman Sachs rakes in profits in credit crisis," *New York Times,* May 19.
8. Packard, D. (1995). *The HP way: How Bill Hewlett and I built our company.* New York: Harper Business.
9. Pfeffer, J. (1998). *The human equation: Building profits by putting people first.* Boston: Harvard Business School Press, chap. 9.
10. Ibid., pp. 278–291.

ACKNOWLEDGMENTS

Upon completion of my doctorate in 1964, I made an unconventional career choice: I decided to take a job at Corning Glass Works (now Corning Inc.). What I thought would be a brief two- or three-year stint in industry became eleven event-filled years. It was a seminal experience that shaped my thinking about organizations, what undermines their effectiveness, employee commitment, and performance. More important, I learned what organizations can become if properly designed, managed, and led. I owe a debt of gratitude to the senior executives of Corning at the time: chairman and CEO, Amory Houghton; my first boss, the late Bud McMahon; and managers who became my internal clients and allowed their organizations to be laboratories for learning. Jim Sabin and Charley Wheatley, who trusted me to help them lead an early experiment in high-commitment management in the Medfield, Massachusetts, manufacturing plant; Tom MacAvoy, who trusted me to help him transform his business unit and later became president of the company and a supporter of my work; and his successor Charles Harwood, who ultimately became president of Signetics. Throughout, the members of my organization research and development department contributed mightily to my learning.

In my years at Harvard, numerous other managers became clients with whom I learned. As CEO of Becton Dickinson, Ray Gilmartin, and Ralph Biggadike, his vice president of strategy and human resources, challenged me to help the company to become capable of implementing its strategy. The ideas about leadership as a collective learning process as well as the learning and governance system we now call the Strategic Fitness Process began there. Clateo Castellini and Ed Ludwig, who followed as CEOs of that company, employed these ideas and methods powerfully as they led the company toward high commitment and high performance (HCHP) organization. All three leaders allowed me to write numerous cases about the company and gave generously of their time. Ed Ludwig was an early supporter and client at BD and has become a valued collaborator and friend. Jim Wessel and Jeff Koeppel in human resources were valued partners in the years when Russ Eisenstat and I worked with the company.

There are many other line managers and their human resource managers whose efforts to build an HCHP organization contributed to the ideas in this book. Among them are Scott Wright, Steve Fossi, Lynne Camp and Jody Edwards at Hewlett-Packard and later at Agilent Technologies, Grey Warner at Merck, and Alan Parker, CEO of Whitbread, and his human resource executive, Angie Risley.

Three companies have played a particularly important role in forming the ideas in this book. My case-writing visit to Hewlett-Packard in 1981 played a foundational role in my understanding of HCHP corporations, and the two Harvard cases about the corporation have been invaluable, the second case made possible by Pete Peterson, HP's vice president of human resources. Archie Norman and Allan Leighton, CEOs of Asda, allowed me access to the company's extraordinary journey to high commitment and high performance. The many conversations we have had, the interviews they gave, and the cases they allowed me to write have richly informed my understanding of corporate transformation. Southwest Airlines is a third company model I have studied in depth. Though my understanding comes primarily through secondary research, an interview with the current CEO, Gary Kelly, contributed to my understanding of this remarkable company.

Because this book is a synthesis of my own work and that of many others in the field of organizational studies, I am indebted to the work of many colleagues in the field, too many to list. I do want to acknowledge, however, the influence of the following: Chris Argyris, the late Rensis Likert, Warren Bennis, the late Richard Beckhard, Ed Schein, Richard Walton, Paul Lawrence and Jay Lorsch, Jeff Pfeffer, Charles O'Reilly, Jim Collins, Jerry Porras, Jim Baron and Michael Hannan, Bob Kaplan and David Norton, Danny Miller, and Nitin Nohria, with whom I developed the ideas about paradox in driving change.

Although I wrote this book alone, I had help from others to whom I am deeply grateful. This book started as an effort by Bert Spector and me to revise *Managing Human Assets*. When other commitments caused him to withdraw from this project, I took the book in a different direction, but some ideas we discussed found their way into this book. Jim Weber, a research associate at the Harvard

Business School(HBS), wrote several cases and helped with secondary research into the HCHP companies listed in chapter 2. I am deeply grateful to the Division of Research at HBS for funding the stream of research that has found its way into this book.

Writing a book would have been a solitary and far less gratifying experience had it not been for the contributions of Russell Eisenstat and Nathaniel Foote, my partners at TruePoint. Our practice and research at TruePoint have informed this book. They read this manuscript several times and offered their reactions and insightful ideas. By shouldering the burden of leading TruePoint on a day-to-day basis, they freed up the time I needed to write this book. Finally, I want to acknowledge the partnership in research and practice that I have had with Russ Eisenstat for the last twenty-five years. Many ideas in this book reflect our joint journey of inquiry during those years.

Several people read drafts of the book or chapters in the book. Chris Argyris's and Danny Miller's reactions to the total manuscript were extremely helpful. Chris Richmond, whose management of General Electric's commercial leasing finance business appears in chapter 8, commented on drafts of that chapter. Jim Detert, Boris Groysberg, Mitch Dickey, and Thomas Rice read and commented on individual chapters. Peter Dunn, a gifted leader, read chapters and offered several important ideas that found their way into the book.

Kathe Sweeny, my editor at Jossey-Bass, who sponsored this project, offered editorial suggestions, edited an early version of chapter 2, and has been unfailing in her support during the several years it has taken to complete this book. Wonderful editorial support was given me by Karen Propp, who went through this manuscript twice and was very helpful in shortening it and straightening out my writing.

This book would not have found its way to completion without invaluable support from the Harvard Business School and the administrative staff to whom I have had access. The Division of Research supported research and analysis in the early stages of the project. My administrative assistant, Jan Simmons found articles and references, handled the permissions process, created figures, and helped me put the final manuscript together. Jan has been helpful well beyond the normal scope of her job, responding to requests for help on workdays and weekends, day or night. Klara Pracher, a temporary assistant, also helped with references.

Last, but by no means least, I want to thank my wife, Cynthia, for being so understanding about the many hours I have spent writing this book, for the many times I have told her I could not do something or another because I had to work on the book. Her last-minute editing help is also much appreciated.

Thank you all for your help.

INDEX

311; evolution and revolution during growth and adaptation, 224*fig*; HCHP assumption regarding, 9–10; Hewlett-Packard Santa Rosa Systems Division, 229–231; iterative redesign process of, 250*fig*; organization design logic of, 231–235; organizations are multilevel and multi-unit, 87–89; self-designing the organization, 242–245; success and failure in navigating, 225–228. *See also* HCHP systems

Oshry, B., 82

P

Pace of change, 304*t*, 320–322

Packard, D., 54, 57, 81, 200, 227, 255, 269, 308–309, 330

Palmisano, S., 140

Palmissano, J., 45

Parker, A., 149, 181, 209

Participation: capacity for learning and change motivated by, 65–67; conditions for appropriate, 171; learning and governance system empirical support for, 170–174; relationship between speed, change and, 166*t*. *See also* Employee voice; Employees

Pay for performance, 281

Pennsylvania Pharmaceuticals (pseudonym), 256, 260

People. *See* Employees

Performance: conscious choice strategy for, 57–59; culture relationship to firm, 275–282; focusing inquiry on inquiry and, 176; human resource management transformation and focus on, 286; learning/change capacity through caring about, 35;

organizing system change lever to increase, 84*fig*, 85, 223–254; Strategic Fitness Process (SFP) improving, 93–94, 160–167*fig*, 173–174; sustaining high commitment and, 323–324. *See also* Financial performance; High performance culture; Strategic performance management system (SPMS)

Performance alignment: consistent organizational design levers for, 27–28; Corning EPD's problems with, 98; distinctive, focused, and values-based strategy of, 25–26; as HCHP pillar, 19, 20*fig*; internal consistency and competitive advantage of, 28–29; motivation for participating to enhance, 65–67; organization-strategy fit for, 26–27; simultaneous solution to HCHP pillars and, 38–40; SMS failure indicated by poor, 192–194; Southwest Airlines demonstration of, 25–29

Pfeffer, J., 7, 331, 332

Pioli, S., 257

Porras, G., 197

Porras, J., 7, 58, 73, 80, 122

Porter, M., 28, 57, 58, 123

Prahalad, C. K., 197

Pricing policies, 62

Priority conflict, 100

Proctor & Gamble, 3

Professional model, 69–70

Progressive Insurance, 244–245

Psychological alignment: Corning EPD's problems with, 98–99; as HCHP pillar, 19; HCHP Psychological Contract for, 29–31*t*; ineffective organizing model as eroding, 225–227; motivation for participating

T

THE AUTHOR

Michael Beer is Cahners-Rabb Professor of Business Administration Emeritus at the Harvard Business School, as well as chairman and cofounder of TruePoint Partners and TruePoint Center for High Commitment and Performance, a not-for-profit research and education institute. He is a world-renowned authority in the areas of organization effectiveness, organization change, and human resource management, and taught in Harvard Business School's Advanced Management Program. Professor Beer is the author or coauthor of nine books, among them *Managing Human Assets* and the award-winning *The Critical Path to Corporate Renewal*. Beer has consulted to top management in dozens of Fortune 500 companies, is a Fellow of the Academy of Management and the Society of Industrial and Organizational Psychology, a member of the National Academy of Human Resources, and is the recipient of numerous professional awards, among them the Academy of Management's Distinguished Scientist-Practitioner Award and the Society for Human Resource Management's Losey Research Award. He began his career at Corning Inc., where he founded and led the Organizational Research and Development department, whose work led to several innovations in organizing and managing the company's business and people.

High Commitment, High Performance Casebook
How to Build a Resilient Organization for Sustained Advantage

Michael Beer

ISBN 978-07879-7438-1 • $35.00 • CD-ROM
www.josseybass.com

This CD draws 33 case studies from Harvard Business School and Stanford Business School that can be used to by instructors to illustrate the principles set forth in *High Commitment, High Performance*. Case studies include:

- Southwest Airlines (A) / *Charles O'Reilly and Jeffrey Pfeffer*
- Southwest Airlines (B): Using Human Resources for Competitive Advantage / *Charles O'Reilly*
- McKinsey & Company (A): 1956 / *Amar Bhide*
- GE… We Bring Good Things to Life. (A) / *James Heskett*
- Human Resources at Hewlett-Packard (A) / *Michael Beer and Gregory C. Rogers*
- Human Resources at Hewlett-Packard (B) / *Michael Beer and Gregory C. Rogers*
- Hewlett-Packard: Culture in Changing Times / *Michael Beer, Rakesh Khurana and James Weber*
- The Lincoln Electric Company / *Norman Berg and Norman Fast*
- Lincoln Electric: Venturing Abroad / *Christopher A. Bartlett and Jamie O'Connell*
- Corning Glass Works: The Electronic Products Division (A) / *Michael Beer*
- Corning Glass Works: The Electronic Products Division (B) / *Michael Beer*
- Corning Glass Works: The Electronic Products Division (C) / *Michael Beer*
- Veridian: Putting a Value on Values / *Rakesh Khurana, Joel Podolny and Jaan Elias*
- Merck Latin America (A) / *Michael Beer*
- Merck Latin America (D): Mexico / *Michael Beer*
- Comcast New England: A Journey of Organizational Transformation / *Michael Beer and Anita Arun*
- Strategic Planning at Sun Life / *Michael A. Roberto*
- Mobil USM&R (A): Linking the Balanced Scorecard / *Robert S. Kaplan*
- Mobil USM&R (A1) / *Robert S. Kaplan*

- Hewlett-Packard's Santa Rosa Systems Division (A): The Trials and Tribulations of a Legacy / *Michael Beer and Gregory C. Rogers*
- Hewlett-Packard's Santa Rosa Systems Division (A1): The Profiling Process and Creation of the Future Model / *Michael Beer and Gregory C. Rogers*
- Hewlett-Packard's Santa Rosa Systems Division (A2): Response to the Employee Task Force / *Michael Beer and Gregory C. Rogers*
- Hewlett-Packard's Santa Rosa Systems Division (B3): Assessing Organizational Fitness Profiling / *Michael Beer and Gregory C. Rogers*
- Leadership Development at Goldman Sachs / *Boris Groysberg and Scott Snook*
- Becton Dickinson (A): Corporate Strategy / *Michael Beer and Alistair D. Williamson*
- Becton Dickinson (C): Human Resource Function / *Russell Eisenstat, Michael Beer and Alistair D. Williamson*
- Becton Dickinson (D): Strategic Human Resource Management Profiling / *Michael Beer and Alistair D. Williamson*
- Becton Dickinson (E): An Assessment of Strategic Human Resource Management Profiling / *Michael Beer and Pamela J. Maus*
- Asda (A) / *Michael Beer and James Weber*
- Asda (B) / *Michael Beer and James Weber*
- Asda (C) / *Michael Beer and James Weber*
- Champion International / *Michael Beer and James Weber*
- IBM's Decade of Transformation: Turnaround to Growth / *Lynda M. Applegate, Robert Austin and Elizabeth Collins*

JB JOSSEY-BASS™
An Imprint of WILEY
Now you know.